CHOICE and PERCEIVED CONTROL

CHOICE and PERCEIVED CONTROL

Sponsored by the U.S. Army Human Engineering Laboratory

Edited by

LAWRENCE C. PERLMUTER
Virginia Polytechnic Institute
and State University

RICHARD A. MONTY
U.S. Army Human Engineering Laboratory

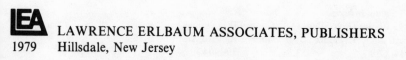

LEA LAWRENCE ERLBAUM ASSOCIATES, PUBLISHERS
1979 Hillsdale, New Jersey

DISTRIBUTED BY THE HALSTED PRESS DIVISION OF
JOHN WILEY & SONS
New York   Toronto   London   Sydney

BF
441
C38

Lawrence Erlbaum Associates, Inc., Publishers
365 Broadway
Hillsdale, New Jersey 07642

Distributed solely by Halsted Press Division
John Wiley & Sons, Inc., New York

Library of Congress Cataloging in Publication Data

Main entry under title:

Choice and perceived control.

Includes indexes.
1. Choice (Psychology) 2. Control (Psychology)
I. Perlmuter, Lawrence C. II. Monty, Richard A.
BF441.C38   153.8   79-19042
ISBN 0-470-26852-2

Printed in the United States of America

This book is dedicated to our parents and teachers, who taught us to understand—after Robert Frost—that "...*freedom is being easy in the harness.*"

Contents

Preface

During the past few years, there has been increasing interest in the concepts of choice and perceived control in a variety of disciplines including philosophy, sociology, and experimental, social, and clinical psychology, as well as political science. There has, however, been a notable lack of communication among these various disciplines, although each has been studying similar phenomena but from different perspectives. Based on our own interests in choice and perceived control as they pertain to human performance, we proposed to Dr. John D. Weisz, Director of the Human Engineering Laboratory, that we conduct a symposium on this topic. Dr. Weisz, an avid supporter of research and interdisciplinary communications, wholeheartedly endorsed the project and provided financial support. Thus, in May 1977 we convened a small planning group. Assisting us were Drs. John H. Harvey, Michael J. Mahoney, Julian B. Rotter, and Jerome E. Singer. By the end of the day, we had collectively prepared a rough outline of a 2½-day symposium and had identified many of the potential speakers. This session eventually led to the conference held at Virginia Polytechnic Institute and State University in Blacksburg, Virginia, on February 13–15, 1978. All the speakers, discussants, and invitees managed to outwit the blizzard of '78 and made the conference a success. The edited papers derived from the conference form the contents of this book.

We wish to thank the U.S. Army Human Engineering Laboratory, especially Dr. John D. Weisz, for both encouraging and sponsoring the symposium. Recognition also goes to the U.S. Army Research Office for encouraging our research efforts that led to the conference. We are indebted to the members of the planning committee for their substantial contributions toward defining a workable format. Thanks are also due to the fine students in the Psychology Department at Virginia Polytechnic Institute and State University who assisted in a variety of duties related to hosting the conference—namely, Susan Ashley, Conway Fleming, and Steve Lovett. In addition, we are grateful to the Department of Psychology and to its head, Charles D. Noblin, for the support we received in conducting the conference and in producing this volume. And finally, a very special word of thanks to B. Diane Barnette of the Human Engineering Laboratory; Jane Roberts, Susan Handy, and Karelle Scharff of Virginia Polytechnic Institute and State University; and Pamela Smith and Julie Demeter of the Veterans Administration Outpatient Clinic in Boston, Mass.; who were responsible for the majority of typing and record keeping surrounding the meeting itself, as well as for retyping most of the final draft of these proceedings.

Of course a book of this kind depends critically on the cooperation and shared wisdom of the contributors and editors. We have made a serious effort to reflect accurately and objectively all the relevant information on freedom and perceived control and were guided by the Talmudic prescription that states that people should cite the source of their ideas in order to increase peace in the world.

LAWRENCE C. PERLMUTER
RICHARD A. MONTY

CHOICE and PERCEIVED CONTROL

Section I

PERCEIVED CONTROL: SOME GENERAL PROBLEMS

Only necessity understood in bondage to the highest is identical with true freedom.
—William James

The papers presented in the opening section of this volume address themselves to methodological, philosophical, empirical, and theoretical issues related to perceived control. They treat both the antecedents and consequences of perceived control. Using a variety of dependent variables, from academic standing and personality measures to self-reports of perceived control, they provide the reader with some of the basic issues as well as some more peripheral matters related to the psychology of perceived control.

Lest the reader be surprised or bewildered by the variety of terminology that relates to the issue of perceived control, it may be helpful to understand that this is to be expected at the initial juncture of disciplines ranging from philosophy to political science and including within these borders a variety of psychologies concerned with normative, idiographic, basic, and applied problems. This is not by way of apology but rather to prepare the reader for the panoptic ideas expressed herein. Further, the reader will soon learn that the notion of perceived control or freedom is referred to by a variety of terms ranging from *power* to *passivity,* from *origin* to *causal agent.* All these terms are connotatively similar. We will probably need to await the next conference on this subject before we can refine our language. However, we don't believe that this terminological babel will prevent the reader from reaching the distillation of the spirit and purpose of this treatise.

The initial paper in this section treats the philosophical implications of perceived control from an empirical perspective. In this paper, Professor Lacey raises some important issues about the notion of control and helplessness. He makes special reference to the Skinnerian view, which receives only limited discussion in the volume. Lacey's discussion of the reciprocal relationship between the controller and that which is controlled raises some interesting theoretical issues. Is it necessary that the controller experience this reciprocity? As is seen in the next section, imitative and vicarious experience are sufficient for producing this reciprocity. The paper by Professor Brown, which extends some of Bandura's (1978) notions, clearly reinforces the idea that this reciprocity need only be perceptual. Further, some recent work by Bailey, Perlmuter, Karsh, and Monty (1978) clearly demonstrates that the control over a nonexistent other presumably satisfies the need to control and thereby motivates the controller. Second, Lacey's discussion of control, using the example of the slave master and the slave, not only shows the sometimes critical interdependency between the controller and the controllee but also raises more fundamental issues about the definition and deployment of *control* as an explanatory term. Having control as master over the construction of the pyramid is not quite the same as deciding which brick should be chosen for each placement in the pyramid.

In the second paper, Professor Steiner proposes a modification of his earlier prominent treatment of freedom and control. Having abandoned the notion of freedom in his current work, Steiner discusses three varieties of choice that are assessed largely by self-report methods. Despite the recent admonitions by Nisbett and Wilson (1977), Steiner proposes some novel approaches to the study of choice. Although not addressing himself to either the consequences of choice or to an elaboration of temporal or sequential factors in choosing, Steiner provides the reader with a parsimonious and clear view of this process.

In the third paper, Professor deCharms continues his intriguing exploration of choice in the educational setting. Expressing concern, as does Lacey, with attempts to study control or personal causation in contrived settings, he distinguishes between the immediate experience of control as causation and the visual experience of control, i.e., perceived control. Although this distinction is relatively easy to operationalize in terms of antecedents, it is difficult to distinguish in terms of consequences. By way of example, the control of a powerful automobile, as Professor Lacey would also argue, certainly has a reciprocal relationship with the controller; however, the question of whether or not it has a consequence that distinguishes it from expected or anticipated control remains to be demonstrated. Again, vicarious (see Brown's paper, Chapter 8) effects can provide similar motivational consequences even when the actual reciprocal relationship is physically impossible. Further, deCharms, in examining individual-difference factors in personal causation as measured by internality scores, does not provide unambiguous support for the expected relationship between these two variables. Although deCharms' program of training is successful in increasing internality in teachers, the change is not reflected by Rotter's I.E. scale. Most interestingly, teachers who are high on the internality score also provide their students with a climate that favors internality. Whether the change in the students' internality scores simply reflects supportive environmental factors or may be attributed to interpersonal social learning factors is not unambiguously clear from these data.

In the final paper in this section, Professor Renshon, a political scientist, provides us with a social learning view of the development of control. Following this is a review of the role of perceived control in political behavior. He points to the potential conflict that can result from the ready use of control by various competing segments of society. Further, he discusses the potential for frustration that exists when individuals believe they are responsible for their behavior and hence are in control while simultaneously they are being deprived of the instruments of control. Finally, he points to the curious fact that whereas voting behavior is in decline, other forms of attempted control, as by protest, tend to increase.

REFERENCES

Bailey, S. E., Perlmuter, L. C., Karsh, R., & Monty, R. A. Choice for others and the perception of control. *Motivation & Emotion,* 1978, *2,* 191–200.

Bandura, A. The self system in reciprocal determinism. *American Psychologist,* 1978, *33,* 344–358.

Nisbett, R. E., & Wilson, T. D. Telling more than we can know: Verbal reports on mental processes. *Psychological Review,* 1977, *84,* 231–259.

1 Control, Perceived Control, and the Methodological Role of Cognitive Constructs

Hugh M. Lacey
Swarthmore College

The principal objective of this paper is to consider various analyses of the concept of "control," and the related concept of "voluntary," in such a way as to locate in the usage of the concept in the literature of "perceived control" an ambiguity that has potentially important consequences. A subsidiary objective is the clarification of the methodological role of cognitive constructs in this literature. The background to my considerations is an attempt to clarify, on one hand, the relationship of these cognitive constructs to the traditional conceptual apparatus in which is posited the capacity of human beings to exert rational control over their actions and their environments, and to the conceptual austerity espoused by radical behaviorism on the other.

PERSONS AS LOCI FOR THE ACTION OF EXTERNAL VARIABLES

According to Skinner (1974), a person is "a locus, a point at which many genetic and environmental conditions come together in a joint effort [p. 168]." Based on this conception of human nature are a number of methodological conclusions, theoretical hypotheses, empirical strategies, and intervention procedures. Among them are views concerning the methodological role of theoretical terms, including cognitive constructs, in psychological inquiry and concerning the concept of control. They are used as foils against which to assess certain features of the literature of "perceived control."

When he challenges the scientific legitimacy of cognitive constructs, Skinner does not deny that there are inner events. Rather he maintains that they are all fully functions of external factors. It follows that an inquiry that relates behavior functionally to inner factors is incomplete, because it fails to relate behavior to those variables—of which it is a function—that are independent with respect to the organism. Conversely, an inquiry that relates behavior successfully to external factors includes, in principle, a functional account of every behavior in terms of independent (and, since they are external, controlling) variables (Lacey, 1974). Moreover, because inner events can only be known through their external indicators, an inquiry that dispenses with reference to inner events in favor of references to the external indicators will lose nothing from the point of view of predictive power and confirmed generalizations (Lacey & Rachlin, 1978).

Regarding "control," we may capture Skinner's conception by defining X to be a controlling factor of a behavior B if and only if X is one of the factors of which B is a function, or if and only if the occurrence of X increases in probability the occurrence of B. Similarly, an organism A can control to some degree an outcome O if and only if A contains within its repertory an operant, the occurrence of a member of which increases the probability of O occurring. To be in control of something is to behave in such a way that its probability of occurrence is changed. From this analysis, Skinner infers that controlling relations are always reciprocal. A's behaviors control C's only if C's behaviors control A's. The controller and the controlled reciprocally control each other's behaviors. "In a very real sense," says Skinner (1971), "the slave controls the slave driver [p. 169]." The slave driver, through the manipulation of reinforcers and punishers, controls the slave's productive activity; the slave, through appropriate productive activity, controls the occasion and the rate with which the slave driver dispenses either reinforcement or punishment.

One might object that this analysis overlooks a crucial asymmetry. The slave driver also controls the contingencies or sets the agenda. He or she brought them into being, has deliberated about them, planned them, designed them, and has the power to change them. They exist and are maintained because of their contribution to the slave driver's goals. Even here, Skinner finds reciprocity. Referring to an experimental space, which in the relevant respects resembles the slave episode, Skinner says (1971): "The behavior of the pigeon has determined the design of the apparatus and the procedures in which it is used [p. 169]." Up to a point, this is uncontroversial, but the experimenter and analogously the slave driver control the fact of confinement to the experimental or labor space, what the procedures in the space are for, and that there be any procedures at all. The design of the controlled space, then, though molded to the organism under control, is a consequence of the controller's choice, and on this there is no reciprocal control exercised by the controlled.[1]

PERSONS AS "RATIONAL ANIMALS"

Opposed to Skinner's conception of human nature is a much older conception (broadly associated with Aristotle and thoroughly embedded in our ordinary moral and legal discourse and in our casual explanations of our own and friends' behavior), according to which persons are not loci for the action of external variables but "rational animals." According to this conception, persons have the capacity to exercise a kind of control upon their environment that is constrained or delimited but not determined by external factors. Moreover, they act in a way most characteristically human when they exercise this capacity. Persons are sources, not merely loci of activity. Choices make a difference. They involve the setting of goals, the hierarchical structuring of goals, planning, the contemplation and assessment of alternative options and their consequences, and rationally informed judgments. They reflect rational processes that are relatively independent with respect to external factors. Any laws that might underlie choices irreducibly contain variables whose values are cognitive events.

Guided by this conception, a person can exercise control when he or she has the power to set and to actualize goals and plans. A precondition is that the individual have the power to control the structure of the immediate environment, including at least some of the contingencies that will modulate his or her behavior. The slave driver controls; the slave does not.[2]

---

[1]In any experimental science, the question arises of the legitimacy and bounds of extrapolations to "natural" situations of principles discovered experimentally. Experimental studies never simply mimic nature. They simplify and restructure, always with the hope that they are bringing into relief factors that do operate in natural situations. In operant experimentation, the key independent variable investigated has been schedule of reinforcement, but rarely has it been investigated as a dependent variable. It may well be the case that the factors that determine the schedule of reinforcement in a particular experiment are the same kind of factors involved in operant-choice experiments, only more complex and difficult to discern. However, there is no experimental support for such a hypothesis. Extending the experimentally confirmed principles to this phenomenon is pure conjecture. Of course it is a very plausible conjecture if one has independent grounds for accepting Skinner's conception of human nature. To the extent that the conjecture is true, reciprocity can be discovered, but the argument in the text suggests that prima facie this is implausible.

[2]Obviously, there are matters of degree connected with control. The slave may attempt to revolt and in certain circumstances will succeed. Also, the distinction between control of structure and functional control of behavior within a structure is not always clear-cut. It is the kind of idealization without which scientists would rarely be able to find regularities.

Paradigmatically, control is of the contingencies or more generally of the standing, but changeable, structures within which the functional and reciprocal interplay of behaviors takes place. Though not denying the explanatory relevance of these functional relations among behaviors, the view emphasizes that an adequate analysis of the location of control in a situation involves specification of the structures and their controllers. In setting up (or acting to destroy) a structure, rational planned choices are characteristically exercised rather than in the consequent behaviors of reaction to the behaviors of the controlled subject, because the latter are merely details in carrying the plan and are of no significance outside the structure. The experimenter, for example, characteristically chooses rationally in setting up the experimental space rather than in dispensing food in response to the pigeon's peck (as is made obvious in the automatization of the procedures of reinforcement).

COGNITIVE CONSTRUCTS

I have sketched two opposed conceptions of human nature, which have widely different implications concerning the likely role of cognitive events in psychological theory, and the appropriate analysis of the concept of control. My intention is to try to locate the literature on "perceived control" within the continuum defined by these two conceptions. In general, I concentrate on several of the writings of Seligman and his associates (Abramson, Seligman, & Teasdale, 1978; Seligman, 1975) that I believe to be exemplars of this literature.

Terms like *perceived control, expectancy,* and *attribution of causality* are clearly intended to refer to cognitive events, and the theoretical and experimental investigations involving them are clearly meant to assign them a causal role. How essential is the causal role assigned to them? In principle, when the theorizing comes to be almost completed, could they be ignored and still every behavior be confirmed as lawful? Or is the lawfulness of some behaviors dependent on their relationships with cognitive events? Do the cognitive events possess any degree of independence with respect to external factors? Or are they fully under the functional control of external factors? And if they are not, to what extent if any are they related to the rational processes posited by the kind of Aristotelian view I have sketched? The point of these questions is probably clear. As a philosopher, I want to know if this domain of psychological research lends more support to a broadly Skinnerian conception of human nature or whether it can be called upon by those who support the centrality and irreducibility of human rationality. This discussion, we will see, goes hand in hand with an analysis of the concept of control.

What, then, is the methodological role of such constructs as *perceived control, expectancy,* and *attribution of causality?* In Seligman's theoretical investigations, they are proposed as causal determinants of the cognitive, emotional, and motivational deficits associated with helplessness and depression and of the generality, chronicity, and type of these deficits. These symptoms and their characteristics are lawful in virtue of their relationships with such constructs. Generalizations such as *L,* for example, are testable, and they can be utilized to make predictions because there are observable indicators of the cognitive events.

L. The expectation that outcomes are noncontingently related to one's own responses is a sufficient condition for the motivational and cognitive deficits (of helplessness) (Abramson, Seligman, & Teasdale, 1978; Seligman, 1975).

What of the causal determinants of the cognitive events themselves? Abramson, Seligman, and Teasdale, (1978) propose the following causal sequence: objective noncontingency, perception of present and past noncontingency, attribution of present or past noncontingency, expectation of future noncontingency, symptoms of helplessness. Precisely what kind of causal connection is proposed between adjacent members of the sequence is not clear. Expectations are suggested as sufficient conditions for the symptoms, but the objective noncontingency is neither sufficient (sometimes it is present, but the perception is not) nor necessary (sometimes the perception has other sources) for the perception.However, the perception seems to be suggested as a necessary condition for the attribution and the attribution as a necessary condition for the expectancy. Clearly, neither is a sufficient condition. For someone with Skinner's outlook, this is highly defective theorizing. Expectation is the key variable, since it is proposed as sufficient for the symptoms, but the framework does not offer sufficient conditions for it; so it can be neither predicted nor brought into being by our deliberate manipulations except to a degree probabilistically. If the latter could be achieved, of course, there would be no need to rely upon a construct like expectation to preserve the lawfulness of the symptoms. On Skinner's outlook, scientific understanding is lacking in the absence of the proposal of manipulable sufficient conditions.

What, in fact, is the scientific point of proposing necessary conditions? Well, if *C* is a necessary condition for *E,* then not *C* is a sufficient condition for not *E.* In other words, if we know sufficient conditions for the nonoccurrence of the perception or the attribution, then we know sufficient conditions for the nonoccurrence of the symptoms. So if our interest is to eliminate the symptoms of helplessness, we need knowledge only of necessary conditions, and we do not need Skinner's "scientific understanding" of the symptoms. This is not an unusual situation in the sciences. It is frequently found, for example, in the medical sciences, where the primary interest is the elimination of diseases. Knowledge of necessary conditions can therefore illuminate therapeutic and preventive practice. Thus, it is practical objectives that justify the role of cognitive constructs in the kind of theory under discussion.

In summary, the cognitive constructs serve at least two methodological roles: (1) they preserve the lawfulness of the symptoms of helplessness; and (2) they represent variables of practical relevance.

What of the argument that they can be dispensed with, without loss of confirmed content, by replacing them with references to their external indicators? Presumably, the number of possible external indicators, independent of the helplessness symptoms, of a cognitive event—such as in L: "expectation that outcomes are noncontingently related to one's own responses"—is finite (say $I_1, \ldots, I_n$). In this case, if we replace L by L_1, we retain a confirmed law (supposing that L is confirmed).

L_1. The occurrence of I_1, or I_2, or . . . or I_n is sufficient condition for the motivational and cognitive deficits.

L is more general than L_1, since the cognitive event could occur without any of the indicators, and L unlike L_1 could represent an explanation of the symptoms. However, any instance that empirically confirms L also confirms L_1, so that L_1 being less general is better confirmed. Thus, if we replace L by L_1, we do retain the lawfulness of the symptoms (with better confirmed, though more complex and nonexplanatory laws; cf. Lacey & Rachlin, 1978).

The general replacement of cognitive constructs, on the other hand, by a list of their alternative indicators does not preserve the practical relevance achieved by the use of the constructs. This is easy to see. Suppose that it is proposed that C is a necessary condition for E and that the external indicators of C are $J_1, \ldots, J_m$. It does not follow that J_1 or J_2 or . . . J_m is a necessary condition for E. The absence of the indicators does not imply the absence of C. Consequently, without using the construct C, there are minimal therapeutic implications. The cognitive constructs, since they represent necessary conditions in the absence of knowledge of sufficient conditions, are thus methodologically indispensable.

Still, it remains an open issue whether or not they are dispensable in principle, and it will remain open so long as we are ignorant of sufficient conditions for the cognitive events. Nevertheless, it is worth querying how rich the domain is that the conceptual framework potentially permits for irreducible rational human action or whether or not the framework on analysis will dissolve into supporting some version of the notion of the person as a "locus." To this end I analyze Seligman's usage of the concept *control*.

VOLUNTARY RESPONSES

An accurate reconstruction of Seligman's (1975) analysis of the concepts *voluntary* and *control* follows. A person A *controls* an outcome O if and only if A makes a voluntary response R such that the probability of O given R is greater than the probability of O given not R. O is *controllable* by A if and only if A can make a voluntary response that increases the probability of occurrence of O. Voluntary responses are identified with members of operants. Seligman (1975) uses a definition that may be paraphrased as:

D_1. A voluntary response is a response that will increase in probability when rewarded and decrease when punished.

What is it to say that A *can make* the voluntary response R? One answer is that it has been established in A's repertoire as a consequence of his or her reinforcement history. A can make R because previously, Rs have been reinforced or punished and their probability of occurrence consequently altered. The advantages of this answer are clear: It is clearly specified that probability of response can, at least in principle, be readily identified with a frequency, and it facilitates experimental inquiry. There is also a disadvantage. The first member of any operant is not explicable in the same terms as subsequent members; yet according to D_1 it is still a voluntary response. To the extent that the occurrence of new operants is always possible, A can thus make voluntary responses that this answer does not account for.

We must be careful not to set up merely verbal problems. Consider another definition of "voluntary response":

D_2. A voluntary response is a response that belongs to a class (operant), the probability of occurrence of a member of which has been altered by the reinforcement or punishment of earlier members; or it is a response whose probability of occurrence is a consequence of earlier members of the class having been reinforced or punished.

D_2 differs from D_1 in that according to it, voluntary responses are those determined (perhaps probabilistically) by the contingencies of reinforcement. According to D_2 (Lacey, 1975), the first member of an operant is not a voluntary response (unless it happens to be also a member of some other relevant operant, as when a response is "shaped"), and so the foregoing analysis of "A can make R" remains complete and coherent. Moreover, it is an analysis that makes the kind of determiner it has the essential thing about voluntary responses. However, it has the consequence that no voluntary behavior can be unique (i.e., not classified in such a way that other members of the class have not been reinforced or punished).

What determines the occurrence of the first member of an operant? One might assign this question to another domain of inquiry (e.g., physiology). Alternatively, a cognitively oriented investigator may see it as goal directed and, as such, explicable in terms of the goals, reasons, motives, plans, etc., of *A*. Of course, in dealing with our friends' behaviors, these are the explanatory categories we use all the time. To the extent that these categories can be incorporated into a workable theory, there are immediate, important consequences.

1. The identification of goal-directed behaviors, or behaviors whose intelligibility is related to their consequences, with behaviors fully explicable in terms of the principles of operant conditioning can no longer be taken for granted.
2. A rethinking of the concept *voluntary* is suggested, so that voluntary behaviors become identified with goal-directed behaviors.
3. This makes it possible both that there be unique voluntary behaviors[3] and that the first member of an operant be voluntary.
4. It permits an analysis that makes the kind of determiner the essential thing about voluntary responses without narrowing the class of voluntary responses in the manner of D_2.
5. The relationship of voluntary behavior to rewards and punishment is now explained rather than definitional. Rewards and punishments are goals to be sought or avoided, alongside other goals. They enter into an agent's deliberation and modify outcomes. On this account it becomes coherent to say that the first and later members of an operant have the same kinds of determiners (whatever the general factors are that determine goal-directed behavior), while maintaining the relevance of reward and punishment to the determination of all except the first member.

The advantage of this way of looking at things is that it connects with the categories we habitually use in our daily life and brings into the voluntary,

---

[3]When an event or behavior is explained, a prerequisite is that it be described. Any event can be described in a variety of different ways and consequently belongs to a variety of different classes. Which description is highlighted in a scientific explanation depends on the theoretical framework within which the explanation is cast. To say that a behavior is unique is to say that it is the only member of the class of behaviors defined by the explanatorily relevant description. For example, the behavior of writing this footnote may well be unique. I have never written this sequence of sentences before, and probably no one will again. Yet it seems plausible to assert that this behavior is explicable in terms of my current goals and motives in reaction to an editor's suggestion. Of course, under another description, but not an explanatorily relevant description, this behavior is not unique. For example, it belongs to the class of behaviors defined by the description, "writing of a sequence of ten sentences." No behavior that is explicable in terms of the principles of operant conditioning is unique in the present sense.

and thence nonanomalous, category such activities with unique products as writing a paper, proposing a theory, constructing a good experiment, making a work of art. On the other hand, there is a loss of a kind of theoretical precision and the difficulty of replicating appropriate situations in the laboratory. Indeed, at this point, the question of the relationship of experimental findings to the explanation of natural phenomena is most heightened. Also, there is no longer an easy way to identify or even to hypothesize about the voluntary responses A "can make" or "cannot make."

PERCEIVED CONTROL

I now relate these considerations to the control that a person may perceive him- or herself to have or not to have. An outcome is controllable by a person if and only if that individual's voluntary activity can change the probability that the outcome will occur. Note that this is a more general analysis than that cited earlier from Seligman. Activities include responses but also ordered sequences of responses. The latter are important when we bear in mind the distinction I drew earlier between controlling responses and controlling contingencies (or situations in which responses occur).

Given a fixed situation, the responses of the slave and slave driver reciprocally control one another. But the slave driver controls the situation; it serves his or her goals, was set up by the slave driver for this purpose, and is maintained so long as it suits those purposes. Setting it up involved more than a single response. Moreover, the slave driver's rational planning and deliberative activity were at a maximum while setting it up. Once set up the individual's role in it is routine and according to the structure he or she has planned and constructed. In such a fixed situation, consider the slave, or the experimental subject. For this individual, the situation is not only fixed but constrained (i.e., it is a situation over which he or she has no control and no available situational options). (Of course, there are great differences concerning how it comes about that the slave and experimental subject are in the relevant situation.) Within the situation, there are a variety of outcomes under the person's control (i.e., contingent on his or her responses). If the contingencies are so constructed that certain "desirable" outcomes are under the person's control, then the symptoms of helplessness will not occur, provided that the right learning has taken place. Observation of behaviors in such constrained situations has provided the experimental support for the claim that the expectancy that highly desired outcomes are uncontrollable is sufficient for the occurrence of the symptoms of helplessness.

Yet another variable is also operative in all these situations: lack of control over the situation.

The word *outcome* carries with it a systematic ambiguity: response-contingent outcomes in a situation and situations or agendas themselves. In the constrained situations we observe in our experiments, the situation is rarely a dependent variable, and so it is easy to ignore. In the literature I have read, this variable has not been directly investigated at all, although some of Abramson, Seligman, and Teasdale's (1978) suggested treatments of helplessness ("Environmental manipulation by social agencies to remove aversive outcomes or provide desired outcomes, e.g., rehousing, job placement, financial assistance, provision of nursery care for children [p. 69]") involve changing situations.

Lack of control over one's situation (or perception or expectancy of this) may be a necessary condition for helplessness, and that the expectancy of lack of response-contingent control over highly desired outcomes is sufficient for helplessness may be *because* there is lack of situational control. Put another way, the expectancy that a desired goal is beyond one's grasp may be sufficient for helplessness because of constraints (real or perceived) upon the scope of one's rational activity that are present when one lacks situational control.

It is a general methodological and theoretical problem to determine the circumstances, without descending into tautology, in which the aforementioned expectancy is sufficient for helplessness. Reference to this variable may offer a way through these difficulties. It also can be used to explain why at times we relinquish control over certain crucial outcomes. Once in the airplane, we have no control over its movements, but we control the situation of which our flight is an aspect. It also explains why commonly, the recognition that certain outcomes cannot be controlled (response-contingent sense) leads not to helplessness but to our rethinking our plans—perhaps our goals, perhaps the situations that we construct to achieve our goals. The slave who learns that nothing he or she does will produce sufficient food cannot do otherwise, but the slave driver who learns that current procedures do not achieve sufficient productivity can change them. When the experimenter fails to obtain interesting results, he or she can design and perform another experiment.

Here we see how concepts and methodological preconceptions shape what we seek. With Seligman's definition of *voluntary,* we look at fixed situations, for only there do we get clear exemplifications of voluntary responses and clear operational measures of probabilities. Thus, we do not look at those contexts in which planning and thence rational activity are maximized. And so, despite methodological liberalism, we are not led very far from the conception of man as a "locus." On the broader conception of *voluntary,* we open up the framework to incorporate the full play of man's rational activity. Questions about causation become refocused but at a price. It is difficult, if not impossible, to investigate situational control experimentally, partly because of the difficulties of making situational control a dependent variable in a circumscribed situation and partly because we may find that relevant situational variables are in fact constant in our society.

Abramson, Seligman, and Teasdale (1978) conclude their recent paper with the following sentence: "A life history which biases individuals to expect that they will be able to control the sources of suffering and nurturance in their life should immunize against depression [p. 70]." This is true even if these individuals do not have such control—as most individuals in fact do not. This truth therefore could be a basis for action in eliminating depression only if either the situation is changed so that the control becomes real or if deception is used. If our knowledge is confined to fixed situations, then the latter is the only possibility. To avoid this, we need to find a way to develop a theoretical framework that can convert a concrete version of man as a rational animal into an empirically confirmed matter. A first step in this direction is to develop, theoretically, the distinction between control of situations or agendas and control over outcomes that are response contingent within an agenda.

CONCLUSION

I have defended, in this paper, the methodological relevance of such cognitive constructs as *perceived control* and *attribution of causality*. More important, I have suggested that the theories of perceived control are marred by an important ambiguity in their usage of the concept of *control*. Control can be of the situation or exercised within a fixed situation. Which is the key variable for the explanation of the symptoms of helplessness is open for further investigation. From the perspective of a conception of human nature founded in the rational capacities of human beings, one would expect that control of the situation would be fundamental.

ACKNOWLEDGMENTS

The writing of this paper was supported in part by a grant from N.S.F. (SOC 75-08464). Discussions with Martin Seligman, Barry Schwartz, Maria I. Lacey, and others have helped to clarify the ideas. Reprints may be obtained from the author, Philosophy Department, Swarthmore College, Swarthmore, Pa. 19081.

REFERENCES

Abramson, L. Y., Seligman, M. E. P., & Teasdale, J. D. Learned helplessness in humans: Critique and reformulation. *Journal of Abnormal Psychology,* 1978, *87,* 49–74.

Lacey, H. M. The scientific study of linguistic behavior: A perspective on the Skinner–Chomsky controversy. *Journal for the Theory of Social Behavior,* 1974, *4,* 17–51.

Lacey, H. M. On operants and voluntary behavior. *Ethics,* 1975, *85,* 349–352.

Lacey, H. M., & Rachlin, H. Behavior, cognition and theories of choice. *Behaviorism,* 1978, *6,* 177–202.

Seligman, M. E. P. *Helplessness: On depression, development and death.* San Francisco: Freeman, 1975.

Skinner, B. F. *Beyond freedom and dignity.* New York: Knopf, 1971.

Skinner, B. F. *About behaviorism.* New York: Knopf, 1974.

2 Three Kinds of Reported Choice

Ivan D. Steiner
University of Massachusetts

INTRODUCTION

Control and *choice* are words with many connotations. Probably they are even more troublesome than many other words we borrow from ordinary speech because they have little denotative meaning. We cannot point to an instance of control or choice with high assurance that others will agree with us. Of course, we can construct our own denotative meaning by decreeing that certain observable events or conditions constitute the referents of our words. Like Skinner (1971), we can say that an agent controls the behavior of a pigeon or child when that agent's actions lead to an increased incidence of a specified behavior. Or, like Bandura (1974), we can assert that choice is indexed by the number of options available to a person. But such observable referents don't necessarily identify the meanings that we want those words to carry.

In this volume, control and choice refer to experiential states. The individual presumably experiences control when feeling that he or she, rather than other people, luck, or unmanageable forces, determines whether desired outcomes will be received. He or she experiences choice when concluding that the self is the agent who decides which of two or more options will be accepted. I suppose most of us believe that control and choice are real and important. Our own subjective experience tells us so, and observation suggests that overt behavior often depends on whether or not they are experienced. But when they are defined as experiential states, control and choice become very difficult to study empirically.

Whether we have dependable access to our own experiential states may be debatable (Schachter, 1964); certainly our access to the experiential states of others is indirect, circumstantial, and often undependable. A wealth of evidence (cf. Tagiuri, 1969) indicates that observers are not ordinarily very accurate judges of others' emotions. Electronic gear that will distinguish between one experiential state and another has not yet been perfected. In the absence of more direct cues, social psychologists often ascribe whatever internal state or process seems consistent with the individual's situation or his or her overt response to it. Dissonance, reactance, or identification are assumed to occur when subjects are exposed to manipulations designed to produce them and when subjects behave in ways that suggest those experiences have occurred.

Inferring internal states from their *known* antecedents or consequences is a commendable practice. But until one knows what those antecedents and consequences really are, inferences of this kind are likely to be distressingly circular. If I think conditions X, Y, and Z are antecedents of choice, I create them for my subjects. If I then observe responses A and B, which I presume to be reactions to choice, I conclude that my manipulations were successful *and* that choice does indeed have the effects I hypothesized. My manipulations must have created choice, for why else would I have observed responses to choice? My subjects' reactions must have been responses to choice, for that is what my manipulations created. Bootstrapping of this kind is excusable when there is lots of ancillary evidence supporting one's guesses about antecedents and consequences, but we usually aren't very sure the experiential state we think we have created actually occurred. Perhaps what my manipulations produced was really arousal, fear, joy, or bewilderment.

On the pages that follow I briefly examine dissonance research as an example of the difficulties that arise when experiential states are too confidently inferred from hunches concerning antecedents and consequences. I then propose a way of minimizing some of these difficulties and summarize some findings generated when the methodology I favor is applied to the study of choice. Finally, I comment on the relationship between choice and control.

COGNITIVE DISSONANCE: A CASE STUDY OF INFERENCE FROM PRESUMED ANTECEDENTS AND CONSEQUENCES

Festinger (1957) conceived dissonance to be a motivational state aroused by the juxtapositioning of two cognitions, X and Y, when *not* X follows from Y. But because a subject's cognitions were no more observable than the dissonance they were presumed to instigate, Festinger's definition did not specify a denotative meaning for either term. In early dissonance research, experimenters exposed subjects to manipulations that were believed to create dissonance and observed responses that could readily be construed to have a dissonance-reducing character. It seemed, therefore, that the manipulations had in fact promoted dissonance, which in turn had been responsible for subjects' overt responses.

Because evidence that dissonance had been aroused was highly circumstantial, other theorists found it easy to suggest alternative explanations of the findings. Chapanis and Chapanis (1964) pointed to possible methodological flaws in the research; Bem (1967) proposed that the data could be understood as consequences of self-perception; and Tedeschi, Schlenker, and Bonoma (1971) contended that self-presentation was the critical intervening variable.

Sporadic failures to observe the hypothesized behavioral effects of dissonance led proponents of the theory to specify major constrictions on Festinger's original statement concerning the antecedents of dissonance. Brehm and Cohen (1962) noted that inconsistent cognitions have strong motivational properties only if the individual is firmly committed to one of them, and Wicklund and Brehm (1976) suggested that it is only when the individual him- or herself has been responsible for juxtaposing contrary cognitions that dissonance-reducing responses occur. Collins and Hoyt (1972) emphasized the necessity that the individual feel he or she has freely chosen among options and is personally responsible for any adverse effects of that decision. Aronson (1968) suggested that dissonance is a significant force only when the self-concept or some other strong expectancy is involved.

In a recent review of the evolution of dissonance theory, Greenwald and Ronis (1978) note that some of the early evidence and many of the early examples of dissonance reduction have been rendered obsolete by contemporary conceptions of dissonance. They suggest that theory and research have steadily coverged with ideas from the tradition of self theory. Whether Greenwald and Ronis believe that *dissonance* is merely another word for ego involvement or self-defensiveness is not entirely clear, but they propose that dissonance studies be viewed as research on self-protective cognitive processing.

Over a period of 20 years, the antecedents of dissonance were drastically redefined, its consequences became more problematical, and serious questions were raised concerning its identity.

A RATIONALE FOR OBTAINING SELF-REPORTS

There is probably no way of guaranteeing that our current conceptions of control and choice will survive or that future research will not make our present efforts seem irrelevant. But we can minimize those possibilities by seeking additional evidence that our hunches concerning antecedents and consequences are correct. One kind of additional evidence that was almost never obtained by dissonance theorists is the subject's own description of his or her experience.

Of course, one must acknowledge that subjects may not always have a clear awareness of dissonance, control, or choice. Even when they do have, they may lack the words or the willingness to communicate about such experiential states. But I think we often overestimate the seriousness of these problems. Subjects in dissonance studies who have had no difficulty reporting their attitudes toward complex political or social issues could undoubtedly have described their feelings about writing a counterattitudinal essay. Had they been asked, they might have said they didn't consider their essays to be counterattitudinal, interpreted their assignment as an intellectual challenge, or thought it too trivial to matter very much. If we were as clever at eliciting subjects' appraisals of our manipulations as we usually are in staging them, we would gain useful information about whether we are really stimulating control and choice. And until we are pretty certain what our manipulations are doing to subjects, we can't be sure our experiments are identifying consequences of control and choice.

In one sense, what I am recommending is already common practice in many areas of social psychological research. There is nothing very novel about the idea of employing self-reports as manipulation checks. But such reports have ordinarily been elicited after subjects' behavioral responses have been observed; they have usually been retrospective accounts that probably reflected subjects' overt actions as well as the experiences subjects were asked to describe. Furthermore, questions concerning the cognitive or emotional impact of manipulations have often been intermingled with inquiries about current attitudes, beliefs, or intentions. Such practices have probably colored subjects' descriptions of the experiential state that preceded their overt conduct.

Interrogation of "throwaway subjects" more closely approximates what I am proposing than does the conventional manipulation check. In this procedure, a subsample of subjects is exposed to experimental conditions before responding to a series of questions concerning their impressions or feelings. They are then "thrown away" because their subsequent actions would almost certainly be influenced by the questions they have been asked and the answers they have given.

I suggest that the use of "throwaway" subjects should be routine during early stages of research on experiential states. But I would go further and propose that we ought somehow to legitimize and dignify research in which all dependent variables are abstracted from subjects' responses to inquiries concerning their feelings of control and choice. Perhaps that seems outrageously phenomenological, but subjects' experiences are what determine whether our manipulations are doing what we want them to do. And until someone discovers a better way of gaining access to those experiences, we ought to listen to what subjects have to say. Perhaps they will tell us that contrary to the assumption of many dissonance theorists, they don't really experience choice when told they are free to reject an experimenter's request. Maybe they will agree with reactance theorists (e.g., Brehm, 1972; Wicklund, 1974) who say a loss of choice is experienced when the availability of one of several options is threatened. But they may not.

As I think this voulme indicates, those of us who investigate control and choice are usually more interested in identifying the behavioral consequences of those states than in determining whether our manipulations have actually had the intended experiential effect. Unfortunately, experimental evidence concerning the consequences of control and choice can be no better than our ability to produce those states permits it to be. Projecting our own phenomenology onto our subjects permits us to bypass uninteresting chores but leaves the critical question unanswered: Are our subjects experiencing the states whose consequences we wish to identify?

The remainder of this paper focuses on procedures of the kind I am recommending. The findings I discuss concern self-reported choice, but it seems probable that parallel research on control would yield similar outcomes.

CHOICE AND COMPARISON LEVELS

When I have asked myself and others to describe situations that prompt a feeling of choice, answers seem always to concern the availability and desirability of options. But replies have tended to suggest that there are at least three kinds of choice, each of which can be coordinated to Thibaut and Kelley's (1959) conception of "comparison level" or "comparison level alt."

Thibaut and Kelly propose that our own past experiences and the actions of others tell us what alternatives we should expect in a given situation. These anticipated options establish our "comparison level"; they serve as the reference points against which we evaluate the goodness of alternatives that become available to us. Our opportunities are good if they are more desirable than those we anticipated and bad if they are less desirable.

Evaluative Choice

Thibaut and Kelley do not link their formulation to an experiential state called "choice," but casual observation suggests there is a linkage. People seem not to report a feeling of choice unless at least one of their available options is at least as desirable as their comparison set. Voltaire's Candide claimed little choice when permitted to select thirty-six lashings across his back or a dozen bullets in his head. The same absence of choice is implied by a Greek legend in which a mother is asked to decide which of her three sons, all of whom are hostages, is to be executed.

I often hear children, and sometimes adults as well, say they have a "good choice" when the alternative they are about to select is more attractive than they might have expected. Consequently, I propose that one variety of choice is experienced when the best available option exceeds the comparison level. The greater the margin by which it exceeds that level, the greater the feeling of choice. Because this experience appears to depend on the individual's evaluation of his or her best alternative, I (Steiner, in press) have called it "evaluative choice."

Before concluding that we can create evaluative choice by providing subjects with a highly attractive option, we ought to elicit the self-reports of subjects who are exposed to our intended manipulation. This is what Solomon and Rodin (1976) did when they asked subjects, "How good is the choice which your options provide?" College students who were permitted to select from four highly attractive options reported a high degree of choice. So also did subjects who could select among two very attractive and two very unattractive alternatives. But subjects whose options were four very distasteful alternatives reported little choice. Parallel results were obtained by Kruglanski and Cohen (1974) in a study involving the selection of hobby clubs by adolescents. The conclusions I draw from these findings are that reported choice is sometimes strongly correlated with the desirability of the best available option and that little or no choice is experienced when no alternative is as good as the individual's comparison level.

Discriminative Choice

Reported choice is not always highly correlated with the attractiveness of the best option. If two or more available alternatives are at least as good as the comparison level, people who want to maximize their benefits will probably compare one such acceptable alternative with another. Under these circumstances, Thibaut and Kelley propose that whichever option seems at the moment to be the best is evaluated against the one that seems second best. Thibaut and Kelley call the second-best alternative "comparison level alt" and emphasize the importance of the margin by which the best alternative exceeds that level. If the margin is small, the individual has little basis for preferring either option and is likely to realize that what seems second best now may turn out to be superior in the long run.

When I have asked subjects to describe situations in which they have experienced choice, some of them tell me of instances in which their best alternative was much more attractive than their second best. They usually go on to explain that they had a "clear choice" or that they felt very free to select the better of the two options. They were not compelled to flip a coin or to choose between Tweedledum and Tweedledee. On the contrary, they felt great confidence in their ability to discriminate between available options. I think they are reporting "discriminative choice."

The experimental literature provides little direct evidence that subjects who are confronted by unequally attractive options report high discriminative choice. Crinklaw (1974) asked college students to read vignettes in which the protagonist was described as finding his options about equally attractive *or* unequally attractive. Subjects who read the latter version of the vignette acknowledged greater freedom to select the better alternative and less freedom to choose the poorer alternative than did subjects who read the vignette in which options were about equally attractive. But Crinklaw did not ask subjects about feelings of choice per se.

My students and I have recently completed the data-gathering stage of a study (unpublished research) that focuses more directly on the issue of choice. Subjects who decided which of two clusters of topics would be covered in an interview with a clinical psychologist were asked: (1) "Do these two clusters provide you with a good choice?" and (2) "To what extent do these two clusters offer you the opportunity to make a meaningful choice?" No attempt was made to manipulate the desirability of the two clusters, but some subjects rated them about equally attractive whereas others found one much more desirable than the other. As expected, "goodness" of choice was positively associated with rated desirability of the more attractive option but was not significantly correlated with the discrepancy between the attractiveness ratings given to the two alternatives. By contrast, reported "meaningfulness" of choice was a positive function of the discrepancy between the two options but was not significantly associated with subjects' ratings of the more attractive alternative. If our questions concerning the "goodness" and "meaningfulness" of choice were successful in focusing attention on evaluative and discriminative choice respectively, it would appear that these two kinds of experiences are quite different. Not only are they uncorrelated with one another; they also reflect different aspects of the subject's phenomenology.

Autonomous Choice

The comparative attractiveness of the individual's first- and second-ranked options also govern another kind of reported choice. When two alternatives are both complex and differ from one another on several dimensions, it may not be immediately clear which is better. To decide the issue, one must compare them on each dimension and decide how important each dimension really is. Is the color of a garment more important than its texture, style, or size? Of course, if one option is markedly superior in almost every respect, comparison will be a perfunctory exercise; one's decision is dictated by the large discrepancy between the overall attractiveness levels of the two options. Under these circumstances, the individual should reach a rapid and confident decision and experience discriminatory choice. But when each alternative has advantages the other lacks, the discrepancy between their overall levels of goodness is likely to be small, and careful deliberation is required. The individual's idiosyncratic preferences guide the evaluative process, and the individual, rather than the obvious qualities of the options, appears to determine the decision. He or she can perceive the self as an autonomous decision-making agent and experience what I would call "autonomous choice."

When I have jokingly told my undergraduate students I was offering them a free trip to Paris or to Rome, they have typically told me that they felt they had a "real choice." Paris and Rome differ in many ways, and students usually feel they are applying their own personal criteria when deciding between such equally attractive options. But when I have offered them a trip to Paris or to Springfield, Massachusetts, they are inclined to say, "What kind of choice is that?" Perhaps they ought to experience discriminative choice, but the discrepancy is apparently so great that they feel there is no real decision to be made. If I press them, they admit to having a good choice, and they aggree that they are very confident of their ability to discriminate between options. But they adamantly disclaim any experience that could be construed as autonomous choice. Apparently none of the three varieties of choice is routinely experienced when one option is vastly superior to the other. Moderate discrepancies seem to encourage discriminative choice and to inhibit autonomous choice, but huge discrepancies probably stimulate no feelings of choice whatever.

The literature includes studies (Harvey & Harris, 1975; Harvey & Johnston, 1973; Steiner, Rotermund, & Talaber, 1974) in which subjects have been asked to report experiences that resemble autonomous choice. And when available options have been complex, findings have rather uniformly supported the conclusion that small discrepancies promote high reported autonomous choice.

It should be apparent by now that research has sometimes yielded a positive correlation between the magnitude of discrepancies and reported choice, and sometimes a negative correlation. What justification can be offered for contending that subjects in these two kinds of studies are reporting different varieties of choice? Is it not possible that all are concerned with the same experiential dimension and that the contradictory findings reflect the effects of extraneous or uncontrolled aspects of experimental situations?

It is possible but not very probable. Studies that have yielded negative correlations have confronted subjects with complex, multidimensional options that, when they were about equal in overall goodness, could be satisfactorily evaluated only by engaging in judgmental activities that ought to encourage the feeling of self-determination of autonomy. Moreover, negative correlations between discrepancies and reported choice have been accompanied by negative correlations between discrepancies and reported ease of making the decision (Harvey & Johnston, 1973), confidence in the correctness of the decision (Steiner, Rotermund, & Talaber, 1974), or subject's impressions of the speed with which the decision was reached (Harvey & Johnston, 1973). By contrast, Crinklaw's (1974) research, which probably comes as close as any to assessing discriminative choice, found that large discrepancies evoked not only strong indications of discriminative choice (e.g., high reported freedom to accept the favored option) but also evidence that the decision required little deliberation because the selected alternative was clearly superior to its rival. Although there is still room for a margin of doubt, it seems almost certain that subjects in the two kinds of studies were describing quite different experiences.

Unresearched Consequences of Three Kinds of Choice

If choice refers to three different kinds of experience that are, in turn, prompted by three different configurations of stimuli, we should be doing whatever we can to differentiate among them. The behavioral consequences of having a "good" choice are probably different from those that follow from experiencing great confidence while deciding. And autonomous choice, the feeling that one is personally very much in charge of comparing and assessing the many assets and liabilities of alternatives, may have behavioral implications that differ from those of either evaluative or discriminative choice. Research into these issues remains to be conducted.

CHOICE AND CONTROL

Finally, it seems appropriate to offer a few speculative suggestions concerning relationships between choice and control. As I have already contended, people experience choice when they seem in one way or another to control the decision-making process: They select an alternative they greatly desire; they confidently select among available options; or by processing and evaluating a mass of information, they identify an alternative that seems best for them. These are three reasons for feeling that one controls the selection process, but none of them guarantees that the ultimate outcome will turn out to be good. I may confidently decide that Dusty Moon will win the fourth race at Aqueduct and lose my bankroll when he doesn't. After careful consideration, I may conclude that a South Pacific tour will be more enjoyable to me than two weeks in the Alps. But the autonomy of my choice will not insure me against hurricanes, the audacity of immigration officials, or an outbreak of malaria. To decide is one thing; to cause the decision to bear fruit is quite another.

Current literature reports many studies (cf. Averill, 1973; Glass & Singer, 1972; Langer & Rodin, 1976; Schulz, 1976; Seligman, 1975) of "personal control." In my judgment some of this research examines control over the selection of options, some concerns control over outcomes, and a few studies (e.g., Ayeroff & Abelson, 1976; Langer, 1975) deal with both. Rotter's (1966) instrument for assessing locus of control and much of the work of Weiner, Frieze, Kukla, Reed, Rest, and Rosenbaum (1971) deal with people's explanations of good and bad outcomes. They do not differentiate very clearly between decision control and outcome control. But perhaps college sophomores don't differentiate either, in which case we should probably ask whether the three kinds of choice subjects report are really three kinds of outcome control as well.

ACKNOWLEDGMENTS

The author's research on choice has been supported by grants from the National Science Foundation (GS-43389) and from the United States Public Health Service, National Institutes of Health (No. MH-20169).

REFERENCES

Aronson, E. Dissonance theory: Progress and problems. In R. P. Abelson, E. Aronson, W. J. McGuire, T. M. Newcomb, M. J. Rosenberg, & P. H. Tannenbaum (Eds.), *Theories of cognitive consistency: A sourcebook.* Skokie, Ill.: Rand McNally, 1968.

Averill, J. R. Personal control over aversive stimuli and its relationship to stress. *Psychological Bulletin*, 1973, *80*, 286–303.

Ayeroff, F., & Abelson, R. P. ESP and ESB: Belief in personal success at mental telepathy. *Journal of Personality and Social Psychology*, 1976, *34*, 240–247.

Bandura, A. Behavior theory and the models of man. *American Psychologist*, 1974, *29*, 859–869.

Bem, D. J. Self-perception: An alternative interpretation of cognitive dissonance phenomena. *Psychological Review*, 1967, *74*, 183–200.

Brehm, J. W. *Responses to loss of freedom: A theory of psychological reactance.* Morristown, N.J.: General Learning Press, 1972.

Brehm, J. W., & Cohen, A. R. *Explorations in cognitive dissonance.* New York: Wiley, 1962.

Chapanis, N. P., & Chapanis, A. Cognitive dissonance: Five years later. *Psychological Bulletin*, 1964, *61*, 1–22.

Collins, B. E., & Hoyt, M. F. Personal responsibility-for-consequences: An integration and extension of the "forced compliance" literature. *Journal of Experimental Social Psychology*, 1972, *8*, 558–593.

Crinklaw, L. D. *Attributed freedom, locus of control and the stimulus person's intrinsic and extrinsic motivations.* Unpublished doctoral dissertation, University of Massachusetts, Amherst, 1974.

Festinger, L. *A theory of cognitive dissonance.* Evanston, Ill.: Rowe, Peterson, 1957.

Glass, D., & Singer, J. *Urban stress.* New York: Academic Press, 1972.

Greenwald, A. G., & Ronis, D. L. Twenty years of cognitive dissonance: Case study of the evolution of a theory. *Psychological Review,* 1978, *85,* 53–57.

Harvey, J. H., & Harris, B. Determinants of perceived choice and the relationship between perceived choice and expectancy about feelings of internal control. *Journal of Personality and Social Psychology,* 1975, *31,* 101–106.

Harvey, J. H., & Johnston, S. Determinants of the perception of choice. *Journal of Experimental Social Psychology,* 1973, *9,* 164–179.

Kruglanski, A. W., & Cohen, M. Attributing freedom in the decision context: Effects of the choice alternatives, degree of commitment and predecision uncertainty. *Journal of Personality and Social Psychology,* 1974, *30,* 178–187.

Langer, E. J. The illusion of control. *Journal of Personality and Social Psychology,* 1975, *32,* 311–328.

Langer, E. J., & Rodin, J. The effects of choice and enhanced personal responsibility for the aged: A field experiment in an institutional setting. *Journal of Personality and Social Psychology,* 1976, *34,* 191–198.

Rotter, J. B. Generalized expectancies for internal versus external control of reinforcement. *Psychological Monographs,* 1966, *80*(1, Whole No. 609).

Schachter, S. The interaction of cognitive and physiological determinants of emotional state. In L. Berkowitz (Ed.), *Advances in experimental social psychology* (Vol. 1). New York: Academic Press, 1964.

Schulz, R. Effects of control and predictability on the physical and psychological well-being of the institutionalized aged. *Journal of Personality and Social Psychology,* 1976, *33,* 563–573.

Seligman, M. E. P. *Helplessness: On depression, development, and death.* San Francisco: Freeman, 1975.

Skinner, B. F. *Beyond freedom and dignity.* New York: Knopf, 1971.

Solomon, S. K., & Rodin, J. *Control-seeking behavior: Are people motivated to attain control?* Unpublished manuscript, Yale University, New Haven, Conn., 1976.

Steiner, I. D. The attribution of choice. In M. Fishbein (Ed.), *Progress in social psychology.* Hillsdale, N.J.: Lawrence Erlbaum Associates, in press.

Steiner, I. D., Rotermund, M., & Talaber, R. Attribution of choice to a decision maker. *Journal of Personality and Social Psychology,* 1974, *30,* 553–562.

Tagiuri, R. Person perception. In G. Lindzey & E. Aronson (Eds.), *The handbook of social psychology* (2nd ed., Vol. 3). Reading, Mass.: Addison-Wesley, 1969.

Tedeschi, J. T., Schlenker, B. R., & Bonoma, T. V. Cognitive dissonance: Private ratiocination or public spectacle? *American Psychologist,* 1971, *8,* 685–695.

Thibaut, J. W., & Kelley, H. H. *The social psychology of groups.* New York: Wiley, 1959.

Weiner, B., Frieze, I., Kukla, A., Reed, L., Rest, S., & Rosenbaum, R. M. *Perceiving the causes of success and failure.* Morristown, N.J.: General Learning Press, 1971.

Wicklund, R. A. *Freedom and reactance.* Hillsdale, N.J.: Lawrence Erlbaum Associates, 1974.

Wicklund, R. A., Brehm, J. W. *Perspectives on cognitive dissonance.* Hillsdale, N.J.: Lawrence Erlbaum Associates, 1976.

3 Personal Causation and Perceived Control

Richard deCharms
Washington University

When you step into a beautiful new sports car and take control, you guide it physically and directly, it responds to your actions, and you experience a feeling of power. When you observe a skillful orator hold an audience in the palm of his hand, you say that he has them under his control. In a sense you see him control them. These two uses of the word *control* are common and recognized in ordinary language, yet there are differences between them. The first is an immediate experience of physical contact. The second is an inference from visually observed phenomena. The first is what I have called the experience of personal causation. The second is perceived control. In some respects, I think the two are quite different, and that is the major theme of my paper.

In comparing the two uses of the word *control*, I make two major points. First, most of our psychological theories and research on control concern perceived control, the second type, and are based on an implicit model of visual perception. In order to understand the experience of personal causation, the first type of control, we may need a radically different implicit model.

Second, I suggest that the study of control is best conducted in the complex situations where it occurs in real life. I propose that we look for the beast in situ rather than try to produce it under artificial conditions.

In support of both major points, I report some research that I have conducted where it is possible to compare Rotter's measure of perceived locus of control of reinforcements with a measure of personal causation.

VISUAL PERCEPTION AND
THE ILLUSION OF CONTROL

The title of this volume highlights the phrase *perceived control*. The phrase indicates some diffidence toward the concept of control and contains a certain amount of ambiguity. Why do we feel it necessary to preface the term *control* with the word *perceived* or even more hesitantly to bury it in the phrase *illusion of control?* The answer may be that the model of perception that we use most easily is the model of visual perception.

There is ample evidence that we fall into the visual metaphor most easily when we use the concept of perception. Our language itself often traps us into the visual metaphor with such phrases as *point of view* or *the way I see it.* . . . From the visual "point of view," the perception of control is indeed an illusion. We never see control directly in the sense that our retinal–cortical hookup directly records control. Further, some of our classical demonstrations of perceived physical control are, in fact, illusions. Think of Michotte's (1963) apparatus for the study of the perception of physical causality. What the subjects saw simulated the well-known billiard ball striking another billiard ball and "causing" it to move. In fact, however, Michotte devised an ingenious method that he called the "disk method" to present this phenomenon visually. A disk with spiral and circular lines on it turned behind a screen with a slit in it. Through the slit the subject saw only a portion of the line that appeared as a moving spot if the line was a spiral or as a stationary spot if the line was a circle of equal radius from the center of the turning disk. The spiral produced a moving spot that appeared to travel horizontally away from the center of the screen in the slit. This moving spot "contacted" another apparently stationary spot that was actually the circle behind the screen. When the first spot (spiral) contacted the second one (circle) in the slit, the second one began to "move" away, because at this point it was drawn on the disk as a spiral. The subject "perceived" causality, but surely it was a visual illusion set up for the control and convenience of the experimenter.

The study of perceived physical causation has served as a foundation in social psychology for work such as that by Heider (1958) and has evolved into perceived personal causation and the field of research now called attribution theory. Attribution theory concerns the processes that the average individual uses in attempting to *infer* the causes of *observed* behavior (Kelley, 1971). Again visual perception is taken as primary in the observation of behavior, but the causes are never perceived directly. The roots of attribution theory lie deep in classical visual perception studies (Michotte, 1963), can be traced through impression formation (Asch, 1946), to person perception (Tagiuri & Petrullo, 1958), and so-called self-perception (Bem, 1972). It can be argued (deCharms, 1968), however, that person perception, especially in the sense of visual perception, is a misnomer. There is a large gap between perception of physical characteristics of a person and the attribution of personal characteristics to that person.

Although there is only a partial overlap between attribution of causality and research on the concept of control, the two share the same inadequacy— the restrictive consequences of basing theory on a model of visual perception.

The crux of the problem is simple. *We do not see control; we feel it.* We never experience it directly by observation of others. We either experience it actively and directly when we control something physically, like the sports car, or we experience it passively when we are controlled by some external force. The *experience* of control is derived far more from touch and kinesthesis than from vision.

In short, we have been studying almost exclusively the observation of objective correlates of control based on what we can see, whereas the only primary evidence that we have for the concept of control comes from personal experience based more on kinesthetic than on visual phenomena. What I am suggesting is that we attempt to study more directly the *experience* of controlling and of being controlled and look for correlates of those experiences in more objective, observable behaviors.

Let me now introduce the concept of personal causation more formally and show more empirically how the foregoing argument grew out of my own work.

The Early Concept of Personal Causation

When I first developed my own conception of personal causation, I defined it in a way that emphasized "perception" and indeed stressed visual perception. The concept came originally from Heider (1958) and hence had roots similar to those of attribution theory. I used Heider's phrase "perceived locus of causality for behavior," which immediately conjures up visual and spatial imagery. The "locus" is either "seen" as internal or external to the observed person. Personal causation implied an internal locus of causality.

In order to avoid the cumbersome phrases involved in spelling out whether the perceived locus of causality for behavior was internal or external, we started using the term *pawn* for a person acting in a situation where the perceived locus of causality was external. We coined the term *origin* for a person acting in a situation where the perceived locus of causality for behavior was internal to the person. Roughly speaking, the pawn is perceived as pushed around, and the origin is perceived as originating his or her own behavior. Since the book *Personal Causation* (deCharms, 1968) used these definitions, they are usually cited when the origin–pawn concept is discussed in the literature. Presumably because the phrases *locus of causality* and *locus of control* bear some resemblance, the concepts of personal causation and locus of control of reinforcements are often used in the literature as almost synonymous. Actually, since the publication of *Personal Causation*, my research has led me away from the perception and toward the experience of personal causation. Let me explain by comparing two studies of personal causation.

One of the first empirical questions that we asked about personal causation was whether subjects could discriminate along the origin–pawn dimension. Put another way, we asked ourselves whether we could devise standard stimulus persons who appeared to be pushed around or to be originating their own behavior and whether subjects could reliably discriminate between them. DeCharms, Carpenter, and Kuperman (1965) designed a typical attribution-type study presenting stimulus persons in short-story vignettes and demonstrated that they were readily "perceived" as different along the origin–pawn dimension by subjects.

When this study was conducted, we had not yet devised a measure of individual differences on the origin dimension, but we did use a version of the Rotter locus-of-control questionnaire and found that internal subjects as compared to external subjects saw the heroes in the short-story vignettes more as origins.

This study, like most attribution studies, showed that people *could* attribute origin–pawn characteristics to others. It did *not* tell us whether they used these characteristics normally when not specifically asked to by an experimenter. Nor did it tell us whether the use of the origin–pawn dimension in attribution made any difference in the subject's own behavior.

In considering the question, "What difference does the origin–pawn dimension make?" our thinking shifted from the perception of locus of causality or origin–pawn characteristics in *others* to the more central question of what difference it makes to experience *one's self* as an origin or a pawn. Kuperman (see deCharms, 1968) and deCharms, Dougherty, and Wurtz (see deCharms, 1968) created origin- and pawnlike situations in the laboratory, where subjects built Tinker Toy models under strict controlling instructions (pawn condition) or under much freer instructions (origin condition). They hypothesized that these conditions would be experienced differently, that the origin condition would be preferred, and that the products of the origin condition would be of higher quality. They even hypothesized that the nonsense-syllable name applied to the origin model would be recalled a month later more frequently than the syllable applied to the pawn model. All these hypotheses were confirmed. In short, origin and pawn conditions could be induced in subjects in the laboratory, and the conditions strongly affected their feelings, their behavior, and even their memory of the experience.

For purposes of comparing the two studies, let us call the first study the "perception study" and the one just described the "experience study." The comparison between these two studies shows empirically the difference between approaching personal causation as a perceptual phenomenon and conceiving of it as an experience that can be induced and has important measurable effects on behavior. Let me emphasize three points of comparison.

First, the perception study asked the subject to "perceive" a stimulus person in good visual-perception-model fashion. The experience study asked the subjects to manipulate and control objects physically (the Tinker Toys). The experience is more physical and actual and kinesthetic. Second, the perception study asked the subjects to react passively to stimulus persons. The experience study asked the subjects to engage actively in production of physical models. Third, data from the perception study were questionnaire reactions only. The experience study measured actual production. A result of some interest was that the questionnaire measure of locus of control of reinforcements was related to the other measures in the perception study but was not related to any of the other measures (not even the questionnaire measures) in the experience study.

These laboratory studies led to a gradual but radical shift in our conception of personal causation based on the distinction between a model based on perception and one that assumes that the basic phenomenon of personal causation, of controlling and being controlled, is personal experience of a kinesthetic sort—in short, a more global experience, not just a perception. We no longer speak of personal causation in terms of perceived locus of causality. Personal causation is the *experience* of causing something yourself, of originating your own actions and controlling elements in your environment. The negative or pawn aspect is the *experience* of being pushed around, of not originating your own actions, of not being in control of elements in your environment. The stress is on the total experience of personal causation rather than on just the perception of it, or just the attribution of it to others, or just the behavioral correlates of it. "Experience" is intended to capture the whole of a complex phenomenon and not reduce it to partial descriptions like perception (Ossorio, 1966). On the positive origin side, the person is seen as an agent (Macmurray, 1957), as a doer, rather than as either: (1) a passive thinker, perceiver, or attributer; or (2) a mere reactor.

In keeping with the more global active concept of experience of originship, we have tried to measure differences in a person's experience through a more global measure than a questionnaire. We have tried to get a sample of a person's thoughts by having them write short stories and then content-analyze such stories for origin ideas such as setting personal goals, working toward them, and at the same time being responsible and realistic. In the second part of this paper I describe some results using this origin measure.

CONTROL IN A PRACTICAL CONTEXT

The second point of my paper is this: In order to clarify the concept of control, we need to study it in a practical context. This is not just another plea for practical relevance. In fact, it is a plea for better theory building. It is based on a deeper meaning that I see in Kurt Lewin's dictum: "There is nothing so practical as a good theory." Put the other way round, one could say the best theories are based on the solid foundation of practical situations. From intensive study of real situations, we can develop a network of related concepts that apply to practical problems. At the formal logical level, we need to ask about the logically possible relations between control and other concepts. The title of this volume takes a step in this direction and suggests a relation between control and choice. Some have suggested a broader scheme (Horosz, 1975). Perhaps choice precedes control and produces responsibility. But the test of such a logical chain is whether it appears in real interactions between people. In order to build the most useful network of concepts, we need to study a common everyday context where control is central and manifest in its complex relations.

One such context is the elementary school classroom. There are many, many classrooms to be observed, and there are enough commonalities among them, and at the same time enough diversity, to make their study fruitful—sufficiently complex, yet potentially comparable. Most important, control seems to be a major component in classrooms. Teachers try to control, pupils are controlled, pupils have to learn to control themselves. In one setting and simultaneously, we can study the controller and the controllee, so to speak.

For the past decade we have turned our attention to this arena. In our early work in the schools, we hypothesized and later confirmed a significant relationship between the origin–pawn variable—as we measured it in thought samples—and academic achievement (for details, see deCharms, 1976). Children who wrote stories about setting their own goals, originating their own behavior, and taking responsibility for it achieved more in school than children who wrote stories about wanting things with no attempt to obtain them by their own efforts. Children who experienced personal causation positively as origins, we inferred, achieved more than those who experienced school as a pawn atmosphere.

It seemed reasonable to believe that the dominant controlling agent in the classroom, the teacher, could do much either to enhance or to inhibit a feeling of personal causation. Based on this reasoning and working in a large inner-city school district, we proceeded to develop training methods designed to enhance the experience of personal causation in students. This longitudinal study that followed the children from fifth to eighth grade was highly successful. Since it is completely reported elsewhere (deCharms, 1976), I only review it as background for our more recent work.

Briefly, we provided extensive origin training to teachers and then collaborated with them in developing techniques for enhancing motivation and personal causation in their pupils. This combination produced large and reliable changes in the pupils' motivation (origin scores) and significantly reversed a trend (typical of these schools) for the pupils to fall further and further behind normal grade placement. Specifically, the academic achievement scores of the trained children began to move back up toward normal grade placement, whereas the achievement of matched untrained children continued to fall off at a rate of nearly 2 months per year (see deCharms, 1976, chap. 8).

It should be noted that the central hypothesis used to design this study was that increasing the pupils' experience of their own control in the classroom, up to a point, and decreasing the teacher's attempts to maintain strict control would enhance the pupils' motivation and ultimately their achievement—a "less control produces more motivation" strategy.

Two footnotes to this study may be inserted here. As in the laboratory studies already discussed, so in this study, we measured the locus-of-control variable in the children. Results were almost completely negative; that is, we found no increase in internality as a function of our training, nor did we find consistent relationships between locus of control and academic achievement. These results are not inconsistent with those reported in a review of locus-of-control data and academic achievement by Lefcourt (1976, chapter 6).

The second footnote worthy of mention here is that two recent follow-up studies indicate that the origin training in the sixth and seventh grades had long-lasting effects on the students. Jackson (1976) sought out a group of previously origin-trained and untrained students when they were in 11th grade (4 years after training) and found the trained students to be still significantly higher on the origin measure than the untrained students. They also had more concrete plans for the future after graduating from high school.

A study in progress at present is attempting to assess whether more of the students who were trained a decade ago in sixth and seventh grades actually went on to graduate from high school than untrained students. The data indicate that significantly more trained boys went on to graduate than did untrained. It is clear that origin training had some long-term effects on their behavior.

This study is a good example of the major point, the importance of studying control in a practical context. It shows also how the context can enhance theorizing. We had worked for 4 years on the effects of enhancing personal causation in pupils, and we had collaborated extensively with the teachers; yet we had very little data about the teachers themselves. In a sense we had studied almost exclusively the pupil, the person who is most often the controllee in the classroom. We had studied neither the controller (the teacher) nor the interactions between controller and controllee. Our recent work has concentrated on this complex controlling and countercontrolling relationship between teacher and pupil.

From the earlier study, we knew that some teachers could enhance personal causation and academic achievement in their students better than others, even without origin training. From this, a chain of questions and reasoning resulted. Were origin teachers good at enhancing motivation in others? Were teachers who were internal on the locus-of-control scale good at helping others?

We began by sketching a theoretical chain of reasoning as follows: Teacher characteristics lead to teacher behavior, which is part of teacher–pupil interaction and, through control, affects pupil motivation and pupil academic achievement. It should be noted that this is not a causal chain. Rather, we use it to visualize some of the events and variables involved in control in the classroom without inferring causal links.

For research purposes, we hypothesized that both origin teachers and internal teachers on the locus-of-control measure would have students with higher academic achievement. The reasoning behind these hypotheses was similar to that used in designing the enhancing motivation project, namely, a "less is more" strategy. Less teacher control (up to a point) should lead to more feelings of personal causation in pupils and hence to greater motivation and academic achievement. Both internal and origin teachers should use fewer controlling measures than external or pawn teachers and should have more of an origin climate in their classrooms. The full model includes a measure of teacher–pupil interaction that is beyond the scope of this paper. So the conceptual chain, for these purposes, simplified to: Origin or internal teachers have more of an origin climate in their classrooms and hence, higher academic achievement.

The origin measure used in this study was a refinement of the earlier measure. The teachers wrote imaginative stories to six verbal cues (such as, "Two men working at a machine"). These thought samples were content-analyzed for an origin score in the same way the children's stories were. We made a new distinction, however, in each subcategory between an *idealistic* orientation and a *realistic* orientation. In the idealistic-type origin story (type A), the hero engages in personal goal setting and the like, untrammeled by the restrictions of any particular context or by authority figures. In the second, more realistic-type origin story (type B), the hero takes responsibility for accepting a context or authority where major goals may be set for him or her. Within that context, the individual engages in setting subgoals. The distinction is not hard to see in stories. In the idealistic-type origin story, the hero may want a bicycle (goal) and sets out to earn the money to get it (activity). In the realistic-type origin story, an authority (teacher or parent) or the context (a dangerous setting) specifies major goals. The hero accepts the inevitability of the setting and the imposed goal (taking an exam), takes ownership of the goal (to do well), and works for it. Note that in both cases, pawn alternatives are clear. The pawn dreams of a bicycle but does nothing to obtain it. The pawn reacts against the situation or authority in negative ways rather than either accepting the imposed goal or making his or her own.

Muir and deCharms (1975) found that scores from these two types of origin stories were uncorrelated with each other. In general, the realistic origin scores (type B) were more highly correlated with academic achievement in pupils. Both idealistic and realistic origin scores were obtained for the teachers in the present study, but only the realistic scores are discussed here.

After writing the imaginative stories, the teachers took the form of the locus-of-control scale presented by Rotter (1966), from which was determined their internal–external scores.

The climate established in the classroom by teacher–pupil interaction was assessed near the end of the school year by a measure developed by Koenigs and Hess (see deCharms, 1976, Appendix B) called the origin climate questionnaire. It is a simple Likert-type scale where pupils are asked to respond to items on a 5-point scale from "never" to "always." The items tap origin categories (e.g., goal setting) that are applied specifically to the pupils' classroom. For instance, a goal-setting item reads, "In this class I can decide how to use the extra time [p. 260]." This measure was related to academic achievement of the classroom and was sensitive enough to discriminate between origin-trained and untrained teachers' classrooms in the earlier study (see deCharms, 1976; Koenigs, Fiedler, & deCharms, 1977). Means of a random sample of students in a classroom are used as a measure of the classroom climate.

The academic achievement measure was the mean class score on the *Iowa Test of Basic Skills* (Lindquist & Hieronymous, 1955). The score for each child was the total of four subscales (vocabulary, language, reading, and arithmetic).

Subjects for the study were 85 teachers, most of whom taught in the inner city. They were fifth-, sixth-, and seventh-grade teachers. Since average class size was approximately 30 pupils, these data represent some 2500 pupils, although sampling within classes reduced the analysis of data to approximately 1000 pupils. The sampling unit, however, is the teacher, so pupils' scores were reduced to means for each class.

The first finding was that there is no correlation between the locus-of-control measure and the realistic origin measure in the teachers. The correlation for the 85 teachers was $r = +.11$, $p < .30$. Despite the apparent similarity of the concepts of origin and internal locus of control of reinforcements, this came as no surprise, since locus of control had not been related to origin scores in the pupils in the earlier study.

One might expect from these data that our hypothesis concerning the teachers' orientation toward control and the pupils' academic achievement

TABLE 3.1
Mean Number of Months
Below Pupil's Normal Grade Placement
(*Iowa Test of Basic Skills*)

		Locus of Control of Teacher		
		Internal	*External*	*Total*
	High	−4.11	−7.33	−6.00
Origin Score		N = 16	N = 23	N = 39
of Teacher	Low	−7.80	−11.98	−9.80
		N = 24	N = 22	N = 46
	Total	−6.33	−9.60	−8.05
		N = 40	N = 45	N = 85

would not hold for one of the measures. But in fact, the hypothesis held for both internal locus of control and for the origin measure. Table 3.1 presents the mean number of months below grade placement for classrooms taught by teachers classified by internal vs. external locus of control and by high- vs. low-realistic origin scores. A 2 × 2 analysis of variance based on the *Iowa Test of Basic Skills* raw scores (i.e., the data underlying these means) revealed a significant difference between internal and external teachers [$F(1, 81) = 4.78$, $p < .04$] and, similarly, a significant difference between high- and low-realistic origin teachers [$F(1, 81) = 6.34$, $p < .02$]. The interaction between these two variables failed to reach significance. Clearly then, although the two orientations toward control of the teachers are uncorrelated, they both contribute independently to academic achievement of pupils.

The question now arises: "By what means do these teachers of different characteristics attain greater pupil achievement?" Following a lead from the earlier study that origin training increased the origin climate of the classroom, we can now insert the origin climate questionnaire in the chain to see if it links either internal locus of control of teacher or origin of teacher to academic achievement of their pupils. It turns out that there is a small but significant ($p < .05$) relationship between teachers' realistic origin scores and the origin climate of the classroom. There is, however, no difference between the origin climate of classrooms taught by internal vs. external locus-of-control teachers.

We can now visualize the empirically established chain of events as follows: Origin teachers do tend to have an origin climate in their classroom and to have higher academic achievement. Internal teachers do not tend to have a higher origin climate, but nonetheless they do have higher academic achievement. The origin teachers, therefore, tend to confirm the "less control leads to more origin climate" hypothesis. The internal teachers do not. We don't know what internal teachers do to increase academic achievement of their pupils. Establishing an origin climate is only one possible way. Perhaps more rather than less strict control also leads to greater achievement, and this kind of control links internality of teacher to pupil achievement. As yet we do not know.

At the broader level, these data show the advantages of studying the concept of control in a practical context. Clearly, we have barely scratched the surface of the complex events that intervene between controller, controllee, and an outcome measure in the classroom.

SUMMARY

Returning to the major themes of this paper—first, the visual perception vs. personal experience distinction—we may conclude that the concept of personal causation and the concept of locus of control appear to be based on two distinct models. Personal causation attempts to tap the experience of controlling and being controlled. Locus of control is more in the "perceived control" tradition. Empirically, both personal causation and locus of control seem important in understanding control in the classroom, but they are statistically and theoretically unrelated and account for independent variance in our studies.

As to the second theme—control in the practical context—I have tried to show the value of studying concepts like control intensively in a practical context to reveal the complex interrelations between concepts that occur in the real setting.

REFERENCES

Asch, S. E. Forming impressions of personality. *Journal of Abnormal and Social Psychology*, 1946, *41*, 258–290.

Bem, D. J. Self-perception theory. In L. Berkowitz (Ed.), *Advances in experimental social psychology* (Vol. 6). New York: Academic Press, 1972.

deCharms, R. *Personal causation: The internal affective determinants of behavior.* New York: Academic Press, 1968.

deCharms, R. *Enhancing motivation: Change in the classroom.* New York: Irvington Publishers, 1976.

deCharms, R., Carpenter, V., & Kuperman, A. The "origin–pawn" variable in person perception. *Sociometry*, 1965, *28*, 241–258.

Heider, F. *The psychology of interpersonal relations.* New York: Wiley, 1958.

Horosz, W. *The crisis of responsibility.* Norman, Okla.: University of Oklahoma Press, 1975.

Jackson, H. *An assessment of the long-term effects of personal causation training.* Unpublished doctoral dissertation, Washington University, St. Louis, Missouri, 1976.

Kelley, H. H. Causal schemata and the attribution process. In E. E. Jones, D. E. Kanouse, H. H. Kelley, R. E. Nisbett, S. Valins, & B. Weiner (Eds.), *Attribution: Perceiving the causes of behavior.* Morristown, N.J.: General Learning Press, 1971.

Koenigs, S. S., Fiedler, M. L., & deCharms, R. Teacher beliefs, classroom interaction and personal causation. *Journal of Applied Social Psychology*, 1977, *7*, 95–114.

Lefcourt, H. M. *Locus of control.* Hillsdale, N.J.: Lawrence Erlbaum Associates, 1976.

Lindquist, E. F., & Hieronymous, A. N. *Iowa test of basic skills.* Boston: Houghton Mifflin, 1955.

Macmurray, J. *The self as agent.* New York: Harper, 1957.

Michotte, A. *The perception of causality.* New York: Basic Books, 1963.

Muir, M. S., & deCharms, R. *Personal causation training and goal setting in seventh grade.* Paper presented at American Educational Research Association meeting, Washington, D.C., April 1975.

Ossorio, P. *Persons.* Boulder, Colo.: Linguistics Research Institute, 1966.

Rotter, J. B. Generalized expectancies for internal versus external control of reinforcement. *Psychological Monographs*, 1966, *80* (1, Whole No. 609).

Tagiuri, R., & Petrullo, L. *Person perception and interpersonal behavior.* Stanford, Calif.: Stanford University Press, 1958.

4 The Need for Personal Control in Political Life: Origins, Dynamics, and Implications

Stanley A. Renshon
City University of New York

As a political scientist interested in the nature and development of character and its implications for the political process, my point of departure in this volume is to raise and examine two primary questions. The first arises out of an observation made by a number of social analysts including many of the present contributors—namely, that in a variety of experimental and real-life situations, individuals prefer to select and travel their own life-paths and that when allowed or able to do so, they will generally perform better and experience concomitant feelings including satisfaction, optimism, and an increased sense of self-worth. The question that arises, given such a finding, is why the individual should have such a preference; that is, what is its origin, nature, and developmental path?

In this paper I wish to argue that there is within each of us a need for considerable influence over the people, events, and institutions that have a substantial impact on our well-being and valued life pursuits. This need, which I have called the need for personal control, is suggested to arise out of the complex interplay between somatically based needs and socially based satisfaction. Furthermore, once acquired, this need gives rise, as conceptual development proceeds, to a series of basic assumptive beliefs about the nature of the world and its operations; among the most important of these are individual beliefs in personal control. These beliefs have implications for feelings, thoughts, and actions in numerous areas of the social process but especially in those areas with direct personal impact. Given that politics is concerned in large part with the authoritative allocation of who gets what—to use Lasswell's (1959) apt phrase—it is no surprise that the political process will act upon and engage, as well as be influenced by, needs for personal

41

control. However, in democratic political systems, there are other forces that engage the need for personal control that may be substantially independent of any real or imagined impact, and these have to do with participatory norms of democratic political cultures and the political myths that arise from them. In this paper, I also argue that the increasing personal impact of public policy decisions, coupled with the normative requirement that citizens ought to have some control over the government, has increased the saliency of this need. Yet at the same time, the corresponding development of individual skills and institutional support that would facilitate such control have been rendered increasingly problematic because of certain patterns in contemporary society that give rise to a number of personal and political double binds.

The second question, then, that I would like to raise and examine concerns the political impact and implications of the need for personal control. However, in constructing a theory of psychological needs and political life, it is necessary to remain aware that the models employed have implications well beyond their ability to explain variance. The concept of needs occupies a central, if not unique, position within both psychology and political science in the explanation of human behavior, but for different reasons. In psychology, the centrality of the need concept arises from the fact that it is the most basic level of psychic organization posited by personality theorists and is regarded by many as a core dimension of individual character. Its uniqueness stems from its dual reference points—one extending inward to the biological mechanisms of the individual, the other extended outward to the social environment in which it operates. It is therefore a biosocial concept that presents the possibility of binding together at one explanatory point two distinct yet crucial levels of human explanation.

For political scientists, the concept of needs represents one method by which the "predisposition-activation" paradigm can be extended beyond the current concern with political attitudes in a way that recognizes the biological nature of human beings. The recognition of the role of individual needs also provides a valuable perspective from which to view and explain political behaviors. This alone would be sufficient to justify careful consideration of needs as an explanatory rubric in political analysis.

But the concept has developed an importance that goes well beyond its explanatory power and arises from its increasing use in the context of political justification. The concept "human needs" has come to occupy a powerful and distinctive position in political discourse and propaganda. Whereas public policy (both democratic and authoritarian) has frequently been justified in terms of "the peoples' needs," the legitimacy of the concept has increased (and therefore, so has its potency as a political symbol) because of its "empirical" basis and more recent association with "scientific" discourse.

It is small wonder, then, that social theorists from a variety of disciplines have grappled with the complexities of need theory in an attempt to resolve some of the conceptual and empirical difficulties surrounding its use. As part of this discussion, therefore, I would like to spend some time examining the political consequences of taking the concept of needs seriously, most especially as they relate to the need for personal control and political choice within a democratic political context. As part of this discussion, it is necessary to discuss briefly the nature and empirical properties of needs, both as theoretical constructs and as operative forces. It is with the former that I would like to begin.

NEEDS OF A CLASS OF MOTIVE EXPLANATIONS

According to Peters (1958): "motives... are a particular class of reasons, which are distinguished by certain logical properties [pp. 27–28]." Among the most important, for present purposes, is that they are reasons of a directed sort: "If (a person) has a motive he must have a goal of some sort, however weak its influence.... [p. 32]." Peters goes on to distinguish four types of motive explanations: (1) "his reason"; (2) "the reason" explanations; (3) causal explanations; and (4) end-state explanations.

Need theories are one type of end-state explanations of human behavior. The latter explain human motivation by reference to requirements of the organism that serve to organize and motivate behavior. Murray's (1938) definition is illustrative in this regard and worth quoting at some length:

A need is a construct (a convenient fiction or hypothetical concept) which stands for a force (the physico-chemical nature of which is unknown) in the brain region which organizes perception, apperception, intellection, conation, and action in such a way as to transform in a certain direction an existing, unsatisfying situation. A need is sometimes invoked by internal processes of a certain kind (viscerogenic, endocrinogenic, thalamicogenic) arising in the course of vital sequences, but, more frequently (when in a state of readiness) by the occurrence of a few commonly effective press[1] (or by anticipatory images of such press). Thus it manifests itself by leading the organism to search for, or avoid encountering, or, when encountered, to attend to and respond to certain kinds of press.... Each need is characteristically accompanied by a particular feeling or emotion.... it may be weak or intense, momentary or enduring. But usually it persists and gives rise to a certain course of overt behavior (or fantasy) which (if the organism is competent and external opposition not insurmountable) changes the initiating circumstances in such a way as to bring about an end situation which stills (appeases or satisfies) the organism [pp. 123–124].

---

[1]A *press* is defined by Murray as a stimulus property of an aspect of the environment perceived by the organism in terms of its threat of harm or promise of benefit.

Murray's definition suggests the crucial nature of needs for the individual—namely, that they will have substantial impact on the perception and organization of "reality" as well as behavioral activities carried out in association with these processes. Yet it is important to emphasize that "needs" are constructs that are proposed "to account for certain objective and subjective facts [p. 54]." As a convenient fiction, they are useful to the extent that they help us to explain variations in human activities and outcomes and are by themselves neither "true" nor "false."

Murray's definition points to several possible criteria for assessing the existence of needs. The first is the typical direction of attempted influence. The organism will attempt to transform the situation in a way that either facilitates the satisfaction of the need or minimizes or postpones deprivations associated with it. A second criterion is the development of a typical mode or action pattern connected with the organization of perception or action. These may be thought of as routinized procedures for dealing with typical need-press situations that develop into personal styles. The third indication might be the person's concern with particular aspects of the environment and not others. This will involve "the search for, avoidance or selection of, attention and response to one of a few types of press (catechized objects of a certain class) [p. 124]." A fourth is the exhibition of particular affect that is connected with particular need-press situations. Thus, when a need has become activated, we would generally (but not always) expect some feeling to be experienced and defined by the person as discomfiture. Last, the existence of a need can be inferred by the state of the organism given a particular need-press-activity outcome. Presumably, the "satisfaction" of a need should lead to expression classifiable as "positive," and the failure to do so should result in dissatisfaction.

There is, of course, one further criterion, which is potentially powerful, yet highly controversial. This is the attempt to adduce the existence and crucial importance of needs by pointing to the pathologies in human development and behavior that result from their systematic or prolonged lack of satisfaction. Thus, Maslow (1954) proposes "the bold proposition that a man who is thwarted in any of his basic needs may be fairly envisioned simply as a sick man or at least less than fully human [p. 57]." Along similar lines, Fromm (1973) contends: "If one of the basic (needs) has found no fulfillment, insanity is the result; if it is satisfied but in an unsatisfactory way—considering the nature of human existence—neurosis (either manifest or in the form of a socially patterned defect) is the result [p. 68]."

Defining needs in terms of "any behavioral tendency whose continued denial or frustration leads to pathological responses" (Bay, 1968, p. 242) involves us at the outset with an enormous set of difficulties. Among the most important is that phrased in this way, the concept of need becomes pointedly normative, for as Peters (1958) has put it, "it usually functions as a diagnostic term with remedial implications [p. 17]." The implication of the normative assumption built into this important explanatory concept is an area to which I return shortly.

THE NEED FOR PERSONAL CONTROL

I began this paper by suggesting that there was within each person a need for personal control. It should be made clear, however, that such a proposition, even if plausible and ultimately theoretically acceptable, provides no more than a foundation for examining the relationsip between personal control and political life. The reason for this is that to propose the existence of a need in no way removes the obligation of the theorist to deal with a number of difficult questions concerning its nature, origin, development, and outplay in the social process. Is, for example, the need for personal control to be thought of as an instinct, as something that is part of the genetically transmitted foundation of human behavior? If so, is it universal and therefore part of a species-wide dimension of "human nature"? To these questions must be added those dealing with the nature of its outplay in the social process. Does a need for personal control have a direct link to public behavior, or is its operation submerged under layers of social learning?

Following Freud, most need theorists begin with the assumption that needs are part of the instinctual equipment present in every person. And although there has certainly been disagreement among need theorists as to the exact number and nature of human needs, there is generally a consensus that the needs are biological "givens," rather than socially induced possibilities. I wish to take a somewhat different approach and argue that the need for personal control is not in itself a biological but rather an existential "given" that—though arising out of the interplay between biological necessity and social experience—is not in itself ultimately reducible to either the former or the latter.

There is general agreement that the human organism enters the world with physical needs but little in the way of innate capacities (except perhaps in embryonic form) with which to satisfy them. The child is from the first, therefore, dependent on the good will, knowledge, and attentiveness of others for the satisfaction of the most basic psychological needs. The child arrives, for example, with hunger drives but no innate knowledge about what constitutes satisfaction or how to go about obtaining it. Although the child apparently arrives with a sucking reflex intact, he or she must be taught that mother's breast is where that innate skill should be applied. Thus, unlike instinctual patterns in other animals, the complete stimulus-response bond is not a biological given for humans.

Freud (1959) suggested that the operative pattern of instincts arose from the gradual building up of tension as the need for gratification increased, followed by quiescence when the need has been satisfied. Freud thought that both the operating dynamics and the content of the needs were biologically based. What Freud and other need theorists have either overlooked or underemphasized to a large degree is that needs can be created as an outcome of a social process rather than necessarily being present at the creation. I would like to suggest that the need for personal control arises in just such a way.

The child is born into the world with basic somatic needs but without the necessary conceptual or physical equipment to satisfy them. Moreover, since needs press for immediate discharge, we would expect that the need for food (hunger) or liquid (thirst) would be experienced as extremely uncomfortable by the child. The child, of course, is not without capacity to influence the behavior of adults, as any parent who has spent a sleepless night will attest; but even among the most concerned and attentive parents, there must of necessity be some delays involved in providing satisfaction. First, by the time the child signals by crying, the discomfort has already begun. Second, even the most attentive parent takes time to respond, thus insuring that there will be at least some delays in satisfaction. Third, even responsive parents can not always tell exactly what need satisfaction is indicated by the child's signals. It may be a cry for food, a change of sheets, or just simply comfort for an unspecified somatic distress.

In all these cases, the inevitability of delay brings with it deprivations. Yet at the same time the child experiences these discomforts, he or she is also experiencing the self (and the degree to which this is so also varies) as a party to the process satisfaction. That cries can bring a response, although delayed, provides the child with an important experience in bringing a part of personal well-being under at least rudimentary control.

It should be clear that there are two related processes at work here. The first involves the distress associated with having a need and lacking control over whether it will ultimately be satisfied, and if so, when. As Erikson (1968) has suggested in connection with this point, the fear is that "eventually" may become "never." Yet as the child begins to associate personal efforts with some satisfactory outcome, however delayed in appearing, a bond is formed between the necessity to insure satisfaction and the experience of having been able to do so. The anxiety of delay, coupled with the real somatic discomfort that accompanies it, gives rise to the need to have more control over the nature, degree, and timing of satisfaction. It is in this sense that the need for personal control arises out of the existential dilemma posed by biologically based needs and socially based satisfactions.

From this perspective, the satisfaction of somatically based needs carries with it three, rather than one, primary sources of gratification. The first and most obvious arises from the satisfaction of the somatic need. The second is the gratification that arises from having reduced (at least momentarily) the fear that delay will be interminable rather than simply inevitable. Third, and for our purposes equally important, is that gratification also comes from having some control over obtaining satisfaction. In short, the experience of control becomes a source of reward not only because it brings about need satisfaction but also because it reduces anxiety. In the course of the thousands of microsequences in which need activation gives rise to satisfaction attempts, a bond is formed between the instrumental activity and these dual rewards. It is not surprising, therefore, that the activity itself soon comes to have reward properties that are related to, but not completely dependent on, full success in either area.

If the need for personal control begins with immediately instrumental activity, it does not long remain limited to it. As the child acquires language, he or she builds an important tool for increasing feelings of personal control. With language, the child is able to name what is needed (wanted) and may also exert greater pressure on those who are responsible for providing gratification. But it is important for our purposes to call attention to the fact that as much control as the child is able to exert, it is exercised within a context that contains a great many "givens." Thus, although children may indicate preferences and more than occasionally get what they want, there are many ways in which parents can control the outcomes without resorting to "dictatorship." Among the most effective ways is to control options, so that choice is presented and control seemingly exercised but within a contextual boundary specified by others.

These more limited exercises in obtaining personal control are not necessarily an impediment to developing feelings of personal control and thus to be avoided. It may be helpful for the child to exercise choice and control in a way that allows practice without severe consequences for mistakes. By making some options unavailable, the parents may forestall the long-term harm that might result from a choice uninformed by longer temporal and experiential perspectives. So, too, consideration must be given to the enormous anxiety that may result from having too much control. To allow free rein may certainly give the child heightened beliefs in his or her control over others, but this will be paid for by the child's incapacity to control personal impulses. Beliefs in personal control arise from internal regulation as well as from external influence.

As maturation proceeds, however, the child becomes increasingly aware of the many different levels at which the gratification process is played out. The realization that there are metascripts (hidden agendas), that set limits and that these limits may themselves (under certain conditions) be up for debate constitutes an expansion of the child's understanding and experience of personal control. It may no longer suffice to have a choice that does not make much of a difference when the real fulcrum of decision is being withheld from control attempts. It is probably the case that this recognition is not explicit;

rather, a model of unfolding realization that operates at latent levels of consciousness seems more appropriate, at least at earlier stages of development.

As the person develops from child to adult, there is a corresponding shift in concerns about personal control. To the extent that maturation, social experience, and perspective permit, the individual may begin to view his or her life in terms of basic personal foundations of the past and to evolve structures of the future. Once this view is taken, the attempt to become the architect of one's own life structures involves the effort to influence diverse domains over temporal periods that may strain, if not erase, the more typical sequences of cause and effect. It is at this juncture that the need for control, coupled with feelings of personal control developed from past success, allows that leap of faith without which life mastery may not be attempted, much less accomplished.

I have reviewed elsewhere (Renshon, 1974) at greater length the studies from comparative (animal) psychology and from psychoanalytic, post-Freudian, and "third force" theory that tend to support the proposition that the experience of personal control is itself rewarding and a basic component of human experience. There now seems to be more powerful experimental evidence from the social psychology laboratories to support this inference. In particular, I refer to Langer's (1975) work on the "illusion of control," which seems to suggest that even in cases where individuals "know" that the contingencies are primarily chance structured, there is a strong tendency to view them as individually controllable. So, too, Seligman's (1975) experiments with the deleterious impact of "learned helplessness" all point to the basic importance of the need for personal control.

However, to propose a need as a basis for social activity is by itself insufficient for two reasons. First, a need, as Murray (1938) metaphorically put it, "may have no inkling of what it needs [p. 403]." That is, granting the existence of a need for personal control, it is not immediately obvious what if anything will satisfy it. A consideration of this point must of necessity involve us in examining the social processes. Second, needs themselves, though they are of obvious importance in understanding social and political behavior, are frequently only indirectly connected with them. For this reason, the concept of needs will be necessary but never sufficient to explain political activity.

The general model that I would like to propose here is that the need for personal control, which originated in the attempt to satisfy other basic needs, gives rise as the organism develops to a series of assumptive beliefs about the nature and operation of the world. These assumptive frameworks arise out of the relative balance between need activation and need-satisfaction experiences. These assumptive beliefs include: (1) beliefs about the nature of the world, whether friendly or hostile; (2) beliefs about the self, whether valuable or not; (3) beliefs about the nature and degree of personal control; (4) beliefs about others, whether and to what extent they can be trusted; and (5) beliefs about location of the self in time and space. I have called these basic beliefs assumptive, because they do in my estimation form the epistemological foundation of the numerous belief and attitude systems that characterize human cognitive structures. These beliefs are not solely cognitive but have emotional valences and evaluative components attached to them. Since they operate at such deep levels of psychic organization and arise out of such early and intense emotional experiences, they would be expected to be highly resistant but not impervious to change.

In general, then, early preverbal experiences give rise to both the need for personal control and some sense of the degree to which it can be exercised. I term the latter beliefs in personal control and suggest that in general, the developmental paths of this and other basic beliefs can be expected to follow from the accumulation of thousands of microexperiences according to the laws of social learning. The development and dynamics of these beliefs are not simply a function of "primacy" as psychoanalytic theory implies (Searing, Schwartz, & Lind, 1973); nor are they solely a function of recency as some would suggest (Hovland, Janis, & Kelley, 1953). Rather they would appear to fluctuate, if at all, in response to the continuity or discontinuity of life experiences. That is, to the extent that later experiences reinforce early experiences, we would expect stability of the basic belief structure; and to the extent that experiences did not, we would expect change. This is one reason why the study of adult socialization (Levinson, Darrow, Klein, Levinson, & McGee, 1978)—including the "milestone" experiences, which come with each stage of development or in any one of them—is so crucial. Until recently, within the social and behavioral sciences, considerably more attention has been paid to early experiences. As a result, we know quite a bit less about later life and the contemporary forces that shape life structures and outcomes. Reaching a "midlife crisis," experiencing the death of a loved one, or living through intense political turmoil—all are experiences that may reshape the individual's assumptive structure including his or her beliefs in personal control. Yet exactly which events operate to what degree for which persons remains unexplored territory. The later-life sources of adult behavior and development are the frontier of personality research.

PERSONAL CONTROL AND POLITICAL LIFE

If I have established at least a plausible case for the existence of a need for personal control, this need still remains to be linked with political processes and outcomes. Politics has been described as the arena in which decisions that are generally accepted as binding are raised, debated, decided, and implemented. It should be clear that societies differ widely on both the range of life pursuits affected by governmental decisions and the legitimacy accorded to whatever decisions are reached. In some societies government authority stops at the village gate. In others, it attempts to reach into every facet of human experience. My own remarks are generally directed toward modernized, democratically oriented societies, althought they are not without application elsewhere.

As a general rule, citizens in technologically advanced democratic societies are connected to the political process by two primary factors. The first is the existence of a highly centralized, technologically sophisticated, governmental apparatus that is increasingly called upon to expand its activities into areas where the problems do not admit of either individual or small group action. Although there has been resistance to this trend, its progression seems relentless. Problems of pollution regulation, national health insurance, and coherent national energy policy are only some of the areas in which substantial government intervention is emerging. Moreover, the experience of the United States since the New Deal suggests that however problematic the initial intervention, there is a tendency for it, once begun, to become institutionalized. Once routinized, such interventions and their supporting frameworks within the political culture soon acquire a legitimacy and normalcy that make them difficult to reappraise, let alone excise. Thus, although Social Security was bitterly contested in the 1930s, not a voice can be heard today in opposition to its continuation.

As the problems of advanced, interdependent societies increase in scope and intensity, the transformation of private needs into public policies will take place at an increasingly rapid pace. It is also true that as this occurs, the scope of the strictly private domain will decrease. The prospect, therefore, is that government and politics will increasingly be a control-relevant domain to the extent that impact increases salience.

There is a second, related way in which politics becomes linked to needs for personal control, and that is through the impact of political events. In concentrating on daily policy outcomes, it is sometimes overlooked that political events themselves can activate control needs and create linkages to the political process. Wars and economic swings are merely the most obvious of a large number of sociopolitical experiences that can function in that way. The reason for this at the individual level is quite clear. Such events may interfere in a very direct way, because they help shape the general social context in which the individual plays out his or her goals and dreams. Indeed the general boundaries prescribed by these kinds of events may have more direct and immediate impact than much government policy, which though restrictive, may occur in areas peripheral to central life concerns.

Aside from these two forms of impact-related linkages, there is a third that has special relevance for democratic political systems. This is the normative linkage between the good-citizen role and political attentiveness, most appropriately, captured by the concept of "citizen duty." Even in the absence of direct impact, citizens would be impelled by civic obligation to pay at least some attention to politics and to discharge their responsibilities periodically by making known their preferences—in short, to vote.

Democratic governments must invest considerable resources in maintaining the acceptable norms that govern the political process. Among the most important in democratic political cultures are beliefs that the government is responsive and that citizens can and do have an impact. The attitudinal constellation conceptualized as "political efficacy"—and operationalized by the SRC's five-item scale—has been studied extensively. (For a review, see Milbrath, 1965.) In general, the finding emerges that greater feelings of political efficacy are associated with greater levels of political participation—in particular, system-supportive, campaign-related activities.

What is more interesting from the standpoint of our present concern is that these feelings apparently begin to emerge in childhood, long before concrete experiences could have given these feelings an experiential foundation. It is not surprising, therefore, that Easton and Dennis (1967), in presenting the results of their path-breaking exploration of the emergence of this constellation in children, entitled their paper, "The Child's Acquisition of Regime Norms: Political Efficacy." Whether norms-based social obligation can be maintained in the absence of confirming experience, however, is open to question. The general decline of voting activity coupled with the rise of the "politics of protest" in the last decade suggest that it cannot. Indeed it seems plausible that unrealistic norms coupled with disconfirming experiences may impel, rather than retard, more direct forms of political activity.

In any event, for reasons already discussed, the political arena is and seems likely to continue to be a control-relevant sphere. However, this does not mean that there is direct, unencumbered linkage between aroused activation and behavior. Beliefs in personal control may arise out of the interplay between needs and satisfaction experiences, but their level and fluctuations are related to and mediated by a number of contextual factors.

In an early paper Julian Rotter (1966) pointed out the generalized expectancies concerning the outcome of events were influenced by attributions of causality to fate, chance, luck, or powerful others. In its most basic form, Rotter's hypothesis was that if a person believed that outcomes were significantly related to his or her own behavior, "then the occurrence of either a positive or negative reinforcement will strengthen or weaken potential for that behavior to reoccur in the same or similar situation [p. 5]." On the other hand, if outcomes were viewed as dependent on "chance, fate, powerful others or unpredictable, then the preceding behavior (would be) less likely to be either strengthened or weakened [p. 5]."

Although Rotter was clearly dealing with a character dimension of basic significance, it is important to recall that his focus was as much directed at the impact of events on individuals and how they were perceived as on the nature of the character dimension itself. That is, the question Rotter asked was: Given either internal or external control attributions, how were new events to be interpreted and acted upon? In his summary, Rotter (1966, p. 26) noted that the perception of situations as chance or otherwise externally controlled resulted in a decreased likelihood of either raising expectations after success or lowering them after failure.

Presumably, therefore, behavior in any particular situation would be a joint function of both individual dispositions (e.g., internal/external generalized expectancies) and attributions of the locus of causality to particular events and tasks (i.e., whether personally controllable or not). The research strategy dictated by such a paradigm would involve, then, two sets of measurements. The first would be of the generalized expectancies of internal vs. external control, whereas the second would be the measurement of the nature of the event or task.

I emphasize this point, simply because most research utilizing concepts of personal control—especially that conducted outside the social psychology laboratory—has emphasized the first of these dimensions, with little attempt to deal seriously with the conjoint influence and importance of both. Although personal control (and related concepts) has been applied to the explanation and analysis of political behavior, there has been very little effort to manipulate systematically the "stimulus properties" of political situations and environments. So although it is clear that individuals are taught to expect some control over political institutions, process, events, and actors, it is not clear how much is expected or believed possible in each case. Nor is the impact of experience in these diverse political arenas very well understood. A major reason for this is that we are accustomed to examining behavior as the dependent variable. Rather than exploring the consequences of behavior, we focus instead on its antecedents. There is nothing inherently wrong in this approach; it simply needs to be strengthened by more systematic efforts to examine internal as well as external consequences.

Attention to the context in which needs develop and operate will alleviate, but not necessarily resolve, all the problems connected with assessing the impact of personal control on political life. This is because there are other, specialized problems involved in transferring concepts developed in the laboratory to larger, less structured, social arenas. These problems are neither inconsiderable nor unimportant in considering the relationship of personal control to political life. Among the issues that must be confronted in any "real-world" analysis are: the specification of exactly what is (and what is not) operating as a reinforcement in any particular circumstance, a consideration of the possibility that multiple reinforcers may be operative, the difficulties involved in operationalizing and measuring these various reinforcements, and the frequent temporal discontinuities between the initiation of an action and some outcome in many nonlaboratory situations.

Whatever the disadvantages of the typical social–psychology experiment, it does provide the experimenter with more control over "stimuli," behavioral sequences, and outcomes than is possible in natural situations. It is certainly true, as Rosenthal (1966) has convincingly demonstrated in his studies of "experimenter effects," that there is a lot more that goes on in experimentation than has previously been appreciated. Still, the social psychology experiment does limit and to that extent allows experimental control not possible under other circumstances. When sequence and stimulus can be controlled, one can make a fairly accurate estimate of what followed from what and why. This control is important in establishing the "rewarding" or "punishing" nature of the stimulus or intervention, as well as in assessing its impact on the subject in terms of intentions, attributions, and resultant outcomes.

Leaving aside the larger issue of desirability, it is clear that such control is not feasible in the larger social arena. In complex social environments, it is exceedingly difficult to single out the stimulus. Given multiple stimuli, it then becomes more difficult to establish just what factor(s) is operating on whom and in what way. This is crucial, because a minimal condition for establishing the "rewarding" or "punishing" nature of a stimulus is the capacity to isolate it. With multiple stimuli comes the possibility that rewards and punishments in any situation are mixed in a way that confounds understanding, let alone prediction. Moreover, in social life, unlike the laboratory, the individual has alternatives available. It is frequently forgotten that even Pavlov's famous canine had to be secured in a harness before conditioning could proceed.

The point here is that what appears to be manifestly obvious (perhaps mistakenly) in the laboratory cannot be so easily assumed in political analysis. The same public policy, for example, may be rewarding to one group, punishing to another, and a neutral stimulus to still another. Moreover, as Edelman (1971) has pointed out, there are large areas of politics that are symbolic in content but important sources of psychic satisfaction for the citizenry. This dimension of social and political life has rarely been tackled in laboratory experimentation.

Lastly, it is important to take note of the enormous differences between the laboratory and social life on the very crucial dimension of temporality. In the laboratory, outcome follows behavior with breathtaking rapidity, but influencing public policy or bringing about political change is a time-consuming process in more ways than one. Advocates of "change now," with the emphasis on the latter, frequently arouse resistance that goes beyond the particular content of their proposals. This is because in politics, as in life, there is a set of durational expectations between the initiation of some action and outcomes. In democracies, the necessity to explore and consider alternative points of view requires a certain tolerance and acceptance of delay. Moreover, it is the nature of the public policy process that "success" in any area is not easily measured. This is in large part because much public policy seeks to provide satisfying gains for the many rather than maximized gains for the few. If policy outcomes in democratic political cultures are characterized by compromise, then success is not easily assessed in either/or terms.

Many of these factors, although reflected in individual beliefs, are more adequately considered as part of a broader social mosaic with roots in both historical and contemporary experience (both real and mythic) whose outcomes are reflected in cultural assumptions. To a large extent individual beliefs are anchored in collective experiences, especially when the group's history has been repeatedly uniform. Given these conditions, a pervasive sense of powerlessness may arise in any of several ways.

The most obvious route is enslavement. In this situation the arena of negotiation is rather small. General goals, means of attainment, sequences of procedure, and rates of accomplishment are constrained only by the conscience of the oppressor (not a noticeably effective barrier to cruelty) or by a rough calculation of sufficient levels of physical well-being to insure continued productivity. Where replacements are not in short supply, these levels may be low indeed. In many cases, exploitation, though present, does not take the severe form illustrated by slavery or forced labor. The major difference lies in the possibility that means, sequences, or pace may be arenas for negotiation, not dictation. What is not negotiable in these cases are general goals or assumptive frameworks. Decisions about where to proceed and why are not subject to any consensual process, a defining characteristic of authoritarian asymmetric relationships. Many colonial experiences fall under this rubric. Colonizers may allow a fair degree of local autonomy, especially if administered under the direction of "loyal natives," but attempted departures from the best interests of the colonizer in any circumstance can rarely be sustained in the absence of force.

A third route to a sense of collective powerlessness is no less effective for being less dramatic. It consists of a systematic policy of governmental nonresponsiveness. Any extended period of "benign neglect" becomes a contradiction in terms, since even the highest levels of personal control beliefs cannot be sustained in the face of chronic ineffectualness.

The development of a sense of shared powerlessness, however, need not arise from governmental activity or inaction. Organizational complexity and technological change may themselves produce the same feelings independent of any governmental activity. Complexity presents at least three problems to those seeking to maintain or enhance feelings of personal control. First, complexity may present comprehension difficulties, especially if there are technical aspects involved. Environmental issues, for example, may require some rather sophisticated knowledge. Complexity may also give rise to difficulties associated with the number of constituent parts that it may be necessary to deal with in order to bring about desired change.

But it is perhaps the diffusion of responsibility in complex systems that presents the most difficult barrier to maintaining personal control beliefs. When power or responsibility is (or appears to be) fragmented, it is difficult to select a fulcrum around which individual or collective activity may be organized. Without visibility, accountability is compromised, and even where visibility exists, it does not facilitate focus in the absence of readily identifiable power centers. This is one reason why the presidency, and not congress, has such enormous symbolic significance in the attachment structures of most citizens.

These mediating factors would be sufficiently formidable by themselves to raise serious questions about the possible scope of experientially based control beliefs for most citizens in mass societies. But the analysis of mediating factors would be incomplete without consideration of two other important contextual elements within which personal control beliefs are embedded. These are rates of social change and the operation of cultural double-bind systems.

Change is a natural dimension of all interpersonal relationships. Even where institutional structures remain stable, the course of human biological and social–psychological development guarantees that individual perspectives will not remain fixed. Yet to say that change is inevitable or even natural does not imply that it is always beneficial or desirable, even when it results in outcomes normally considered favorable. The reason for this lies in the complex relationship between change, environmental stability, personal control, and stress.

The development of personal control arises in its most basic and realistic forms from concrete accomplishments. The experience of having attempted and succeeded in bringing about some result is an indispensable foundation for this belief structure. As individual maturation proceeds, the further development of this belief requires continued social accomplishments, which are dependent on an increasingly diverse range of skills. But skills remain most effective when environmental conditions remain stable or similar. If there is sufficient change, old skills may not only be ineffective but counterproductive.

Every change therefore represents a challenge to coping capacity. Among the many questions raised under these circumstances are whether old skills can be made useful and whether new, more effective skills can be developed. The answers to these questions have fundamental implications not only for beliefs in personal control but also for estimations of the self and others. The failure to develop and maintain such skills is likely to result in a fundamental restructuring of beliefs about both the potential for control in the world and one's place in it. These challenges arise even in cases where change is assumed to be beneficial. Holmes and Rahe (1967), in developing their life experiences stress scale, include such obvious and profound shocks as the death of a loved one, but they also include such "positive experiences" as upward occupational mobility. The reason for this is clear. Even beneficial change brings with it challenges as well as potential rewards. Indeed, it might be argued that in many such situations, the greater the latter, the greater the former. It is important to emphasize, however, that stress per se is not inherently deleterious, for both its degree and nature are important considerations. What is being argued here is that novelty results in stress primarily because of the questions it raises about the integrity and continuity of the self in term of both control and esteem.

We can also view this process at work in a somewhat larger social context. It is frequently pointed out, for example, that traditional societies maintain sufficient environmental continuity to make skills learned early in life appropriate for decades and perhaps lifetimes. One result of social change in transitional or modernizing societies has been a discontinuity between skills that facilitated personal control beliefs at one point in the life cycle and those found necessary later. What is not frequently emphasized, however, is that even "modern" societies are transitional and indeed may be so in a more fundamental way than many so-called developing countries. The reason for this has to do with the diversity of relational (interpersonal) possibilities and the enormous impact of technological change.

Perhaps the most dramatic statement of this position is found in Toffler's *Future Shock* (1970), which argues that rates of social change, fueled by technology but exacerbated by an increasing number of diverse "life-styles," ensure that social and political environments will become increasingly transient and that corresponding institutional and ritual arrangements will cease to provide the stable structure within which personal control may be more easily attempted, developed, and maintained. This is not to argue that experientially based beliefs in personal control can not be developed; rather, they have been made more problematic. The implications of this position for public policy are a point to which I return shortly.

The last general mediating factor examined here doubtlessly exists in many political cultures but arises out of unique circumstances and has special significance in democratic societies. It consists of at least two widely promoted and generally accepted but inconsistent (if not mutually exclusive) "messages" that the individual is unable either to integrate or transcend without running afoul of other norms and power sanctions. These cul-de-sacs of life trajectories may be thought of as cultural double binds that replicate at a societal level what Bateson, Jackson, Haley, and Weakland (1950) implicated many decades ago in the genesis of interpersonal impairment, and that, somewhat later, Merton (1957) suggested as a causative factor in the development of anomie.

The cultural double bind that mediates beliefs in personal control arises from the injunction to participate in political life, which when coupled with the assumption that government and public officials will be responsive and that citizens ought to feel (and are) efficacious, runs a substantial risk of contradicting other messages learned in many, if not most, institutional frameworks.

The norm of citizen duty (or participatory obligation) is widely held and continually reinforced in both public and private arenas. Textbooks, parents, teachers, and media all exhort the citizen to exercise his or her participatory rights (obligations), especially as they relate to voting and other campaign-related activities. Missing, of course, is any exhortation to carry this obligation much beyond the most conventional paths, but this need not be of great concern here. Coupled with this exhortation is the assumption—taught rather early in many classrooms—that in democracies, governments are responsive to the wishes of the citizenry, not only in a collective but also in an individual sense (for an excellent discussion of this point in connection with the socialization of children, see Connell & Goot, 1972-1973, p. 169). The acquisition of feelings of political efficacy as a norm has already been mentioned, and it is sufficient (for illustrative purposes) to note that those feelings begin to emerge as early as the fourth grade.

The strands of these multiple messages combine to produce a powerful impetus to belief that citizens ought to, can, and do exercise substantial personal control in the political arena. Running parallel, however, are experiences that subvert, if not nullify, the intent as well as the actual and potential reality of these messages. For many people, the major socialization agencies—family, schools, and jobs—are laboratories for compliance, not autonomy. Nowhere has this point been more extensively examined than in schools (Patrick, 1977). A number of studies have suggested that the overt subject matter taught is only part of what is being learned. Within the traditional classroom, along with more typical subjects, there is what has been termed a "hidden curriculum," which has to do with power and control. The degree of initiative encouraged, the (limited) conditions under which authority may be challenged, and the boundaries of acceptable discourse are not frequently left to student discretion. So, too, family authority relationships frequently reinforce rather than discourage the symmetry of power that arises naturally from adult skills and perspectives. These and similar experiences combine to produce anomalous messages, and inconsistent results. Whereas one set of culturally sanctioned exhortations stress activity and mastery, many other experiences, culturally produced if not sanctioned, result in the opposite. One plausible outcome of these incompatible directives is a deep sense of confusion and a pervasive feeling of powerlessness. The latter arises from the understanding that ultimately, the experience of personal control cannot rest on normative expectations for it.

These factors illustrate but do not exhaust the ways in which beliefs in personal control are mediated by and a part of the macroenvironment in which individual behavior and experience are embedded. Raising these issues, however, still leaves unanswered, except in an indirect way, exactly why beliefs in personal control are of such crucial importance for the individual's relationship to government in democratic societies. The evidence I present can be considered no more than suggestive; it does, however, represent one of the few attempts to assess systematically the impact of feelings of personal control on political orientations and behaviors. In the fall of 1970 and again in the spring of 1971, interviews were conducted with a random sample of undergraduates at an urban Ivy League university. The project was intended to uncover the nature, development, and political implications of beliefs in personal control, and to this end data were gathered on a number of (political) attitudes and behaviors. The results, which have been reported in greater detail elsewhere (Renshon, 1974, 1975), are certainly not exhaustive. Nonetheless, they are at least highly suggestive.

The basic independent variable, beliefs in personal control, was measure by a modified form of Rotter's I/E Scale. The data suggested that low levels of personal control beliefs were associated with a low willingness to trust others, which carried over to a lack of faith in government. Those with low feelings of personal control tended to view the political system as ineffective, to evaluate the policy outcomes of the government as personally punishing, and to attribute the responsibility for the undesirable outcomes to "the system," rather than to assume any of it themselves. Not surprisingly, such respondents were highly politically alienated, tended to view the government as inaccessible and unresponsive, and were highly impatient for political change.

In the area of political participation, I found that individuals with low feelings of personal control were more (rather than less) likely to be politically participant than those whose needs for personal control had been satisfied. Yet there was an interesting pattern to this participation. Individuals with low levels of personal control were overwhelmingly drawn to the more "unconventional" forms for participation, including sit-ins, mass demonstrations, and political violence. Moreover, they were much more willing than those with high or moderate degrees of personal control to accept violence as a tool of political change. It hardly needs to be emphasized that such attitudes and behaviors raise serious questions about the nature of support for democratic procedures among this group and about the nature of political circumstances that brought them to this position.

My point here is neither to assess nor assign blame but rather to point out that beliefs in personal control have important implications for the public order. When individuals do not feel as if they have sufficient control over events, processes, institutions, or individuals that they come to feel affect their lives, an outcome of satisfied quiescence cannot be expected. These findings lead to a presumption that democratic societies would benefit by taking the need for personal control seriously. Exactly how this might be done is not immediately obvious and requires that at least some thought be given to the issues raised by basing public policy on human needs. It is to this last area that I turn in the final section of this paper.

A CONCLUDING NOTE ON NEED THEORY
AS THE BASIS FOR PUBLIC POLICY

The possibility of an empirically validated theory of human needs contains within it the most profound implications for public policy. Part of the reason for this lies in the complex interrelationship between private needs and public rights. To have demonstrated a need is to have established a presumptive claim for satisfaction. As Minogue (1963) points out, "(A) desire (or want) may be capricious; need always claims to be taken seriously [p. 103]." It is only a small distance from this view to the assumption that having established the existence of a need, one has also established a prima facie case for its public-based satisfaction. This view is shared by Abraham Maslow (1954), who notes that "it is legitimate and fruitful to regard instinctive basic needs and metaneeds as *rights* [p. xiii]." The impact of this doctrine may be seen in the expansion of the conceptualization of citizenship from strictly legal and political definitions to an inclusion of what Prewitt and Verba (1977) have referred to as "social-right citizenship [pp. 71–72]." Here the major questions do not revolve around "due process," or even questions of leadership selection but rather around "rights" that previously were left to the "unseen hand," such as freedom from economic fears because of old age, or the right of every family to a decent home.

The expansion of private needs into public rights has not met with universal acceptance either among political theorists or practitioners. In the former category, for example, Fitzgerald (1977) writes, "Even if one can identify universal needs, there is another further problem of why ought human beings, let alone governments, feel obliged to satisfy such needs ... [p. 46]?" There is, of course, an excellent self-interest argument from the government's standpoint in response to Fitzgerald's question.

Insofar as the legitimacy of the regime rests on at least minimal satisfaction of citizen wants, and insofar as these wants reflect real needs, the greater the degree of governmental responsiveness, the higher the level of allegiance and legitimacy (accorded to the government) ought to be. Admittedly, this is easier to see when one discusses more "basic" needs such as food, clothing, shelter, personal security, and control. Moreover, governments that have not provided these necessities for large portions of their citizenries have remained in power for long periods. But the study of revolution strongly suggests that when large numbers of citizens feel deprived of "necessities" and when this coincides with deprivations of higher needs among at least a portion of the elite (e.g., status deprivation), governments cannot long endure without extraordinary good fortune, or an extremely effective security apparatus. If the gap between wants (which are presumably based at least in part on felt needs) and satisfaction leads to the potential for violence, as every variation of the frustration–aggression hypothesis (and my own data) has suggested, then a case might be made for the self-interest-based policy of need satisfaction.

Just how this would be done, especially in the case of higher needs, is of course a legitimate question. Yet Fitzgerald's (1977) illustration (using Bowlby's [1970] attachment needs as an operational indicator of Maslow's [1954] need for affection) provides a slightly misplaced analogue. Certainly, few would argue that the government ought to become the surrogate "mother" for each of its citizens. Yet it is not too difficult to think of public policies designed to foster the sense of inclusion in a political system, which would provide its own kind of emotional satisfaction.

The relationship of public policy to feelings of personal control, especially in the political arena, poses special difficulties. In a general sense, it is not too difficult to design promotional policies or to restructure environments to facilitate the development of feelings of personal control. In the schools, for example, this would entail encouraging and supporting attempts based on individual's initiative and choice while decreasing (but not eliminating) concern with components of the "hidden curriculum." So too in the family, the value of initiative, choice, and responsibility as a basis for developing these important life-relevant beliefs could be made more widely known, and thus encouraged.

In the political arena, too, it is possible to think of policies designed to decrease feelings of powerlessness. In the area of social change, for example, Toffler (1970) has recommended a series of programs including education for the future and specially designed communities in which social and cultural change are more strictly controlled. One can also envision centers, available to any child or adult, where time and professional assistance are made available for people to "work through" reactions to either impending or preceding personal or interpersonal change.

Yet this is not to say that the relationship of political processes to feelings of personal control does not raise special issues for public policy. One reason for this is that once politics is viewed as a control-relevant sphere because of a particular policy (or lack of it), the maintenance of personal control beliefs will require at least some evidence of success in the form of particular public programs. Since the nature and direction of the desire will always vary as a function of individual or group concerns, it appears that governments can never be expected to be wholly successful in supplying such evidence. This will be increasingly the case as public policy is conducted in a context of scarcity, rather than abundance. Where expansion or intervention has been the rule, as I have argued it has been in the United States, government will face a particularly difficult transition period. Not only will politics become control relevant because of the desire for new initiatives but also to keep old ones from disappearing. Under these circumstances, pressure will be enormous, feelings of dissatisfaction high, and feelings of personal control perhaps marginal.

No immediate solution to this dilemma is obvious. The increasing intervention and expansion of government activity has played a large role in generating both the need for personal control, and the expectation that satisfaction in the form of public policy that provides either personal or group relief will be forthcoming. Perhaps the best that can be done in the immediate short run is to lower expectations with straightforward disclosures of the difficulties to be expected during the "politics of scarcity." So, too, government can capitalize on the ambiguity of estimations of success that must accompany large-scale policy in any area by promoting an appreciation that in some circumstances, other fractions must be added to the saying, "Half a loaf is better than none." Additionally, the temporal expectations of citizens must also be addressed. A more realistic understanding of political responsiveness must include attention to the time-consuming nature of public policymaking, especially when diverse and frequently contradictory aims must be integrated.

But beyond these immediate possibilities lie some very fundamental questions about the nature of democratic government and its relationship to individual character and the collective moods generated by public processes and events. Lasswell (1959) once argued that "the stability of the constitution depends upon the molding of the appropriate form of character [p. 3]." This was an argument that suggested that democratic government could not long survive in the absence of sufficient numbers of democratically oriented character structures among the citizenry. Yet it is equally true, as Maslow (1957) has pointed out, that "healthy character alone will not guarantee democratic behavior [p. 128]," because the right social and political structures are also necessary. Just what these structures are and how they would operate are questions that Maslow never confronted and other need theorists have only begun to approach. But there can be no question that to the extent that empirical linkages are forged between multiple-need gratification and the facilitation of those characteristics that are supportive of democratic forms (e.g., tolerance, flexibility, feelings of personal control, etc.), government policy aimed at facilitating such development is not merely a luxury but a necessity.

REFERENCES

Bateson, G., Jackson, D. D., Haley, J., & Weakland, J. H. Toward a theory of schizophrenia. *Behavioral Science*, 1950, *1*, 251-264.

Bay, C. Needs, wants and political legitimacy. *Canadian Journal of Political Science*, 1968, *3*, 241-245.

Bowlby, J. *Attachment and loss* (Volume 1). London: Hogarth, 1970.

Connell, R. W., & Goot, M. Science and ideology in American political socialization research. *Berkeley Journal of Sociology*, 1972-1973, *27*, 165-193.

Easton, D., & Dennis, J. The child's acquisition of regime norms: Political efficacy. *American Political Science Review*, 1967, *61*, 25-38.

Edelman, M. *Politics as symbolic action*. Chicago: Markham, 1971.

Erikson, E. *Identity: Youth and crisis*. New York: Norton, 1968.

Fitzgerald, R. Abraham Maslow's hierarchy of needs—An exposition and evaluation. In R. Fitzgerald (Ed.), *Human needs and politics*. Rushcutters Bay, NSW, Australia: Pergamon, 1977.

Freud, S. Instincts and their vicissitudes. In J. Strachy (Ed.), *Collected papers*. New York: Basic Books, 1959.

Fromm, E. *The sane society*. London: Routledge & Kegan Paul, 1973.

Holmes, T. H., & Rahe, R. H. The social readjustment rating scale. *Journal of Psychosomatic Medicine*, 1967, *11*, 213-218.

Hovland, C. I., Janis, I. L., & Kelley, H. H. *Communication and persuasion: Psychological studies of opinion change*. New Haven, Conn.: Yale University Press, 1953.

Langer, E. J. The illusion of control. *Journal of Personality and Social Psychology*, 1975, *32*, 311-328.

Lasswell, H. D. Political constitution and character. *Psychoanalysis and the Psychoanalytic Review*, 1959,*46*, 4-18.

Levinson, D. J., Darrow, C. N., Klein, E. B., Levinson, M. H., & McGee, B. *The seasons of a man's life*. New York: Knopf, 1978.

Maslow, A. H. *Motivation and personality*. New York: Harper, 1954.

Maslow, A. H. Power relationships and patterns of personality development. In W. Kornhauser (Ed.), *Problems of power in American democracy*. Detroit: Wayne State University, 1957.

Merton, R. *Social theory and social structure*. New York: Free Press, 1957.

Milbrath, L. *Political participation*. Chicago: Rand McNally, 1965.

Minogue, K. R. *The liberal mind*. London: Methuen, 1963.

Murray, H. *Explorations in personality: A clinical and experimental study of fifty men of college age*. New York: Oxford University Press, 1938.

Patrick, J. Political socialization and political education in the schools. In S. A. Renshon (Ed.), *Handbook of political socialization: Theory and research*. New York: Free Press, 1977.

Peters, R. *The concept of motivation*. New York: Humanities Press, 1958.

Prewitt, K., & Verba, S. *An introduction to American government* (2nd ed.). New York: Harper & Row, 1977.

Renshon, S. A. *Psychological needs and political behavior: A theory of personality and political efficacy*. New York: Free Press, 1974.

Renshon, S. A. Personality and family dynamics in the political socialization process. *American Journal of Political Science*, 1975, *19*, 63-80.

Rosenthal, R. *Experimenter effects in behavioral research.* New York: Appleton-Century-Crofts, 1966.

Rotter, J. B. Generalized expectancies for internal versus external control of reinforcement. *Psychological Monographs,*1966, *80*(1, Whole No. 609).

Searing, D. J., Schwartz, J., & Lind, A. E. The structuring principle: Political socialization and belief systems. *American Political Science Review,* 1973, *67,* 415–432.

Seligman, M. E. P. *Helplessness: On depression, development and death.* San Francisco: Freeman, 1975.

Toffler, A. *Future shock.* New York: Bantam, 1970.

Section **II**

CONSEQUENCES OF CHOICE ON LEARNING AND PERFORMANCE

All theory is against the freedom of the will—all experience for it.
—Dr. H. Johnson

Despite the exhortations of some of the writers in the previous section regarding the advisability of studying the perception of control in laboratory settings, all the papers in this section employed experimental settings. The first paper, by Professor Kehoe, is an elaborate attempt to determine whether choice between options of varying degrees of desirability directly influences the perception of control or whether the perception of control is a secondary effect dependent on the initial evaluation and processing of the options. Kehoe's work grows out of a number of both empirical and theoretical attempts to understand how the similarity of available options can influence the individual's judgment of perceived control. The major contribution of this work is in showing that when studying how dissimilarity of the options affects decision time and perceived choice, it is also necessary to control for the average attractiveness of the options as well.

The second paper in this section, by Professor Moyer, is concerned primarily with the issue of countercontrol. Moyer's paper has significance not only for those interested in assessing the effects of perceived control and its relationship to internality but also for investigators more generally concerned with learning and memory processes. Moyer's paper clearly points to the real difficulty in assessing how subjects who are given instructional sets not only may fail to accede to these but actually show behavior that is opposite to the instructional efforts.

The third paper in this section, by Savage, Perlmuter, and Monty, is basically concerned with how the elimination of a potential opportunity to choose can demotivate subjects. Their experiment also examined how the similarity of the options from which subjects are enabled to choose can serve to moderate the effects of perceived control. A choice between dissimilar options is apparently equivalent to no choice at all. Whether this effect is attributable to the dissimilarity in the options or to the lower average desirability, as Kehoe would predict, cannot now be determined.

The fourth paper, by Professor Brown, treats the problem of perceived control from the helplessness perspective and shows how subjects' performance can be debilitated simply by their observing failure in a co-actor whom they believe to be of similar competence. This paper as well as the previous one (Savage et al.) nicely complement each other in showing how expectation for control or conversely for failure can predictably modify behavior.

Finally, in this section Professor Newman summarizes and critically evaluates the contributions provided by the four previous papers. In addition to pointing to the important similarities and discrepancies among these papers, Newman discusses the potential contributions of choice and perceived control to the burgeoning area of learning and memory. Cautioning investigators in memory to begin to examine potential influences of motivation, individual differences, and countercontrol in their studies, he discusses by specific example how one or more of these variables can dramatically influence and even distort the outcome of an investigation.

5 Choice Time and Aspects of Choice Alternatives

Jerard F. Kehoe
*Virginia Polytechnic Institute
and State University*

INTRODUCTION

The research on the antecedents of perceived choice has focused largely on manipulations of the choice options. Generally, the more and the better the options, the greater the perceived choice (e.g., Harvey & Johnston, 1973; Jellison & Harvey, 1973). Theoretical analyses and research interest have tended to focus on processing variables rather than on the effects of the options themselves. Examples of these processing variables are uncertainty (Harvey & Johnston, 1973; Jellison & Harvey, 1973), competence (Jellison & Harvey, 1973), processing time (Harvey & Jellison, 1974), control (Harvey, Barnes, Sperry, & Harris, 1974; Harvey & Harris, 1975), and volition (Steiner, 1970).

Each of these is a quality of the psychological experience of choosing. The typical strategy for testing the explanatory value of these mediating variables has been to manipulate the characteristics of the available choice options, observe the extent to which judgments of perceived choice are related to these option manipulations, and finally, assume that the option manipulation affected processing variables that in turn affected perceived choice. Thus manipulations are generally of options' characteristics, but interpretations and conclusions are generally about one or more processing variables.

The question can be raised, however, whether the effects of such processing variables have been empirically distinguished from whatever effects could be directly attributed to the charcteristics of the choice options. This question is directly related to a larger theoretical question. Is the experience of choice a consequence of the quality of processing, a chooser characteristic, or a consequence of the options' characteristics? It is clear that if any of these processing variables are to have explanatory force, it is necessary that they vary with perceived choice independent of the way in which option characteristics vary with perceived choice. In order to evaluate whether this has been the case, let us consider three studies that offer processing-type interpretations based only on manipulations of the characteristics of the options. In addition to these studies that suggest the legitimacy of the proposed distinction, a fourth study is considered that highlights the importance of the question.

These four studies are largely involved in testing Mills' (cf. Jellison & Harvey, 1973) analysis of perceived choice, in which perceived choice exists to the extent that alternatives to the most preferred option are perceived to exist. Mills suggests that an option is perceived to be an alternative to the extent that its attractiveness is similar to but different from the most preferred option and to the extent that there is uncertainty that the preferred option will result in the best outcome. Jellison and Harvey (1973) manipulated uncertainty and difference independently in a study in which the respondents had to choose which of two football teams was the winner in a game between them. Respondents were given information about the teams by a series of seven rating scales indicating the various strengths and weaknesses of the teams. In the small-difference conditions both teams had an average rating of 5.35, whereas in the large-difference conditions the two teams had average ratings of 2.15 and 5.35. Uncertainty was manipulated by including additional information about game-time weather conditions and player injuries. Both the certainty factor and the difference factor resulted in the changes in perceived choice predicted by Mills' analysis. The first point to be made is that the effect of the difference factor cannot be unequivocally attributed to the *difference* in overall team skill. In the small-difference conditions the two teams had an overall average rating of 5.35, whereas the teams in the large-difference conditions had an overall average rating of 3.75. If the desired outcome was choosing a potential winner, then we might say that the small-difference conditions offered more instrumental value than the large-difference conditions. This confounding exists whether the difference is presumed to be mediated by some processing variable such as uncertainty, as suggested by Jellison and Harvey (1973) and Harvey and Harris (1975), or is directly a function of the characteristics of the choice options. The second point to be made is that the effect of the uncertainty manipulation cannot be unequivocally attributed to the psychological state of uncertainty, although it seems the most plausible interpretation. Poor weather conditions and injuries to important players may well be interpreted as changing the skill levels of the competing teams so as to change their instrumental value. Again, the basic problem seems to be that if uncertainty is manipulated by changing option characteristics, then one cannot distinguish between explanations in terms of the processing variable uncertainty on one hand and variables representing option characteristics on the other.

In the second study Harvey and Johnston (1973) replicated Jellison and Harvey (1973) using the same football team paradigm and also used gambles as choice options. In the gambles experiment, respondents were asked to judge how much choice others reported having when offered a given set of gambles. Each gamble consisted of a specific probability, p, of winning an amount of money, X; otherwise, no money would be won. Certainty was increased by increasing the probability of winning. High-certainty conditions resulted in less perceived choice than low certainty. My interpretation of this manipulation echoes the empirically based conclusions of Steiner, Rotermund, and Talaber (1974). Instead of explaining the probability effect as an uncertainty effect, Steiner et al., in a more complex gambles design, conclude that "attributed choice is affected by the expected values themselves rather than by the components that create those expected values [p. 561]." Clearly the argument is, again, that manipulations of option charcteristics do not necessarily imply an effect of processing variables.

In the third study Harvey and Harris (1975) examined the valence of options as well as the difference between options' valences. The two options, visual stimuli, were described to the respondents in an ambiguous fashion, and the valence of each option was conveyed to the respondents by informing them of alleged average pleasantness ratings. In the large-difference condition there was a 2.51 unit difference in rated pleasantness. In the small-difference condition the difference was .03 units. Once again it was found that the smaller the difference, the greater the perceived choice. As in the research already reviewed, this difference effect was interpreted in terms of uncertainty. Unfortunately, however, in this design the average pleasantness ratings in the small-difference conditions were 1.24 units greater than the average pleasantness ratings in the large-difference conditions. Therefore, choosing an uncertainty explanation over an explanation in terms of the attractiveness of the options is arbitrary.

Lastly, a study by Kehoe (1977) highlights the importance of the empirical distinction between the effects of processing variables and the effects of characteristics of the options. This study specifically attempted to determine whether perceived choice is at all a function of the *difference* in attractiveness—which would be necessary for an uncertainty explanation— or whether one could account for perceived choice solely as a function of the attractiveness values of the options in the choice set—which would disallow an uncertainty explanation. Let us call the former possibility the difference hypothesis and the latter possibility the choice-set-attractiveness hypothesis. Although these are similar hypotheses, they can be distinguished in that the difference hypothesis predicts that the impact an option has on perceived choice is, in part, a function of the other options (i.e., what the difference is between options); whereas the choice-set-attractiveness hypothesis predicts that the impact an option has is independent of other available options. Kehoe's data supported the choice-set-attractiveness hypothesis more strongly than the difference hypothesis. That is, changes in perceived choice that occur as a consequence of manipulations of options' attractiveness could be accounted for by the proper scaling and weighting of the individual options independent of other options in the choice set. Thus, it was not necessary to know how different one option was from another in order to know its impact on perceived choice. This study did not directly assess the impact of any processing variable but only suggested that the apparent difference effect that has been interpreted in terms of uncertainty might well be the effect of merely having more attractive options available. This suggests that one need not invoke processing variables that involve comparison processes such as uncertainty.

The objective of this current research is to assess directly a processing variable to determine what its *independent* contribution is. This might be accomplished in two ways. The first consists of directly manipulating processing variables without changing option characteristics. Harvey and Jellison (1974) investigated the effect of perceived choice time on perceived choice in this way by informing respondents that they took relatively more or less time than the average respondent. One criticism of this approach is that dissonance theory predicts the same result as Mills' analysis. And if judgments of perceived choice are dependent on dissonance reduction, then one does not have unambiguous evidence about the relationship between perceived choice and choice time. A second criticism is that this procedure only assesses whether individuals *can* use explicitly presented processing information and not whether they *do* use real processing cues. A second research strategy is to manipulate option characteristics independently and measure processing variables. A relationship between *perceived choice* and some measure of *processing* would support a processing interpretation of perceived choice so long as the processing variable is independent of option manipulations. The research reported here uses this second strategy.

A potential difficulty with this strategy is that in a given design, processing variables and option manipulations may be not at all independent. In this case this approach would be useless. A prerequisite for the design, then, is that the manipulations of option characteristics and the measure of processing be chosen so that the option manipulations are in some part independent of the processing variable. Research by Harvey and Johnston (1973) and Steiner, Rotermund, and Talaber (1974) and preliminary work by myself suggest a solution to this problem. In their research the manipulations of level of option attractiveness and differences in option attractiveness are both related to perceived choice. My observation in preliminary work has been that the processing variable *choice time* is related to the differences in option attractiveness but not related to the level of option attractiveness. This implies that manipulations of option attractiveness will be in part independent of choice time. For this reason, choice time seems to be a particularly good process measure for our objective of separating process effects from option effects. Also, choice time is likely to be closely related to variables such as uncertainty and competence, which allows this research to bear on studies using those terms.

The objective of this research, then, is to determine what the relationship is between perceived choice and choice time independent of the relationship between perceived choice and level of option attractiveness and difference in option attractiveness.

Three studies were designed using different kinds of choice options (occupations, movies, meals). In each of these studies, respondents were separately presented several pairs of choice options. For each pair, the respondents indicated their selection while being unobtrusively timed, and they judged how much choice they felt the particular pair allowed them.

METHOD

The occupations, movies, and meals selected were chosen on the basis of preliminary information about their recognizability and attractiveness. In each domain the stimuli were selected to provide a wide range of attractiveness and to be uniformly recognizable. Since it has been demonstrated that qualitative dissimilarity is positively related to perceived choice, I wanted to hold it constant in the choice pairs presented for judgment. In order to do this, a multidimensional scaling analysis was done of the dimensions underlying each of the three kinds of options. Three pilot studies were conducted that defined the dimensional structure underlying 48 movies, 48 occupations, and 48 meals, respectively. Four-dimension solutions were judged best for each of the three stimulus domains.

These four-dimension solutions provided the definition of the qualitative dissimilarity of choice options in the experiments reported here. Pairs of choice options were defined as qualitatively dissimilar to the extent that there was a large Euclidean distance between them in the four-dimensional space. All choice pairs were chosen to be maximally close to the modal distance for that particular kind of option.

The three domains were selected for particular distinguishing characteristics. Movies represent common, perceptually integral, generally positive choice options for which it is easy to construct a choice scenario, and there are relatively few choice constraints such as prohibitive cost or social expectations. Occupations, again, represent common, perceptually integral options for which it is easy to construct a choice scenario. However, the 48 occupations used here represented a wide range of attractiveness with both very positive and very negative occupations. Certainly what are positive and negative options depends on the respondent, but it has been the case in prior work that respondents virtually always identify very positive and very negative occupations from the list of 48. In addition to this difference, movies and occupations are different in terms of real choice constraints. That is, many occupations are rated as very attractive, but because they demand either high skill levels or costly training, etc., they are seen as less likely choices. We included this kind of option, because it was felt that the presence of choice constraints would allow an additional opportunity for perceived choice and choice time to vary independently of the manipulated option characteristics.

Lastly, meals were chosen because they offered options that are common, perceptually separable (as presented here), and convenient for choice scenarios. The particular aspect of meals that we were interested in was their perceptual separability. Meals were presented as a list of four parts: (1) a main dish; (2) a starch; (3) a green vegetable; and (4) a refreshment. It was felt that the presentation of two separable choice options would increase the salience of the comparison process over two integral choice options and allow an opportunity for the processing variable choice time to increase in importance.

The subjects volunteered for this research from the Introductory Psychology course at Virginia Polytechnic Institute and State University. The subjects received credit toward the final course grade for their participation. Eighteen male subjects participated in the occupations study, 24 subjects (12 male and 12 female) participated in the movie study, and 23 subjects (11 male and 12 female) participated in the meals study. Each subject was run individually.

As the individual subjects entered the experiment room, they were seated in front of a desk and handed a set of written instructions. The instructions told the subject to sort each of 48 cards into one of five attractiveness categories. Each card had either a movie, a meal, or an occupation typed on it depending on the kind of option that the subject received. Five squares were drawn on a mat in front of the subject labeled (from left to right): "Very unattractive (1)," "(2)," "Neutral (3)," "(4)," "Very attractive (5)." After the subjects had sorted the 48 stimuli into the attractiveness categories, they were handed a second set of written instructions describing the choice portion of the session. During this time the experimenter, seated beside the subject and in front of a cathode-ray-tube-type computer terminal, entered the subject's attractiveness ratings into a computer program that controlled the choice portion of the session.

When the subjects finished the choice instructions, they were seated in front of the computer terminal, and the experimenter verbally reiterated the written instructions for operating the terminal. The subjects were instructed that a pair of stimuli would appear on the screen and that they were to indicate which of the two they would choose if they were in the hypothetical situation described in the instructions. For occupations, this was that the subject was in a career training program and there were openings in the training program for only these two careers. For movies, the subject had decided to see one of two movies showing in town that evening. For meals, the subject was in a family restaurant for dinner, and these were the two meals available. In all cases the subjects were choosing only for themselves.

When a choice pair appeared on the screen, subjects chose by pressing one of two keys at the side of the computer terminal. The computer program controlling the presentation of choice pairs recorded which was chosen and the amount of time that expired between the time the pair instantly appeared on the terminal screen and the time the choice was made.

After choosing one of the options, subjects were asked to judge, "How much choice did these two options allow you?" using a number scale ranging from 10—labeled "very little choice"—to 90—"a great deal of choice."

The choice pairs were constructed by an interactive computer program on the bases of the subject's attractiveness judgments and a measure of qualitative dissimilarity derived from the prior multidimensional scaling analyses. The objective was to hold qualitative dissimilarity constant and to vary systematically the attractiveness of the two choice options. Given five levels of attractiveness, there are 15 possible attractiveness pairs. The 15 conditions are schematically represented in the triangle shown in Fig. 5.1.

This triangle-shaped design indicates the way in which the two attractiveness factors, level and difference, are manipulated. Each diagonal of conditions represents a particular difference category. For example, the dotted conditions on the main diagonal all correspond to a difference of 0 while varying in level of attractiveness. The striped conditions all correspond to an average level of 3 while varying in difference. Although this is not a factorial combination of the level and difference factors, these two factors are not correlated so long as each subject receives an equal number of choice pairs

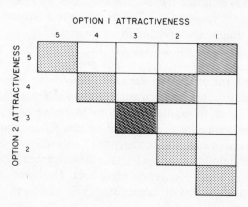

FIG. 5.1. Schematic representation of 15 possible attractiveness choice pairs.

from each condition. The program attempted to define three separate option pairs for each of the 15 possible attractiveness combinations ranging from (5,5), (5,4), (5,3), and so on through (1,1). Thus a subject could be presented, at most, 45 option pairs. However, if a subject placed no stimuli in a particular attractiveness category, then the five conditions involving that category could be disallowed, and only 30 pairs could be constructed. Likewise, if only one stimulus is placed in an attractiveness category, then the program is limited in what pairs it can construct.

There were two reasons for presenting three pairs for each attractiveness combination. The first was to enhance the possibility of variance in perceived choice that is not related to attractiveness characteristics. Variance of this kind could potentially be related to choice time without being related to option characteristics. The second was to estimate better the relationship between perceived choice and option characteristics.

RESULTS

Let us first consider those results that affect the characteristics of the design. Two design factors and their correlation are of interest here. The first is the difference in attractiveness of a pair of options, and the second is the level of attractiveness of the pair of options as measured by their average attractiveness. When a subject has received all possible pairs in the triangular design, then among those pairs there is a 0 correlation between difference in attractiveness and average attractiveness. However, it may not be possible to construct all 45 option pairs for each subject. The question then can be raised: To what extent did missing choice sets affect the correlation between the two attractiveness characteristics? In the occupations study, respondents averaged 37.5 pairs; in the movies study, 38.0 pairs; in the meals study, 38.7 pairs. The resultant average correlations between difference in attractiveness and level of attractiveness are .009, .075, and .007 for occupations, movies, and meals, respectively. Clearly, these two attractiveness characteristics remain virtually uncorrelated in all three studies.

Second, let us consider the relationships between manipulated design characteristics (i.e., average attractiveness and difference in attractiveness) and the processing variable, choice time. Figure 5.2 presents the aggregate relationship between attractiveness difference and average choice time. There is a clear negative relationship between choice time and attractiveness difference for each kind of option. Root-mean-square correlations for this relationship across individual respondents describe the extent to which straight lines approximating these aggregate lines in Fig. 5.2 are representative of individual respondent data. The correlations between choice time and attractiveness difference are $-.307$, $-.332$, and $-.263$ for occupations, movies,

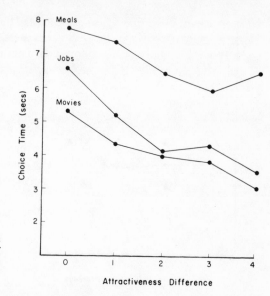

FIG. 5.2. Average choice time (in seconds) as a function of the type of option and the attractiveness difference between two options.

and meals, respectively; and all are significantly different from 0 ($p < .01$). On the other hand, there is no consistent relationship between choice time and average attractiveness. The root-mean-square correlations across individuals for occupations, movies, and meals are .196, .105, and .162, respectively. Only in the occupations data is there a significant ($p < .01$) relationship between choice time and average attractiveness—due almost exclusively to those pairs in which the options are equally attractive.

There are two implications of these results relating choice time to option characteristics. First, the relationship between choice time and attractiveness difference serves to validate the attractiveness manipulations. Second, over 90% of choice-time variance is independent of manipulations of option attractiveness. Since much of the choice-time variance in this design is independent of both option manipulations, there is a very real opportunity to observe whatever independent relationship between time and perceived choice may exist.

The third category of results to be considered is that describing the relationships between perceived choice, attractiveness manipulations, and choice time. Figure 5.3 presents the aggregate relationship between perceived choice and attractiveness difference for the three kinds of options. The relationships are slightly positive but not significant ($p > .01$) for movies and meals, whereas much more positive and significant ($p < .01$) for occupations. The root-mean-square correlations across individuals are .405, .049, and .207 for occupations, movies, and meals, respectively. Attractiveness difference, when independent of average attractiveness, uniformly affects choice time but affects perceived choice only for occupations. It seems clear that the

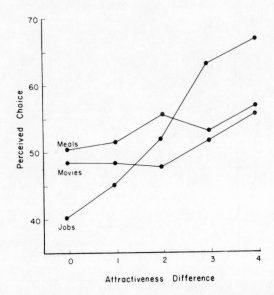

FIG. 5.3. Average perceived choice (self-reported on a 10–90 number scale) as a function of the type of option and the attractiveness difference between two options.

occupation data are behaving differently than either the movies or meals data. A possible explanation is offered in the "Discussion" section.

Figures 5.4, 5.5, and 5.6 represent the relationship between perceived choice and average attractiveness for each of the kinds of options. These are all significant ($p < .01$) and the strongest relationships in the studies. The root-mean-square correlations across individual respondents are .599, .547, and .505 for occupations, movies, and meals, respectively. Two aspects of

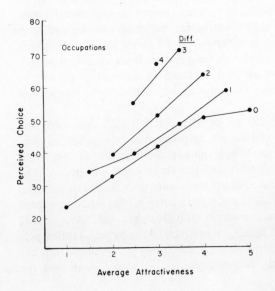

FIG. 5.4. Average perceived choice (self-reported on a 10–90 number scale) as a function of the attractiveness difference between two occupation options and the average attractiveness of the options.

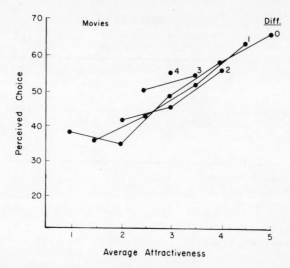

FIG. 5.5.   Average perceived choice (self-reported on a 10–90 number scale) as a function of the attractiveness difference between two movie options and the average attractiveness of the options.

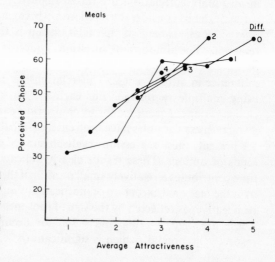

FIG. 5.6.   Average perceived choice (self-reported on a 10–90 number scale) as a function of the attractiveness difference between two meal options and the average attractiveness of the options.

these relationships should be noted. First, they are clearly positive *regardless* of the level of difference in attractiveness. Each line connects a set of choice pairs of the same attractiveness difference. All these lines have a positive slope. Second, there is a striking difference between occupations and both movies and meals. For occupations at a given level of average attractiveness, the choice set of *larger* difference always represents greater perceived choice. This is not the case for movies or meals.

TABLE 5.1

Average Percentage of Perceive-Choice Variance Accounted for by Design Factors and Choice Time

Options	Design Factors Only	Design Factors Plus Choice Time	Increment Due to Choice Time
Occupations	56.62[a]	62.44	5.82[d]
Movies	42.00[b]	45.25	2.25[e]
Meals	34.02[c]	42.52	8.50[f]

[a]17 of 18 significant ($p < .01$)
[b]18 of 24 significant ($p < .01$)
[c]15 of 23 significant ($p < .01$)
[d]7 of 18 significant ($p < .01$)
[e]2 of 24 significant ($p < .01$)
[f]7 of 23 significant ($p < .01$)

We might also point out that this relationship between level of attractiveness and perceived choice is not likely mediated by the processing variable, choice time. When choice time is statistically controlled for, all root-mean-square correlations are raised slightly.

Lastly, let us consider the relationship between perceived choice and choice time. The assessment of this relationship is the primary objective of this research. The important question concerns the relationship between perceived choice and choice time independent of average attractiveness and difference in attractiveness. This relationship can be explicitly represented using multiple regression. For each subject, the proportion of perceived choice variance accounted for by choice time can be determined after the two attractiveness variables have been entered into the prediction equation. Table 5.1 presents these regression results, averaged over subjects, for each of the kinds of options. These results clearly indicate that on the average, choice time contributes a relatively small portion of the variance of perceived choice, with the marginal exception of the meals options. These contributions tend to be negative, as reflected by the signed root-mean-square simple correlations. These are −.207, −.106, and −.246 for occupations, movies, and meals, respectively, none of which is significant ($p > .01$).

DISCUSSION

The important results of this study are:

1. There is a minimal negative relationship, if any, between choice time and perceived choice independent of the attractiveness characteristics of the options.

2. There is a moderate, positive relationship between perceived choice and average attractiveness for each kind of option.
3. There is a small, negative relationship between choice time and difference in attractiveness for each kind of option.

The primary contribution of this study is that having controlled for the option characteristics' level of attractiveness and difference in attractiveness, the relationship between perceived choice and actual choice time was not what previous studies suggested it would be. Most directly, Harvey and Jellison (1974) demonstrated a positive relationship between perceived choice and relative choice time. However, choice time was a manipulation in their study. That is, subjects were told that they had taken more (or less) time to choose than typical. The manipulation was independent of actual choice time, even though, presumably, they generalized their result to actual choice time. Results from other studies are indirectly related to our results. Those studies that explained perceived choice in terms of either uncertainty or competence would likely predict a positive relationship between perceived choice and choice time. This is because choice time is likely a measure of processing difficulty or complexity, which in turn is likely a salient cue for the experiences of uncertainty and competence.

Having unconfounded the relationship between perceived choice and the processing variable, choice time, we might speculate on why choice time had on the average only minimal, if any, cue value for the perception of choice in the research presented here. Three issues suggest themselves. The first two are largely methodological, the third is substantive. First, what are the salient characteristics of the choice situation in the experimental setting? Any circumstances that would minimize the *salience* of the processing required to make a choice would presumably also minimize the effect processing has on the perception of choice (or certainty, competence, or control, for that matter!). In this study it is likely that the familiarity of the options, the number of choices to be made, the rapidity of the presentation of choices, and the hypothetical nature of the choice all mediate against the psychological salience of the processing characteristics of the choice problem. This argument gains some strength when one considers that the relationship between choice time and perceived choice among meals in our samples is more than twice as strong as that of either movies or occupations. The decision to present meal pairs as two lists of four parts each was specifically for the purpose of emphasizing the comparison process. Of course, it is not necessary that our results be considered incompatible with those of Harvey and Jellison (1974). One need only assume that the two studies represent opposite ends of the processing salience continuum and, further, that processing salience is positively related to the cue value of choice time for the perception of choice. Neither our results nor theirs dispute these assumptions.

A further question could also be asked, however. Is the processing salience of typical, everday, choice behavior similar to that in our study or to that in Harvey and Jellison? That is, which research is more generalizable? There is no direct evidence on this issue, but we suspect that task and situation variables will be shown to interact with the relationship between processing characteristics and the perception of choice.

Second, what is the impact of individual differences? Our primary interest was in the aggregate strength and direction of effects. However, it may be instructive to consider the simple relationship between choice time and perceived choice at an individual level. Choice time accounted for more than 10% of the variance of perceived choice in 29 of 65 respondents. (Effects of this magnitude are often *very* significant in an analysis of variance framework.) Unfortunately, for our primary interest in strength and *direction* of aggregate effects, nine of these 29 substantial relationships (or nearly one-third) were in the positive direction, whereas the remaining 20 were in the negative direction. After working by now with several hundred subjects, each of whom had been asked, "How much choice did these options allow you?" I believe that the typical subject is somewhat confused by the question and seeks to formulate lay hypotheses about what the experimenter means by "choice," and that a variety of hypotheses may be formed and acted upon. Although this is a generally acknowledged criticism of much laboratory research, perceived-choice research seems particularly susceptible to it. Other less reactive measures of perceived choice are surely needed. One potential solution is based on the assumption that perceived choice imposes felt responsibility. A less reactive measure of perceived choice may be the amount of evaluation or self-disclosure risk felt in making public or social choices. A related suggestion is that further research address itself to consequential choices rather than to the hypothetical or inconsequential choices that have typically been used in past laboratory research.

Third, if processing difficulty and complexity as measured by choice time have no cue value for the perception of choice, how does one interpret previous research that invoked processing characteristics such as uncertainty and competence? In this regard, we are primarily concerned with the explanation of those previous results that demonstrated a relationship between perceived choice and difference in attractiveness. We are concerned with this relationship, because one interpretation of it is that processing difficulty or complexity is a cue for the perception of choice; but we have discounted this interpretation. Are there other interpretations of the attractiveness-difference effect that are compatible with our interpretation of this choice-time effect? We believe there are two possible interpretations, which were alluded to in the introduction. The first is that some studies have confounded attractiveness and have gotten exactly the results we would predict on the basis of level of attractiveness alone (cf. Harvey & Harris, 1975; Harvey & Johnston, 1973; Jellison & Harvey, 1973). The second possible interpretation is that perceived choice is simply a function of the weighted sum of the attractiveness values of the indiviudal options. This effect can be confused with an attractiveness-difference effect if the combination weights are such that any time two choice sets have the same unweighted average of option attractiveness, the choice set with more similarly attractive options has a higher (or lower) *weighted* sum than the less similarly attractive options. This would be the case if weights were related to attractiveness values by either a smooth negatively accelerating curve or a smooth positively accelerating curve. Kehoe (1977) provided some evidence that the so-called attractiveness-difference effect is better described as a weighted-sum-of-attractiveness effect for occupations and movies. The evidence also indicated that the relationship between weights and attractiveness is not the same for occupations as for movies. The present results indirectly support this finding, since the relationship between what we labeled attractiveness difference and perceived choice is not the same for occupations and movies.

This weighted-sum interpretation does not require or even allow a comparison-process effect as does the attractiveness-difference interpretation. The fact that our results demonstrate very little relationship between choice time and perceived choice lends further support to the general conclusion that processing variables do not directly affect the perception of choice.

More generally, the question is whether the perception of choice is a function of the quality of the processing necessary to choose or a function simply of what the potential outcomes are. That is, is the perception of choice a perception of chooser characteristics or a perception of option characteristics, or both? The two results of this research—that choice time is a relatively unimportant predictor of perceived choice and that occupations yield different results than movies or meals—seem to give more weight to explanations in terms of option characteristics than chooser (processing) characteristics.

REFERENCES

Harvey, J. H. Barnes, R. D. Sperry, D. L., & Harris, B. Perceived choice as a function of internal–external locus of control. *Journal of Personality*, 1974, *42*, 437–452.

Harvey, J. H., & Harris, B. Determinants of perceived choice and the relationship between perceived choice and expectancy about feelings of internal control. *Journal of Personality and Social Psychology*, 1975, *31*, 101–106.

Harvey, J. H., & Jellison, J. M. Determinants of perceived choice, number of options, and perceived time in making a selection. *Memory & Cognition*, 1974, *2*, 539–544.

Harvey, J. H., & Johnston, S. Determinants of the perception of choice. *Journal of Experimental Social Psychology,* 1973, *9,* 164–179.

Jellison, J. M., & Harvey, J. H. Determinants of perceived choice and the relationship between perceived choice and perceived competence. *Journal of Personality and Social Psychology,* 1973, *28,* 376–382.

Kehoe, J. F. *How options combine to determine perceived choice.* Presented at the 1977 convention of the American Psychological Association, San Francisco, California.

Steiner, I. D. Perceived freedom. In L. Berkowitz (Ed.), *Advances in experimental social psychology* (Vol. 5). New York: Academic Press, 1970.

Steiner, I. D., Rotermund, M., & Talaber, R. Attribution of choice to a decision maker. *Journal of Personality and Social Psychology,* 1974, *30,* 553–562.

6 Countercontrol in Cognitive Performance

William W. Moyer
Millersville State College

OVERVIEW

Countercontrol in human behavior is studied under many rubrics. Developmental and educational literatures refer to "noncompliance" and "passive-aggressive" behavior. Studies in behavior modification concern themselves with "oppositional children" and "negative behavior." Psychoanalytic theory refers to "resistance" in psychotherapy. All these terms describe behavior that is either opposite to or seemingly unrelated to the expectations, hypotheses, or contingencies of the experimenter, teacher, or parent.

The study of noncompliance in children has shown that oppositional behavior can be changed by using time out from reinforcement and contingent reward (Bucher & Davidson, 1974). The naturalistic causes of noncompliance have not been as well documented. It has been shown that noncompliance can be instrumentally conditioned, generalizes easily, and is relatively resistant to extinction. The studies that show this, however, fail to document etiology (Bucher & Davidson, 1974).

Brehm's (1966) theory of reactance dominates the social psychological literature in countercontrol. Reactance is a motivational state caused by loss of choice or freedom. The behavior resulting from that motivation will be directed at restoring or demonstrating freedom of choice. A communication that attempts to force opinion change in the subject can push opinion in the direction opposite to that espoused by the communicator. Additionally, Snyder and Wicklund (1976) conclude that both the exercise of freedom and the observation of a model exercising freedom can reduce reactance.

Freedom of choice has been shown to ameliorate reactance (Heilman & Toffler, 1976) but only in interpersonal settings, not in nonsocial situations. This would imply that an interpersonal conflict, real or imagined, is necessary for countercontrol to occur.

One interpersonal situation that involves a dominance relationship capable of arousing this conflict is the hypnosis relationship. Milton Erickson (1964) used the oppositional behavior and attitudes of skeptical subjects to overcome resistance to hypnosis. The relationship between hypnotist and subject is often viewed as a power struggle, and the wielding of that power invariably limits the freedom of the subject.

The research presented herein was designed to test the limits of countercontrol in verbal learning and the use of mnemonic strategies. The first study demonstrated that unhypnotized control groups were not merely neutral to controlling instructions but reacted negatively toward them. The second study investigated the subjects' abandonment of suggested mnemonic strategies in a free-recall paradigm. Finally, the third study investigated the effects of loss of choice on paired-associate learning in subjects of internal or external locus of control of reinforcement.

Data I've reported previously (Moyer, 1976) demonstrated that waking subjects given suggestions to increase their memorial capacity actually reduced recall below that of a neutral-suggestion control group. This behavior was clearly counter to the perceived intent of the experimenter. Additionally, the intention and attitudes of the subjects were measured by a postexperimental questionnaire. On this measure, 57% of the subjects given suggestions to decrease recall professed attempts or intentions to countercontrol. Of a group given hypermnesia suggestions, 21% professed intent to decrease recall or to decrease recall effort.

The mechanism for the reduced recall of the countercontrolling subjects was shown to be the active withholding of remembered material. There was no attempt made to account for the reason the countercontrol occurred other than the empirical conclusion that the instructions had caused the behavior. The process can be seen as subjects reacting negatively to one kind of attempt to control their behavior. In this particular study the type of control exerted (i.e., the suggestions to increase or decrease recall) was blatant and not exercised in a social context likely to be effective. In the context of this study, it is not possible to conclude that the saliency or blatant nature of the suggestions alone caused the countercontrol. The effect may also be dependent on the subject's perception that the suggestions would not be effective.

The abandonment of memorization strategies was of concern to me in a second study that I describe in more detail, as it is not reported elsewhere. In many verbal learning experiments, mnemonic strategies of imagery, verbal mediation, and/or rehearsal are required of subjects. Since models of memory are developed from the results of such research, it is imperative that the subjects actually be using the strategy required by the experimenter. Paivio and Yuille (1969) have investigated the shift of these strategies and found that subjects quickly abandon the use of rehearsal, for example, when learning easily imageable material. Another of their anecdotal findings was the reported abandonment of imagery as well as all other strategies by some of their subjects. The authors state that this is reflective of a "negative relation to learning." This attitude is of importance in studying countercontrol. Although the subjects were reminded after every trial of what strategy they were to implement, they used either no strategy or some other strategy for more than 50% of the material in all conditions. Paivio and Yuille concluded that the compelling nature of concrete nouns caused the use of imagery as a learning strategy when it was not the suggested technique. However, the hypothesis that there is an increase in the spontaneous use of imagery gains little support from the fact that imagery was abandoned at the same rate as other techniques.

This research and some pilot work completed by Moyer (1973) lead to the hypothesis that qualities of verbal material, type of strategy required, and difficulty of applying the strategy might all affect the subjects' compliance with instructions. In the present study, three mnemonic strategies were investigated: interactive imagery, separation imagery, and rehearsal. The hypothesis derived from Paivio's research was that abandonment of the suggested strategy would be greatest with rehearsal or separation imagery subjects and least in the interactive imagery subjects. Additionally, the material learned was either categorizable or not and was presented as word groups of either eight or four words per group. These manipulations were designed to provide some interference to the use of imagery as a mnemonic. It was hypothesized that abandonment of an imagery strategy would be greatest in the subjects who learned categorized material, particularly when presented as eight-word groups.

Two hundred and forty undergraduates at The Pennsylvania State University who received course credit for their participation served as subjects in the study. Males and females were evenly divided among groups.

Subjects learned 40-item lists that were made up of concrete nouns. The lists were either categorizable or not (the dimension of list structure), the categories being made up of 8 words each. There were no category repetitions within any word group.

The experiment had three independent variables: mnemonic strategy (rehearsal, interactive imagery, separation imagery), list structure (categorized versus uncategorized material), and the number of words per slide as presented to the subject (eight versus four).

Each subject was taught and practiced in a particular mnemonic strategy. A special plea to follow instructions was made, emphasizing that it was more important to use the suggested strategy than to maximize recall. A 40-item list was then presented, either as five groups of eight words per group or as 10 groups of four words per group. Total time per trial spent viewing each list was equal for all groups (80 sec). For groups seeing five stimulus slides, the slides were each shown for 16 seconds with an interstimulus interval of 2 seconds. For groups seeing 10 stimulus slides, the stimulus slides were exposed for 8 seconds each with a 2-second interstimulus interval. After the entire list had been presented, subjects spent 3 minutes in free recall. This presentation–recall sequence was repeated for a total of four trials, order being counterbalanced across trials. After the final recall trial, the subjects filled out a questionnaire asking them to describe the suggested learning strategy and to rate their overall use of that strategy and any other they might have used.

All but one subject could correctly identify what strategy had been called for. Of all the subjects, 96% testified to having used some other technique to some extent. The subjects' rating of the use of this "other" technique was subtracted from their rating of the use of the suggested technique, and a single score was thus derived. The higher the positive value of the resultant number, the greater the use of the suggested technique.

Analysis of these scores showed significant effects of suggested learning strategy $F(2,216) = 11.49$, $p < .001$, list structure, $F(2,216) = 4.01$, $p < .02$, and an interaction between list structure and word group size, $F(1,216) = 6.50$, $p < .02$. Post hoc analysis revealed that the abandonment of the suggested strategy increased from interactive imagery ($\bar{X} = 1.80$) to rehearsal ($\bar{X} = 1.70$) and was greatest in separation imagery groups ($\bar{X} = 1.10$). There was greater abandonment when learning categorized ($\bar{X} = 1.20$) versus uncategorized lists ($\bar{X} = 2.36$).

The subjects who learned categorizable material shown in four-word groups (10 slides) had an average of 1.47; those who learned categorizable material in eight-word groups (five slides) had an average of .93. Subjects learning uncategorized material presented in four- and eight-word groups had averages of 1.63 and 3.10, respectively. High positive values indicated greater use of the suggested strategy over other strategies.

To summarize these results—when categorizable lists were learned, the subjects abandoned the suggested strategy, particularly when the number of words per slide was high. If, however, there was no list structure and eight-word groups were learned, abandonment of the suggested strategy was low.

The type of alternate strategy reported by the subjects was also recorded and for the most part reflected the categorized nature of some of the material. Spontaneous shifting to imagery by those subjects using rehearsal was low. Most comments written by the subjects indicated that they felt unable to use only the suggested strategy.

There are, therefore, two factors that affect the degree of countercontrol in this situation. The first is the suggestion of the experimenter. The second is the type of material learned. If the material is seen as unsuited to the suggested strategy, that strategy is abandoned. It is unclear whether this results from a cognitive processing limitation or from the negative learning set postulated by Paivio and Yuille (1969).

Countercontrol in many situations operates as if motivation to be noncompliant was present. It may be possible, then, to have a situation that can produce both motivation to countercontrol and motivation to comply. The difference in reactions of subjects could then be related to stable personality differences.

One theory of differences among people is the social learning theory of Rotter. In particular, Rotter's (1966) theory of internal and external locus of control offers predictions about behavior in situations of varying degrees of external control over behavior. There is, for example, emprical evidence that internals resist vicarious learning to a greater extent than do externals (McColley & Thelen, 1975).

Thus, in a third study (Moyer, 1978), a verbal learning paradigm patterned after that described by Perlmuter and Monty (1977) was used to relate countercontrol to an overall motivational concept.

In their paradigm, external control is varied by manipulating the degree of choice that subjects have over what material is to be learned. The repeated result of this manipulation has been to increase learning in groups given even small amounts of choice.

It was the hypothesis of my study (Moyer, 1978) that motivational forces in this situation were mediated by the locus of control of the subjects. Externals expect to be controlled by external forces, and there is little theoretical reason for them to react to a choice manipulation. Internals should certainly be more reactive. An internal expects choice, acts as if he or she has it, and is reluctant to give it up (McColley & Thelen, 1975). Because of these attitudes, internals should be more responsive to a choice manipulation. When choice is given to an internal, we should expect highly motivated compliant performance. When choice is removed from an internal, we should expect either poorly motivated compliant responding or noncompliant performance. Specifically, in the Perlmuter and Monty (1977) paradigm, internals not given freedom of choice should learn materials slowly, whereas internals given choice should learn relatively quickly. The effect of varying choice of externals should be minimal.

To test this hypothesis, internals and externals either were given choice of material to learn or were not offered a choice. Countercontrol was documented in this study in internals (as hypothesized) in the form of reduced recall of a paired-associate list of nouns. There was no statistically reliable superiority in learning for internals given choice over externals given choice. The variance in recall for internals and externals given choice was large and accounted for the lack of statistical significance in amount of recall. The average number of words correctly recalled on the first anticipation trials was 6.00 for internals given choice, 1.60 for internals denied choice, 4.60 for externals given choice, and 3.70 for externals denied choice.

The countercontrol effect disappeared after the first anticipation trial. This was originally interpreted in Phares' (1976) terms of the internal's concern for "current demands of the situation [p. 83]," (i.e., the task of learning the words). A behavioral learning interpretation of the transitory nature of the countercontrol effect may also be made.

Skinner (1972) has stated that the use of punishment as a behavior control technique has emotional concomitants that make it unattractive in use. One of the results of the emotional effects of punishment would be to counter the perceived attempt at external control. If the lack of loss of choice in internals is viewed as a punishing stimulus, the lower performance of internals who are not given choice can be seen as an example of response suppression. Since the punishing stimulus occurs only on a single trial, the decrease in performance extinguishes over further trials.

A reinforcement analysis of the positive aspects of choice would predict an initially higher rate of recall for internals given choice, a statistically unreliable finding in this study (Moyer, 1978).

GENERAL CONCLUSIONS

There appears to be more than one type of countercontrol, and the implications of each type are very different. One type involves an inability of the subject to follow instructions such as in the present experiment on mnemonic strategies. This is theoretically of little interest but of great practical importance to the study of cognitive ability. Seemingly simple instructions that involve control over cognitive processes may be impossible for subjects to comply with, even when motivated to do so.

The second type of countercontrol demonstrated is when subjects actively opposed the perceived intent of the experimenter. There are emotional concomitants present that may be the cause of the countercontrolling behavior. These reactions relate to Skinner's (1972) contention that attempts at aversive control will result in countercontrol. Examples of this type of countercontrol include the present studies on reactions of waking subjects to hypnotic suggestion and the response of internals to loss of choice. Perhaps the perceived control in these situations is aversive to the subject.

Countercontrol is, therefore, an important force in research on cognitive abilities. Although we usually attempt to control this by enjoining the cooperation of the subjects, at time their active, even enthusiastic, participation is not sufficient. The rigors of the task and constraints on behavior, both formally stated and informally a part of the laboratory situation, all can have a profound effect on individual performance.

REFERENCES

Brehm, J. W. *A theory of psychological reactance.* New York; Academic Press, 1966.

Bucher, B., & Davidson, P. Establishment and generalization of non-compliant responding in children. *Canadian Journal of Psychology,* 1974, *28,* 69-78.

Erickson, M. H. The confusion technique in hypnosis. *American Journal of Clinical Hypnosis,* 1964, *6,* 183-207.

Heilman, M. E., & Toffler, B. L. Reacting to reactance: An interpersonal interpretation of the need for freedom. *Journal of Experimental Social Psychology,* 1976, *12,* 519-529.

McColley, S. H., & Thelen, M. H. Imitation and locus of control. *Journal of Research in Personality,* 1975, *9,* 211-216.

Moyer, W. W. *Mnemonic imagery and the effect of categorized material in multitrial free recall.* Unpublished manuscript, The Pennsylvania State University, 1973.

Moyer, W. W. Countercontrol in hypnotic control groups. *Psychological Reports,* 1976, *39,* 1083-1089.

Moyer, W. W. Effects of loss of freedom on subjects with internal or external locus of control. *Journal of Research in Personality,* 1978, *12,* 253-261.

Paivio, A., & Yuille, J. C. Changes in associative strategies and paired-associate learning over trials as a function of word imagery and type of learning set. *Journal of Experimental Psychology,* 1969, *79,* 458-463.

Perlmuter, L. C. & Monty, R. A. The importance of perceived control: Fact or fantasy? *American Scientist,* 1977, *65,* 759-765.

Phares, E. J. *Locus of control in personality.* Morristown, N.J.: General Learning Press, 1976.

Rotter, J. B. Generalized expectancies for internal versus external control of reinforcement. *Psychological Monographs,* 1966, *80* (1, Whole No. 609).

Skinner, B. F. *Beyond freedom and dignity.* New York: Bantam, 1972.

Snyder, M. L., & Wicklund, R. A. Prior exercise of freedom and reactance. *Journal of Experimental Social Psychology,* 1976, *12,* 120-130.

7 Effect of Reduction in the Amount of Choice and the Perception of Control on Learning

Ricky E. Savage
Lawrence C. Perlmuter
*Virginia Polytechnic Institute
and State University*

Richard A. Monty
U.S. Army Human Engineering Laboratory

It has been several years since we first demonstrated that allowing subjects to choose materials they are going to learn *may* benefit their performance on various learning tasks (Perlmuter, Monty, & Kimble, 1971). We emphasized the word *may* because more recent research has shown that improvements in learning and retention are by no means assured from the opportunity to exercise choice. Rather, the consequences of choice on learning have proved to be complex and sometimes evasive. Our pursuit of how and when choice enhances learning has often seemed tortuous and even frustrating.

In the experiments conducted to date, we have most frequently used a paired-associate (PA) learning paradigm. Basically, two conditions were employed, one of which was the *choice condition* in which subjects were shown a slide with a set of verbal materials consisting of a single stimulus word presented on the left and up to five potential response words on the right. Typically, an experiment used 10 to 14 such slides, each containing unique words. The subjects were instructed to read aloud both the stimulus and response words and to choose the response word they wished to learn to associate with each stimulus word. This procedure was repeated until all the S–R pairs were constructed. The subjects then proceeded to learn the word pairs by the conventional anticipation method. That is, they were shown only a stimulus word and asked to recite aloud the response word that went with it; afterward they were shown the stimulus and the correct response together and subsequently moved on to the next stimulus word. After each set of words in the list had been shown, the procedure was repeated for a predetermined number of trials as the subjects learned to anticipate the response to each stimulus.

The subjects in the *force condition* also read aloud the stimulus and potential response words. Following this reading, the experimenter announced the response to be learned and thereby designated the S–R pairs. The response words assigned to the subjects in the force condition were the response words chosen by the previous choice subject, and thus the subjects in the force condition were yoked to those in the choice condition.

Using this technique, Perlmuter, Monty, and Kimble (1971) found that choice subjects learned more rapidly and to a higher level than did force subjects. Thus allowing subjects the opportunity to choose the responses they wished to learn seemingly benefited performance.

This early discovery led to a series of more elaborate studies that have recently been summarized by Perlmuter and Monty (1977) and need not be repeated here. By way of background, however, it might be helpful to review briefly a few of the major conclusions, one of which was the finding that when the subject is given the opportunity to choose and is subsequently denied the opportunity to learn the chosen materials but rather is required to learn a list substituted by the experimenter, performance is worse than it is for subjects offered no choice at all (Perlmuter, Monty, & Cross, 1974). This finding led us to speculate that there are two consequences of choosing. First, following choosing, the subject's general level of motivation is enhanced. Secondly, a potential for frustration simultaneously develops that, if activated (as by substitution of a nonchosen list), serves to heighten motivation to a nonoptimal level and hence disrupts performance in the manner discussed by Brown (1961). Interestingly, in a subsequent series of studies, it was found that if the imposition of the nonchosen material is delayed for 24 hours after the choice is made, the disruptive effects are not noted. In other words, the potential for frustration dissipates rapidly with time (Monty & Perlmuter, 1975). However, the beneficial effects noted earlier persist over this 24-hour interval (Monty & Perlmuter, 1975).

Another series of studies explored the role of the amount and locus of choice. We found that if subjects are allowed to choose only 3 responses in a 12-item list, performance is as good as when all 12 responses are chosen *provided* that the choice occurs early in the choice phase of the experiment. If choice was offered only at the end of the choice phase, no beneficial effects were found (Monty, Rosenberger, & Perlmuter, 1973). Further, choice is equally effective whether subjects choose either the stimulus or the response in the absence of the other member of the S–R pair (Monty & Perlmuter, 1975). This finding is especially important because the learning theorists among you are probably thinking (as we previously did) that most of the results presented to this point can be explained simply by postulating that offering the subjects S–R pairs of their own choosing affords them the opportunity to form associative hookups of their own liking and that motivational mechanisms may not even play a role. Clearly these studies, as well as those in which only some of the S–R pairs are chosen, all argue against the associative hookup notion. In other words, the associative hookup explanation cannot account for the enhanced learning of the nonchosen S–R pairs when only three of 12 items were chosen; nor can it account for the enhanced learning of chosen responses or stimuli when the other member of the S–R pair was absent during the choosing. This latter situation would not allow any associations to be formed, because either the stimulus or the response was absent during the choice phase. Therefore, due to the inadequacy of the associative hookup notion in accounting for these data, a motivational interpretation appears to be preferable.

You have probably noticed that up until this point, we have implied that it is choice per se that leads to heightened motivation and hence altered performance. There is nothing in these early data to suggest otherwise. More recently, however, we have found that it is not the act of choosing per se that activates the proposed motivational mechanism. Rather, perceptual factors seemingly play a critical role. Hence we were required to distinguish between the act of choosing and what we have referred to as the perception of control. We are by no means the first to embrace this notion of perceived control. Both Mills (as reported by Jellison & Harvey, 1973) and Steiner (1970) proposed similar concepts. In a test of the perceived control hypothesis, Harvey and Johnston (1973) showed that choosing prospective winners in a football contest resulted in self-reports of greater perceived control when the teams were described by the experimenters as being similar on relevant dimensions. Thus a choice between similarly attractive alternatives should result in a larger amount of control than will a choice between dissimilar alternatives. However, in their research, the perception of control was assessed only by self-report data. By contrast, Savage and Perlmuter (1976) sought to extend the perceived control paradigm to the behavioral domain or, more specifically, to the learning situation. Savage and Perlmuter observed that if subjects in a paired-associate learning task were offered a choice of two response alternatives similar in meaningfulness or "m" (and presumably attractiveness) as determined by Locascio and Ley (1972), they significantly outperformed subjects offered response alternatives dissimilar in meaning-fulness. Presumably, the former subjects perceived a greater degree of control, which in turn heightened their motivation and their performance. An example of a choice between similar alternatives would involve a stimulus (e.g., GALAX) and two high-m responses (e.g., WAGON and SALAD). On the other hand, a choice between dissimilar alternatives would provide an identical stimulus, GALAX, and one high- and one low-m response, e.g.,

WAGON and ZOBEL. Further, some of the subjects who were offered a choice between dissimilar response alternatives actually chose one or two of the responses rated low in meaningfulness. Their data were separately analyzed. The performance of these maverick subjects fell closer to that of the subjects offered similar response alternatives than to that of the subjects offered dissimilar alternatives, although it was not significantly different from either. It would have to be argued (after the fact) that the maverick subjects viewed the alternatives as constituting a meaningful choice and thus developed a perception of control that in turn elevated performance marginally.

In an attempt to gain information regarding the feeling of control, a questionnaire was administered following the experiment, and as expected, the group offered a choice between similar alternatives reported a greater feeling of control and was more satisfied with their performance than the group that chose only high-m alternatives in the presence of dissimilar alternatives. Monty, Geller, Savage, and Perlmuter (1979) have recently replicated these results in a slightly different context and reached essentially the same conclusions—it is not the act of choosing per se that leads to enhanced motivation but rather the subject's perception of the choice situation.

EXPERIMENT 1

At this point we examine the notion of perceived control from a slightly different perspective. Before getting into specifics, let us propose a simple metaphor to communicate some of the rationale for the present experiment. A small child says to you, "See my box of chocolates." At that point, you expect that some future opportunity for choice is present. But then the child continues, "You may have *that one*, the rest are for me." Now your anticipated freedom to choose has been withdrawn or "reduced," and you may experience a feeling of disappointment or frustration. It is with this idea of *reduction in freedom* that we are concerned. Let's turn now to our latest observations. In the first of these experiments, both of which used a modified PA task, we sought to investigate the effects of offering the subjects more than one variety of choice. Thus in contrast to previous experiments—in which subjects were presented with a single list of stimuli and were allowed to choose from alternative responses—in the present experiment, all subjects read *two* lists each containing stimuli along with response pairs, and some were allowed to choose the list as well as the responses within the chosen list. Whereas responses were entirely unique, the stimuli in the first list were identical with those in the second list. The complete design was as follows. After the reading of the two lists, each of the subjects was randomly assigned to one of nine groups (20 subjects to a group) shown in Table 7.1. Reading

TABLE 7.1
The Arrangement of the Nine Experimental Groups
According to Number of Choices and
Meaningfulness of the Response Alternatives

Choice of List and Responses (Two Choices)	Forced on List Choice of Responses (One Choice)	Forced on List and Responses (No Choice)
High-High Choice	High-High Choice	High-High Force
High$_H$Low Choice	High$_H$Low Choice	High$_H$Low Force
High$_L$Low Choice	High$_L$Low Choice	High$_L$Low Force

across the top of the table, it can be seen that there were three basic conditions: choice of list and response words (two choices); forced on list but with a choice of response words on the forced list (one choice); and forced on both the list and the response words (no choice). Within each of these conditions, meaningfulness or m of the response alternatives was also manipulated as follows: In column 1 we see that subjects could choose responses from pairs consisting of two high-m responses in each list (designated High-High Choice), or they could choose responses from pairs consisting of one high-m response and a low-m response in each list where subjects selected exclusively the high-meaningfulness responses (designated High$_H$Low), or they could choose responses from between pairs consisting of one high-m response and a low-m response in each list where subjects, based on their own preference, selected *some* (usually one or two) low-m responses (designated High$_L$Low). Subjects in the high-low-choice condition were not required to choose low-m responses; and thus, as in the previous experiments (Monty et al., 1979; Savage & Perlmuter, 1976), about 35% of the subjects choosing between high- and low-m response alternatives actually chose some low-m responses, presumably to increase their perceived control over the choice situation. Therefore, 59 subjects had to be run in high-low conditions in order to obtain 20 subjects who chose only high-m alternatives and 20 subjects who chose some low-m alternatives. In order to equalize the number of subjects per group, the data of the remaining 19 subjects were not analyzed. Moving across to column 2—where the *list* was forced—we have three corresponding groups, each yoked to its counterpart in column 1 (i.e., the list chosen by the subjects in column 1 was forced on the subjects in the corresponding condition in column 2). And finally moving over to column 3, where the subjects were forced on both the list and the words, we see the three corresponding force groups in which subjects were yoked to their counterparts in column 1 with respect to both list and words.

As in some of the earlier experiments on meaningfulness, all materials were presented in test booklets rather than with slides, and subjects were tested in groups of various sizes. On test trials, subjects were provided with a list of stimuli and were required to recall the appropriate responses. The six test trials alternated with five study trials during which subjects studied their respective S-R pairs. The response measure was the percent of high-m responses recalled correctly on each trial.

These scores were subjected to an analysis of variance with number of choices (0, 1, or 2) and level of meaningfulness (i.e., high-high vs. high$_H$low vs. high$_L$low) as between-effects and trials as a within-effect. The significant main effect for trials, $F(5,855) = 647.34$, $p < .0001$, simply indicated that performance improved with practice, as would be expected. More importantly, the significant main effect for number of choices, $F(2, 171) = 7.19$, $p < .001$, indicated that generally speaking, two choices led to better performance than one choice, which in turn led to better performance than no choice (being forced), with a mean percent correct per trial of 72, 68, and 59, respectively. Even more importantly, however, was the significant Number of Choices × Meaningfulness × Trials interaction, $F(20, 855) = 2.78$, $p < .0001$, which required subsequent analysis to aid in interpretation.

Ceiling effects were apparent in the last three trials; consequently, all further analyses were limited to the first three trials only. The data underlying these analyses are shown in Fig. 7.1.

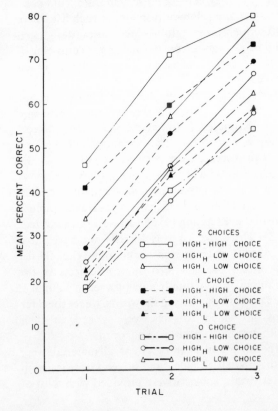

FIG. 7.1. Mean percent correct per trial as a function of number of choices offered, meaningfulness, and trials (Exp. 1).

Two Choices Versus One Choice

Without going into too much detail, let's look at some of these major analyses and conclusions. First using a 2 × 2 × 3 factorial, looking at the two-choice vs. one-choice conditions, we compared the groups offered two high-m responses with the groups offered high- and low-m alternatives that elected to learn some low-m alternatives. These data were evaluated over the first three trials and revealed a significant main effect for meaningfulness, $F(1, 76) = 6.43$, $p < .01$, indicating that choosing between similar alternatives led to better performance than choosing between dissimilar alternatives. Secondly, we found a significant main effect for number of choices, $F(1, 76) = 5.16$, $p < .03$.

Looking at Fig. 7.1, it is apparent that when the opportunities for choice are reduced by forcing the subjects to limit their choices to one of the lists, performance declined for both the high-high-choice condition and the high$_L$low-choice condition. By contrast, a second analysis of variance revealed there was no significant decrement in performance for the high$_H$low-choice condition when subjects were required to limit their choice to one of the lists. Presumably, the subjects in the latter condition never perceived they were offered the freedom to choose in the first place, since the alternatives were dissimilar. Hence the potential for perceived control never developed, and thus no frustration was evinced from the reduction in freedom to choose. In short, then, two major conclusions follow from the differential effects occasioned by the reduction in choice. First, the perception of control is not dependent on the act of choosing per se, but rather it can be established merely by providing the subject with a potential opportunity to choose. This represents a major modification to our previous thinking (Perlmuter & Monty, 1977) in that it now appears that perceived control develops *prior* to the act of choosing rather than following it, as we had previously implied. Second, harmful consequences from reducing future opportunities to choose affect behavior only if the perception of control has been established previously, as it was for the high-high and high$_L$low conditions. Conversely, subjects who elected only high-m alternatives (high$_H$low), when provided with dissimilar response pairs, neither anticipate nor develop the perception of control and hence are unaffected by reductions in the opportunity to choose. It is probably important, before moving on, to mention that we recognize that this anticipation of control and consequent reduction in freedom is a learned phenomenon. That is, in the present experiment the subjects were provided with a practice trial containing two practice items prior to being exposed to the two lists. Choice subjects were permitted to choose responses during the practice trial in order to illustrate the paired-associate procedure. Following the practice trial, they were exposed to the two lists. Presumably, the practice trial established the set in the subjects that they would be allowed to make choices during the experiment. Had they not been exposed to the practice trial, it is possible that the observed results would not have ensued.

Two Choices Versus No Choice

Next we compared the two-choice condition with the no-choice (force) condition. In both of these, the alternatives were similar in meaningfulness. We found a highly significant difference, $F(1,38) = 13.11$, $p < .001$, presumably stemming from the opportunity to choose, which benefited the choice subjects. More importantly, however, when subjects in the two-choice situation were presented with pairs of dissimilar responses and selected all high-m alternatives, they performed no better than their counterparts in the no-choice situation. In other words, we again see there is a complete lack of any benefits of choosing when no viable choice is perceived between the available response pairs. By contrast, subjects in the two-choice (dissimilar) condition who elected to learn some low-m responses performed significantly better than their forced mates, $F(1, 38) = 4.74$, $p < .05$.

One Choice Versus No Choice

When we compared the one-choice situation with the no-choice situation, the only difference that resulted was that the high-high-choice subjects performed better than their forced counterparts, $F(1, 38) = 7.31$, $p < .025$. This finding reinforces the previous conclusion that only when the situation is perceived as offering a real or viable choice will performance be enhanced.

Performance With Two Choices

Now let's look at the relative performance of subjects offered two choices. Here we found that performance was significantly higher when the alternatives were similar (that is, the high-high-choice condition) than when they were dissimilar, $F(1, 38) = 6.98$, $p < .025$ (i.e., the high$_H$low condition). Once again, we see that subjects in the high-high condition perceive that they were offered a real choice, which in turn led to heightened motivation and hence improved performance. These findings can also be embraced in terms of Steiner's (1970) notions of outcome freedom and decision freedom. Perceived outcome freedom is reflected in the individual's *judgment* of the availability and desirability of the outcomes he or she wishes to obtain. Perceived decision freedom refers to the volition the individual believes him- or herself to exercise when deciding whether or not to seek a specific outcome or when deciding to seek one outcome rather than another. In terms of our data, we would conclude that subjects in the high-high condition were presumably provided with both decision freedom and outcome freedom. However, subjects in the high$_H$low condition presumably perceived that the dissimilar alternatives constrained or limited their decision freedom, and thus their choosing did not constitute a real choice; hence they did not develop the perception of control, and their performance was not facilitated. Performance of those subjects who elected to learn a few low-m alternatives was at an intermediate level (i.e., not significantly different from either of the other two groups). Since these subjects selected a few low-m alternatives, they also experienced decision freedom, which in turn moderately benefited their learning. However, the failure of these subjects actually to reach the performance levels of those who chose between similar high-m alternatives may have resulted from a lesser amount of outcome freedom due to the subjects' misjudgment of the desirability of the chosen low-m responses in that they were in fact more difficult to learn than anticipated.

Finally, one last comment on the similarity variable. It is now apparent that the similarity of the alternatives provides only a necessary but not a sufficient condition for the development of perceived control. This conclusion is based upon an evaluation of the two-choice situation in which subjects chose between two lists, each comprised of pairs of dissimilar alternatives. Subjects in the high$_H$low condition who selected all high-m alternatives learned no better than their yoked mates who were forced both on the list as well as on the specific responses. Apparently, the dissimilarity within the pairs of alternatives contained in each list was more salient than the overall similarity between the lists, and thus a choice between these two lists did not lead to the perception of control.

Performance With One Choice

Let's now move on to an examination of the relative performance of the three groups of subjects offered only one choice (i.e., their choice of responses on the forced list). It may be recalled that in our initial analysis, we found a significant Number of Choices × Meaningfulness × Trials interaction. Here, in dissecting this analysis, we found that subjects choosing between pairs of similar responses tended to outperform subjects choosing between responses dissimilar in m irrespective of whether they chose all high-m responses, $t(38) = 2.14$, $p < .05$, Trial 1 only, or a combination of high- and low-m responses, $F(1,38) = 5.30$, $p < .05$. All other differences failed to reach significance. In short, these results differ from the two-choice situation in that the slight elevation in performance for the subjects selecting some low-m responses was not apparent.

Performance With No Choice

When the opportunity to choose was eliminated (the no-choice situation), there were no significant differences as a function of meaningfulness. Presumably, the subjects in these conditions did not have the opportunity to develop the perception of control. Note that during the practice trial, these subjects were assigned responses and thus would not then be expected to anticipate an opportunity to choose.

Questionnaire Data

At the completion of the PA trials, a questionnaire was administered to each subject. A series of questions were posed including one concerned with the subject's perception of control over the events in the experiment. The subjects responded on a 25-point scale, and those in the two-choice condition who chose from similar alternatives reported being more in control than either the yoked forced subjects, $t(38) = 2.41, p < .03$, or the subjects in the two-choice condition who chose from dissimilar alternatives, $t(38) = 2.62, p < .02$. Also, subjects in the one-choice condition who chose from similar alternatives reported being more in control than their forced counterparts, although this result just failed to reach significance, $t(38) = 1.87, p < .06$. There were no other significant differences. These results are generally consistent with the performance data and show that the perception of control may lead to effects that subjects can evaluate and report. Of course, it must be recognized that the questionnaire data were gathered following the PA trials and thus may not purely reflect only differences in perceived control.

EXPERIMENT 2

Before summarizing the results of the first experiment, let's turn to another recent study of how perceptual factors affect performance when *no* choice is provided. Specifically, in this experiment we tested the hypothesis that being forced to learn low-m materials in the context of high-m materials would have a depressing effect upon performance relative to forcing subjects to learn these identical low-m responses in the presence of other low-m responses.

Two groups of 20 subjects each were presented with a paired-associate task in which they were initially exposed, in booklet form, to a single common list of 12 stimulus words each paired with two response words. One group, designated the low-force group, was presented with stimulus words each accompanied by two low-m responses; whereas the second group, high-low force, was shown the identical stimuli each paired with one high-m and one low-m response. By way of example, the stimulus word POLYP was paired with VUTAW and GEMOT in the low-force group, whereas in the high-low-force group, the stimulus word POLYP was paired with VUTAW and MEDAL. On the following page of the booklet, one response word in each pair appeared with a circle around it. The circled word designated the response to be learned. For both groups, identical low-*m* alternatives were learned exclusively.

Since subjects were required to learn low-*m* responses, a demonstratively more difficult task than learning high-*m* responses, they were provided with seven study trials that alternated with test trials rather than the five study trials used in the previous experiment.

The measure of performance was the percent of correct responses on each trial. The results are shown in Fig. 7.2. An analysis of variance revealed no main effect for groups; however, there were both a significant trials effect, $F(7, 266) = 119.51$, $p < .01$, and a significant Trials × Group interaction, $F(7, 266) = 3.40$, $p < .01$. As can be seen, the low-force group outperformed the high-low-force group on the latter trials, thereby confirming the hypothesis that being forced to learn low-*m* materials in the context of high-*m* material has a depressing effect upon performance. A questionnaire administered after the learning trials showed that the low-force group felt more in control than the high-low-force group, $t(38) = 2.13$, $p < .05$, and felt more satisfied with their performance, $t(38) = 2.18$, $p < .05$. Therefore, we

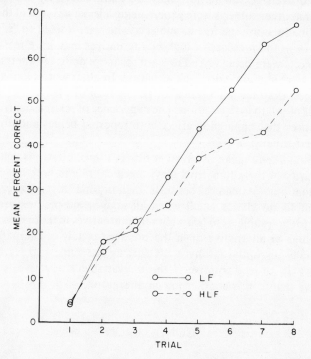

FIG. 7.2.   Mean percent correct per trial as a function of groups and trials (Exp. 2).

concluded, based on both performance data and the subjective feelings expressed on the questionnaire, that the perception of control is also important even when no overt choice is possible. That is, the mere presence of more desirable alternatives may lead the subjects to recognize that they might have been better off had they had the opportunity to learn the other response. They thus experience despair or possibly frustration, which degrades performance relative to that of subjects forced in the presence of similar alternatives. These results also seem to be harmonious with those found in the first experiment, in which the mere exposure to certain alternatives led subjects to anticipate the opportunity to choose. The negative consequences attributable to the reduction in the opportunity to choose are in a sense analogous to being forced to learn only low-m alternatives when both low- and high-m alternatives have been present. Thus the relatively poorer performance in the high-low-force group may have resulted from the systematic exclusion of all the high-m alternatives. These results seem compatible with the observations of Glass and Singer (1972), who introduced the concept of relative deprivation. They found that when subjects were exposed to aversive stimulation, they were more severely affected if they believed that other subjects were experiencing a lesser amount of the aversive stimulation. In our experiment, subjects who were forced to learn low-m alternatives in the presence of high-m alternatives may have reasoned that other subjects were being forced to learn the more desirable alternatives and therefore were in a more desirable situation. In other words, being forced to learn the less desirable alternative further weakens the perception of control as a result of relative deprivation. The experience of relative deprivation has consequences that apparently affect both reported beliefs about control as well as performance.

We would like to make two further observations. First, it is apparent that the similarity of the alternatives plays a critical role in both the choice and force situations. A choice between high-m and low-m alternatives is equivalent to no choice at all when all high-m alternatives are selected. Further, forcing subjects to learn high-m alternatives in the presence of either another high-m alternative or in the presence of low-m alternatives is not differentially disruptive. Conversely, forcing the subject to learn a low-m alternative is more disruptive if the unavailable alternative is a high-m alternative than if it is another low-m alternative.

CONCLUSION

In conclusion, these experiments have made three major contributions to an understanding of choice. Merely exposing subjects to alternative sets of materials under specifiable conditions can lead to an anticipation that choice will be offered subsequently. Thus the initial locus of perceived control resides not in the act of choosing but rather in the anticipation of the opportunity for choice and control. Second, given that the situation generates the anticipation that choice will be offered, the chooser then becomes demonstratively vulnerable to the negative consequences of reductions or eliminations in the opportunity to choose. The reduction in freedom is procedurally and theoretically distinct from the abrogation of choice (Perlmuter et al., 1974) that follows the overt act of choosing and apparently is less adverse in its consequences than is the abrogation of choice. Third, as shown in Experiment 2, even subjects who are provided with no opportunity to choose continue to maintain a degree of perceived control. Evidence for this observation is based on the fact that being forced to learn the less desirable of two responses (one high-m and one low-m) is more disruptive to the reported perception of control and to performance than is being forced to learn the identical low-m responses that have been presented along with other similar low-m alternatives.

In summary, and in the interest of reducing confusion, we introduce a pictorial summary of the results discussed here in a simple fashion as shown in Fig. 7.3.

On the extreme left can be seen two fundamental starting points—one for those subjects who are shown materials and anticipate they will be exercising the option to choose at least some of these materials and the other starting point for subjects who are given a list that they are forced to learn. Looking first at those subjects who are forced, we see that one of two things will happen. If they are forced to learn from similar options or if they are forced to learn the more desirable of two dissimilar options, they report a relatively low perception of control, and they perform at what we will call the baseline level. By contrast, if they are forced to learn the less attractive of two dissimilar responses, they recognize that they might have been better off had they had the option of learning the other response. Thus they experience despair or frustration, which depresses performance to a subbaseline level.

The situation is much more complicated if the subjects are shown material and anticipate a choice. If no choice is offered, they experience a reduction in freedom, and thus performance is reduced to a baseline level. Similarly, if subjects are offered a choice but fail to accept it as a real choice, there is no perception of control, and hence baseline performance results. By contrast, if subjects see the choice as real, they develop the perception of control and a potential for frustration. If they are subsequently offered the opportunity to choose but the choice occurs late in the procedure, the potentially beneficial effects are negated, and they perform similarly to those offered no choice at all. Conversely, if the act of choosing occurs early, they retain the benefits until the chosen materials are either utilized or abrogated. If their choices are abrogated immediately following choosing, the potential for frustration is

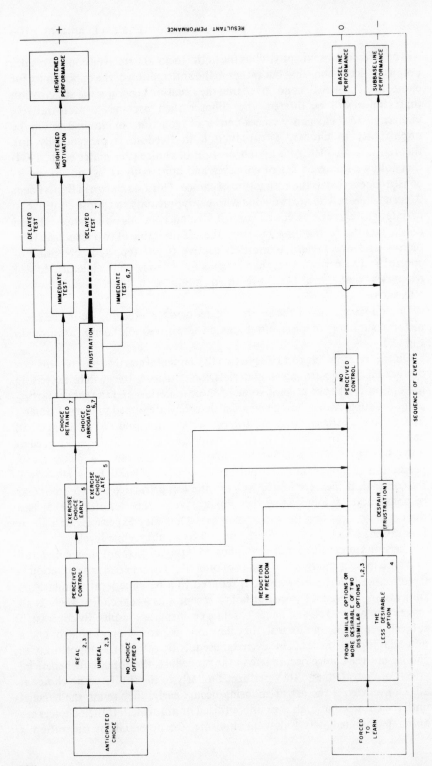

realized, and if they are required to immediately learn material not of their own choosing, performance is degraded to a level *below* that of subjects who were forced initially. However, if the imposition of the nonchosen materials is delayed for a period of 24 hours, the potential for frustration dissipates, and heightened motivation and subsequently heightened performance are realized. Subjects simply allowed to learn their chosen materials either immediately or 24 hours following choice show heightened motivation and enhanced performance. Apparently, the positive consequences of choice do not readily dissipate with time. This is intentionally a simplistic summary that does not in fact even reflect all our own experiments—just the ones of interest here.

We have seen, then, that even in our relatively simple experimental setting, choice can result in a variety of outcomes depending in part on the subject's perception of the situation; however, our results are by no means limited to such simple settings. One of our colleagues, for example, demonstrated that it is possible to improve reading-comprehension test scores in the classroom simply by offering children the opportunity to choose, from a list of titles, the stories to be read during the test (White, 1974). We would hasten to add, however, as we have previously stated (Perlmuter & Monty, 1977), that in an area as complex as this, it may be easier to misapply these principles in the classroom than to use them prudently, and manipulations could be destructive.

In closing, although our research has been limited to only one aspect of behavior—namely, enhancing learning—it is reasonable to speculate that providing choice in other contexts might also lead to improved performance. This volume should serve to elucidate many of them.

ACKNOWLEDGMENTS

This research was supported in part by a grant from the U.S. Army Research Office to the second author and in part by the Behavioral Research Directorate of the U.S. Army Human Engineering Laboratory.

REFERENCES

Brown, J. S. *The motivation of behavior*. New York: McGraw-Hill, 1961.
Glass, D. C., & Singer, J. E. Behavioral aftereffects of unpredictable and uncontrollable aversive events. *American Scientist*, 1972, *60*, 457–465.

FIG. 7.3.   (*Opposite page*) A pictorial summary of the data discussed in the text. The numbers in the cells denote the original published source references: (1) Perlmuter, Monty, & Kimble, 1971; (2) Savage & Perlmuter, 1976; (3) Monty, Geller, Savage, & Perlmuter, 1979; (4) Savage, Perlmuter, & Monty (see text); (5) Monty, Rosenberger, & Perlmuter, 1973; (6) Perlmuter, Monty, & Cross, 1974; and (7) Monty & Perlmuter, 1975.

Harvey, J. H., & Johnston, S. Determinants of the perception of choice. *Journal of Experimental Social Psychology*, 1973, *9*, 164–179.

Jellison, J. M., & Harvey, J. H. Determinants of perceived choice and the relationship between perceived choice and perceived competence. *Journal of Personality and Social Psychology*, 1973, *28*, 376–382.

Locascio, D., & Ley, R. Scale-rated meaningfulness of 319 CVCVC word paralogs previously assessed for associative reaction time. *Journal of Verbal Learning and Verbal Behavior*, 1972, *11*, 243–250.

Monty, R. A., Geller, E. S., Savage, R. E., & Perlmuter, L. C. The freedom to choose is not always so choice. *Journal of Experimental Psychology: Human Learning and Memory*, 1979, *5*, 170–178.

Monty, R. A., & Perlmuter, L. C. Persistence of the effects of choice on paired-associate learning. *Memory & Cognition*, 1975, *3*, 183–187.

Monty, R. A., Rosenberger, M. A., & Perlmuter, L. C. Amount and locus of choice as sources of motivation in paired-associate learning. *Journal of Experimental Psychology*, 1973, *97*, 16–21.

Perlmuter, L. C., & Monty, R. A. The importance of perceived control: Fact or fantasy? *American Scientist*, 1977, *65*, 759–765.

Perlmuter, L. C., Monty, R. A., & Cross, P. M. Choice as a disrupter of performance in paired-associate learning. *Journal of Experimental Psychology*, 1974, *102*, 170–172.

Perlmuter, L. C., Monty, R. A., & Kimble, G. A. Effect of choice on paired-associate learning. *Journal of Experimental Psychology*, 1971, *91*, 47–53.

Savage, R. E., & Perlmuter, L. C. *Choice and control: Perceptual determiners.* Paper presented at the meeting of the Southeastern Psychological Association, New Orleans, 1976.

Steiner, I. D. Perceived freedom. In L. Berkowitz (Ed.), *Advances in experimental social psychology* (Vol. 5). New York: Academic Press, 1970.

White, A. M. *The effects of choice upon paired-associate learning and reading comprehension.* Undergraduate honors thesis, Virginia Polytechnic Institute and State University, 1974.

8 Learned Helplessness through Modeling: Self-Efficacy and Social Comparison Processes

Irvin Brown, Jr.
Stanford University

I am reminded of a recent counseling experience with a college student who had aspired since his elementary school years to become a physician. Although a combination of events, some historical and others current, appeared to have precipitated his inability to cope at that time, one particularly traumatic experience was the suicide of a physician from his small Midwestern hometown. The two men did not know each other personally, but as a member of the same ethnic group, the physician had been the young man's most esteemed model since childhood. Such instances, in which one person's sense of direction and efficacy are influenced by the outcome of another's behavior, are quite common in a society so complex that we must look to the experiences of others to determine the feasibility of personal goals and standards.

Observations such as the foregoing example have led me to combine two separate interests, one of which is theoretical and the other practical. The theoretical interest concerns the social learning processes through which we are influenced by, and learn from, the behavior of others. The applied interest concerns motivational problems such as those presented by "high-risk children." These are children who, because of social or personal disadvantages, fail to achieve self-fulfilling and rewarding lives. The separate interests in these issues have been brought together under the rubric, "Learned Helplessness through Modeling." Our research in this area, and that of other investigators, has shown that people can develop a sense of futility through witnessing failure by others as well as through their own experience of failure or uncontrollability (Brown & Inouye, 1978; DeVellis, DeVellis, & McCauley, 1978).

Research on motivation has traditionally focused either on the effects of direct success or failure or on person-related variables such as perceived locus of control (Phares, 1976) and achievement motivation (Atkinson, 1964). Results of experiments that have examined the interaction of person and situational variables generally support the view that failure undermines motivation and that this effect is strongest for persons low in achievement motivation (e.g., Feather, 1966) and low in perceptions of control (Hiroto & Seligman, 1975). Conversely, it is people high in achievement motivation and perceived control who benefit most from success experiences.

Studies of learned helplessness in humans have demonstrated that a variety of experiences, the most typical being aversive consequences for failure at insoluble tasks, can undermine subsequent performance (e.g., Dweck & Bush, 1976; Hiroto & Seligman, 1975; Roth & Kubal, 1975). Although the wide range of operations employed in these studies makes it difficult to conceptualize learned helplessness as a unitary phenomenon, Maier and Seligman (1976) have proposed that the various effects that characterize learned helplessness are mediated by subjects' expectations of controllability. That is, as a result of being subjected to uncontrollable events, people come to expect that they cannot affect outcomes through their actions in other situations as well. This expectation, in turn, is believed to debilitate performance through cognitive and emotional effects as well as undermining motivation.

The general viewpoint expressed by Maier and Seligman is consistent with Bandura's (1977) social learning view that performance is mediated by self-efficacy expectations. From the social learning perspective, however, lowered efficacy expectations may result not only from direct failure experiences but from vicarious experiences as well. This is consistent with the common observation that people develop expectations about how well they will perform on tasks at which they have had no direct experience.

Vicarious influences have especially important social implications, because the experiences of a salient model can adversely affect large numbers of people. In the case of children who indentify strongly with peer groups, or persons who belong to economically and politically disadvantaged minority groups, witnessing failure by members of the group may have devastating effects on feelings of *self*-efficacy. Low perceived efficacy in turn may lead people to shun activities and fail to exert the effort necessary to acquire essential skills. Such vicarious experiences could have all the deleterious effects commonly associated with avoidance patterns of behavior, in which one's potential efficacy is not adequately tested and hence not fully developed.

In addition to personal and vicarious experiences, performance expectations may develop through other modes of influence. These would include the social judgments others make of one's performance capabilities, which in many instances may be based on characteristics other than actual abilities, such as sex, race, and social class. This is of course the Pygmalion issue revisited.

From the self-efficacy perspective, the direct and vicarious experiences of "helplessness" are mediated by similar processes. People's perceptions of their capabilities are undermined when they expend a high degree of effort and fail to affect outcomes by their actions. Similar inferences may be drawn from observing others work hard at a task and fail. However, vicarious influence operates through a social comparison process. The extent to which observed failure will exert an effect should vary depending on comparability of the performer's competence, amount of effort expended by the performer, and uncertainty about one's own skill at the task. The vicarious experience of uncontrollability is thus complicated by the fact that performers vary widely in competence, and observers do not have direct access to other people's levels of motivation and capabilities. When people undergo similar experiences, however, or otherwise view a model as similar, it is likely that some degree of competence similarity will be inferred.

THE ROLE OF PERCEIVED SIMILARITY
IN COMPETENCE

The initial experiment in this program of research was designed to evaluate the role of perceived similarity in competence in developing a sense of helplessness through modeling (Brown & Inouye, 1978). Male college students observed a model perform unsuccessfully at anagram tasks under conditions of presumed similarity in ability, assumed superiority, or they received no information concerning their competence relative to that of the model. Subjects' efficacy expectations for each anagram and their persistence on unsolved anagrams comprised the primary dependent measures. Control subjects performed anagram tasks without any prior treatment. In order to assure comparability in solution rates for the different groups, and not confound the measurement of persistence, the anagrams were very difficult with one-third being insoluble.

Results of the experiment provided support for the "vicarious learned helplessness" hypothesis that self-perceptions and motivation can be undermined by exposure to modeled failure. The effects of exposure to modeled failure on subjects' persistence are summarized graphically in Fig. 8.1. Because the subjects' experiences were vicarious, the results of the experiment also provided strong evidence for the view that it is the expectation of "uncontrollability" that is critical in producing helplessness effects.

After observing modeled helplessness, subjects reduced their persistence in the face of task difficulty but only when they perceived themselves as similar

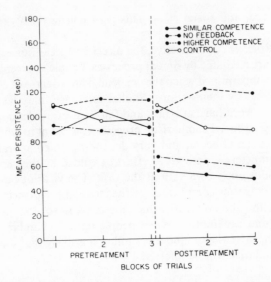

FIG. 8.1. Mean persistence during pretreatment and posttreatment anagram tasks.

in competence to the ineffectual model. Observers who perceived themselves as more competent than the model were unaffected in their persistence by exposure to modeled helplessness. If anything, the vicarious experience enhanced their motivation in the face of failure. Subjects in the control and the perceived superiority conditions did not differ in persistence in the initial posttreatment phase. However, on subsequent trials these two groups diverged significantly: The controls reduced their effort, whereas subjects who perceived themselves to be of higher competence than the unsuccessful model boosted their effort. Subjects who had no comparative knowledge about the model's competence showed an intermediate reduction in persistence as a function of exposure to modeled helplessness. A post-experimental questionnaire revealed that many of these subjects assumed that the model, who was also a college student, was comparable to themselves in ability.

The effects of exposure to modeled helplessness on expectations of personal efficacy were likewise mediated by perceived similarity in competence (Fig. 8.2). Subjects who perceived themselves as more competent than the helpless model maintained uniformly high expectations throughout the trials. In contrast, modeled helplessness had a devastating effect on subjects' self-judged efficacy when they perceived themselves of comparable ability to the model. These subjects expressed an extremely low sense of personal efficacy in solving the challenging anagrams. Subjects who were given no feedback on the model's competence displayed an intermediate level of self-judged efficacy.

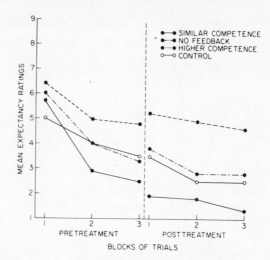

FIG. 8.2. Mean expectancy ratings during pretreatment and posttreatment anagram tasks.

Perceived similarity continued to exert an influence on subjects' persistence and judgments of self-efficacy throughout the experiment. Differences in motivation and self-perception were maintained despite the fact that subjects did not differ in their actual ability to solve the anagrams.

The hypothesis that the behavioral effects of exposure to modeled failure are mediated through changes in expectations of self-efficacy also received support. When subjects entered the experiment, they had little idea what the anagrams were like, so they had no basis for judging their efficacy at the task. However, after sampling a few items, self-efficacy became a good predictor of persistence regardless of treatment conditions (Fig. 8.3). The higher their perceived efficacy, the longer the subjects persisted on the tasks. The magnitude of this relationship increased across experimental trials, suggesting that subjects relied more heavily on their judgments of self-efficacy in regulating their expenditure of effort as the experiment progressed.

The dynamic quality of the relationship between expectations and persistence is illustrated by the behavior of subjects who perceived themselves to be superior to the ineffectual model. The results were generally consistent with less formal studies of labeling and segregation of children as "superior" and "inferior" in classrooms on the basis of such incidental characteristics as eye color (Zimbardo & Ruch, 1977, pp. 13a–13d). Results of these studies have not only shown diminished performance and self-esteem by children who were labeled and treated as inferior but also enhanced performance and self-esteem by members of the group arbitrarily designated as "superior." In our experimental study, the "superior" subjects showed enhanced self-efficacy expectations immediately after witnessing the model fail, although their level of persistence was initially no higher than that of control subjects. Because the anagrams were very challenging, "superior" subjects in some

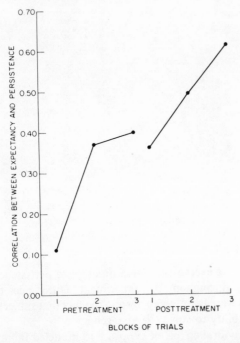

FIG. 8.3. Correlations between expectancy and persistence at different phases of the experiment.

sense had their high expectations disconfirmed when they confronted the task. When faced with the choice, however, of lowering their expectations or working harder, these subjects tended to persist even longer, as if to confirm their perceived superiority.

In addition to the posttreatment anagrams being very challenging, all subjects in the experiment worked on a set of pretreatment anagrams that were equally difficult. The question thus arises as to the impact of subject's low pretreatment performance outcomes on their susceptibility to vicarious helplessness. Although this aspect of the experimental design does not account for the differential effects of perceived similarity, people should be less susceptible to vicarious helplessness when their direct experiences have been favorable. In the example of the aspiring physician, the impact of suicide by his hometown doctor may not have been so devastating if the student himself had not been experiencing difficulty and uncertainty in his studies.

EFFECTS OF PRIOR LEVEL OF ACCOMPLISHMENT AND SEX DIFFERENCES

The present experiment was designed to explore the influence of prior level of accomplishment on susceptibility to modeled failure. Sex differences in susceptibility to modeled failure were also examined. Male and female high school students (N = 36) observed a male model fail at anagram tasks under conditions of assumed similarity in ability, or they were given no information about the model's level of competence. Control subjects performed the anagrams without any intervening treatment. As in the previous study it was predicted that similar-competence subjects would show lower expectations and persist less than control subjects and less than subjects given no feedback on the model's competence. Subjects who performed well during the pretreatment were expected to have higher efficacy expectations during the posttreatment and be more persistent than subjects who were less competent at solving the pretreatment anagrams. On the basis of previous research on sex differences in learned helplessness (e.g., Dweck & Bush, 1976), it was further predicted that girls would be more influenced by modeled helplessness than boys.

Because the posttreatment anagrams were very difficult and subjects would invariably perform more poorly than during pretreatment, modeled failure and perceived similarity were expected to result in diminished persistence and expectations over posttreatment trials. Control subjects, on the other hand, who did not witness the model fail would maintain their effort and sense of efficacy in the face of difficulty. No predictions were made in this regard for subjects who observed the unsuccessful model but were given no feedback on his level of competence.

The subject and the model performed word-anagram tasks in adjoining but separate testing booths. The anagrams were projected onto screens in the testing booths by a standard slide projector. Each subject had a handswitch that simultaneously advanced the slide projector and activated an electronic clock. Circuits were designed such that the handswitch activated, stopped, or reset the clock to allow precise measurement of the amount of time subjects worked on each anagram.

The number of anagrams solved during pretreatment provided the measure of each subject's prior level of accomplishment at the task. The pretreatment anagrams, although of varying levels of difficulty, were all soluble, but only three of the posttreatment anagrams were soluble. The insoluble anagrams were used during posttreatment to keep the solution rates relatively low across conditions so as not to confound the measure of persistence through differential success rates. Subjects recorded on a 10-point scale their expected ability to solve each anagram before viewing it, with a rating of 1 meaning complete inability and a rating of 10 signifying complete certainty in their ability to solve the subsequent anagram.

After the pretreatment task was completed, subjects assigned to the similar-competence condition were led to believe that they and the model attained similar scores on the task. In the no-feedback and control conditions, no competence feedback was given.

Modeling of Failure

Following the similarity induction, the subject and the model were informed that in the next part of the experiment, they would have to perform separately and that the model had been chosen by a random procedure to go first. The subject was asked to wait quietly seated, out of view of the model's screen, because he/she would be working on the same anagrams after the model finished. The model then began the posttreatment task, giving the appearance initially of trying hard. After the fourth anagram, he began to mutter to himself about his ineffectiveness, saying, "These are really hard for me." As the session progressed, the model began to manifest additional signs of defeat, spending an average of 15 seconds on each of the last five anagrams. Finally, after having gone through the list, he remarked, "These are definitely impossible for me to solve." Subjects in both the similar-competence and no-feedback conditions watched the model fail.

The posttreatment procedures were identical to those used in the pretreatment task. The main dependent measures were the number of seconds that subjects persisted before giving up on the anagrams they did not solve and their self-judged ability to solve each anagram before it was presented.

Data Format and Preliminary Analyses

Solution rates, persistence scores, and expectations were analyzed in blocks of five trials yielding two pretreatment blocks and two posttreatment blocks. The pretreatment and posttreatment results were analyzed separately using a $3 \times 2 \times 2$ analysis of variance, with the three experimental conditions and sex as fully crossed factors and with repeated measures on the two trial blocks. Also, t tests were used for comparison of differences between particular groups, including posttreatment comparisons of subjects who performed well during pretreatment with those who performed poorly. Because of high variability, logarithmic transformations were performed on subjects' persistence scores prior to analyzing the data. All results reported as significant are at the .05 level or beyond.

The analysis of variance revealed no pretreatment differences between conditions on either measure. Nor were there any significant changes across pretreatment trials on the different measures. Boys and girls showed no difference in their ability to solve pretreatment anagrams, nor did they differ in their expectations of self-efficacy. However, girls showed a significantly higher level of persistence than boys on the pretreatment anagrams for which they were unable to find solutions. As intended, posttreatment solution rates did not differ as a function of conditions, sex, or trial blocks. Thus comparisons between groups on persistence were not confounded by solution rates.

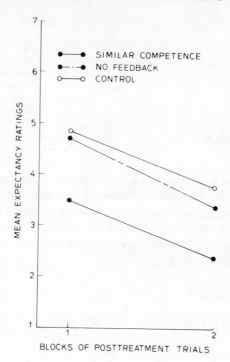

FIG. 8.4. Mean expectancy ratings during posttreatment.

Efficacy Expectations

Figure 8.4 shows subjects' efficacy expectations for the two experimental groups and the control group during the blocks of posttreatment trials. The analysis of variance revealed that the main effect for groups was statistically significant. Subsequent between-group comparisons showed that subjects who perceived the ineffectual model to be of equal competence judged themselves to be less efficacious than did the control subjects. Subjects who received no information on the model's level of competence exhibited an intermediate level of expected efficacy and did not differ significantly from the other groups. Trial blocks were also a significant source of variance. Regardless of condition, subjects' efficacy expectations decreased as they worked on the difficult task.

Table 8.1 shows expectancy ratings for males and females in the three conditions. Boys had somewhat higher expectations about being able to solve the anagrams than girls. Although an analysis of variance revealed that these differences were not statistically significant, the Sex × Condition interaction was significant. Between-group comparisons showed that boys who were not given feedback on the model's level of competence had significantly higher expectations than boys in the control group. Girls who were not given such

TABLE 8.1
Mean Expectancy Ratings for Males and Females
by Conditions

| | Treatment Conditions | | |
	Similar Competence	No Feedback	Control
Males	3.44	5.40	3.73
Females	2.41	2.70	4.88

feedback showed lower expectations than control girls. Thus, girls who observed the model fail lowered their expectations regardless of whether or not comparative information was provided. The boys, on the other hand, became more confident in their ability to solve the anagrams following exposure to modeled failure when they had no knowledge of the model's competence level.

Persistence

Figure 8.5 shows the persistence scores for the two experimental groups and the control group during the two blocks of posttreatment trials. Although the

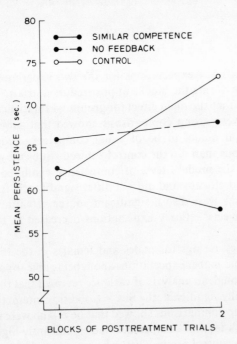

FIG. 8.5.   Mean persistence during posttreatment anagram tasks.

analysis of variance revealed no overall effect for perceived similarity, the Condition × Trial interaction was statistically significant. After working on pretreatment anagrams of varying levels of difficulty, subjects' motivation appeared uninfluenced by modeled failure as they began the posttreatment task. But when further confronted with the challenging posttreatment anagrams, subjects who had been led to believe that they and the unsuccessful model were similar in competence showed progressively less persistence. Between-group comparisons revealed that by the second half of the experimental trials, these subjects were persisting significantly less in their attempts to solve the anagrams than control subjects, who in turn became progressively more persistent in the face of task difficulty. As predicted, subjects who observed the model fail but were given no feedback on his level of competence showed an intermediate level of persistence.

It should be noted that although control subjects showed a progressive decrease in efficacy expectations, they increased their persistence over trials. It would appear that these subjects were not convinced that they were unlikely to find solutions for the anagrams. Given additional experimental trials, perhaps subjects' expectations and persistence would have converged as shown in the previous experiment (Brown & Inouye, 1978). In the earlier study, subjects received more performance trials. In the present experiment, there was no significant relationship between subjects' expectations and persistence in any of the conditions.

Table 8.2 shows persistence scores for males and females in the three conditions. No overall sex differences were found for subjects' persistence at the anagram tasks. Although the Sex × Condition interaction also fell short of statistical significance, it can be seen that there was a trend for girls who had no knowledge of the model's level of competence to exhibit less persistence than their control counterparts and to be as strongly affected as girls who observed a failing model of similar ability. Boys who had no information on the model's level of competence tended to show higher persistence than controls during the initial block of trials, though overall these groups did not differ.

TABLE 8.2
Mean Persistence Ratings for Males and Females
by Conditions

	Treatment Conditions		
	Similar Competence	No Feedback	Control
Males	57.28	70.48	59.77
Females	63.14	63.26	75.41

TABLE 8.3
Mean Posttreatment Persistence
as a Function of Pretreatment Solution Rates

| | Trials | | | |
| | Block 1 Pretreatment Solution Rate | | Block 2 Pretreatment Solution Rate | |
Conditions	High	Low	High	Low
Similar	84.27	55.70	73.21	52.37
competence	(*n* = 3)	(*n* = 9)	(*n* = 3)	(*n* = 9)
No feedback	74.43	57.80	76.39	58.91
	(*n* = 6)	(*n* = 6)	(*n* = 6)	(*n* = 6)
Control	67.37	59.41	63.57	80.24
	(*n* = 5)	(*n* = 7)	(*n* = 5)	(*n* = 7)

Table 8.3 shows subjects' persistence on the posttreatment anagrams depending on their level of pretreatment performance on the anagram task. Subjects are divided into those who solved six or more anagrams correctly and those who solved five or less.

Between-group comparisons showed that after observing the model fail, subjects who had performed well on the pretreatment anagrams persisted significantly longer than subjects who had performed poorly. These results were obtained for both the first and second blocks of trials. Consistent with the general pattern of results, experimental subjects who performed poorly on the pretreatment anagrams persisted significantly less than their control counterparts during the second block of trials. Thus, exposure to modeled helplessness undermined motivation when prior performance level was low but if anything, enhanced motivation when prior performance level was high. Although this same pattern of results appeared to hold for subjects' efficacy expectations, the findings generally fell short of statistical significance.

These results were consistent with the view that efficacy information based on direct experiences is likely to be more influential than vicariously based information. However, the complex interplay of these sources of information is demonstrated by the delayed motivational effects of modeled helplessness and perceived similarity. Subjects tended to be persistent despite failure by a model of similar ability until they themselves had been sufficiently challenged. But even in the face of such challenge, subjects who had experienced high levels of success were undaunted by witnessing the model fail.

Results of the present experiment are also consistent with previous research on sex differences in learned helplessness, which shows that girls tend to be more susceptible to failure influences than do boys (Dweck & Bush, 1976). Although boys and girls were equally influenced by seeing a model of similar ability fail, the girls' motivation and efficacy expectations were also undermined by modeled failure when no information on the model's level of competence was provided. In view of the fact that the model for the girls was of the opposite sex and presumably low in social comparison, these results may be interpreted as strengthening the view that girls are more susceptible than boys to vicarious failure influences. However, the lack of sex differences when subjects were exposed to a model of similar ability suggests that the difference is accounted for within the social comparison process. Girls appear more willing than boys to assume that a male model is competent, and hence the model's performance outcomes have relevance for judging self-efficacy.

Social comparison influences on efficacy expectation would appear to be an issue of considerable theoretical and practical interest. Although perceived similarity in competence has been shown to be a critical factor in developing a sense of helplessness through modeling, in the absence of explicit information about a performer's level of competence, it must be inferred from salient characteristics of the performer and the task at hand. When knowledge of relative competence is lacking, social stereotypes may come to influence judgments about the relevance of an observer's performance accomplishments for one's own efficacy. Girls in the present experiment appear to have adopted the view that males are at least as competent as they in the type of problem-solving task employed.

In the present view, as well as in Festinger's (1954) original formulation of social comparison theory, it is assumed that people look to others for information about their own abilities to the extent that they are uncertain about their level of accomplishment. This may account for the discrepancy in the performances of males in the present study vs. those in the Brown and Inouye (1978) study in their response to observing repeated failure by a model whose relative competence is unknown. In the present experiment, subjects' efficacy expectations were boosted, and to some extent so was their persistence. Males undergoing the same treatment in Brown and Inouye's (1978) study behaved much like those who were led to believe that they were of similar ability to the model. Since subjects in the present experiment experienced much higher personal success prior to observing the model fail, they would be less dependent on modeling cues for information about their own ability. Although this receives further support in the findings that subjects who performed well on the pretest did not have their self-perceptions and motivation undermined by modeled failure, this issue requires further investigation. A systematic test of this notion would require a factorial design in which subjects are blocked according to pretreatment performance level as well as according to sex.

Though somewhat tentative, the foregoing findings are also consistent with a recent study by Paulus, Gatchel, and Seta (1978), which shows that modeled failure can enhance performance under certain conditions. In the present view, the conditions necessary for such effects are perceived superiority or the competitive opportunity to establish superiority to an ineffectual model. Perceived superiority may result from subjects' comparisons of their prior successes with the model's ineffectiveness or from explicit information that the model is less competent. Future research in this program will explore the factors that determine whether modeled failure will undermine or enhance the self-conception and motivation of observers. It is also of considerable interest to explore the efficacy and motivational effects of modeled success. Findings of such studies should provide knowledge on how vicarious sources of influence might be enlisted in the development of favorable self-perceptions and competencies.

ACKNOWLEDGMENTS

The activities reported herein were supported by funds from Boys Town. However, the opinions expressed and the policies advocated do not necessarily reflect those of Boys Town. Special thanks go to Elaine M. Curran and Bob Forman, who assisted with the project.

REFERENCES

Atkinson, J. W. *An introduction to motivation.* Princeton, N. J.: Van Nostrand, 1964
Bandura, A. Self-efficacy: Toward a unifying theory of behavioral change. *Psychological Review,* 1977, *89,* 191–215.
Brown, I., & Inouye, D. K. Learned helplessness through modeling: The role of perceived similarity in competence. *Journal of Personality and Social Psychology,* 1978, *36,* 900–908.
DeVellis, R. F., DeVellis, B. M., & McCauley, M. The vicarious acquisition of learned helplessness. *Journal of Personality and Social Psychology,* 1978, *36,* 894–899.
Dweck, C. S., & Bush, E. S. Sex differences in learned helplessness: Differential debilitation with peer and adult evaluators. *Developmental Psychology,* 1976, *12,* 147–156.
Feather, N. T. Effects of prior success and failure on expectations of success and subsequent performance. *Journal of Personality and Social Psychology,* 1966, *3,* 287–298.
Festinger, L. A theory of social comparison processes. *Human Relations,* 1954, *7,* 117–140.
Hiroto, D. S., & Seligman, M. E. P. Generality of learned helplessness in man. *Journal of Personality and Social Psychology,* 1975, *31,* 311–327.
Maier, S. F., & Seligman, M. E. P. Learned helplessness: Theory and evidence. *Journal of Experimental Psychology: General,* 1976, *105,* 3–46.
Paulus, P. B., Gatchel, R. J., & Seta, J. J. Enhancement and reduction of task performance by psychological modeling. *Personality and Social Psychology Bulletin,* 1978, *4,* 126–130.
Phares, E. J. *Locus of control in personality.* Morristown, N. J.: General Learning Press, 1976.
Roth, S., & Kubal, L. The effects of noncontingent reinforcement on tasks of differing importance: Facilitation and learned helplessness. *Journal of Personality and Social Psychology,* 1975, *32,* 680–691.
Zimbardo, P. G., & Ruch, F. L. *Psychology and life.* Glenview, Ill.: Diamond Printing, 1977.

9 Comments on Section II: Consequences of Choice on Learning and Performance

Slater E. Newman
North Carolina State University

My comments are divided into four parts. First, I indicate some of the main points of the four papers presented in this section. Next, I mention some of the questions that these papers have suggested to me. Then I indicate some types of experiments in memory and verbal learning for which the concept, "perception of control," may be useful in explaining some of the results. Finally I suggest briefly some kinds of information that those of us working in memory might wish to gather. First, then, for the summaries of the papers.

Jerard Kehoe was concerned with the relationships in perception-of-choice experiments between the level of attractiveness of the options, their difference in attractiveness, perception of choice, and choice time. By using a combination of multidimensional scaling and partial correlation, he was able to demonstrate: first, that perceived choice and level of attractiveness are positively related, as he suspected; second, that choice time and difference in attractiveness are negatively, though not substantially, related; and third, and rather surprisingly perhaps, that choice time and perceived choice are almost independent of one another, at least in situations that—as in those he used—the actual processing in the choice situation is not salient for the subject. He called also for the development of less reactive measures of perceived choice than those currently in use and for additional research on the effects of various option characteristics on perceived choice.

William Moyer discussed his recent research, which demonstrated that subjects may not always do our bidding and that, in fact, under some circumstances they may attempt to undermine what they believe the experimenter is attempting to do. Subjects who were led to believe that they would learn faster and recall better (that is, the so-called hypermnesic subjects) actually recalled more poorly than either those subjects who were given no such information or those who were led to believe that they would not perform well (the so-called amnesic subjects). Subsequent analysis of the data suggested that those hypermnesic subjects may have been withholding some responses and that the amnesic subjects (at least many of them) felt challenged to perform well. Moyer also showed that instructions to use a particular mnemonic technique were not always followed and that the difficulty in using the mnemonic technique with a particular memory task was determinative of the extent to which the instructions were followed. Finally, Moyer demonstrated that restricting a subject's choice in a learning experiment on a paired-associate task similar to that reported by Savage and his colleagues might also lead to countercontrol, particularly if the subject was rated as an "internal" on a locus-of-control scale. In these experiments countercontrol appears to have been demonstrated.

The paper by Savage, Perlmuter, and Monty summarized some of their findings from previous experiments in which they have demonstrated that subjects who are given the opportunity to choose either the stimulus terms or the response terms of paired associates, even if only for a few pairs, will learn all the pairs faster than subjects given no such choice, at least when the choice occurs for early items. They have interpreted their findings in terms of the notion of "perception of control." The greater that perception, the better the performance. In the two experiments they presented here, they have demonstrated the utility of that position. In their first experiment they showed, generally, that the greater the number of choices (when subjects perceived they had a real choice), the better the performance; and they demonstrated also the importance of similarity of options on both perception of control and on performance. In their second experiment, they showed that when subjects were forced to choose a low-meaningfulness item, performance was better if the accompanying alternative item was also a low-meaning-fulness item than if it was an item of higher meaningfulness. Finally, they emphasized the importance of the subject's perception of the choice situation in determining perception of control and its influence on performance.

In the final paper, Irvin Brown also summarized some of his experiments, which were aimed at studying the effects of perceived similarity in competence on persistence on a problem-solving task. He demonstrated that subjects who believe themselves to be more competent than a not-very-competent model persisted longer in trying to solve the problems than those who believed themselves of equal competence to the model. In this study, too, there was a strong correlation, particularly in the later trials, between expectation of success and persistence. In another experiment, Brown's subjects were given easier tasks during the first part of the experiment (that is, tasks that were easier than in the early part of the previous experiment), and doubtless they felt more competent prior to their exposure to the model than did those in his previous experiment. Subsequently, however, subjects again became less persistent after they had observed the model whom they believed to be of similar competence to themselves, although the effect was not as great as in the earlier experiment, presumably because in the latter experiment they had experienced greater success on the preliminary task. In addition, and rather surprisingly perhaps, though the model was a male, the female subjects were less persistent on the criterion task than were the male subjects. This was true even though on the initial task, the female and male subjects were equivalent in ability and the females were the more persistent.

Here are a few questions that these papers have suggested to me. First, I wonder about the generality of the relationship noted by Kehoe (Chapter 5), namely that there is a positive relationship between the level of attractiveness of options and perception of choice. Apparently, this is not the case when—as in the second experiment of Savage, Perlmuter, and Monty (Chapter 7)— subjects who were forced to learn the low-m item in the presence of a high-m item did more poorly (presumably because they perceived less control) than subjects who were forced to learn a low-m item in the presence of another low-m item. (The level of attractiveness would presumably be higher for the high–low than for the low–low pair.) It is interesting to note also that in their first experiment, forced choice of the high-m item in the presence of another high-m item, when compared with forced choice of the high-m item in the presence of a low-m item, did not facilitate performance.

A second question, deriving from the countercontrol work reported by Moyer (Chapter 6), asks about the relationship between the kind of subject pool we use in our experiments and the tendency for countercontrol to occur. (I'm not asking about their locus of control or aptitude characteristics but rather about how they come to serve in the experiment in the first place.) Will there be differences in perception of control and perhaps concomitantly in the tendency for countercontrol to occur among subjects who are paid to serve in an experiment as contrasted with true volunteers? And how about the differences between those who are serving to fulfill the course requirement as compared with those who have points added to their final grade?

A third question relates to the need mentioned by Kehoe for better measurement of perception of choice and of control. I would assume this would be particularly important for Savage, Perlmuter, and Monty, who, I would think, would want to measure perception of control throughout the various stages of their experimental cycle: from the time that subjects appear for the experiment, then following the practice trials, then at various stages during the choice trials, at various stages during the training trials, and even after. Are the kinds of self-report questions that ask directly about choice and perception of control adequate; or are there better ways to do this? Kehoe suggests that there may be. Also, since "frustration" and "despair" appear in the model proposed by Savage, Perlmuter, and Monty, should an attempt be made to assess these also and to relate both "perception of control" and "frustration" to the various independent variables they have found to affect performance?

Another question is related to the work reported by Brown (Chapter 8). In one study, he found that female subjects who watched a male model judged to be of similar competence to themselves were more likely to be affected by the model than were male subjects. How can a finding such as this be handled by social comparison theory, or can it?

A final question again relates to the work of Savage, Perlmuter, and Monty. If it is the case that perception of control affects performance on a learning task, how does it do so? That is, in what way does the person with a high perception of control behave differently during the learning task (i.e., in what way does the subject process the information differently) from someone with a lower perception of control? Is it a difference in type of rehearsal—in what, for example, Craik and Lockhart (1972) might call "elaborative rehearsal" as compared with "maintenance rehearsal"? Or is it a difference in the amount of elaborative or maintenance rehearsal? Is it a difference in dealing with response learning, with associative learning, or with stimulus-term discrimination [some of the stages postulated to occur during paired-associate training (e.g., McGuire, 1961)] or with one of the many other processes that Battig (1968) and others (e.g., Greeno, 1970) have proposed? Are these questions that are worth trying to answer?

Next let me turn to a number of experiments in memory in which the subject's perception of control may differ as a function of experimental treatment. Among those that I have in mind are experiments in what is called "extralist cuing," such as those used to evaluate the validity of the encoding specificity hypothesis (Santa & Lamwers, 1974; Thomson & Tulving, 1970), experiments on associate symmetry (Newman, 1972), and on stimulus selection (Richardson, 1972). The general format in these experiments is that the subject is led to believe that he or she will be tested in a particular way, but on the test, some of the subjects are tested as they thought they would be, whereas others are not. For example, in the extralist cuing experiments, some subjects are presented at the time of recall either with a cue that they had never seen before in the experiment or with no retrieval cue at all; in the associative symmetry experiments, subjects may be tested in the B-A or backward direction, though they may have expected to be tested in the A-B or so-called forward direction. And in the stimulus selection experiments, some part of the nominal stimulus (that is, the entire stimulus term that is presented to the subject) may not be present on the test, and this may be the part of the nominal stimulus that the subject was using as his or her functional stimulus. In each of these instances, the subject's performance has usually been poorer on the unexpected test than if the subject had been tested in the way that he or she had expected. The usual explanation has emphasized the cue properties of the missing-cue or altered-cue situation. But is it possible that the subject's poor performance, when surprised, derives at least to some extent from a loss in perceived control? Perhaps we should attempt to ascertain, if we can, the extent to which this might be a factor.

Another situation in which perception of control might be of some consequence is in attribute-identification experiments in which some subjects are allowed to test their hypotheses by selecting individual examples (the selection procedure) whereas for other subjects the experimenter selects the examples (the reception procedure). Though the results from these experiments favor neither the selection nor the reception procedure (Bourne, Ekstrand, & Dominowski, 1971), it seems reasonable to assume that allowing subjects to select the instances to test their hypotheses would tend to foster greater perception of control than not allowing such selection and would thus tend to facilitate performance.

Finally, let me mention another more applied study in which perception of control may have played some role. The study (Newman, 1957) was one for which I asked some colleagues of mine, each of whom is an expert in the paired-associate learning task, to design a program to be used in teaching airmen to learn a list of names for electrical symbols. A training program was agreed upon, and we then compared the learning of subjects who were exposed to this expert-designed training program with the performance of subjects who were allowed to use their own procedures in studying the pairs. These latter subjects were given the same amount of time to study the items that the other subjects had had. As you may have guessed, the subjects who were allowed to select their own learning procedures did much better than those exposed to the program designed by the experts. Although we sought the explanation for this difference mainly in the differences between the stimulus characteristics of the subject-designed programs and the expert-designed program, it is possible that the subjects who used their own procedures felt more in control of their learning and thus performed better.

In closing, let me mention some possible implications for research on memory and perhaps on other aspects of cognition that have been suggested by the four papers presented in this section—which have described experiments on perception of choice, on countercontrol, on locus of control, on perception of control, and on expectation of success. It has been the case that research in the memory laboratory has generally paid little attention either to individual differences among the subjects or to motivational factors. There have been occasional reminders over the years and some demonstrations, but most of us have continued looking for the processes common to all of our appropriately motivated subjects as they process the information in our experiments. Perhaps our neglect of individual differences and motivational variables has been due in part to our distrust of self-reports as data. The papers presented in this volume suggest, however, that it might be of some value if, in addition to looking at the stimulus, response, and performance variables, we try to get at least some information in our memory experiments about several other subject-related variables. We might attempt, for example, to ascertain the expectations of our subjects about how they will perform and the interrelationships between these expectations and performance. We may wish, also, for information about the extent to which the hypotheses that we are testing are discernible by our subjects, and the degree to which this differs for the different treatments in our experiment and for subjects of different characteristics. Concomitantly, we may wish to determine the relationship of each of these factors to the subject's tendency to engage in countercontrol. Finally, we might wish to obtain information about the extent to which our subjects—at various stages of our experiment—perceive that they have or do not have control, about the relationship between perception of control and our stimulus and response variables, and about the contribution of each of these to the various processes that affect performance.

These are some problems that have been and continue to be of concern to many of you. Perhaps it is desirable for those of us who study memory, as well as other aspects of cognition, to share this concern.

REFERENCES

Battig, W. F. Paired-associate learning. In T. R. Dixon & D. L. Horton (Eds.), *Verbal learning and general behavior theory*. Englewood Cliffs, N.J.: Prentice-Hall, 1968.

Bourne, L. E., Ekstrand, B. R., & Dominowski, R. L. *The psychology of thinking*. Englewood Cliffs, N.J.: Prentice-Hall, 1971.

Craik, F. I. M., & Lockhart, R. S. Levels of processing: A framework for memory research. *Journal of Verbal Learning and Verbal Behavior*, 1972, *11*, 671–684.

Greeno, J. G. How associations are memorized. In D. A. Norman (Ed.), *Models of human memory*. New York: Academic Press, 1970.

McGuire, W. J. A multi-process model for paired-associate learning. *Journal of Experimental Psychology*, 1961, *62*, 335–347.

Newman, S. E. Student vs. instructor design of study method. *Journal of Educational Psychology*, 1957, *48*, 328–333.

Newman, S. E. In search of associative symmetry. In C. P. Duncan, L. Sechrest, & A. W. Melton (Eds.), *Human memory: Festschrift for Benton J. Underwood*. New York: Appleton-Century-Crofts, 1972.

Richardson, J. Encoding and stimulus selection in paired-associate verbal learning. In A. W. Melton & E. Martin (Eds.), *Coding processes in human memory*. Washington, D.C.: Winston, 1972.

Santa, J. L., & Lamwers, L. L. Encoding specificity: Fact or artifact? *Journal of Verbal Learning and Verbal Behavior*, 1974, *13*, 412–423.

Thomson, D. M., & Tulving, E. Associative encoding and retrieval: Weak and strong cues. *Journal of Experimental Psychology*, 1970, *86*, 255–262.

THE ROLE OF
PERCEIVED CONTROL IN
CLINICAL AND EDUCATIONAL
SETTINGS

So free we seem, so fettered fast we are.
—Robert Browning

The first paper in this section investigates the role of perceived control in the classroom. Rather different in orientation and methodology from deCharms' approach to this problem, Professor Brigham's paper adopts a Skinnerian approach toward understanding how students' control over their work schedules can serve to facilitate academic learning. Children preferred self-selected reinforcers over those selected by the experimenters despite the fact that the reinforcers were identical to those selected by the experimenter. They maintained this preference even when having to work harder to earn self-selected reinforcers. Thus, these data point to the intrinsically rewarding aspects of choice. That is, it's not what is chosen that is important; rather, it's the exercise of choice that benefits the chooser. Interestingly, Brigham finds an additive effect of choice that shows that when children could choose whether they themselves or their teachers would select the reinforcers, they performed even better than when merely selecting their own reinforcers. As can be seen in the paper by Schulz and Hanusa (Chapter 21), these additive effects occur only in situations where subjects can generally utilize or enjoy additional freedoms. Environments that are by their nature generally impoverished in freedom tend to make the experience of augmented freedom either unpleasant or of no value to the chooser. Thus, in certain situations, increases in freedom may actually be debilitating and constraining rather than liberating. Apparently, the environmental conditions in Brigham's classroom situation nurtured increased freedom for his students.

The second paper in this section raises some important questions about the reported tolerance that staff may be expected to display toward increased control and freedom granted to institutionalized mental patients. Using a Heiderian framework, Houts, Quann, and Scott examined, through the use of scenarios, the conditions that encourage staff to provide their clients with the use of control, and those conditions in which antagonism between staff and patient may be engendered by augmenting patient control. These results suggest, as do those of deCharms, Brigham, and Schulz and Hanusa, that environmental factors can set very critical limits on the use and potential benefits of control and that under specifiable conditions, the establishment of control may cause negative repercussions for the controller.

The third paper in this section weaves both experimental and clinical perspectives into an intriguing pattern. Following a nearly exhaustive examination of the ways in which the term *control* has been used, Arnkoff and Mahoney discuss a number of psychological disorders in which deficiencies of perceived control may have played a critical role. They also discuss Becker's (1973) treatment of control, which suggests that individuals actually employ the myth of control in order to keep themselves motivated. This idea importantly contrasts with the more common conception that the need to exercise control takes precedence and that its satisfaction (real or imagined) serves to heighten motivation. In the final section the authors critically discuss treatments that have been employed to treat a variety of control-related psychological disorders.

The final paper in this section, by Professor Wilson, reviews the pervasive relationship between perceived control and therapeutic progress. In discussing a variety of therapies from biofeedback to stress inoculation therapy, Wilson underlines the role of perceived control in clinical practice. He points out that permitting subjects to make choices in the therapeutic situation may attenuate countercontrol efforts on the part of the subject, thereby increasing the probability of successful treatment. Similarly, he argues that relaxation therapy, for example, cannot be imposed on the patient but rather is a self-regulated activity that clients may choose. He points to an interesting paradox in relaxation therapy that suggests that the perception of control increases as the subject "begins to let go." Further, he discusses the successful application of his therapy program with a patient who was taught to understand that his exhibitionist behavior was not irreversibly automatic or mindless (see Langer, Chapter 20) and that control (real or perceived) can interrupt the maladaptive reflexlike response of the subject.

Wilson also takes a rather dim view of laboratory studies of perceived control, as did Lacey and deCharms earlier. The laboratory does not permit reality testing by subjects because their control is merely illusory, he contends. However, one might inquire by rejoinder whether control in the clinic or in the real world is anything but illusory. The final portion of his chapter examines the treatment of alcoholism and shows that the effectiveness of the treatment may depend on increasing feelings of internality and self-efficacy in the patient. However, he cautions against overreliance on this relationship because of its correlational nature. Finally, in keeping with his behavioral approach to therapy, he stresses what he considers, as deCharms previously did, to be an important distinction between perceived and actual control and avers that real control is the more effective procedure clinically.

REFERENCE

Becker, E. *The denial of death*. New York: Free Press, 1973.

10 Some Effects of Choice on Academic Performance

Thomas A. Brigham
Washington State University

Before dealing with some research on the effects of choice on academic behavior, it is appropriate to review briefly the history of choice in experimental psychology. Until very recently, choice has been treated almost exclusively as a dependent variable. That is, the experimenter would manipulate some independent variable and observe: the rat's choices in a maze; the pigeon's choice of response keys in a concurrent schedule; the subject's choice of alternatives on a concept formation task; and so on. As a consequence, the individual's choice of response alternatives has been treated in experimental psychology as a measure of the effects of other more important psychological processes—e.g., discrimination, deprivation, perception, motivation, generalization, etc.—rather than as a potentially important variable in and of itself. Choice has been a dependent variable in experimental psychology from Wundt and the beginnings of scientific psychology to the present. The "mental chemistry" structuralism of Wundt (1904) and Titchener (1897) was deterministic, with no place for volition except as a perception caused by other psychological stimuli. This general approach has been adopted by the experimental psychologies that have followed structuralism, whether they were behavioral, cognitive, or eclectic. It is not surprising, therefore, that choice, with its implications of volition, was replaced by the more neutral term *preference* in most instances in the psychological literature.

Operant learning theory has been somewhat inconsistent in the treatment of voluntary behavior. Skinner often appears to suggest that the individual can affect the environment and in turn his or her own behavior, only later to reaffirm a strictly deterministic position (see Skinner, 1953, pp. 227–241). The

131

issues involved are far too complex to be dealt with in depth here and are presented only as a context for the development of the research program. One way to deal with complex problems is to ignore them temporarily and to work with limited aspects of the phenomenon in the hope that by systematic approximations, it will be possible to increase our understanding of the complex issues. As a consequence, the definition of choice we have used is very simple and in terms of observable events. Choice is the opportunity to make an uncoerced selection from two or more alternative events, consequences, or responses. By uncoerced, we mean there are no programmed implicit or explicit consequences for selecting one alternative over the others except for the characteristics of the alternatives themselves.

The first efforts in the analysis of choice had to do with choice of reinforcers and who does the choosing. The original concern was with the analysis of why well-designed and operated token systems of reinforcement improve performance. Although such characteristics as the immediacy of reinforcement and the generalized reinforcer aspects of tokens were heavily emphasized in the literature from watching children exchange the tokens they had earned, it seemed possible that something else was involved also. In a good token system, when children earn a number of tokens, they can exchange them for their individual choice of a number of desirable activities. Children often spend as much time choosing as they do engaging in the chosen activity. It was decided to examine the role of choice in token systems by bringing children into a lab and having them press a key for reinforcers. Choice was isolated by comparing how children responded for self-selected reinforcers versus the same reinforcers selected by the experimenter. As can be seen in Fig. 10.1 (Brigham & Stoerzinger, 1976) in the multiple schedule format where the opportunity to earn self-selected consequences alternated with the chance to earn experimenter-selected consequences, the children earned equal numbers of self-selected and experimenter-selected consequences. But in the concurrent schedule format where the children could press a second key to determine which type of consequence was available, they worked almost exclusively for self-selected reinforcers. This preference was maintained even when it was demonstrated to the children that the reinforcers were the same whether they picked the consequences or the experimenter did, and also when the children had to work much harder to earn self-selected reinforcers.

These studies and others led to the theoretical speculation that the opportunity to choose might itself be a positive reinforcer. A prototype study was designed to investigate the effects of choice reinforcers on math performance (Hockstra & Brigham, 1976). The subjects were students in an academic preschool, and the math materials were the Singer *Sets and Numbers* kindergarten and first-grade books (Suppes & Suppes, 1968).

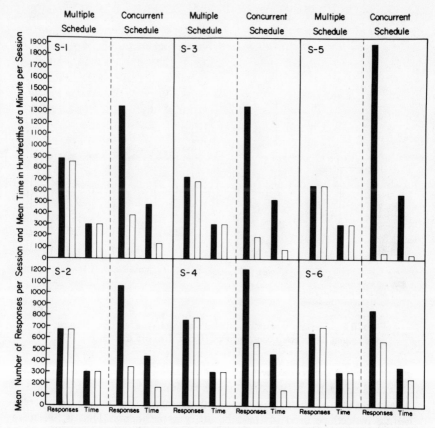

FIG. 10.1. Mean number of responses and time spent in each component as a function of experimenter-selected and self-selected consequences. (From Brigham & Stoerzinger, 1976.)

After a baseline period, during which consequences were delivered noncontingently, we began by simply alternating conditions between sessions where subjects selected their own consequences and those where the teacher selected the consequences. Also in this study, rather than using consumable reinforcers as consequences, enjoyable math games were used. The activities were tested, and it was found that the children liked them and would work to play with them.

As expected, there was an increase in the children's rate of working math problems when a contingency was introduced requiring the completion of so many problems before the children could play with the activities. These increases can be seen in Fig. 10.2. Both the teacher-select and the child-select conditions resulted in increased rates, but the children did work faster when

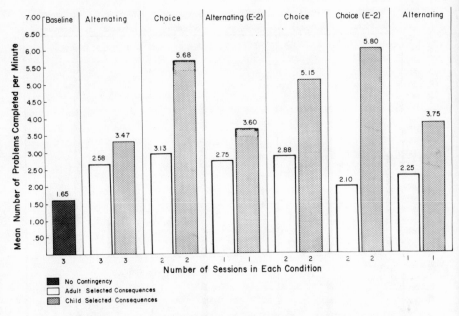

FIG. 10.2.   The rate of working arithmetic problems as a function of teacher-selected and self-selected consequences. (From Hockstra & Brigham, 1976.)

they got to select the consequences. Next the children were allowed to choose who would select the activities after the session.

The choice procedure was instituted as an analog to the concurrent schedule procedure used in the laboratory experiments. That is, we were interested in finding out if the children preferred to select their own consequences. The eight children were each given two opportunities to choose who would select the consequences for their work. In 14 of those 16 trials, the children chose to select their own consequences. This result was not surprising, but the change in the children's performance was. In those sessions where the children chose to select their own consequences, there was a tremendous acceleration in response rate (true of all subjects and statistically significant as well). This result was not only surprising, it was also worrisome, because it did not seem to be a reasonable outcome. There were, of course, a number of factors that could have produced these results other than the choice procedure. First, the children might have all hit easy sections of the book. This was unlikely, since they all had been individually placed in the book and were now all in different sections of the book. A second related possibility was that the children were all simply improving in math and this had produced the increase in speed. Finally, it seemed possible that perhaps Dr. Hockstra, imbued with enthusiasm for choice as an important variable, was somehow unintentionally influencing the students' behavior. We tested these possiblities by introducing a second teacher, who was completely unfamiliar with the research. Her first sessions alternated between child-select and adult-select conditions, and the response rate dropped back to its previous level. This indicated to us that the children had not simply improved in math. Subsequently, the second teacher ran some choice sessions, and the earlier results were replicated (Choice E-2). In these sessions, the children again decided to select the consequences themselves, and their rate of working problems was accelerated over that found in the regular self-select sessions. Over the course of the study, there was an increase in the students' rate of working math problems, but there were also easily discriminated accelerations of that rate associated with the choice condition.

These results indicated that there was more to choice than simply some sort of effect on the value of reinforcers as suggested by the earlier research. That is, the procedure didn't appear to have anything to do with reinforcement per se. In fact, it finally became apparent that choice could be separated from the self-selection of consequences and used as an antecedent condition to the performance of some task.

After this study, an extensive series of research projects examining the effects of various aspects of choice on academic performance in public middle school classrooms were undertaken. Students were given control over such procedures as self-scoring their work, self-pacing, self-monitoring their work, and self-scheduling work periods. Although the results of these were quite positive, the details of a study of self-determined reinforcement are presented, because previous research in this area has produced conflicting results. For example, Bandura and Perloff (1967), Felixbrod and O'Leary (1973), Glynn (1970), and Parks, Fine, and Hopkins (1976) all found important differences in the results of letting children determine their own reinforcement schedules and came to different conclusions about the desirability of procedures. Unfortunately, all these studies used different response measures, research designs, and lengths of treatment as well as children who differed tremendously in many important characteristics.

Leaping into the breach, Farnum and I designed yet another study that differed in terms of subjects, response measures, research design, and length of treatment (Farnum, Brigham, & Johnson, in preparation). But the subjects were students in a regular classroom, the dependent measure was performance in the regular math program, and the study lasted nearly a full year. Thus the results may have greater generality than those of the earlier studies.

In detail, 23 fifth-grade students in a regular classroom located in a middle-class neighborhood participated in the study. Another fifth-grade class with 24 students in the same school served as a *control classroom*. Math periods were conducted daily in the experimental classroom for 40 minutes during baseline and 4 days a week during the manipulations. The control classroom had daily 40-minute math sessions, but no experimental manipulations were conducted. The text was *Mathematics Around Us Series, 1975* (Bolster et al., 1975). Students in both classrooms began on page 1 of the text at the beginning of the school term.

In general the experimental classroom operated in the following manner. After a thorough training procedure, for all conditions each student in the experimental classroom recorded in a folder the following information: page number, step number, number of problems completed, number of problems correct, and the time the student started and ended each step. All students started on page 1 of the text and were allowed to proceed through the assigned material at their own rate. The assignment sheets were prepared by the classroom teacher and were posted on the bulletin board. Assignment sheets consisted of the following information:

1. Step number: Steps were the assignment number and were numbered consecutively.
2. Assignments: Assignments included the page number, pretest or posttest, number of problems to be worked, and any special instructions. Special instructions included: see M.J. (classroom teacher), see M.J. before correcting, study page and see M.J.

The daily procedure for the students was as follows: After checking the math assignment sheet, the students recorded in their folders the step number, page number, and the time started. Then they worked the math problems, entered the time finished, and brought their work to the experimenter. The experimenter corrected each student's work, recording the page number, the number of problems completed, and the number of problems correct on the experimenter's record sheets. The students corrected any errors, recording in their folders the time started and the time ended for all corrections. At the end of the math period, all student folders were turned in. The times that each student started and ended each step were recorded by the experimenter on the experimenter record sheets.

During a 5-week baseline period, the students were allowed to proceed through the material at their own rate. No contingencies were in operation. Math periods were held 5 days a week for 40 minutes each day.

The first experimental condition consisted of 6 weeks where the teacher set a goal for the number of steps each student was to complete for each week. The goal took into consideration the number of steps the student had completed on the average during the last 3 weeks of baseline and increased the number of steps by two. On Monday morning of each week, the students received slips of paper with their names and the number of steps they were to complete by the end of the math period on Thursday. The daily math sessions followed the general procedure already outlined. On Friday mornings, a list of those students who did not make their goals and the number of steps they lacked was written on the blackboard. These students worked on math during Friday's math period. The steps completed during Friday's math period were recorded by the students but were not included in the experimenter's records. For those students who did not make their goals, the goals were adjusted the next week. Therefore goals did not remain constant over weeks. The students who reached their goals received free time during Friday's math period. These students could select to participate in any of the following activities: cards, games, catching up on work in other academic areas, committee meetings, free reading, and library time. During this condition, math periods were conducted 4 days a week for 40 minutes each period with a free 40-minute period on Friday for those students who had finished all their steps for the week.

Next the procedures were changed, so that students could choose their own goals; all other procedures remained the same as in Condition I. On the first day of the condition, students received slips of paper stating the average number of steps they had been required to complete during the teacher-set condition. It was explained to the students that the averages were calculated by adding the number of steps required each week and dividing this number by 6. An example was done on the blackboard. Each student then determined how many steps he or she would complete that week. It was made clear to the students that they could choose a goal that had as many or as few steps as they wished. They were told that they would receive their free time on Friday if they made their goals whether the goal was one step or 20 steps. This condition lasted for 6 weeks.

To evaluate the effects of the student-set-goals condition, the teacher-set-goals procedures were reinstated. The first day of this condition, the students were told that the teacher would be setting the goals again. This condition was a replication of Teacher-Set Goals I and lasted for 4 weeks.

The preceding conditions were analogous to the multiple schedule format in the earlier studies; now the students were given the opportunity to choose who would set the goals. The students were informed that they could set their own goals or that they could have the teacher set their goals for the week. Each student received a slip of paper with his or her name on it. They were instructed to either set their own goal or put M.J. on the paper if they wanted the teacher to set their goal. It was stressed that M.J. did not care which they did. If the student put M.J. on the paper, the goal was filled in and the paper returned to the student within 5 minutes. This condition lasted for 3 weeks.

The results of the study were analyzed both in terms of individual and group results. Overall, there was a very close match between the individual results and the group data, with the variations being mainly in terms of magnitude of effects and not in the pattern of results. As a consequence, the results presented in Table 10.1 are representative of both individual and

TABLE 10.1
A Comparison of the Average Number of Steps Set for Goals
and a Comparison of the Number of Steps Completed Across Conditions

	Baseline[a]	Teacher-Set I	Student-Set	Teacher-Set II[b]	Choice[b]
Average number of steps set	X	7.22	7.32	7.32	7.37
Average number of steps completed	6.02	8.60	9.11	7.87	8.8

[a]Based on five 40-minute math periods per week, the rest of the data represent the work done in four 40-minute math periods per week.
[b]These data represent only 19 students, because four of the students completed the fifth-grade mathematics book. Although they began the sixth-grade book, the material was not divided into steps and was not directly comparable.

138

group responses to the procedure. As can be seen in Table 10.1, there was a substantial increase in performance with the addition of teacher-set goals and consequences. There was also a subsequent increase when the students were allowed to choose their own goals. Although there were no statistically significant differences between performance under the student-determined-goals condition and the teacher-set-goals condition, the students consistently completed more work in the former condition. It is also interesting to note that the additional work was accomplished while the students were setting essentially the same goals as the teacher.

In the 3-week choice condition, an average of 20 of the 23 students chose to set their own goals. A chi-square analysis of this preference indicates that it was significant at the .01 level ($\chi^2 = 34.08$, $p < .01$, $df = 1$).

A comparison of the year's progress revealed placements in the experimental classroom from page 183 to four students completing the book (page 386), whereas the range in the control classroom was page 78 to two students at page 301. The placements were such that the two distributions almost did not overlap. The difference in progress between the two classrooms was statistically significant, $t = 4.65$, $p < .01$, $df = 45$.

Based on essentially theoretical arguments, social psychologists (e.g., Levine & Fasnacht, 1974) have suggested that the use of external rewards may undermine student motivation and feelings of accomplishment. In this classroom, rewards were used in all academic areas and resulted in clearly superior performance in comparison to the control classroom. Across academic areas, these students accomplished almost twice as much work as their peers in the control classroom. But in addition to monitoring academic performance, several pre- and postmeasures of student attitudes toward school and themselves (Crandall–Katkovsky, Piers–Harris, Coppersmith, and Likert scales) were administered. Although there were no statistically significant differences in the pre–post scores, all the changes were in the positive direction. Not only was there no decrease in student motivation or self-esteem, there were small positive changes. It is true that we have not systematically looked at the performance of students after they have left our classrooms, but the feedback we have received has been all positive. Based on the overall results of this study and others, I believe that it is both possible and practical to design reinforcement systems that actively involve the student in their operation, and that such well-designed programs will result in increased student self-confidence and performance.

Before summarizing our research on choice, it must be noted that choice is not an unlimited blessing. All our research has been conducted in fairly structured situations where the response alternatives were positive and where individuals were limited in the opportunity to make choices that might have long-term detrimental effects on their lives. This obviously is not the case in every situation where the individual has a choice of multiple response alternatives. For instance, in many problems of consummatory abuse (self-control problems), the individual clearly chooses a detrimental alternative. Similarly, in unstructured "free" school environments, children frequently make choices for short-term gains that may have long-term negative effects. As a consequence, the following conclusions about choice are limited to situations we have studied. First, regarding choice of reinforcers, subjects have preferred to choose their own consequences; they have worked hard for the opportunity to choose their own reinforcers and have reacted strongly when this privilege was constrained; and they have worked faster when they were able to choose their own reinforcers. Overall, there is something about choosing one's own reinforcer that people have found to be reinforcing in and of itself. Second, but possibly more important, when subjects were given the opportunity to make a choice about some aspect of a situation before responding, they worked harder, faster, and reacted more positively to the situation than when they were unable to make such choices. In this role, choice appears to function as a setting event. Kantor (1959) defined setting events as antecedent stimulus–response interactions that—because they have occurred—affect the frequency or topography of responses that follow. When we have allowed students in our classroom research to make choices about instructional procedures, they have worked better and seemed to like the classroom more. Certainly they were reinforced for their performance, but that reinforcement had been delivered in the procedures prior to the choice condition. Choice appears to be the key ingredient, the setting event that leads to these changes in behavior.

ACKNOWLEDGMENTS

The preparation of this manuscript was partially supported by grants to the Self-Control Research and Training Unit, Department of Psychology, Washington State University, Pullman, Washington 99164.

REFERENCES

Bandura, A., & Perloff, B. Relative efficacy of self-monitored and externally imposed reinforcement systems. *Journal of Personality and Social Psychology*, 1967, *7*, 111–116.

Bolster, L., Cox, G., Gibb, E., Hansen, V., Kirkpatrick, J., Rabitaille, D., Trimble, H., Vance, I., Walch, R., & Wisner, R. *Mathematics around us*. Glenview, Ill.: Scott, Foresman, 1975.

Brigham, T. A. & Stoerzinger, A. An experimental analysis of children's preference for self-selected rewards. In T. A. Brigham, R. Hawkins, J. Scott, & T. F. McLaughlin (Eds.), *Behavior analysis in education: Self-control and reading*. Dubuque, Iowa: Kendall/Hunt, 1976.

Farnum, M., Brigham, T. A., & Johnson, G. *A comparison of the effects of teacher-determined and self-determined contingencies of reinforcement on arithmetic performance.* Manuscript in preparation.

Felixbrod, J. J., & O'Leary, K. D. Effects of reinforcement on children's academic behavior as a function of self-determined and externally imposed contingencies. *Journal of Applied Behavior Analysis,* 1973, *6,* 241–250.

Glynn, E. L. Classroom applications of self-determined reinforcement. *Journal of Applied Behavior Analysis,* 1970, *3,* 123–132.

Hockstra, C., & Brigham, T. A. *The effects of choice of consequences and procedures on preschool children's rate of working arithmetic problems.* Paper presented at the annual meeting of the Midwestern Association of Behavior Analysis, Chicago, May 7, 1976.

Kantor, J. R. *Interbehavioral psychology.* Bloomington, Ind.: Principia Press, 1959.

Levine, F. M., & Fasnacht, G. Token rewards may lead to token learning. *American Psychologist,* 1974, *29,* 816–820.

Parks, L., Fine, M., & Hopkins, B. A study of teacher-managed and self-managed reinforcement with young children on an academic task. In T. A. Brigham, R. Hawkins, J. Scott, & T. F. McLaughlin (Eds.), *Behavior analysis in education: Self-control and reading.* Dubuque, Iowa: Kendall/Hunt, 1976.

Skinner, B. F. *Science and human behavior.* New York: Macmillan, 1953.

Suppes, P., & Suppes, J. *Sets and numbers.* New York: Random House, 1968.

Titchener, E. B. *An outline of psychology.* New York: Macmillan, 1897.

Wundt, W. *Principles of physiological psychology.* New York: Macmillan, 1904.

1 Staff Perception of Client Initiative and Control

Peter S. Houts
Patricia Quann
Robert A. Scott
The Pennsylvania State University

Much of this volume has been concerned with the behavior of individuals: how the individual learns or does not learn to choose and control self and environment, as well as the behavioral effects of perceiving oneself as in control of oneself and one's environment. As we all recognize, however, a person's behavior is as much controlled by his or her environment as by personal skills, perceptions, and motivation. Therefore it is essential, in order to develop a comprehensive understanding of these behaviors, that we study how a person's environment reacts to his or her choosing behavior as well as how that environment reinforces or punishes those behaviors.

The current situation of the institutionalized mentally handicapped (both mentally ill and mentally retarded) provides a unique opportunity to study these variables. Within the past 5 years political and legal changes have radically altered the requirements for choice by residents of these institutions. Staff are now being required not only to allow choice and self-initiative on the part of the clients; they also must actively encourage those behaviors. This is a change from past practices and shows promise of having widespread effects on the lives of the residents of these institutions. These changes, which are just beginning to occur, provide a natural laboratory for studying response to choosing behaviors as well as how this response affects the behavior of clients. The implications of such research are both practical (e.g., how can we best accomplish this change to maximize client growth?) and theoretical (e.g., what are the cognitive mechanisms used by staff to deal with the inconsistencies implicit in viewing a client as dependent on staff and, at the same time, choosing and directing staff's work?)

The study discussed here is a beginning in this area. It is an attempt to identify some of the variables that affect staff perceptions regarding initiating behavior on the part of the clients. In this study we hoped to identify some of the important parameters in this situation and to identify directions for future research.

BACKGROUND

The current interest in developing client initiative and choice in institutional settings has historical, social, and legal roots. Institutions for the mentally handicapped were founded in this country in the middle of the past century to alleviate the deplorable conditions in which these people were kept. It was intended, at that time, that institutions would reflect the "moral treatment" philosophy of Pinel and Tuke (Misiak & Sexton, 1966), where the disturbed person was provided a maximally supportive environment in order to regain his or her abilities. Client choice and self-control were central in moral treatment programs, and those behaviors were encouraged by institution staff. However, the ideals of moral treatment were soon obscured by overcrowding combined with underfunding; by the pressures for bureaucratic efficiency, which reduced clients to objects of treatment rather than active participants in treatment; and by the medical rationale applied to these clients, namely, that they were "sick" and therefore should be "good" patients and passively accept "treatment." The result was a passive, compliant institutional population of clients who forgot whatever skills they had for choice or control of their lives or who, if they had lacked these skills before entering the institution, never learned to develop them.

Social scientists, to their credit, were among the first to recognize and publicize the fact that the behavior of institutionalized persons was as much the effect of the institutional environment as of their handicaps. Stanton and Schwartz (1954), Goffman (1961), Wolfensberger (1972), and Blatt (1973), among others, raised these issues publicly, which helped to reawaken public concern for humane care. Concurrent with, and to some extent influenced by, the awareness of these issues among professional social scientists, the courts have become increasingly concerned with institutional conditions and their effect on clients, especially on their rights to self-determination (Martin, 1975). The courts now require that clients must have as much control as possible over the treatment and program decisions that affect them. The courts have ruled that this is basically a civil rights issue under the "equal protection" provisions of the 14th amendment. Equal protection requires that agreement must be obtained before one attempts to intervene or affect another person's life. In addition, this agreement must be both voluntary and informed. The effect of these rulings is that institutional staff will be expected to change their behavior toward clients in fundamental ways: doing with instead of doing to, asking instead of ordering, and encouraging initiative instead of squelching it.

How these changes are to be implemented is now the issue. Institutionalized persons remain handicapped and therefore dependent on staff. Under these conditions, will staff be willing or even able to carry out these mandated changes? Or, as has happened in the past, will these reforms become distorted and twisted by the bureaucratic structure of institutions and by the existing attitudes of staff? Of particular interest is whether staff will perceive increased client control as necessarily decreasing their own control. If they do perceive this as a power struggle, clients are likely to be the losers, because they have the least power to start with.

This study is a first step in identifying variables that affect staff response to client control and what can be done to insure positive, supportive responses on their part. In this research we have focused on the cognitive responses of staff to client control. We were interested in how staff perceive "controlling" clients, how staff are influenced by others' perceptions of these clients, and how staff respond to reward vs. punishment programs for clients. Since controlling and choosing behaviors by clients are not the norm in institutions, we would expect that these behaviors will create a certain amount of cognitive imbalance for staff. This in turn may result in cognitive changes that could support the new behavior toward clients or could distort perception to justify old habits and procedures. The questions we specifically asked were as follows:

1. Does staff approval or disapproval of a client's attempt to control or influence his or her environment generalize to how they perceive the client in other respects? Cognitive balance theories suggest that there will be generalization, especially to liking or disliking the client. Heider (1958), for example, has postulated a need for balance between how one feels about a person and how one feels about that person's actions. This would suggest that if staff disapprove of a client's controlling behaviors, they will disapprove of him or her in other ways as well.

2. Does staff approval or disapproval of a client's controlling behaviors influence whether they support punishment- or reward-type programs for the client? Cognitive balance theory would suggest that support for punishment programs will be greatest when staff disapprove of a client's controlling behaviors and that support for reward programs will be greatest when staff approve of his or her controlling behaviors.

3. Will staff perceptions of a client be different when attitudes toward client control and type of client program are congruent (i.e., positive attitude

and reward or negative attitude and punishment) than when they are incongruent (positive attitude and punishment or negative attitude and reward)? Balance theory suggests that the incongruent situations will be uncomfortable for staff and may result in cognitive distortion to lessen this discomfort. Distortion could occur in the traits assigned to the client (e.g., "He isn't really so nice, and so he deserved punishment") or in how much intention the client displays (e.g., "She doesn't really intend to be so bothersome, so it's alright to reward her").

Answers to the foregoing questions will indicate some of the patterns of responses we can expect from institutional staff as they attempt to implement these new mandates.

METHOD

The subjects were 48 volunteers from the day-shift staff at an institution for the mentally retarded. All were direct-care staff (i.e., aides, nurses, and other professionals working directly with clients).

The subjects were first asked to read background information about a client at an institution for mentally retarded persons. There were four elements to this description, some of which were the same for all subjects and some of which were different for different groups of subjects, as follows:

1. The client was described as an active, initiating client who volunteered, questioned, led, and in general sought to control his circumstances and the behaviors of others. All subjects received this same description, which was based on an earlier, unpublished study in which staff of an institution for the mentally retarded were asked to give semantic differential (Osgood, Suci, & Tannenbaum, 1957) ratings for two matched clients—one who took initiative in trying to control events in his life, and one who did not. Fourteen semantic differential scales showed statistically significant differences between these two descriptions. These 14 scales were used as the basis for describing the controlling client in this study.

2. The staff reactions to the client's behavior were also described. For half the subjects, staff reaction was described as positive, with the staff being pleased with the client's efforts to control his life. Staff appreciated his help when he volunteered, and they believed that it was therapeutically good for him to be demonstrating such independence. The other subjects were told that staff reacted negatively to the client's initiative. They were told that the staff were concerned that the client's questioning, challenging behavior could cause him problems when he moved into a community placement.

Furthermore, staff said that his controlling behavior made their jobs more difficult.

3. A problem situation involving the client was described. This was the same for all subjects and included some facts about a second client who felt that he was "bossed around" by the controlling client. This made the second client very angry, and he had created a scene that included throwing furniture. The staff of the unit felt that they should work with the controlling client to avoid further problems of this sort.

4. A plan, developed by the staff to deal with this problem, was then described. For half the subjects, the plan involved helping the controlling client to develop more effective ways to work with the second client and rewarded him as he developed and used these new skills. For the other half of the subjects, the plan involved punishing the controlling client whenever he upset the second client. This punishment plan was given a therapeutic rationale—that he must change his behavior if he is to be able to live in a group home in a community. Thus, both plans were described as sincere efforts by staff to help the client.

The experimental design can be summarized in the following 2 × 2 matrix in Fig. 11.1. Note that cells 1 and 4 in the chart are "congruent" in that the staff's attitudes toward the client's behavior and the methods used to change the behavior are consistent. Cells 2 and 3 are incongruent in that the attitudes toward the client's behavior do not match the method used to change that behavior.

There were two types of dependent variables in the study. First, subjects were asked how much they approved or disapproved of the plan as well as

	Reward Program	Punishment Program
Positive staff attitude toward client's controlling behavior	1	2
Negative staff attitude toward client's controlling behavior	3	4

FIG. 11.1.

how likely it was that the plan would succeed. Both ratings were on a 10-point scale. Second, subjects were asked to rate the controlling client on the 39 semantic differential scales. Of the scales, 29 were selected from Osgood et al.'s (1957) original factor analysis on the basis of appropriateness for describing a mentally retarded client. An additional 10 scales were added consisting of terms frequently used by institution staff to describe clients. Left-to-right scoring was counterbalanced within each of the Osgood factors. The 10 additional scales were also directionally counterbalanced for positive–negative tone.

A 2 × 2 factorial design was employed to analyze the data. The row main effects (staff approval or disapproval) indicated how subjects were influenced by the staff reaction to client's controlling behavior. Column main effects (reward or punishment program) indicated how subjects responded to the type of program. The interaction term indicates how subjects responded to the combination of staff attitudes and client programs (congruence or incongruence between attitudes and program).

RESULTS

Response to the Client Program

Three scores were indicative of subject response to the client program: approval of the plan, likelihood of success, and the sum of both these measures. Results showed no statistically significant main effects or interactions. However, the sum of the two measures did have an interaction term at the .10 level of confidence, which indicates a trend that may warrant further research. This trend was as predicted, namely, that the combined approval–likelihood-of-success scores were greatest when the staff attitude and the client program were congruent (e.g., approval–reward and disapproval–punishment). The lack of statistical significance may, in part, be due to the restricted range of the approval scores. Only 8 out of 48 subjects indicated disapproval of any plan.

Perception of the Client

Table 11.1 reports the analysis of variance results for the 39 semantic differential client ratings. Row main effects show that when staff approve of the client's controlling behaviors, subjects perceived the client as more cooperative, kind, contented, courteous, gentle, congenial, respectful, grateful, calm, safe, obedient, happy, careful, and strong. With the exception of the trait *strong*, this list describes a client who is well adjusted to institutional life and whom staff can work with easily. Where staff disapprove

TABLE 11.1
Statistically Significant Findings in Semantic Differential Scales

Semantic Differential Scales	Row Main Effects With $p < .05.$[a]	Column Main Effects With $p < .05.$[b]	Interactions With $p < .05.$[c]
cooperative–manipulator	cooperative		
unwilling–willing			
cruel–kind	kind		
contented–discontented	contented		
uncomfortable–comfortable			
useless–useful			
unattentive–attentive			
careful–careless	careful		
orderly–disorderly			
courteous–discourteous	courteous	courteous	
volunteers–forced			volunteers
indifferent–eager			
gentle–vicious	gentle		
following–leading			leading
argumentative–congenial	congenial		
disrespectful–respectful	respectful		
yielding–strong willed			
aimless–motivated			motivated
grateful–ungrateful	grateful	grateful	grateful
stable–changeable		stable	
humble–proud			proud
not helpful–helpful			
cooperative–uncooperative	cooperative		
uninvolved–involved			
unselfish–selfish			
aggressive–unaggressive			
calm–excitable	calm		
safe–dangerous	safe		
insensitive–sensitive			
unemotional–emotional			
disobedient–obedient	obedient		
active–passive			
humorous–serious			
free–not free			
happy–sad	happy		
friendly–unfriendly			
sneaky–open			
intentional–unintentional			
strong–weak	strong		

[a]Positive attitude toward client control associated with client rated as more.
[b]Punishment program associated with client rated as more.
[c]Congruence associated with client rated as more.

of the client's controlling behaviors, the client is perceived as a more difficult person to work with. These results indicate that staff's response to a client's behavior does influence general traits that they ascribe to that client.

Three column main effects were statistically significant, indicating that the type of program prescribed for a client also affects how staff view the client. If a punishment program was given, subjects viewed the client as more courteous, grateful, and stable.

Five interactions were statistically significant. Four of these interactions showed that when staff attitudes and client programs were congruent (approve–reward and disapprove–punish), the client was viewed as more volunteering, motivated, leading, and proud; whereas in the incongruent conditions, he was seen as more forced, aimless, following, and humble. This suggests that the purposefulness and intentionality of the client is viewed as higher in the congruent conditions and lower in the incongruent conditions.

There was one additional interaction that showed a somewhat different pattern from the others. The grateful–ungrateful scale showed a particularly high (ungrateful) score in cell 3 (disapprove–reward), whereas the other three cells and lower scores were very similar to one another. This suggests that if staff disapprove of a client's controlling behavior, they will be especially negative toward that client if he or she is rewarded. On the other hand, if they approve the behavior, the reward versus punishment makes little difference.

DISCUSSION

There was only weak $(p < .10)$ evidence for a relationship between congruence and support for the plan. As was noted earlier, this trend is consistent with attribution theory, since it is more "balanced" to support a program for a client when one's attitude toward the client and the method used for the plan are congruent, whereas it is less balanced to support a program when these attitudes and methods are incongruent. The weakness of these results may be due partly to a limited range of scores, since most subjects approved the plan. It was surprising, and somewhat disappointing, that more subjects did not challenge the punishment plans, since rewards are generally agreed to be more effective than punishment in helping clients to grow. It is likely that subjects took the view that this was someone else's client and that they shouldn't interfere. This is the rationale frequently used by staff for not speaking up in meetings when another staff member proposes a program for a client. When this happens, the client is the loser in two ways: (1) the client's program is not carefully considered against alternatives; and (2) staff, having acquiesced in accepting the plan, must fall back on cognitive distortions to deal with any discomfort they feel with the plan. The semantic differential data indicate that they did just that.

The semantic differential data indicated that clients who were punished were viewed as more courteous, grateful, and stable than were clients who were rewarded. One explanation is that subjects were anticipating that punishment would make the client more comfortable to work with. On the other hand, seeing a punished client in this way may be a cognitive compensatory mechanism whereby liking someone makes up for hurting them. Heider (1958) has suggested this as a strategy for dealing with cognitive inconsistency. Both interpretations suggest that the subjects were looking for a way to feel more comfortable about punishment. If so, this could have the unfortunate effect of making it easier for them to administer punishment. This finding suggests the need for additional research on how staff justify punishment programs for clients.

Perceptual distortion was also evident in four of the interactions indicating that the client was seen as less leading, proud, volunteering, and motivated when staff's attitudes and treatment were incongruent than when they were congruent. This may also indicate perceptual distortion to help staff deal with uncomfortable situations. As Heider has pointed out, intentionality is central to person perception. To be intentional is to be human. To the degree that a client can be viewed as having less intentionality, he is less of a human being, and therefore there is less need to maintain cognitive consistency. In other words, this finding may indicate that subjects are viewing the client as having less intentionality in order to reduce their discomfort with the inconsistency between that client's program and their attitudes toward his or her behavior. If this is the case, such situations could have the effect of reducing staff's perceptions of the client as a choosing, initiating person at the very time when the courts and others are trying to reverse these attitudes. It is important that further research be carried out to determine if this interpretation is correct and what effects these perceptions have on staff behavior toward the client.

The finding that clients are seen as especially "ungrateful" in cell 3 (disapprove, reward) suggests that if we used reward programs for clients where staff disapprove of their controlling behavior, this may backfire in creating even more dislike for the client.

Finally, it was found that subjects did attribute different traits to clients whose controlling behavior was approved relative to clients whose controlling behaviors were disapproved (row main effects). These results suggest that when control is viewed negatively by staff, clients will be seen as less respectful and less cooperative than when control is viewed positively. We do not know, from these data, how these cognitive differences will affect how staff treat clients. If, as is likely, staff expectations influence client behavior, this may spiral into more noncompliant behavior and even stronger feelings on the part of staff. This is an important question for future research.

These findings have several important implications for practitioners. First, it is important to consider staff attitudes toward client control before mandating greater client control and choice. If staff attitudes toward these behaviors are negative, this may backfire into increased antagonism toward clients. It may also result in staff's supporting punishment programs for clients. Second, incongruence between attitudes toward the client and his or her program led to viewing the client as less controlling. This particular way of dealing with cognitive inconsistency could have serious implications for client growth. If the result of mandating client choice and control is that staff view clients as less able to fulfill these expectations, the result could be even less growth.

This study also points to several areas for future research. First, it is important that we better understand why staff acquiesce in accepting plans, as did 40 out of 48 subjects in this study. This is a critical question for clients, because if staff do not express their discomfort with plans openly, they are likely to resort to cognitive distortion. This distortion can affect staff expectations of clients and can result in staff becoming comfortable with punishment programs. It may be that in order to support client efforts at choice and control, we first must be concerned with staff exercising control through participation in program decisions for clients.

A second question for future research is how staff response to clients' choosing, controlling behaviors influences therapeutic outcomes. There is evidence that the social climate of a ward, including support for client autonomy, is related to therapeutic outcomes (Moos, 1974). It is therefore important that we understand how staff perceptions of client autonomy are translated into the social climate that they create for those clients and how this, in turn, affects client growth.

In conclusion, this study has shown that staff perception of mentally retarded clients is influenced by: (1) staff attitudes toward clients' controlling, choosing behaviors; (2) the use of punishment versus reward programs; and (3) the congruence between 1 and 2. Cognitive balance theory has proved a useful framework for interpreting these findings. Further research in this area can contribute to understanding cognitive balance processes and also to an important humanitarian goal: autonomy and choice for mentally handicapped persons.

ACKNOWLEDGMENTS

The authors would like to express their appreciation to Dr. Joseph Stewart and the staff of Polk Center for their help in data collection.

REFERENCES

Blatt, B. *Souls in extremis: An anthology on victims and victimizers.* Boston: Allyn & Bacon, 1973.

Goffman, E. *Asylums: Essays on the social situation of mental patients and other inmates.* Garden City, N.Y.: Anchor Books, 1961.

Heider, F. *The psychology of interpersonal relations.* New York: Wiley, 1958.

Martin, R. *Legal challenges to behavior modification.* Champaign, Ill.: Research Press, 1975.

Misiak, H., & Sexton, V. S. *History of psychology: An overview.* New York: Grune & Stratton, 1966.

Moos, R. *Evaluating treatment environments.* New York: Wiley, 1974.

Osgood, C. E., Suci, G. J., & Tannenbaum, P. H. *The measurement of meaning.* Urbana, Ill.: University of Illinois Press, 1957.

Stanton, A. H., & Schwartz, M. S. *The mental hospital.* New York: Basic Books, 1954.

Wolfensberger, W. *Normalization: The principles of normalization in human services.* Toronto, Canada: National Institute on Mental Retardation, 1972.

12 The Role of Perceived Control in Psychopathology

Diane B. Arnkoff
Michael J. Mahoney
The Pennsylvania State University

Each individual has a network of beliefs about the self and the world, a "model" that serves to organize experience and guide behavior (Arnkoff, in press; Frank, 1961; Kelly, 1955; Kreitler & Kreitler, 1976). A key aspect of the individual's model of the world is a set of beliefs about *control*. There is a cultural consensus regarding what aspects of one's life are controllable, and each individual also has a set of beliefs about his or her personal control. These two sets of beliefs can conflict. Persons who are regarded as psychopathological may be characterized according to the manner in which their model of personal control is discrepant from the shared societal assumptions. An examination of the relationship between perceived control and psychopathology may shed light both on generalized beliefs about control and on the nature of maladaptive behavior.

In this paper we examine the meanings of the term *control* and how the meanings relate to our commonly shared beliefs about the nature and extent of personal control. The cultural norms are reflected in current psychological theories regarding perceived control. They are also central to the process of labeling behavior as abnormal. The various recognized types of behavioral deviance are related to deviations from cultural standards of beliefs and behavior regarding control. We will see that the individual's phenomenology and the *meaning* of control for that individual (Averill, 1973) are correlated with the type of abnormal behavior exhibited. Such a relationship has implications for understanding the organization and treatment of psychopathology.

THE MEANING OF CONTROL

The term *control* is used in several different ways, and it is easy to become confused about the concept of perceived control if these meanings are left implicit. An examination of these meanings will aid in delineating some of our assumptions regarding personal control. There are four related meanings of the term *control* that are important here:

1. skill;
2. power;
3. direction, regulation, and coordination; and
4. restraint or reserve.

Control as Skill

When we speak of an individual's belief in control over events, we are often referring to control as a *skill*, a choice of possible actions. Control here refers to *internal* capabilities. This is the sense in which we refer to a dancer's control over her body—a set of skills that give her the capability or choice to use her body in a manner that others cannot. Skills have a developmental character. Many types of skills, like reasoning, are thought to increase during development, and skills can be cultivated.

Therapy is often conceived of as a training in skills. For example, Bandura (1977a) hypothesizes that treatment has its effect in strengthening the client's expectancy of personal effectiveness. These beliefs in personal capability are called *self-efficacy* expectations. According to Bandura's formulation, successful treatment of certain disorders may involve a change in the individual's perceived ability to act effectively.

Control as Power

Skills involve control over internal choices. *Power*, on the other hand, involves control over the *external* world. It is the capacity to control resources or reinforcements. Power can be experienced as "residing" in the self, in which case it is the individual's use of skills to obtain consequences from the environment. But power to control the individual's reinforcements can also be perceived as residing in other people. Finally, power can be experienced as residing outside of human control. In this case consequences may be perceived to be randomly programmed, or they may be seen as having a regular pattern that is unrelated to human actions. An example of the latter is the weather. It is generally believed to follow regular rules, but with rare exceptions, these rules are not governed by human actions.

Power is the meaning of control referred to in the well-known work of Rotter and his colleagues on internal vs. external control of reinforcement

(Rotter, 1966; Rotter, Chance, & Phares, 1972). There is a difference, however, between the present analysis of power and that found in Rotter's I–E scale (1966). Whereas we have delineated three perceptions of the locus of power—in the self, in others, or outside of persons—Rotter's I–E scale deals with only two of the three: the belief in self-determined consequences vs. the belief in randomly generated outcomes. The belief that others have power over us is clearly important to a full consideration of perceived control. For example, it is clear that the persecutory delusions of the paranoid schizophrenic involve the belief that others have an inordinate degree of power over him. It is this belief about the control of others that is the hallmark of the persecutory type of paranoid schizophrenia.

Skills and power are often considered as one concept. Steiner (1970) joins "may" and "can" into one concept, which he calls outcome freedom. However, a differentiation of the two may be necessary for an adequate understanding of the concept of control. The possession of skills is thought to be unequivocally positive. The same cannot be said for power. For example, the power of behavior therapy to induce change has led some to criticize it on ethical grounds (Mahoney, Kazdin, & Lesswing, 1974). Even unexercised power can be morally condemned, as when homosexual schoolteachers are fired because it is believed that they could contaminate young minds. This example also illustrates our belief that power, like skills, has a developmental aspect. Presumably, parents who demand the firing of homosexual teachers would claim that they are not afraid of being influenced themselves, but children are believed to be less powerful than adults. Personal power is believed to increase during development, parallel to the development of skills but not synonymous with it. By the time they reach adulthood, people are thought to have extensive power over their own outcomes. Adults who believe they possess little power—as described in the term *learned helplessness* (Seligman, 1975)—are thought to be neurotic or psychotic.

The exercise of power can be stressful. In the well-known study by Brady, Porter, Conrad, and Mason (1958), "executive" monkeys who had power over the delivery of shock developed ulcers and died, a fate not experienced by other monkeys who received uncontrollable shocks. Weiss (1971) has investigated the process behind this phenomenon. As summarized by Averill (1973), ambiguity or delay of feedback regarding responses can result in power being stress inducing. Analogies to childrearing are tempting, and we succumb to the temptation later when we discuss the double-bind theory of schizophrenia.

Control as Regulation

Skill and power refer to choices in actions. *Regulation, direction, and coordination* refer to management of these choices. To meet both short- and long-range personal goals, choices must be coordinated, and there must be a balance between self and societal concerns. The capacity to regulate can itself be seen as a type of skill, and it can serve to increase personal power. Thus self-control training involves training in skills to achieve a balance between short-term and long-range goals (Mahoney & Arnkoff, in press; Thoresen & Mahoney, 1974). Control here is the capacity to manage both skills and power.

Control as Restraint

A related aspect of control is that of *restraint or reserve*. In this case, control is the inhibition of some behaviors in order to meet a goal. Self-control in the lay sense of willpower often falls into this category (Thoresen & Mahoney, 1974). However, as already noted, a more useful conception of self-control is that of regulation, the balance of immediate and long-term goals (Thoresen & Mahoney, 1974). We tend to link control in the sense of reserve to the term *responsibility*. We are acting responsibly when we restrain or regulate our use of skills or power. Responsibility itself has numerous meanings. In this context, the most applicable definition is that of the 19th-century philosopher Alexander Bain, who substituted "punishability" for responsibility (cited in McKeon, 1957). According to Bain, to be responsible means to be capable of answering an accusation and therefore capable of being punished. In this sense, control means responsibility for exhibiting restraint in order to avoid punishment. Also relevant is Locke's use of responsible as "trustworthy" (cited in McKeon, 1957). Thus the trustworthy use of skills and power involves restraint in their exercise. The practice of control in this sense makes the individual worthy of praise rather than blame. The individual who is "out of control" is not acting with responsible restraint.

THE CULTURAL IDEOLOGY OF CONTROL

It is clear that the four meanings of the term *control* just outlined are closely linked. A consideration of their relations reveals the dual nature of control. Skill and personal power imply *freedom* in the choices available for action. Skill is the internal capability to act, power the capability to achieve an external effect. Thus treatment can be said to enlarge skills and personal power by increasing the number and range of options available to the individual (Bandura, 1977b; Mahoney, Kazdin, & Lesswing, 1974). Regulation and restraint, on the other hand, imply *limits* on freedom. In order to accomplish goals and avoid punishment, actions must be balanced and responsible. Both freedom and limits on that freedom are essential to the notion of control.

The dual nature of control is an important aspect of our shared beliefs regarding control. Western culture embraces the belief that the individual controls much of his or her life. Whether or not the belief is an "illusion," it is central to the Western model of the world (Immergluck, 1964; Lefcourt, 1973). We have an "ideology" built around the perception of control (Brim, 1974). This ideology of control is part of our shared theory of social structure. The belief regarding control is that we have control—skill plus power—over much of our lives, especially those aspects of our lives that involve relationships with other people and achievement. According to the ideology, our control is substantial but not infinite. Consistent with the dual nature of control, the ideology also places restraints on the exercise of control. Responsibility to regulate and restrain activity is part of the cultural ideal.

According to Brim (1974), there is a developmental sequence that characterizes belief in personal control. A person's perceived control coincides with the cultural norms only during middle adulthood. Small children believe both in their personal omnipotence, as Piaget has shown, and in their helplessness (Becker, 1973; Brim, 1974). According to Brim, children are socialized to link the satisfaction of needs with personal mastery. He reviews studies showing a gradual increase in the sense of perceived control through childhood and adulthood, up to about the age of 50. From then on, the sense of perceived control gradually declines. As Brim (1974) summarizes it:

> During the lifespan segment from around age five or six to the mid-life period, changes in the sense of personal control correspond in a common sense way to the realities of life, namely, an increase from early childhood up through the adolescent expansion—the feeling of great power, of "I cannot fail"—through the next several decades of mastery of the key tasks of life—and then the inversion point and the gradual erosion of the sense of control during the later years. . . . As one is forced to set aside, or to suppress, components of the self. . . . somehow the elderly have grown not just old, but perhaps wise too, for they seem to have shucked off some of their sense of responsibility over matters clearly outside of their span of control [pp. 14, 16, 17].

There is a predictable sequence, then, of accord with the cultural ideology. Even though Brim suggests, at the end of the passage quoted, that the prevailing ideology may not be wholly consonant with reality, it influences many aspects of social conduct. The sense of personal control, whether valid or not, is prized in our culture.

The value placed on the sense of mastery is reflected in psychological writings on control. Actual mastery is seen as adaptive, as in White's (1959) hypothesis of a drive to competence. Likewise, contemporary psychologists generally see *perceived* control as adaptive. For example, deCharms (1968) discusses the value of the experience of personal causation. According to Brehm's (1966) reactance theory, perceived freedom is so important that if alternatives are threatened, the individual will take action to regain the sense of control. It is common to conclude from the research on Rotter's internal vs. external control of reinforcement research that the internal side of the continuum is "better." The research programs of Perlmuter and Monty (1977), Glass and Singer (1972), and Schulz (1976), among others, have pointed to the positive effects of a sense of mastery. The careful review of research on control and aversive stimulation by Averill (1973) catalogs the occasional stressful aspects of control. Nevertheless, Averill concludes that the experience of control is adaptive in the long run, even if there is a short-term increase in stress.

There are exceptions to the generally held position that control is possible and is striven for. Some individuals or groups may actually have meager skills or scant personal power to achieve goals. For example, there is a consistent relationship found between belief in perceived control and socioeconomic status as well as other indications of achievement (Brim, 1974; Lefcourt, 1972). Those who are unsuccessful often have little faith in their control over events. These individuals may still subscribe to the belief that control is possible for some people—but not for them.

In a different type of dissent from the prevailing cultural view, Fromm (1941) argues that human beings may not wish to be masters of their fate. He reasons that as our species became more free from economic constraints, the result was not an increased sense of mastery. Instead, the realization of being alone generally has led to a sense of isolation and powerlessness, most often resolved by an "escape from freedom" to a new authority. Bartley (1962), too, writes of the "retreat to commitment," in that an irrational leap of faith in an authority is at the heart of virtually every contemporary Western belief system.

Becker's (1973) exposition of control issues is strikingly at odds with the cultural ideology. His position regarding that ideology, in fact, is that it is a myth that we use to keep ourselves motivated. If we faced the real truth—our massive fear of our weakness to combat death—we could not act to keep ourselves alive. According to Becker (1973):

> The fear of death must be present behind all our normal functioning, in order for the organism to be armed toward self-preservation. But the fear of death cannot be present constantly in one's mental functioning, else the organism could not function. . . . Reality and fear go together naturally [pp. 16–17].

In order to survive, we repress our fear. "Repression is normal self-protection and creative self-restriction" (Becker, 1973, p. 178). In the Oedipal "project," children attempt to assert themselves as the masters of their fate. But the attempt cannot wholly succeed. Becker (1973) quotes Maslow: "We are simultaneously worms and gods [p. 51]." Our defenses allow us some feeling of control, but anxiety and fear are bound to remain. Neurotics are those whose defenses are particularly ineffective. As a result, they may be too constricted. Or they may be stripped of comfortable illusions of mastery, coming close to the truth of human "creatureness."

Becker's view of the neurotic as having a more accurate model of reality than "normals" is clearly irreconcilable with the cultural norms of believing that true control is possible. Neurotics may in fact be closer to the truth; but we will continue to *label* them as being further away. We have no method of determining the absolute truth regarding our skills and power. Therefore we make judgments based on the prevailing belief. Sometimes the deviant is a member of a large group, such as urban, poor Blacks. Most observers agree that these people truly lack both skills and power. As a group, they are therefore given the deviant label, "disadvantaged." If a person's control beliefs or actions are idiosyncratically deviant, however, the person is labeled psychopathological or mentally ill. We do not *know* that our conception of control is symmetrical with reality, but we take action as if it were.

An example of judgments we make can be seen in the phenomenon of learned helplessness (Seligman, 1975). As noted earlier, this is the belief that one's actions are independent of consequences—a lack of personal control. It has been linked with depression. The paradigm for this phenomenon is a laboratory demonstration with animals, particularly dogs. The initial stage is experience with shock that is in reality uncontrollable for the animal (the experimenter maintains control). After this experience of helplessness, the animal is found to be slow to learn to avoid shock when the avoidance is actually controllable. In tne animal paradigm, the true state of affairs regarding power is known. Such is not the case, of course, in clinical practice—yet we label depressives as pathological partly on the basis of a discrepancy between cultural beliefs and personal beliefs. Wortman and Brehm (1975) point out that there is a danger in assuming that learned helplessness is in conflict with reality. Treatment aimed at "immunizing" against helplessness beliefs may be unwise; in the face of real uncontrollability, "the most adaptive response may be to give up" (Wortman & Brehm, 1975, p. 331). A more appropriate type of treatment, they suggest, would be to train the individual to differentiate between situations that are controllable and those that are not.

In the case of the grandiosity of the paranoid schizophrenic or hypomanic, the individual gets labeled because of a belief in greater personal power or skill than is culturally the norm. For example, the senior author once treated a woman who was consumed by the self-imposed task of documenting her thoughts and outside events. During virtually every moment of her day, she was engaged in keeping a stream-of-consciousness diary or in noting recent events in newpapers and magazines. Her small room was jammed to the ceiling with notebooks filled with her thoughts. She had held a job steadily for the past ten years, but it was well below her capabilities and education. Her social life was limited solely to her co-workers, and she rarely socialized even with them outside of work.

To this point, the description of the woman is certainly abnormal. It would possibly earn her the label of schizoid or obsessive-compulsive. But one simple addition changes the diagnosis: She believed that her thoughts *caused* world events. This type of power is discrepant even from our culture's sanguine notion of personal control. Her diagnosis clearly becomes that of paranoid schizophrenic, grandiose type. It is a label based on a shared belief, not certainty, that such personal control is not possible.

A different kind of control pathology is seen in the diagnosis of the sociopath. In this case the individual's perception of skill and power is consistent with the common perception. But the impulsivity and lack of emotional commitments of the sociopath are at variance with the cultural notion of responsibility. Ordinary lawbreakers are not usually labeled psychopathological. Their priorities are seen as deviant, but they share in the framework that governs social interactions. However, those who are called sociopaths not only have inverted priorities; they also operate out of a different framework. They do not act responsibly in the sense that they do not fear the interpersonal aspects of punishment (e.g., Schmauk, 1970). The McNaughten rule, long used as a basis for deciding insanity, asks whether the individual knows right from wrong—whether the lawbreaker shares in the notion of responsibility. The criminal behavior itself is not considered psychopathological; the belief system and its associated behaviors are.

Once an individual has been labeled psychologically abnormal, public and professional behavior is consistent with the ideology of control. The ideology has a dual nature: Skills and power are joined to restraint and balance. If an individual shows an idiosyncratic distortion of the norms, then our response is predictable: We see the individual as having both no choice and no responsibility. We often say that deviants are "out of control"—outside of our shared framework of control. Because they are not accountable or trustworthy, we may assume responsibility and assert power over them, institutionalizing them. If they do not share in our assumptions, they are not allowed to share in our social process.

We do not mean to imply, as Scheff (1966) does, that the labeling process merely assigns some people arbitrarily to the crazy role. Plainly some behavior is maladaptive. The vegetative apathy of the severe depressive, the preoccupation of the paranoid schizophrenic, and the impulsivity of the sociopath are clearly at odds with our standards for adaptive behavior. But an awareness of the relativity of our cultural ideology should enable us to avoid the excesses of the labeling process.

PSYCHOPATHOLOGY AND
THE MEANING OF CONTROL

We have observed that shared beliefs about control influence our perceptions of psychopathology. A further delineation of the relationship between types of psychopathology and perceived control issues may shed light on both control and deviance. Three types of disorders may be identified. They are not completely independent, but they appear to be meaningfully separable. The types of disorders include:

1. psychopathology in which there is deviance from cultural beliefs about control, with attendant symptomatic behavior;
2. psychopathology that may be characterized as deficits in skills or regulatory functioning; and
3. psychopathology in which the manner in which the individual asserts control is seen as inappropriate or maladaptive.

Deviant Beliefs About Control

Several categories of abnormal behavior include deviation from cultural norms regarding perceived control as part of the pathology. The deviations are both in beliefs about personal freedom and in beliefs about restraint. Paranoid persecution and grandiosity, phobias, and depression are types of abnormal behavior that will serve as examples.

Paranoid or manic grandiosity, as already noted, may be conceived of as entailing beliefs about skills and power that are discrepant from the norm. The client described earlier, who believed she could determine world events by her thoughts, perceived herself as having power that others would not attribute to her. An example of a deviant belief about skills is the common hypomanic belief that if only the person could reach the president with his plan, world peace would surely follow.

Paranoid persecution, on the other hand, is a deviant ascription of power to others. As Shapiro describes it (1965):

> While the normal person feels not only competent, but also free to exercise his will, and, in that sense as well, self-directing, in charge of his own life, and, master of himself, the paranoid person is continuously occupied and concerned with the threat of being subjected to some external control or some external infringement of his will [pp. 81–82].

A recently proposed theory by Colby (1977) suggests a provocative relationship between paranoid persecution and control beliefs. Colby calls his theory the shame-humiliation perspective. According to the theory, the paranoid individual is sensitive to signs of inadequacy. When a perception of shame signals inadequacy and an impending feeling of humiliation, the paranoid instead attributes wrongdoing to others. In the terms used here, when there is danger of perceiving inadequate skills, the paranoid makes an incorrect attribution of power to others. If others can be held responsible for the person's negative affect, no acknowledgment of inadequacy is necessary. A computer simulation of paranoid inference has been devised (Faught, Colby, & Parkison, 1977). The results of the simulation are consistent with the shame-humiliation theory.

This theory is also consistent with a program of research on stress in animals, summarized by Averill (1973). In this paradigm the experimenter creates a situation in which punishment is inevitable. Interestingly, the animal tends to exhibit more distress when the onset of punishment is also explicitly signaled than when it is unsignaled. It is the "added pinprick of vigilance" (Liddell, 1950, p. 195) that seems to be especially stressful. In the paranoid, the parallel in Colby's (1977) theory is that the "pinprick" of shame is prior to the punishment of humiliation. The paranoid exercises the maladaptive escape route of blaming others.

In the case of both grandiosity and persecution, it is possible to argue that the meaning of the symptoms may not be a straightforward extrapolation from the phenomenology. Such is the case with Colby's (1977) shame-humiliation theory. The choice of treatment for a disorder would depend on the therapist's judgment—first regarding the validity of the client's beliefs and then regarding the meaning of the beliefs for the client. Most therapists recall with amusement their novice days when they tried and failed miserably to directly dissuade a paranoid schizophrenic to give up delusionary beliefs. More sophisticated persuasion techniques may be necessary. But it may also be necessary to choose techniques based on the *meaning* of the phenomenology to the client. If a realistic skills deficit is behind the power delusion, the choice of treatments would be different from the case in which it is a particular type of deviant belief. Such is the situation with every disorder: The overt behavior may suggest one type of formulation, the covert phenomenology another.

In the case of phobias, the phenomenology suggests an exaggeration of the power attributed to the feared object. To the dog phobic, all dogs are potential killers. However, Bandura (1977a) has hypothesized that even if the phobic has realistic knowledge that danger can be avoided by taking certain actions (such as petting the dog), she may not feel that she is capable of doing what is necessary. She may not have the self-efficacy expectation that she can approach the dog. In the vocabulary we have proposed, self-efficacy expectations correspond to perceived skills. Bandura (1977a) further hypothesizes that behavioral treatments for avoidance patterns operate by altering self-efficacy expectations. He and his colleagues have presented evidence that improvement in avoidant behavior is accompanied by an increase in self-efficacy expectations (Bandura & Adams, 1977; Bandura, Adams, & Beyer, 1977).

It was noted earlier that the apparent process involved in the disorder may be different from the meaning of the deviation to the individual. In the case of the phobic, Bandura (1977a) hypothesizes that skills expectancies may play a more important role than the power of consequences. He makes the further point that the process of change need not be identical with the procedures used to effect that change. Although a change in the phobic's cognitions regarding skills is the *process* of change in treatment, it does not necessarily follow that a verbal persuasion *procedure* will be most effective. In fact, Bandura (1977a) hypothesizes that the overt behavioral tasks involved in participant modeling will make participant modeling a more effective treatment than verbal persuasion. A careful analysis of a disorder, then, may reveal different processes operating than appear from a casual look at its topography. Similarly, Bandura (1977a) argues that the best treatment may not be that which appears most direct. Just as the disorder must be studied thoughtfully, so the best approach to treatment must be analyzed carefully.

Nowhere is this advice more applicable than in the disorder of depression. Judging by the volume of research being generated, depression may be called the most popular pathology of the decade. There are almost as many viewpoints on the disorder as there are researchers. The conceptualization of depression that is most clearly related to perceived control is the learned helplessness formulation of Seligman and his colleagues (Maier & Seligman, 1976; Seligman, 1975). As already described, the theory rests on experimentation with animals in which there is an initial independence of responding and aversive stimulation. In the present formulation, learned helplessness in humans involves a maladaptive belief regarding the individual's personal power. The person who has learned to be helpless believes that his or her actions have no bearing on reinforcement or punishment. The cultural belief, in contrast, is that one's actions do indeed have a powerful effect on outcome.

Learned helplessness involves the independence of responses and outcomes. Mandler (1975) and Rehm (1977) have proposed a different type of helplessness. In this case, there *is* a relationship between actions and outcomes, but the individual either does not have the necessary behavior available (Mandler) or believes that he or she cannot perform it (Rehm). The latter formulation is similar to Bandura's (1977a) notion of perceived self-efficacy as central to behavioral disorders. Helplessness here refers more to perceived lack of skill, whereas learned helplessness is involved more with power. The conceptualization of helplessness that is most accurate may vary from individual to individual. As Rehm (1977) points out, for example, the importance of self-evaluation in the depressed person's phenomenology may make it likely that the perceived helplessness is more related to lack of skill than to lack of power.

Lack of control is seen differently in other conceptualizations of depression. Lewinsohn's (1974) behavioral conceptualization involves a lack of power. For Lewinsohn, the low rate of activity in depression is explained by a lack of positive reinforcement. Depression is often a loss of power, in that previous reinforcements are no longer forthcoming, as when someone close to the person dies. The Freudian position (Freud, 1917/1957) may also be recast into a loss of power formulation. The theory may be oversimplified as follows: A severe loss engenders hostility at the loss of power to obtain gratification. Since the ego has introjected or incorporated the lost object as a means of avoiding the pain of loss, the hostility is actually turned against the self.

Beck's (1967, 1976) conceptualization of depression also emphasizes perceived loss of power to obtain reinforcements. Instead of anger as in Freud's formulation, Beck theorizes that feelings of loss predominate. But he also places considerations of skill in the center of the disorder. A part of the cognitive triad typical of depression (Beck, 1967) is devaluation of the self (as well as the world and the future). The individual concludes that the loss occurred because of defects in the self. Self-blame and self-criticism may be seen as taking responsibility—punishability—for not having certain skills.

The results of a study by Golin, Terrell, and Johnson (1977) are consistent with Beck's conception of depression as involving both skill and power. In this study, mildly depressed and nondepressed subjects took part in a gambling game in which either the subject or the experimenter threw the dice. In the terms used here, power to determine the outcome rested in the person who threw the dice. Since the outcome depended solely on the roll of the dice, there was no skill involved. Nevertheless, subjects may have interpreted the task as reflecting abilities. (The subjects' interpretations of the task were not assessed in the study.) Before each throw, subjects rated their confidence in winning, which was defined as the appearance of certain numbers. The results showed that both depressed and nondepressed subjects were "irrational" in their confidence in winning. That is, for each group there was a condition in which subjects rated their likelihood of success as higher than was rational in this game of chance. This is the type of error that Ross (1977) calls the "fundamental attribution error"—overestimating the importance of personal influences relative to environmental factors. For nondepressed subjects, this optimistic irrationality came when they themselves threw the dice and therefore had the power to control outcomes. When the experimenter threw the dice, the subjects' evaluation of outcome was approximately consistent with the actual likelihood. For depressed subjects, however, the opposite was the case. When they rolled the dice themselves, they rated the likelihood of success as only slightly below the likelihood by chance, but they rated their confidence of success as higher than chance when the experimenter rolled the dice.

For nondepressed subjects, the results are interesting in light of Becker's (1973) position that people protect themselves from reality by believing the *illusion* that they control their destiny. Depressed subjects in the Golin et al. (1977) study were realistic regarding their own power or skill. This is consistent as well with Becker's (1973) claim that neurotics have fewer illusions about their control than normals. But depressed subjects in this study had their own distortion—that others have more power or skill than they.

An added perspective on power and depression is provided by Wortman and Brehm (1975). They argue that self-blame is preferable to the sense of powerlessness and therefore may be chosen by depressives. For example, Chodoff, Friedman, and Hamburg (1964) found that the parents of children with leukemia blamed themselves rather than believing in the uncontrollability of the world. In the terms used in this paper, Wortman and Brehm (1975) hypothesize that the self-blame allows the individual to retain some sense of power in the situation by asserting responsibility for it.

This analysis suggests a possible explanation for a paradox posed by Abramson and Sackeim (1977). Whereas the learned helplessness model of depression proposes a belief in the independence of responses and outcomes, many researchers including Beck (1967, 1976) point out the importance of self-blame in depression. These two aspects of depression seem to be incompatible. However, they are incompatible only if depressives are wholly logical. Even "normals" do not act in an entirely logical fashion (e.g., Ross, 1977; Tversky & Kahneman, 1974), and Beck (1976) proposes that neurotics have even more distorting thinking patterns than nonneurotics. Both perceived uncontrollability and self-blame could exist side by side if the individual perceives a lack of power but prefers the self-attribution of responsibility to a full acceptance of helplessness.

It is interesting in light of the complex issues surrounding depression that there are methods that show great promise for treating it, such as cognitive therapy (e.g., Rush, Beck, Kovacs, & Hollon, 1977). Phobias, another disorder involving deviant beliefs about control, also can be successfully treated by techniques such as participant modeling (Bandura, 1976). Treatment of paranoid schizophrenia, on the other hand, has been less spectacularly successful (May, 1975). In the next section, disorders involving a deficit in skills or regulation are discussed. Here, too, there is great variability in success of treatment.

Deficits or Perceived Deficits
in Skills or Regulation

The second type of deviance from norms about perceived control is not wholly orthogonal to the first. Deficits or perceived deficits may involve deviant beliefs. For example, the overlap with the first category can be clearly seen in the case of phobias. To the extent that phobias involve a mistaken perception of lack of self-efficacy (Bandura, 1977a) or a mistaken belief regarding the power of the feared object, they belong in the first category. But in some cases there is an informational deficit that can be called a skills deficiency. Phobias for small animals, for example, often involve a lack of information on how to handle them. Treatment such as participant modeling (Bandura, 1976) can be seen as instruction and skill rehearsal. Sexual dysfunctions can also be conceived of as partly a deficit in skills, although the influence of expectations regarding control of sexual response is clearly significant as well. Recently developed treatments for disorders such as orgasmic dysfunction in women have been remarkably successful (e.g., Masters & Johnson, 1970). These treatments appear to operate by training skills, by conveying information, and by altering beliefs regarding sexual response and its control.

Treatment for the remainder of the disorders that are discussed in this section has not been as unequivocally successful. Obsessive-compulsive neurosis is one of the most puzzling of the behavior disorders. Obsessive ruminations can be conceived of at least partially as a deficit in perceived self-regulation. The ruminations consist of unwanted, intrusive, and repetitive thoughts regarding doubts and impulses that are abhorrent to the individual. For example, typical obsessions are repetitive doubts about whether the gas is turned off or the temptation to murder a family member. The phenomenology is of being controlled by the intrusive thoughts. Persons labeled as obsessive-compulsive fear that they cannot restrain themselves from performing unwanted acts and/or often experience great anxiety when prevented from executing their rituals. Theories on the source of the disorder range from organic defect to anal fixation to learning history (Nemiah, 1975). Treatments such as psychoanalysis or thought stopping do not stand out in their promise of efficacy (e.g., Mahoney, 1974).

In the case of addictive behaviors and obesity, some recently devised treatment procedures do show promise. Nevertheless, these disorders of regulation have also been resistent to theoretical explanation or consistent therapeutic success. Whereas obesity has been traditionally seen as a lack of restraint in the sense of willpower, more recent formulations portray it as a lack of skills in self-management of physical activity and eating behavior

(Mahoney & Mahoney, 1976). Although training in self-control techniques is a promising therapy for obesity, evidence for long-term success is not yet strong (Mahoney & Arnkoff, 1978).

Alcoholism is defined in part by the individual perceiving that drinking is out of control (Nathan, 1976). Control here again refers to self-regulation or restraint. An interesting recent development in the treatment of alcoholism is the finding that some alcoholics can learn to drink moderately—a finding that is in opposition to the long-held assumption that one drink would render the alcoholic out of control (e.g., Sobell & Sobell, 1977). In the controlled drinking program, alcoholics are taught to discriminate blood alcohol levels, with positive and negative consequences for their success at drinking moderately. At least for some alcoholics, it appears that self-regulation can be taught. The self-perception that the individual is no longer "out of control" may be an important aspect of their success.

For the psychophysiological disorders such as hypertension and ulcer, the dysfunction may again be conceptualized at least partially as a disorder of self-regulation. Theories of psychophysiological disorders generally refer in one manner or another to stress being expressed physically. Selye (1956), for example, conceives of many of the disorders as the result of an imbalance in the body's reaction to stress. Perceived control over demands may be an important component in the psychophysiological disorders. Experimental evidence is available to the effect that a perceived lack of skills or power is correlated with physical symptoms. For example, Hokanson, DeGood, Forrest, and Brittain (1971) allowed some subjects to choose the time and duration of rest breaks during a task in which periodic shock was administered. Other subjects were given the same rest times but were not allowed to determine their timing or length. Subjects who had power over their rest had lower blood pressure during the task than subjects for whom the power resided in the experimenter.

Control is an issue not only in relation to environmental events but also in regard to the course of the psychophysiological disorder itself. It is commonly believed that actions taken by the individual such as relaxation and diet can result in improvement of the disorder. But even if power is perceived, the person may have the belief that he or she lacks the skills to self-regulate. Techniques such as biofeedback, with their elaborate equipment and training, may serve to persuade the individual that he or she has learned a skill for controlling the disorder.

In summary, several diverse disorders may be conceptualized at least partially as exhibiting a deficiency or perceived deficiency in skills or self-regulatory ability. Treatment may involve training in skills as well as persuasion that the individual is capable of controlling the behavior.

Inappropriate Assertions of Control

A deficit of control was hypothesized in the disorders just discussed. For some individuals, however, the behavior that leads to being labeled abnormal can itself be seen as an assertion of control. In the individual's perception of his or her life situation, the behavior may appear to be the most rational available. By social criteria, however, it is abnormal. Some of the most refractory disorders may be construed in this manner. Treatment may require a drastic "reframing" of the individual's life (Watzlawick, Weakland, & Fisch, 1974).

Psychological defenses, by definition, are examples of this type of control process. Defenses involve a distortion of reality as it is consensually agreed upon. Denial, for example, is a primitive type of defense in which the conflict is negated by the claim that it does not exist. Opinions vary as to whether defenses are an inevitable human psychological mechanism or whether the self-actualized individual can function without them (Jourard, 1974). Freud, for example, thought that just as conflict is unavoidable, so distortions of reality are inevitable. As Becker (1973) says in regard to neurosis, illusions or defenses allow the individual to assert control but at a high price.

In the case of the obsessive-compulsive neurotic, the price of control is rigid, stereotyped behaviors known as compulsions. Engaging in rituals relieves anxiety, apparently by restraining temptation, and so they allow the individual to feel in control. But the price is an exceedingly narrow range of options; if 3 hours of every day are consumed in rituals surrounding getting dressed, for example, the time for constructive activity is greatly reduced. Successful treatment for compulsions would seem to require not only the interruption of the ritualistic act but also a change in other behaviors or beliefs so that its function is no longer needed. For successful treatment, the obsessive-compulsive may need to perceive that rituals are no longer necessary for self-regulation.

In hysterical neurosis, Lefcourt (1973) has hypothesized that the "secondary gain" in the physical symptoms is that they allow the person to assert power over others. Physical disability is an acceptable escape from difficult interpersonal situations. The hysteric's "belle indifference" results from the gain in power. Symptoms are an acceptable trade-off for control. Successful treatment might again involve interrupting the system so that the symptoms are not necessary. The needs might be met with other coping mechanisms, or the hysteric's model of the world might be altered so that control is no longer equated with escape.

According to the double-bind theory of schizophrenia, the symptomatology of psychosis also serves the function of allowing the individual to assert control (Bateson, Jackson, Haley, & Weakland, 1956). The double bind is an impossible situation in which the individual must choose to respond to one of two conflicting messages, and either choice entails punishment for not choosing the other. For example, the child's mother may verbally express love while nonverbally communicating withdrawal. If the child responds to either, the other is violated. The response to the child can never be wholly positive.

The double-bind situation is similar to the research already described regarding power and stress in animal studies. As Averill (1973) summarizes the research, ambiguous or conflicting feedback is stressful. In the human case, according to the double-bind theory, the stage is set for schizophrenia if the conflict occurs repeatedly and if escape is forbidden. The child may perceive no option but to communicate in metaphor, a level on which the mother may "read in" what she wants. Such a move brings safety, according to the theory, and also a measure of power. It allows survival. The schizophrenic pathology arises when the metaphoric communication is so standard that the individual does not recognize it as metaphor. It follows from the double-bind position that successful therapy for schizophrenia may involve a dramatic reinterpretation of interpersonal communication, so that control can be maintained in a more adaptive fashion.

The disorders described in this section involve assertions of control that are reasonable maneuvers from the individual's perspective but deviant in the view of behavioral norms. The therapeutic goal is to intervene to change the individual's perceptions, his or her pathological model of the world.

SUMMARY

Our culture's ideological position on the issue of personal control is that the individual has extensive control over his or her life, with attendant responsibility. Control may be divided into the four components of skill, power, regulation, and restraint. An examination of these four components reflects the dual nature of control: freedom plus limitations. There is no objective source of validation for the "true" degree of personal control. Labels indicating that an individual's model of control is not in accord with reality therefore involve evaluating the individual in terms of social norms. Processes relating psychopathology and control include deviant beliefs about control, deficits in control skills, and an inappropriate assertion of control. The presenting symptomatology of a disorder may be related in a complex fashion to its meaning for the individual. Although uncovering the meaning may facilitate understanding of the disorder, it does not dictate in an obvious fashion a preferred treatment technique. It is apparent, however, that these procedures may be most effective when they alter the individual's "model" of the world (Arnkoff, in press).

REFERENCES

Abramson, L. Y., & Sackeim, H. A. A paradox in depression: Uncontrollability and self-blame. *Psychological Bulletin*, 1977, *84*, 838–851.

Arnkoff, D. B. Psychotherapy from the perspective of cognitive theory. In M. J. Mahoney (Ed.), *Cognition and clinical science*. New York: Plenum, in press.

Averill, J. R. Personal control over aversive stimuli and its relationship to stress. *Psychological Bulletin*, 1973, *80*, 286–303.

Bandura, A. Effecting change through participant modeling. In J. D. Krumboltz & C. E. Thoresen (Eds.), *Counseling methods*. New York: Holt, Rinehart & Winston, 1976.

Bandura, A. Self-efficacy: Towards a unifying theory of behavioral change. *Psychological Review*, 1977, *84*, 191–215. (a)

Bandura, A. *Social learning theory*. Englewood Cliffs, N.J.: Prentice-Hall, 1977. (b)

Bandura, A., & Adams, N. E. Analysis of self-efficacy theory of behavioral change. *Cognitive Therapy and Research*, 1977, *1*, 287–308.

Bandura, A., Adams, N. E., & Beyer, J. Cognitive processes mediating behavior change. *Journal of Personality and Social Psychology*, 1977, *35*, 125–139.

Bartley, W. W. III. *The retreat to commitment*. New York: Knopf, 1962.

Bateson, G., Jackson, D. D., Haley, J., & Weakland, J. Toward a theory of schizophrenia. *Behavioral Science*, 1956, *1*, 251–264.

Beck, A. T. *Depression: Clinical, experimental, and theoretical aspects*. New York: Harper & Row, 1967.

Beck, A. T. *Cognitive therapy and the emotional disorders*. New York: International Universities Press, 1976.

Becker, E. *The denial of death*. New York: Free Press, 1973.

Brady, J. V., Porter, R. W., Conrad, D. G., & Mason, J. W. Avoidance behavior and the development of gastroduodenal ulcers. *Journal of the Experimental Analysis of Behavior*, 1958, *1*, 69–72.

Brehm, J. W. *A theory of psychological reactance*. New York: Academic Press, 1966.

Brim, O. G., Jr. *The sense of personal control over one's life*. Paper presented at the meeting of the American Psychological Association, New Orleans, September 1974.

Chodoff, P., Friedman, S., & Hamburg, D. Stress defenses and coping behavior: Observations in parents of children with malignant disease. *American Journal of Psychiatry*, 1964, *120*, 743–749.

Colby, K. M. Appraisal of four psychological theories of paranoid phenomena. *Journal of Abnormal Psychology*, 1977, *86*, 54–59.

deCharms, R. *Personal causation: The internal affective determinants of behavior*. New York: Academic Press, 1968.

Faught, W. S., Colby, K. M., & Parkison, R. C. Inferences, affects, and intentions in a model of paranoia. *Cognitive Psychology*, 1977, *9*, 153–187.

Frank, J. D. *Persuasion and healing*. Baltimore: Johns Hopkins University Press, 1961.

Freud, S. Mourning and melancholia. In *The collective works of Sigmund Freud: The standard edition* (Vol. 14). London: Hogarth Press, 1957. (Originally published, 1917.)

Fromm, E. *Escape from freedom*. New York: Holt, Rinehart & Winston, 1941.

Glass, D. C., & Singer, J. E. *Stress and adaptation: Experimental studies of behavioral effects of exposure to aversive events*. New York: Academic Press, 1972.

Golin, S., Terrell, F., & Johnson, B. Depression and the delusion of control. *Journal of Abnormal Psychology*, 1977, *86*, 440–442.

Hokanson, J. E., DeGood, D. E., Forrest, M. S., & Brittain, T. M. Availability of avoidance behaviors in modulating vascular-stress responses. *Journal of Personality and Social Psychology*, 1971, *19*, 60–68.

Immergluck, L. Determinism-freedom in contemporary psychology: An ancient problem revisited. *American Psychologist*, 1964, *19*, 270–281.

Jourard, S. M. *Healthy personality*. New York: Macmillan, 1974.

Kelly, G. A. *The psychology of personal constructs*. New York: Norton, 1955.

Kreitler, H., & Kreitler, S. *Cognitive orientation and behavior*. New York: Springer, 1976.

Lefcourt, H. M. Recent developments in the study of locus of control. In B. A. Maher (Ed.), *Progress in experimental personality research* (Vol. 6). New York: Academic Press, 1972.

Lefcourt, H. M. The function of the illusions of control and freedom. *American Psychologist*, 1973, *28*, 417–425.

Lewinsohn, P. M. A behavioral approach to depression. In R. M. Friedman & M. M. Katz (Eds.), *The psychology of depression; Contemporary theory and research*. New York: Wiley, 1974.

Liddell, H. The role of vigilance in the development of animal neurons. In P. H. Hoch & J. Zubin (Eds.), *Anxiety*. New York: Grune & Stratton, 1950.

Mahoney, M. J. *Cognition and behavior modification*. Cambridge, Mass.: Ballinger, 1974.

Mahoney, M. J., & Arnkoff, D. B. Cognitive and self-control therapies. In S. L. Garfield & A. E. Bergin (Eds.), *Handbook of psychotherapy and behavior change*. New York: Wiley, 1978.

Mahoney, M. J., & Arnkoff, D. B. Self-management: Theory, research, and application. In O. F. Pomerleau & J. P. Brady (Eds.), *Behavioral medicine: Theory and practice*. Baltimore: Williams & Wilkins, in press.

Mahoney, M. J., Kazdin, A. E., & Lesswing, N. J. Behavior modification: Delusion or deliverance? In C. M. Franks & G. T. Wilson (Eds.), *Annual review of behavior therapy: Theory and practice* (Vol. 2). New York: Brunner/Mazel, 1974.

Mahoney, M. J., & Mahoney, K. *Permanent weight control*. New York: Norton, 1976.

Maier, S. F., & Seligman, M. E. P. Learned helplessness: Theory and evidence. *Journal of Experimental Psychology: General*, 1976, *105*, 3–46.

Mandler, G. *Mind and emotion*. New York: Wiley, 1975.

Masters, W. H., & Johnson, V. E. *Human sexual inadequacy*. Boston: Little, Brown, 1970.

May, P. R. A. Schizophrenia: Evaluation of treatment methods. In A. M. Freedman, H. I. Kaplan, & B. J. Sadock (Eds.), *Comprehensive textbook of psychiatry* (2nd ed., Vol. 1). Baltimore: Williams & Wilkins, 1975.

McKeon, R. The development and the significance of the concept of responsibility. *Revue Internationale de Philosophie*, 1957, *11*, 3–32.

Nathan, P. E. Alcoholism. In H. Leitenberg (Ed.), *Handbook of behavior modification and behavior therapy*. Englewood Cliffs, N. J.: Prentice-Hall, 1976.

Nemiah, J. C. Obsessive-compulsive neurosis. In A. M. Freedman, H. I. Kaplan, & B. J. Sadock (Eds.), *Comprehensive textbook of psychiatry* (2nd ed., Vol. 1). Baltimore: Williams & Wilkins, 1975.

Perlmuter, L. C., & Monty, R. A. The importance of perceived control: Fact or fantasy? *American Scientist*, 1977, *65*, 759–765.

Rehm, L. P. A self-control model of depression. *Behavior Therapy*, 1977, *8*, 787–804.

Ross, L. The intuitive psychologist and his shortcomings: Distortions in the attribution process. In L. Berkowitz (Ed.), *Advances in experimental social psychology* (Vol. 10). New York: Academic Press, 1977.

Rotter, J. B. Generalized expectancies for internal versus external control of reinforcement. *Psychological Monographs*, 1966, *80* (1, Whole No. 609).

Rotter, J. B., Chance, J. E., & Phares, E. J. *Applications of a social learning theory of personality*. New York: Holt, Rinehart & Winston, 1972.

Rush, A. J., Beck, A. T., Kovacs, M., & Hollon, S. Comparative efficacy of cognitive therapy and pharmacotherapy in the treatment of depressed outpatients. *Cognitive Therapy and Research*, 1977, *1*, 17–37.

Scheff, T. J. *Being mentally ill: A sociological theory.* Chicago: Aldine, 1966.

Schmauk, F. J. Punishment, arousal, and avoidance learning in sociopaths. *Journal of Abnormal Psychology,* 1970, *76,* 443-453.

Schulz, R. Some life and death consequences of perceived control. In J. S. Carrol & J. W. Payne (Eds.), *Cognition and social behavior.* Hillsdale, N.J.: Lawrence Erlbaum Associates, 1976.

Seligman, M. E. P. *Helplessness: On depression, development, and death.* San Francisco: Freeman, 1975.

Selye, H. *The stress of life.* New York: McGraw-Hill, 1956.

Shapiro, D. *Neurotic styles.* New York: Basic Books, 1965.

Sobell, M. B., & Sobell, L. C. *Behavioral treatment of alcohol problems.* New York: Plenum, 1977.

Steiner, I. D. Perceived freedom. In L. Berkowitz (Ed.), *Advances in experimental social psychology* (Vol. 5). New York: Academic Press, 1970.

Thoresen, C. E., & Mahoney, M. J. *Behavioral self-control.* New York: Holt, Rinehart & Winston, 1974.

Tversky, A., & Kahneman, D. Judgment under uncertainty: Heuristics and biases. *Science,* 1974, *185,* 1124-1131.

Watzlawick, P., Weakland, J. H., & Fisch, R. *Change: Principles of problem formation and problem resolution.* New York: Norton, 1974.

Weiss, J. M. Effects of coping behavior in different warning signal conditions on stress pathology in rats. *Journal of Comparative and Physiological Psychology,* 1971, *77,* 1-13.

White, R. W. Motivation reconsidered: The concept of competence. *Psychological Review,* 1959, *66,* 297-333.

Wortman, C. B., & Brehm, J. W. Responses to uncontrollable outcomes: An integration of reactance theory and the learned helplessness model. In L. Berkowitz (Ed.), *Advances in experimental social psychology* (Vol. 8). New York: Academic Press, 1975.

13

Perceived Control and the Theory and Practice of Behavior Therapy

G. Terence Wilson
Rutgers University

To those who identify therapy with the strict behavioristic philosophy of applied behavior analysis (cf. Baer, Wolf, & Risley, 1968), a concern with such an unabashedly cognitive construct as *perceived* control might appear misplaced. However, even a cursory survey of the clinical practice of behavior therapy with adults suggests that it is viewed as an important phenomenon. The notion of perceived control and its implications for therapeutic progress seem to crop up here, there, and everywhere. Some clinical illustrations may be mentioned.

ILLUSTRATIONS FROM CLINICAL PRACTICE

Training in progressive relaxation is a basic behavioral technique that is a component part of other procedures (e.g., systematic desensitization) and is a useful anxiety-reducing method in its own right (Bernstein & Borkovec, 1973). Many a novice behavior therapist has experienced difficulty in teaching clients to relax because of the clients' apprehension about the sense of losing personal control. In fact, it is often this type of client for whom relaxation training is especially indicated. Appropriate therapeutic groundwork is necessary in order to overcome this fear and to facilitate relaxation training. Clients may have to be reassured that in the ultimate analysis, they are always in control. Relaxation training is not a form of therapeutic influence that is imposed on clients but a self-regulated process that clients *choose* to engage in. Clients are given the rationale that they are actually acquiring greater personal control over their emotions by deliberately letting go and relaxing themselves. The frequent result of this therapeutic intervention is enhanced perceived control on the part of clients and greater willingness to confront anxiety-eliciting sources of their problems.

Cognitive restructuring is a widely used technique in behavior therapy. In essence, the procedure involves assisting clients to identify and then modify negative thought patterns or self-statements that are assumed to be the cause of emotional disturbance (e.g., Beck, 1976; Ellis, 1970; Meichenbaum, 1977). The assumption that negative thought patterns are responsible for psychological disorders is far from established (cf. Wilson & O'Leary, in press). However, although they acknowledge an absence of hard data that would support such an assumption, Goldfried and Davison (1976) nonetheless advocate the therapeutic use of the rationale and methods of cognitive restructuring. Undoubtedly echoing the sentiments of other behavioral practitioners, the justification they offer is "clinical and pragmatic: it may be that *believing* that one's negative self-statements cause emotional turmoil can be useful in helping people change their feelings [p. 163]." Moreover, an examination of the content of the sort of self-statements or internal dialogues behavior therapists tend to encourage in their clients reveals an overwhelming preponderance of statements emphasizing both perceived and actual personal control, mastery, and coping ability in the face of threatening circumstances. For example, in his stress inoculation therapy for treating anger disorders, Novaco (1977) has clients actively rehearse such coping self-statements as "This could be a rough situation, but I know how to deal with it" and "As long as I keep my cool, *I'm* in control of the situation."

Yet another example of the role of perceived control in clinical practice can be drawn from a recent case of mine involving the treatment of an exhibitionist. Not atypical of such cases, the client was convinced that his acts of exposure were caused by an involuntary drive over which he had no control. A fundamental facet of treatment consisted of demonstrating to the client through a painstaking behavioral assessment that the automaticity of his exposures was only apparent. Intensive interviewing was used as a means of indicating how he contributed directly to his behavior by attending to inappropriate stimuli, rehearsing specific thoughts, and embellishing deviant fantasies related to exposure. Since critical precursors in the behavioral chain leading to ultimate exposure were *self*-generated, it was suggested that he could engage in alternative cognitive activities and develop self-regulatory skills that would enable him to control any exhibitionistic urges. Throughout assessment and subsequent treatment, his perceived control of his actions was fostered and his role as an active agent of his own behavioral change emphasized. The effect of such a strategy was to revive hope of therapeutic success in a client who, as a result of numerous previous treatment failures, had come to accept the diagnosis that he was incorrigible. And with hope came renewed motivation, without which any treatment program is doomed to failure and which eventually powered his acquisition of a demonstrably effective capacity to control his hitherto unchecked deviant behavior. As Davison (1969) has observed, regardless of its ultimate validity, this sort of social learning conceptualization of the maintenance and modification of deviant behavior may have therapeutic properties in encouraging realistic hope of personal control and ultimate treatment success.

As a final clinical example, I wish to draw attention to the significance of perceived control in an infrequently discussed but vitally important aspect of behavior therapy, namely client "resistance" or "countercontrol." A great deal of behavior therapy involves instructing clients to carry out homework assignments—practice relaxation, rehearse specific self-statements, engage in assertive behavior, self-monitor daily caloric intake, and so on. In the event that the client fails to comply with these requests, treatment cannot be successful. Contrary to some opponents and proponents of behavior modification alike, the much vaunted notion of unilateral therapist control over the client is largely a myth (Bandura, 1977b; Wilson & Evans, 1977). The image of the behavior therapist as "a social reinforcement machine" or "behavioral engineer" who automatically shapes desired responses in otherwise passive clients is manifestly false. Although the therapist's influence is considerable, he or she is not a controller but a consultant who requires the client's active participation in the treatment process.

The reasons for lack of client compliance with the therapist's requests (i.e., "countercontrol") are far from clearly understood. Current conceptual analyses of the lack of compliance and clinical strategies for combating it are discussed by Davison (1973) and by Wilson and Evans (1976, 1977). Suffice it to note here that many clients react negatively or are unresponsive to conspicuous attempts at external control. Efforts to instigate desired behavior by the use of externally regulated methods such as therapist-administered contingency contracts are frequently unsuccessful for this reason. Deliberately fostering the client's perceived control in the therapeutic process, perhaps by providing a *choice* between therapeutic prescriptions, is one way of avoiding resistance to external direction (Mahoney, 1974). To the extent that clients perceive themselves as having *choice*, it is possible that what Brehm (1966) has called psychological reactance is reduced. Reactance is assumed to be aroused when individuals perceive their choices as being restricted or threatened by an external authority. In a related proposition, Johnson and Matross (1977) argue that clients will be less resistant to influence they attribute as deriving from themselves than from the therapist. Fortunately, this appears to be consistent with the recent emphasis in behavior therapy on self-control of behavior change.

ATTRIBUTION THEORY, ILLUSORY CONTROL,
AND BEHAVIOR THERAPY

From its beginnings in the late 1950s to the late 1960s, behavior therapy was rooted in the principles and procedures of the animal conditioning laboratory. Serious attention was first focused on the cognitive construct of *perceived* control when attribution theorists attempted to eliminate avoidance behavior by directly altering the cognitive labeling of emotional arousal. The logic and ultimate fate of this extrapolation from attribution theory to clinical treatment can be summarized by an analysis of the first and perhaps most important experiment in this tradition by Valins and Ray (1967).

Valins and Ray (1967) hypothesized that if phobic subjects were led to *believe* that they were resting nonfearfully in the presence of previously anxiety-eliciting stimuli, irrespective of whether or not they experienced actual autonomic arousal, they would relabel those phobic stimuli as nonthreatening and subsequently behave less fearfully. To test this possibility, subjects who had indicated that they were fearful of snakes were alternately exposed either to the sight of a snake or slides of the word *shock* that were paired with an uncomfortable but not painful shock. Experimental subjects heard what they were erroneously led to believe was their heart rate increasing noticeably to the shock slides but not to the snake presentations. Control subjects heard the same sounds but were told that they were extraneous noise. Experimental subjects showed a greater amount of posttreatment approach behavior toward the snake than control subjects.

Unfortunately, subsequent methodologically superior studies failed to replicate these results (cf. Davison & Wilson, 1973). Specifically, it was shown that false feedback of a lack of autonomic arousal does not result in cognitive relabeling of arousal unless that arousal is somewhat ambiguous and weak. Intense anxiety of the sort experienced by phobic individuals cannot be overcome by artificially induced cognitions of perceived control unsupported by reality-based corrective learning experiences (Borkovec, 1973; Kent, Wilson, & Nelson, 1972; Rosen, Rosen, & Reid, 1972). The same conclusion holds for those studies on the misattribution of emotional arousal in which subjects are deceived into attributing their arousal to a nonemotional source (e.g., Ross, Rodin, & Zimbardo, 1969). This sort of practice of deceptive labeling is inappropriate and ineffective in the treatment of clients with high anxiety (Singerman, Borkovec, & Baron, 1976).

Perceived Versus Actual Control

The obvious lesson that was laboriously learned from the failure of the so-called attribution therapy just described is that debilitating fears or phobic disorders cannot be eliminated solely on the basis of nonveridical cognitive relabeling. This finding has to be borne in mind in evaluating the practical significance of much of the laboratory research on the effects of perceived or illusory control.

In general, this body of research has been interpreted to indicate that the illusion or expectation of control is effective in reducing behavioral and psychophysiological stress reactions to aversive circumstances (Averill, 1973; Jones, 1977). Consider, for example, the frequently cited Glass and Singer (1972) study on the role of controllability in the attenuation of stress. In what was described as an analog investigation of urban stress, the effects of an aversive noise on problem solving and proofreading were investigated under three experimental conditions: (1) the *actual control* group members were able to terminate the noise by pressing a button; (2) the *perceived control* group members were told that they had the same option but were encouraged not to because their physiological adaptation was allegedly being measured; and (3) a *yoked control* group was in a circumstance in which the noise was uncontrollable. Subjects in the perceived control group performed as well as those in the actual control group, and both were superior to the group for whom the noise was uncontrollable. This latter group fared more poorly in problem solving and proofreading and experienced the identical noise as more aversive.

What studies such as this do not address are the consequences of reality testing and the subjects' discovery that their perceived control is illusory. What would have happened had Glass and Singer's (1972) subjects tried to terminate the noise by ineffectually pressing the button? Would they have performed like the yoked control group, or might their performance not have deteriorated even more than that of those subjects who knew that the noise was uncontrollable from the outset? I am suggesting that such a discovery might result in something akin to a "negative rebound effect." Averill (1973) makes an important point in this connection. He wisely cautions that:

> Most laboratory studies have allowed subjects only arbitrary and artificial responses (e.g., pressing a button)... in order to prevent or terminate a noxious stimulus. Although such responses may be convenient from the experimenter's point of view, they probably have little inherent significance for the subject. This fact is bound to influence the extent to which many laboratory studies of personal control can be generalized to real-life situations [p. 301].

One may speculate that the "negative rebound effect" just alluded to is more likely, the more realistic the aversive circumstances are that the subject is confronted with and the more personally significant the illusory control is that subjects perceive themselves to have.

Expectations of control can be assumed to function like other therapeutic expectations. They comprise a double-edged sword. On one hand, positive expectations appear to facilitate outcome; on the other hand, if subsequent experience is not consonant with the expectations the therapist has created and success does not immediately follow, the client may see in this disconfirmation of expectations yet another affirmation of the hopelessness of his or her plight (Wilson & Evans, 1976).

PERCEIVED CONTROL:
A SOCIAL LEARNING ANALYSIS

The fact that deceptive labeling designed to create the illusion of personal control has an insignificant effect on relevant behavior in the natural situation hardly implies that cognitive appraisal of one's actions is unimportant in behavioral change. Abundant evidence exists demonstrating the influential role of cognitive factors in human behavior and need not be discussed here (Mahoney, 1974, and in press). What is required is a conceptual framework that directly ties cognitive mediating processes to observable action. Behavior is a function of interdependent influence processes, and cognitions do not operate independently (Bandura, 1977b). Furthermore, a complete analysis of the cognitive control of behavior necessitates that the determinants of internal mediating processes be spelled out. In the present context, a theoretical model is needed that relates perceived control to actual control in the maintenance and modification of problem behaviors. Elsewhere, I have suggested that Bandura's (1977a) social learning framework in general, and self-efficacy theory in particular, provide one such heuristic approach (Wilson, 1978b, and in press). The remainder of this paper indicates how this social learning approach might be usefully applied to the analysis of personal control as it affects the generalization and maintenance of treatment-produced change.

SELF-EFFICACY: TOWARD AN INTEGRATIVE
THEORY OF PERSONAL CONTROL

In this theory Bandura (1977a) proposes that psychological treatment methods are effective because they increase the client's expectations of *personal efficacy*. Efficacy expectations reflect the individual's subjective estimate that he or she has the capacity to cope successfully with a threatening situation. They are differentiated from *outcome expectations*, which are defined as the client's belief that a particular action will result in a certain outcome.

Efficacy expectations are hypothesized to play a major part in the initiation, generalization, and maintenance of coping behavior. Take the agoraphobic client, for example, who avoids public situations in which she fears she will become anxious, losing personal control and the ability to cope. To the extent that therapy strengthens or restores efficacy expectations, it is predicted that the client will cease avoiding and confront the previously feared situations. Efficacy expectations are based on four major sources of information: behavioral performance (e.g., participant modeling), vicarious experience (e.g., symbolic modeling), physiological arousal (e.g., systematic desensitization), and verbal persuasion (e.g., traditional psychotherapy).

In an experimental test of self-efficacy theory, snake-phobic subjects received treatments designed to create differential levels of efficacy expectations and relate them to behavioral change (Bandura, Adams, & Beyer, 1977). The three treatment methods were participant modeling, symbolic modeling, and a no-treatment control group. Predictably, participant modeling produced significantly stronger efficacy expectations of coping successfully with the phobic object and more generalized behavioral changes than symbolic modeling. The latter resulted in greater expectations of personal efficacy and behavioral change than the control condition. The degree of behavioral change was closely related to an increase in efficacy expectations. The greater the increase in self-efficacy, the greater the reduction in phobic behavior. Consistent with the theory, increases in efficacy expectations were predictive of behavioral change irrespective of whether they were induced by participant or symbolic modeling methods.

Generalization of Behavioral Change

Expectations of self-efficacy also generalize to other situations and help explain the process of generalized behavioral improvement. In the Bandura et al. (1977) study, for example, generalization of treatment effects was assessed at posttreatment by exposing subjects to snakes that were either similar or dissimilar to the snake used in treatment. Strength of efficacy expectations predicted subsequent approach behavior toward similar and dissimilar snakes equally well. Subjects' past behavioral performance during treatment successfully predicted posttreatment approach behavior toward the similar but not the dissimilar snake. This predictive superiority of efficacy expectations over simple overt past behavior shows that treatment-produced improvement cannot be explained solely on the basis of specific behavioral cues or stimulus similarity but is attributable to enhanced personal control or efficacy.

Traditionally, generalized behavioral change has been explained on the basis of the learning principles of stimulus and response generalization. These well-known principles were derived from animal conditioning research in the laboratory and have been developed into a technology for generalization in applied behavior analysis (Stokes & Baer, 1977). However, it has always been difficult to account adequately for the generalization of behavior change in one specific situation to radically different situations solely on the basis of stimulus and response similarity. For example, Bandura, Jeffery, and Gajdos (1975) showed that after snake-phobic subjects had been successfully treated using participant modeling, they coped more effectively with fears of other animals as well as their social anxieties. This is an example of *mediated generalization*. Bandura (1977a) suggests that the mediating process in this type of generalization is an increase in self-efficacy. As one of the subjects in the Bandura et al. (1975) study said, "The biggest benefit to me of the successfulness of the treatment was the feeling that if I could like snakes, I could lick anything. It gave me the confidence to tackle, also successfully, some personal stuff [pp. 141–152]."

Efficacy expectations are not automatically increased as a result of the successful behavioral performance of a formerly threatening task. Self-attribution of increased personal mastery is a necessary element in the development of strong self-efficacy. Unlike earlier extrapolations from attribution theory, however, successful self-attribution of therapeutic change does not demand an ambiguously structured treatment process or preclude the use of powerful therapeutic techniques. In the treatment of phobic clients with participant modeling, for example, gradually withdrawing the supportive presence of the therapist and ensuring that the client engages in self-directed rehearsal of nonfearful approach behavior results in the attribution of treatment change to a sense of personal competence that generalizes to other situations (Bandura et al., 1975). Since most forms of contemporary behavioral treatment emphasize self-regulatory processes, structuring the appropriate attributional set for generalized behavior change poses little problem.

In its present form, self-efficacy theory does not enable one to make specific predictions about generalization following particular treatment interventions. It simply asserts that changes in fears that appear to be unrelated to the target or treated fear depend in some way on increments in efficacy expectations. An enhanced sense of personal efficacy is assumed to be a necessary but not always a sufficient condition for the sort of quantum leap in generalization that is frequently observed following a key therapeutic event. The precise manner in which this occurs and the boundary conditions of the generalized changes produced by alterations in self-efficacy remain to be investigated.

Maintenance of Treatment-Produced Change

According to self-efficacy theory, the strength of efficacy expectations is a major determinant of clients' persistence in active coping behavior when faced with the "slings and arrows of outrageous fortune." As such, this theoretical tenet has critically important implications for the analysis of the phenomenon of "relapse," a major problem for all forms of psychological treatment including behavior therapy. Unquestionably, the relative absence of compelling outcome data indicating the long-term efficacy of behavioral methods constitutes a major inadequacy in the behavior therapy literature (Kazdin & Wilson, 1978). The relevance of self-efficacy theory to maintenance may be illustrated by reference to a clinical disorder such as alcoholism.

Alcoholism would seem to be a particularly appropriate clinical disorder to analyze in terms of expectations of personal control or efficacy. One reason is that it is a form of addictive behavior that is notorious for a high relapse rate. Another reason is that what proponents of the disease model of alcoholism refer to as "loss of control" is usually held to be a defining feature of alcoholism (Jellinek, 1960):

> Recovered alcoholics in Alcoholics Anonymous speak of "loss of control" to denote that stage in the development of their drinking history when the ingestion of one alcoholic drink sets up a chain reaction so that they are unable to adhere to their intention to "have one or two drinks only" but continue to ingest more and more—often with quite some difficulty and disgust—contrary to their volition [p. 41].

Yet a third reason for taking a closer look at alcoholism is that drawing from McClelland's (1972) theory, Marlatt (1976) has proposed that alcohol acts to increase the drinker's sense of perceived power or control. With obvious relevance to an explanation of alcohol abuse, Marlatt (1978) goes on to suggest that "the attractiveness of alcohol as a coping strategy would increase in situations where the individual feels powerless or otherwise lacking in personal control [p. 294]."

It is not difficult to understand the wide acceptance of the "loss of control" construct among those working in the area of alcohol use and abuse. The sudden, often devastating return to uncontrollable drinking by a former alcoholic who had been abstinent for a period of months or even years is a relatively common and perplexing occurrence. The appeal to a physiological addictive process that is triggered by a single drink and that unleashes a bout of involuntary, compulsive drinking filled an explanatory void. Over the past few years, however, a number of lines of experimental evidence have seriously challenged the validity of the disease model of alcoholism and the notion of "loss of control" as a physiologically based addictive process in the speculative sense (e.g., Jellinek, 1960; Nathan & Marlatt, 1978; Pomerleau, Pertschuk, & Stinnet, 1976). Alternative psychological interpretations of the clinical phenomena that the "loss of control" construct was invoked to explain have recently been put forward by Marlatt (1978) and Wilson (1978a).

In most forms of lay and professional treatment, the alcoholic is virtually inculcated in the belief of suffering from an irreversible disease. The alcoholic learns that he or she is qualitatively different from nonalcoholics and uniquely vulnerable to the addictive effects of alcohol, and that recovery hinges upon lifelong abstinence. In terms of self-efficacy theory, the alcoholic's efficacy expectations about coping with alcohol are reduced to zero. Outcome expectations are created stressing the certainty of a return to uncontrollable alcohol abuse in the event of a transgression from the rigid code of abstinence. In short, it can be argued that a self-defeating, self-fulfilling prophecy is developed—first drink, then drunk! Furthermore, it is the rare treatment program that systematically equips the alcoholic client with improved self-regulatory and social skills with which to resist the innumerable social pressures or to cope with the sources of anxiety or frustration that are often associated with relapse. This combination of factors leaves the alcoholic extremely vulnerable to the potentially deleterious effects of a drinking transgression. The significance of this lies in the rarely discussed and often vehemently denied fact that a majority of alcoholics seen in abstinence-oriented therapy, including those who are successfully treated, engage in sporadic posttreatment drinking (cf. Armor, Polich, & Stambul, 1978; Orford, Oppenheimer, & Edwards, 1976).

Thus the alcoholic is likely to take a drink or two following therapy regardless of the customary treatment goal of total abstinence. It is suggested here that it is not so much the actual ingestion of alcohol during the posttreatment abstinence period that may be responsible for relapse but the meaning that the act of drinking has for the client. Given the likely deficits in specific behavioral coping strategies, a drastically diminished sense of personal mastery, and outcome expectations that predict relapse, the client may well react to transgression by interpreting his or her drinking as further proof of a lack of personal control. Lacking the necessary efficacy expectations, the client may fail to persist in the attempt to remain sober despite the various psychological and environmental pressures that seem to invite a return to drinking and may "blow" the entire treatment program.

It follows from this theoretical analysis that durable treatment effects will be a function of the development of strong efficacy expectations with respect to coping with alcohol-related situations in the posttreatment period. A realistic sense of personal efficacy that is based on authentic personal control would also eliminate or reduce alcohol's hypothesized reinforcing valence of artificially boosting perceived power or control (Marlatt, 1976). As I have discussed elsewhere (Wilson, 1978a), this is most likely to be accomplished using performance-based treatment methods similar to those that have yielded such encouraging success in the treatment of phobias (Bandura, 1977a; Leitenberg, 1976) and obsessive-compulsive disorders (Rachman & Hodgson, in press). More controversially, such a treatment strategy would include an explicit emphasis on teaching the client to cope with the effects of posttreatment transgression. In other words, treatment would involve exposing the client to specific high-risk stimuli that were associated with alcohol abuse in his or her natural environment. The consumption of alcohol under carefully structured circumstances would be one source of high-risk stimulation. Marlatt (1978) has referred to such a treatment as a "programmed relapse." Its purpose is to minimize the negative consequences of any posttreatment drinking mishap and to ensure that the client returns to the treatment program strictures as rapidly as possible.

The foregoing analysis has assumed that the goal of treatment is total abstinence. Treatment directed toward abstinence need not develop expectations of personal control (or the lack thereof) that inadvertently maximize the self-defeating consequences of posttreatment program violations. Of course, this analysis also applies to treatment methods that have controlled drinking as their goal. It should also be noted that self-efficacy theory is clearly not the only theoretical framework that generates recommendations of the sort discussed here aimed at facilitating the maintenance of treatment-produced sobriety. Marlatt (1978), for example, derived cognitive maintenance strategies essentially the same as those discussed here on the basis of cognitive dissonance and attribution theory. What is important is the extension to the problem of maintenance of sobriety that places a primary emphasis on actual control of drinking (e.g., self-regulatory skills) complemented by cognitive appraisals of perceived control (e.g., efficacy expectations). The application of these proposals to the problems of alcohol abuse should provide testing ground for competing psychological theories as well as helping to break down the conceptual insularity that has surrounded the field of alcoholism.

The preceding analysis is speculative, and the necessary tests of the different predictions that may be derived from the analysis have yet to be conducted. Few existing studies bear directly on the hypothesized role of personal efficacy in the maintenance of treatment-produced outcomes. In a study of the effects of relaxation methods on alcohol consumption in heavy drinkers, Marlatt and Marques (1977) found no differences among meditation, progressive relaxation, or an attention-placebo condition ("sitting quietly for 20 minutes twice a day"). All three conditions, however, produced a significantly greater decrease in alcohol consumption than no treatment. The three treatment conditions were associated with a shift toward internal locus of control on the Rotter (1966) scale, whereas the no-treatment control group showed no change. In interpreting these findings, Marlatt and Marques (1977) argue that the locus-of-control changes indicate an increase in perceived control that mediated a decrease in drinking.

Caution must be exercised in interpreting these data. First, an alternative explanation in terms of demand characteristics cannot be ruled out. Second, as the authors themselves observe, the relationship between internal locus-of-control scores and alcohol consumption is only correlational; cause cannot be determined. It is quite plausible that subjects who reduced their alcohol consumption felt more in control as a consequence. Third, the follow-up assessment in this study was only 7 weeks, too short a period to permit an acceptable test of the influence of perceived control on maintenance. Fourth, findings from the behavioral treatment of obesity consistently show that the internal–external locus-of-control scores do *not* predict weight loss (e.g., Tobias & MacDonald, 1977; Weiss, 1977). It is not clear why the situation should be any different for problem drinking. Finally, it is questionable whether an increase in internality on the Rotter scale can be accurately interpreted as an increase in perceived power or control. In this connection, more specific measures of self-efficacy—a construct that is directly related to perceived control—might provide a better test of the hypothesized relationship between perceived control and the effective treatment of addictive behaviors like alcoholism and obesity.

COGNITIVE PROCESSING
AND PERCEIVED EFFICACY

A major emphasis of this paper is that perceived control will be therapeutic only to the extent that it is at least partly based on actual control of previously threatening situations. This is one reason why performance-based treatment methods are more effective than those that rely on symbolic procedures. Performance-based methods provide the most dependable source of information about actual control. Control that is merely perceived will have transitory effects on behavior at best.

However, there is no one-to-one relationship between actual and perceived control. Behavioral competence does not necessarily ensure high self-efficacy or perceived control. A fairly common example is the depressed client who appears to be functioning competently to outside observers but who suffers from overwhelming feelings of inadequacy and helplessness. In terms of self-efficacy theory, the cognitive processing of efficacy information from performance is distorted. Or as Seligman (1975) has suggested, the client believes that significant life events are beyond personal control—that he or she is helpless. In this case, perceived control is desynchronous with actual or potential control.

Happily, although this cognitive processing of efficacy and outcome information is as yet poorly understood, Beck (1976) has developed a cognitive-behavioral treatment method that is demonstrably effective in reducing depression (e.g., Rush, Beck, Kovacs, & Hollon, 1977). This form of therapy can be viewed as restoring greater synchrony between perceived and actual control of significant life events. Essentially, the method involves the skillful use of the client's own behavioral efforts to modify negative thought patterns. In Socratic fashion, clients are encouraged to prove to themselves the inaccuracy and inappropriateness of their negative cognitions. Future research on this interdependency between cognitive and behavioral change processes—or, in the present context, between perceived and actual control—should have important implications for the understanding and treatment of a wide variety of clincial disorders.

ACKNOWLEDGMENT

Preparation of this paper was assisted in part by NIAAA Grant No. 00259-05.

REFERENCES

Armor, D. J., Polich, J. M., & Stambul, H. B. *Alcoholism and treatment.* New York: Wiley, 1978.

Averill, J. R. Personal control over aversive stimuli and its relationship to stress. *Psychological Bulletin,* 1973, *80,* 286–303.

Baer, D. M., Wolf, M. M., & Risley, T. R. Some current dimensions of applied behavior analysis. *Journal of Applied Behavior Analysis,* 1968, *1,* 91–97.

Bandura, A. Self-efficacy: Toward a unifying theory of behavioral change. *Psychological Review,* 1977, *84,* 191–215. (a)

Bandura, A. *Social learning theory.* Englewood Cliffs, N.J.: Prentice-Hall, 1977. (b)

Bandura, A., Adams, N. E., & Beyer, J. Cognitive processes mediating behavioral change. *Journal of Personality and Social Psychology,* 1977, *35,* 125–139.

Bandura, A., Jeffery, R. W., & Gajdos, E. Generalizing change through participant modeling with self-directed mastery. *Behaviour Research and Therapy,* 1975, *13,* 141–152.

Beck, A. T. *Cognitive therapy and the emotional disorders.* New York: International Universities Press, 1976.

Bernstein, D. A., & Borkovec, T. D. *Progressive relaxation training.* Champaign, Ill.: Research Press, 1973.

Borkovec, T. D. The role of expectancy and physiological feedback in fear research: A review with special reference to subject characteristics. *Behavior Therapy,* 1973, *4,* 491–505.

Brehm, J. W. *A theory of psychological reactance.* New York: Academic Press, 1966.

Davison, G. C. Appraisal of behavior modification techniques with adults in institutional settings. In C. M. Franks (Ed.), *Behavior therapy: Appraisal and status.* New York: McGraw-Hill, 1969.

Davison, G. C. Counter-control in behavior modification. In L. A. Hammerlynck, L. C. Handy, & E. J. Mash (Eds.), *Behavior change: Methodology, concepts, practice.* Champaign, Ill.: Research Press, 1973.

Davison, G. C., & Wilson, G. T. Processes of fear-reduction in systematic desensitization: Cognitive and social reinforcement factors in humans. *Behavior Therapy,* 1973, *4,* 1–21.

Ellis, A. *The essence of rational psychotherapy: A comprehensive approach to treatment.* New York: Institute for Rational Living, 1970.

Glass, D. C., & Singer, J. E. *Urban stress: Experiments on noise and social stressors.* New York: Academic Press, 1972.

Goldfried, M. R., & Davison, G. C. *Clinical behavior therapy.* New York: Holt, Rinehart & Winston, 1976.

Jellinek, E. M. *The disease concept of alcoholism.* New Brunswick, N.J.: Hillhouse Press, 1960.

Johnson, D. W., & Matross, R. Interpersonal influence in psychotherapy. In A. S. Gurman & A. M. Razin (Eds.), *The therapist's contribution to effective psychotherapy: An Empirical Assessment.* New York: Pergamon Press, 1977.

Jones, R. A. *Self-fulfilling prophecies.* Hillsdale, N.J.: Lawrence Erlbaum Associates, 1977.

Kazdin, A. E., & Wilson, G. T. *Evaluation of behavior therapy: Issues, evidence and research strategies.* Cambridge, Mass.: Ballinger, 1978.

Kent, R. N., Wilson, G. T., & Nelson, R. Effects of false heart-rate feedback on avoidance behavior: An investigation of "cognitive desensitization." *Behavior Therapy,* 1972, *3,* 1–6.

Leitenberg, H. Behavioral approaches to treatment of neuroses. In H. Leitenberg (Ed.), *Handbook of behavior modification and behavior therapy.* Englewood Cliffs, N.J.: Prentice-Hall, 1976.

Mahoney, M. J. *Cognition and behavior modification.* Cambridge, Mass.: Ballinger, 1974.

Mahoney, M. J. *Cognition and clinical science.* New York: Plenum, in press.

Marlatt, G. A. Alcohol, stress and cognitive control. In I. G. Sarason & C. D. Spielberger (Eds.), *Stress and anxiety* (Vol. 3). Washington, D.C.: Hemisphere Publishing, 1976.

Marlatt, G. A. Craving for alcohol, loss of control, and relapse: A cognitive-behavioral analysis. In P. E. Nathan & G. A. Marlatt (Eds.), *Experimental and behavioral approaches to alcoholism.* New York: Plenum, 1978.

Marlatt, G. A., & Marques, J. K. Meditation, self-control, and alcohol use. In R. B. Stuart (Ed.), *Behavioral self-management: Strategies, techniques and results.* New York: Brunner/Mazel, 1977.

McClelland, D. C. Examining the research basis for alternative explanations of alcoholism. In D. C. McClelland, W. N. Davis, R. Kalin, & E. Wanner (Eds.), *The drinking man.* New York: Free Press, 1972.

Meichenbaum, D. *Cognitive behavior modification.* New York: Plenum, 1977.

Nathan, P. E., & Marlatt, G. A. *Alcoholism.* New York: Plenum, 1978.

Novaco, R. W. Stress inoculation: A cognitive therapy for anger and its application to a case of depression. *Journal of Consulting and Clinical Psychology,* 1977, *45,* 600–608.

Orford, J., Oppenheimer, E., & Edwards, G. Abstinence or control: The outcome for excessive drinkers two years after consultation. *Behaviour Research and Therapy,* 1976, *14,* 409–410.

Pomerleau, O., Pertschuk, M., & Stinnet, J. A critical examination of some current assumptions in the treatment of alcoholism. *Journal of Studies on Alcohol,* 1976, *37,* 849–867.

Rachman, S., & Hodgson, R. *Obsessions and compulsions.* Englewood Cliffs, N.J.: Prentice-Hall, in press.

Rosen, G. M., Rosen, E., & Reid, J. B. Cognitive desensitization and avoidance behavior: A re-evaluation. *Journal of Abnormal Psychology,* 1972, *80,* 176–182.

Ross, L., Rodin, J., & Zimbardo, P. G. Toward an attribution therapy: The reduction of fear through induced cognitive-emotional misattribution. *Journal of Personality and Social Psychology,* 1969, *12,* 279–288.

Rotter, J. B. Generalized expectancies for internal versus external control of reinforcement. *Psychological Monographs,* 1966, *80* (1, Whole No. 609).

Rush, A. J., Beck, A. T., Kovacs, M., & Hollon, S. Comparative efficacy of cognitive therapy and pharmacotherapy in the treatment of depressed outpatients. *Cognitive Therapy and Research,* 1977, *1,* 17–37.

Seligman, M. E. P. *Helplessness: On depression, development, and death.* San Francisco: Freeman, 1975.

Singerman, K. J., Borkovec, T. D., & Baron, R. S. Failure of a "misattribution therapy" manipulation with a clinically relevant target behavior. *Behavior Therapy*, 1976, *7*, 306–313.

Stokes, T. F., & Baer, D. M. An implicit technology of generalization. *Journal of Applied Behavior Analysis*, 1977, *10*, 349–367.

Tobias, L. L., & MacDonald, M. L. Internal locus of control and weight loss: An insufficient condition. *Journal of Consulting and Clinical Psychology*, 1977, *45*, 647–653.

Valins, S., & Ray, A. Effects of cognitive desensitization on avoidance behavior. *Journal of Personality and Social Psychology*, 1967, *7*, 345–350.

Weiss, A. R. Characteristics of successful weight reducers: A brief review of predictor variables. *Addictive Behaviors*, 1977, *2*, 193–202.

Wilson, G. T. Booze, beliefs, and behavior: Cognitive processes in alcohol use and abuse. In P. E. Nathan & G. A. Marlatt (Eds.), *Alcoholism*. New York: Plenum, 1978. (a)

Wilson, G. T. Cognitive behavior therapy: Paradigm shift or passing phase? In J. P. Foreyt & D. P. Rathjen (Eds.), *Cognitive behavior therapy: Research and application*. New York: Plenum, 1978. (b)

Wilson, G. T. The importance of being theoretical: Comments on Bandura's "Self-efficacy: Toward a unifying theory of behavioral change." In H. J. Eysenck & S. Rachman (Eds.), *Advances in behaviour research and therapy*. Oxford: Pergamon, in press.

Wilson, G. T., & Evans, I. M. Adult behavior therapy and the therapist–client relationship. In C. M. Franks & G. T. Wilson (Eds.), *Annual review of behavior therapy: Theory and practice* (Vol. 4). New York: Brunner/Mazel, 1976.

Wilson, G. T., & Evans, I. M. The therapist–client relationsip in behavior therapy. In R. S. Gurman & A. M. Razin (Eds.), *The therapist's contribution to effective psychotherapy: An empirical assessment*. New York: Pergamon, 1977.

Wilson, G. T., & O'Leary, K. D. *Principles of behavior therapy*. Englewood Cliffs, N.J.: Prentice-Hall, in press.

THE EFFECTS OF
INDIVIDUAL DIFFERENCES
ON PERCEIVED CONTROL

On free will—
There is no such thing... the mind is induced to wish this or
that by some other cause, and that cause is determined by
another cause, and so on back to infinity.
—Baruch Spinoza

The development of perceived control depends critically on a number of cognitive-perceptual factors, not the least important of which is expectancy. This concept has received extensive investigation following the introduction of Rotter's social learning theory. It therefore seems reasonable to expect that a greater understanding of the expectancy notion will be propaedeutic for the increased understanding of perceived control. Thus the first four papers of this section provide an intensive review of the concept of internality. Professor Rotter's critical discussion of these papers concludes the section.

In the initial paper, Professor Phares provides two major observations. First he strengthens the notion that the individual's perception of control is only minimally dependent on the objective characteristics of the situation. Secondly, as he and others have shown, simply administering the I–E scale to an individual may provide us with only a partially accurate or even myopic view as to how the individual will react to environmental influences. It is only by the use of additional conjugate moderator variables that we will be able to predict with more accuracy how an individual's behavior will be affected by perceived control. Despite this somewhat optimistic view regarding increased understanding of perceived control through the conjoint application of properly used measures of internality, there remain a number of aspects that continue to be resistant to resolution; especially to be noted are sex differences—as Professors Phares, Lefcourt, Strickland, and Ryckman verify.

Professor Lefcourt, in the second chapter, reviews a series of studies showing relationships between internality and various indices of well-being. Following this, he argues persuasively that measures of internality should be more differentiated and goal specific, and he shows how a variety of specific I–E scores are related reliably to a variety of other behaviors varying from affiliation and achievement to posture shifting. He concludes his chapter on a hopeful theme, which suggests that the clinical use of specific subscales may provide the therapist with predictive tools that could enable the patient to be fortified against certain concerns revealed by the patient on these scales.

Examining both laboratory and clinical studies, Professor Strickland reviews the relationship between perceived control and health status. Using internality measures as an index of control, a number of studies of cardiovascular dysfunction are reviewed. A series of plausible hypotheses are proposed, all of which generally suggest that internals may be somewhat less susceptible to cardiovascular infarct and if stricken, may recover with a greater success rate than externals. However, internals may be more vulnerable to cardiovascular problems if they persist in their attempts to control uncontrollable events, and they may show a lower recovery rate than externals if the treatment conditions do not match their general personality needs. In contradistinction to the approaches of Phares and Lefcourt, Strickland's approach tends to rely almost exclusively on the overall I–E scale without having to resort to the more convoluted approach of Phares and the subscale approach of Lefcourt.

In an extensive review of the literature on internality, Professor Ryckman provides an updated and critical assessment of the field. In addition to discussing Rotter's social learning theory, he also provides a comparison with one competing theoretical formulation (cf. Weiner, Nierenberg, & Goldstein, 1976). He also provides a potential resolution of the often found and unwanted interaction of sex and internality measures that has plagued this entire research area. Finally, he discusses the effect of internality on behavior in group settings. As we have seen earlier (e.g., deCharms, Chapter 3), there are some complex interactions between internality and perceived control in situations that require actors and co-actors to share power.

In concluding this section, Professor Rotter not only comments on the papers of Phares, Lefcourt, Strickland, and Ryckman but also points toward the resolution of some problems that have increasingly vexed those concerned with the problem of internality. He concludes his paper with a discussion of the relationship between internality and perceived control.

Rotter cautions investigators about the application or misapplication of his test and suggests that the very prevalent, but unwanted, Sex × I–E interaction may be attributable to the use of ill-chosen tasks to which females and males may respond differentially. Further, he comments on the not always significant relationship between internality and performance measures. He indicates that the occasional superiority of externals may be attributable to the countercontrol (see Moyer, Chapter 6) efforts of internals, whose scores may suffer thereby from this attempt. Finally, he speaks of the shift, over the years, in the mean scores of subjects on the I–E scale, with the consequence that the results of previous studies may differ from current studies unless investigators take account of these shifting criteria.

Finally, in discussing the generally positive motivational consequences of allowing subjects to make choices, he avers that we cannot simply assume that internals will necessarily benefit more from this opportunity than will externals. A number of variables such as task meaningfulness, complexity, and the like must be taken into account. In summary, it appears as if the I–E scale can provide some critical and helpful insights into the perception of control and its effects on behavior; however, the application of the I–E test to this—as well as to other situations—should be executed cautiously and discreetly.

REFERENCE

Weiner, B., Nierenberg, R., & Goldstein, M. Social learning (locus of control) versus attributional (causal stability) interpretations of expectancy of success. *Journal of Personality*, 1976, *44*, 52–68.

14 Defensiveness and Perceived Control

E. Jerry Phares
Kansas State University

INTRODUCTION

At least since our ancestors have been walking upright, the notion of reward or reinforcement has been central in everyone's life. Whether we are generals or corporals, clerks or presidents, we all realize that our behavior, and that of others as well, is to a large extent controlled by reinforcement. But if the concept of reinforcement has occupied a ubiquitous role in the everyday perceptions of us all, it has been no less so in the theoretical and empirical attempts of psychologists to account for human behavior. As an example of this widespread use, Rotter's social learning theory (Rotter, 1954; Rotter, Chance, & Phares, 1972) utilizes reinforcement along with expectancy and situational variables as major concepts in predicting human behavior.

But, like anything else, the role of reinforcement is not absolute or invariant. Its value and effects are conditioned by many factors. One of these factors is the perception of control. The role of reinforcement will be quite different when people perceive that a reward has occurred because of their own efforts or skill as compared to when they perceive it as due to chance or caprice (Phares, 1957). Lefcourt (1976), Phares (1976), and Rotter (1966) have all summarized a great deal of research demonstrating that when people adopt the expectancy that they do not control the occurrence of reinforcement, they will generalize less from the past and will fail to use increasing experience to develop better strategies or more accurate expectancies.

But perceived control as a moderator of reinforcement effects is not just a situational variable. A veritable mountain of evidence supports the notion that there are measurable individual differences in the extent to which people see themselves or other forces as exerting some generalized control over the occurrence of reinforcements (Lefcourt, 1976; Phares, 1976; Rotter, 1966, 1975). For example, using Rotter's (1966) Internal–External Control Scale (I–E Scale), it is possible to order individuals along a dimension in terms of the degree to which they regard themselves or other forces (chance, luck, powerful others, etc.) as the agents controlling the occurrence of reinforcements. Persons scoring low on this scale (so-called internals) have been shown to be: (1) more likely to exert efforts to control their environment; (2) less susceptible to social influence; (3) more oriented toward achievement; and (4) better adjusted than are externals.

These relationships are but the tip of the iceberg; there are a host of other complex correlates of the I–E Scale that space prevents us from dealing with here. Indeed, the amount of research on internal–external control (I–E) has been phenomenal (Phares & Lamiell, 1977; Prociuk & Lussier, 1975; Thornhill, Thornhill, & Youngman, 1975). Phares and Lamiell (1977) have observed that there are at least three possible reasons for this interest. First, there are several short, easy-to-score, and objective scales to measure individual differences in perceived control. Second, some investigators have an unflagging compulsion to correlate these scales with anything available. But the third and, hopefully, most important reason is that investigators recognize that individual differences in the attribution of responsibility for reinforcement are singularly important in providing a crucial link between the occurrence of reinforcement and its effects. But there is more to I–E than a simple catalog of its correlates. To fully comprehend the nature of the construct, we must also understand why it is that a person endorses external rather than internal alternatives on an I–E scale. This question leads us to a consideration of the role and functions of an external belief system. And that is the principal focus of this chapter.

Perhaps this chapter would be more appropriately entitled, "Defensiveness and *Lack of* Perceived Control," since it is external orientations with which we are chiefly concerned. These external beliefs could logically arise from several possible antecedents. For example, they could arise in part from lack of parental nurturant behavior. Equally plausible are explanations that attribute the stable external control beliefs of the adult to a history of inconsistent or unpredictable reinforcement encountered during childhood. Even ordinal position in the family (later born) has shown a modest relationship to externality. And of course there are a variety of important social factors that could presage the establishment of external beliefs. For example, factors of race, lower socioeconomic status, or lack of access to power can easily be construed as fertile (and even veridical) ground for the learning of external generalized expectancies. Both Lefcourt (1976) and Phares (1976) have discussed at length these antecedents and the research evidence for them. But an additional basis from which individuals might choose to express external beliefs involves considerations of defensiveness.

It is the contention of this paper that many individuals express an external expectancy in order to guard against the negative effects of failure. Failing and at the same time admitting to a belief in internal control frequently imply personal inadequacy. But failure coupled with an avowal of external beliefs would enable the individual to evade personal responsibility, thereby mitigating some of the unpleasant effects of that failure. In Rotter's (1966) paper on the development and rationale of the I-E Scale, he raised the question of defensive elements when he stated: "Externality may act as an adequate defense against failure, but very high scores toward the external end may suggest, at least in our culture, a defensiveness related to significant maladjustment [p. 16]."

Possibly, too, there may be more than one "kind" of external. If this is so and if we can reliably identify them, opportunities for increased prediction from the I-E construct are immediately suggested. For example, the behavior of two individuals, even though they possess identical I-E scores, ought to be quite different in non-I-E situations. Therefore, to fail to distinguish between what we shall call defensive externals and congruent externals could easily lead to a lowered efficiency in prediction.

In developing this theme of a relationship between externality and defensiveness, we shall pursue two paths. First, we shall examine the possibility that merely being an external permits one the opportunity to react defensively and thereby to soften the discomforting effects of negative reinforcement. The second path we shall explore is the possibility that there are indeed two kinds of externals: defensive ones and congruent ones.

EXTERNALITY AND THE DEFENSIVE FUNCTION

There is a variety of evidence that suggests the defensive function of external beliefs.

Differential Recognition and Retention

Efran (1963) observed that high school subjects tended to forget failure and moreover, that internal subjects were more prone to such forgetting than were externals. In a study with the physically disabled, Lipp, Kolstoe, James, and Randall (1968) found that disabled internals showed a higher threshold for the tachistoscopic recognition of disabled people than did externals. Therefore, it is possible that an external orientation provides individuals a ready-made mechanism to reduce the effects of threat and thus to perform at higher levels of perceptual or recognition acuity in certain situations. Work by Burnes, Brown, and Keating (1971) also suggests that internals are not as likely to admit to personal inadequacies.

It was the foregoing kind of results that led Phares, Ritchie, and Davis (1968) to study specifically the differential retention of internals and externals under conditions of threat. They provided both positive and negative feedback to subjects regarding the results of personality and intelligence tests previously administered. Subsequently, a measure of retention of this feedback was taken. Generally, better retention of both positive and negative material was shown by external subjects. The interpretation offered by the authors was that subjects' external beliefs afforded them less need to deny unpleasant information by forgetting and also lessened anxiety that may have interfered with cognitive processes. This work showing reduced retention on the part of internals (Efran, 1963; Phares et al., 1968) is particularly interesting since other work (Seeman, 1963; Seeman & Evans, 1962) has produced better retention on the part of internals. It is surely not accidental that the latter work did not involve directly threatening situations.

In one sense, the foregoing work seems contradictory to the thesis linking defensiveness and externality. That is, if internals show higher recognition thresholds, poorer retention, and a reduced willingness to admit to personal problems, perhaps they are the defensive ones. But if so, it is only because the internal's generalized expectancy lessens the opportunity to reduce the effects of failure. The consequent anxiety then propels the internal into a kind of temporary or situational pathology. The external, already in possession of a generalized belief that serves nicely as a constant defense against threat from failure, can easily escape such situational pathology. However, as we move to another kind of experimental situation, we can see how things reverse themselves.

Attribution of Responsibility

Rationalization has long been included in lists of defense mechanisms. Therefore, if indeed externals are outfitted with defensive raiments, it should follow that they will often attribute failures in important need areas to factors other than themselves.

Phares, Wilson, and Klyver (1971) failed subjects on several tasks previously described to them as measures of intellectual ability. Half the subjects failed in the presence of environmental distractions; the other half failed without such distractions. After failure, all subjects completed a blame-attribution scale. With no distractions, internals were significantly less likely than externals to blame forces outside themselves for their failure. But there was no difference between internals and externals under the distractive conditions. Such results are consonant with the hypothesized greater defensive potential of an external orientation. This study also demonstrates that when highly visible cues are present in the situation (distractions in this case), they will dampen the effects of individual differences.

Lacking in the foregoing study was a success condition. This is significant, since differential attributions for success and failure on the part of internals and externals should be particularly revealing as regards defensiveness. Fortunately, Davis and Davis (1972) remedied this problem. They observed that although internals and externals were equally prone to accept responsibility for success, externals were significantly less likely to accept personal responsibility for failure. This study is especially interesting because it illustrates the complexity of I–E beliefs. That is, they are not beliefs that operate uniformly and inevitably in every situation. As Davis and Davis have shown, internals tend to accept responsibility for both success and failure; they behave in concert with the presumed properties of the internal construct. Externals do not. They behave like externals in a failure situation but like internals in a success condition. This suggests the defensive component of external beliefs. More precisely, it illustrates how the situation will engage certain properties of the I–E construct differentially in internals and externals.

Sour Grapes

Another defensive gambit is the old "sour grapes" approach. How many times have we all heard someone remark after a failure, "Oh, that's alright, it wasn't that important anyway." To see whether externals would be more likely to adopt this strategy, Phares (1971) told internal and external subjects that they were participating in a study to determine the effects on intelligence test performance of differential preferences for success on certain subtests. Prior to their performance, the subjects were asked to indicate how important it was to succeed on each of four intelligence subtests. All subjects were failed on the two subtests on which they wished most to succeed. Following their failure, subjects were allowed to change the preferences they stated earlier on the pretext that the experimenter wanted information that was as correct as possible ("Perhaps with actual experience, your preferences might have changed"). Sure enough, externals showed a greater devaluation (i.e., change in preference) of the subtests on which they failed than did internals. This kind of sour grapes behavior suggests a greater defensiveness in externals.

Give Me an Out

If externals are indeed frequently defensive, they might also be expected to employ strategies prior to task performance that would give them an explanation for any subsequent failure. Phares and Lamiell (1974) offered internals and externals a choice of several kinds of intellectual tasks on which to perform. Two of the tasks contained "built-in" rationalizations for any subsequent failure (e.g., "Some of the symbols or characters on this sheet did not print out very well—they are rather dim. . . . I hope it won't affect your performance too much but there is always that possibility"[Phares & Lamiell, 1974, p. 874]). The other two tests did not contain such potential rationalizations. As expected, externals more frequently chose to perform on the "rationalizable" tests than did internals.

Activity Preferences

A number of years ago, Rotter and Mulry (1965) showed that internals preferred to succeed on skilled tasks whereas externals preferred to succeed on chance tasks. Such findings would appear to be consistent with the presumed construct properties of the I–E dimension. Not only that, but such findings also suggest that there may be a value component to I–E aside from its expectancy elements. Subsequent work by both Julian and Katz (1968) and Schneider (1968, 1972) would support the Rotter and Mulry conclusions. However, there is a potential alternative to these conclusions—an alternative that involves defensive considerations. Suppose, for instance, that certain externals choose chance tasks, not because they value success on them, but because they have a low expectancy for success on skilled tasks. Thus, chance preferences would only reflect a defensiveness born out of fear of failure in activities that depend on ability.

In effect, we have two competing hypotheses to account for these activity preferences. One (the value hypothesis) states that externals, perhaps in order to be considered "lucky people," prefer chance activities. The other asserts that such perferences reflect a defensive posture. Perhaps, then, the reinforcement value of success on skilled tasks has been confused with expectancy for success. To help disentangle this potential confound and perhaps to shed further light on defensiveness and externality, Phares and Lamiell (1975) carried out the following study.

Subjects were solicited by a college newspaper ad and paid to "assist in the development of several tests." The first test was described as a "pure" skill test (i.e., one on which scores were entirely a matter of ability). The second was likewise described as involving skill but as one that also contained "bugs" or defects that could randomly distort scores and thereby provide a somewhat less than accurate index of ability. The third test was supposedly one to identify persons who were characteristically lucky on intelligence tests. The fourth was presented as one on which scores were entirely due to transient luck.

The last three tests were all described as ones on which the probability of success was .50. For the pure skill test, however, one-third of the subjects were told that probability of success was .85, one-third .50, and one-third .15. After reading the test descriptions and normative information, subjects were asked to state their expected scores for each test. Next, they were asked to indicate that test on which it was most important for them to succeed. Finally, each subject was told to distribute 48 minutes across the four tests, thus indicating how much time they were willing to devote to each.

Several results are of interest here. First, the stated expectancies for the pure skill test revealed that the instructions were successful in controlling the subjective expectancies of both internals and externals. A chi-square analysis was made on subjects' responses to the question, "Which test is it most important for you to do well on?" Results indicated that internals' preferences for the pure skill test *increased* as probability of success *decreased*, whereas externals' preferences for the skill test *decreased* with *decreasing* probability of success $[X^2(2) = 7.92, p < .05]$. For the distribution of time measure, however, regression analyses revealed a significant negative relationship between probability of success and time devoted to the pure skill test by internals, $F(1, 52) = 6.90, p < .05$, but no significant relationship for externals $F(1, 46) = .06$. A pairwise comparison of cell means indicated that internals were willing to devote significantly more time to the skill test when probability of success was .15 than were externals in the same condition.

Results obtained with the importance of success measure would appear to support a defensive view of stated external beliefs. Both chi-square and regression analyses revealed a decline in the importance assigned by externals to success on the skill test as probability of success decreased. The time distribution measure was not as clear-cut. But if it is viewed as a measure of effort rather than reinforcement value, then the results are more coherent. Nothing in the results suggested that externals have a need to be considered lucky. In summary, if externals really prefer external reinforcement (such as success on chance tasks over success on skilled tasks), their preferences should not be affected by probability of success on the skill tests. The fact that they were affected supports the notion that the stated activity preferences of many externals (particularly in a college sample) are defensive in nature.

THE CONGRUENT-DEFENSIVE DISTINCTION

To strengthen the basis for believing that there are two kinds of externals, the first thing one might look for is evidence of heterogeneity on the part of external samples. In comparing internals and externals on a variety of measures of personality, Hersch and Scheibe (1967) observed this very thing and were moved to comment: "Individuals scoring low on the I–E Scale (internals) are more homogeneous on their test performances than are high scoring subjects. This may suggest a diversity in the psychological meaning of externality [p. 612]." These comments are entirely consistent with the informal observations of investigators who have been repeatedly struck by the pronounced variability in the performance of externals (Phares, 1976). Given all the foregoing discussion and evidence, it would seem plausible to consider distinguishing two kinds of externals. First there are *congruent* externals (CEs), whose life experiences have taught them that reinforcements occur independently of their own efforts. Then there are *defensive* externals (DEs), who verbalize an external orientation as a characteristic defense against anticipated failures but who often behave more like internals when placed in actual performance situations that offer reinforcements that appear contingent upon behavior.

Indentification of DEs and CEs

Two chief methods have been proposed to distinguish between CEs and DEs. Davis (1970), in a study involving the academic recognition need area, defined DEs as those who not only achieve external scores on the I–E Scale but who also profess a willingness to take action to improve their academic skills. The latter willingness was measured by a device modified from an action-taking questionnaire developed by Gore and Rotter (1963). CEs were defined by external I–E scores and low action-taking scores, thus fitting the classical definition of externality.

Hochreich (1968), however, defined CEs, or "true" externals as individuals who score high in both externality and in interpersonal trust. DEs, however, were seen as high in externality but low in trust. In effect, she used the Interpersonal Trust Scale (Rotter, 1967, 1971) to moderate I–E scores. From this view, low-trust externals are striving, ambitious people who are prone to employ blame projection to explain their expected failures. In competitive, achievement situations, DEs are expected to behave like internals, but their attributional behavior should be characteristic of externals. Consistent with this general theme, Hamsher, Geller, and Rotter (1968) found that low-trust externals are more likely to impute incompetence and malevolence to authority figures.

There are a variety of other potential methods for distinguishing between CEs and DEs, but none has yet been systematically pursued. For example, DEs might be expected to show higher minimal-goal levels or need value scores in certain areas. Another method might adapt the strategy of Crandall, Katkovsky, and Crandall (1965). That is, on a questionnaire inquiring about I–E beliefs regarding both failure and success, DEs would be expected to endorse external beliefs for failure situations but internal beliefs for success situations. CEs should be consistent across both classes of situations. Another method might ask subjects to distinguish between expectancies for internal versus external control and the value of that control. DEs might be expected to state external expectancies but internal values. Again, CEs would be congruent across both values and expectancies. Still another potential method is illustrated by the work of Levenson (1973a, 1973b). She has distinguished between beliefs in the chance determination of events versus influence from powerful others and has developed several scales for this purpose. There is the likelihood that her distinction overlaps the CE–DE dichotomy. Prociuk and Breen (1975) used the powerful-others scale as a measure of defensiveness. They determined that the academic achievement of internals was superior to that of those who believed in either chance or powerful others. However, the academic achievement of those scoring high on the powerful-others scale (defensives) was significantly greater than those believing in chance (congruents).

The Evidence

Davis (1970) found several sources of support for the CE–DE distinction. First, she noted that DEs placed a higher value on the need for academic recognition (ACR) than did CEs. They also evidenced a greater discrepancy between need for ACR and the expectancy of achieving it than did CEs. In addition, during an experimental session, DEs and internals were no different in information-seeking behavior calculated to help solve an ACR problem; but both were superior to CEs. In general, there was little difference between high- and low-action-taking internals, which suggests that the action-taking scale was effective in enhancing prediction only for external subjects. In any event, her research supports a view of DEs as people who often behave like internals but who, on the I–E Scale, profess external beliefs as a verbal defense.

A study by Lloyd and Chang (1977) also employed Davis' method of distinguishing CEs and DEs. They provided positive and negative feedback to both male and female subjects regarding their performance on a social sensitivity scale. They found that DEs varied their causal attributions as a function of outcome (accepted responsibility for success but not for failure) but that CEs did not. Furthermore, DEs accepted significantly less personal responsibility following failure than did any of the other groups (high-action internals, low-action internals, high-action externals, low-action externals). These investigators stress the utility of a three-category construct of I–E (internals, DEs, CEs).

Hochreich (1968, 1974, 1975) has carried out a series of studies employing interpersonal trust as a moderator variable. In her first study (Hochreich, 1968), she used an angle-matching task with skill-competitive instructions. For males, she found that low-trust externals (DEs), as compared to high-trust externals (CEs), were much more responsive to feedback concerning their performance. For females, the reverse was found.

In a subsequent study, Hochreich (1974) asked subjects to read several TAT stories and then attribute responsibility for the success or failure of the story heroes. Again, for males (but not for females), she found that DEs attribute less responsibility in the case of failure than do either CEs or internals. Further, this difference was most prominent in achievement situations. On several scales of an adjective checklist, DEs endorsed fewer favorable adjectives and more unfavorable adjectives, and they achieved poorer defensiveness and adjustment scores. Thus, DEs seemed to acknowledge personal inadequacies without taking responsibility for them. For females, however, the results were either inconsistent or nonsupportive.

In Hochreich's (1975) third study, subjects actually experienced failure. As expected, DEs rated the test procedures as less adequate than did either internals or CEs. They also blamed their poor performance on the nature of the test more than the other groups did. In a related study, Evans (1973) also manipulated actual performance outcomes and found that CEs and internals attributed both success and failure to external and internal factors, respectively, whereas DEs assumed credit for success but attributed failure to external forces.

On a level of aspiration task, Hochreich (1978) found that both DEs and internals behaved in a striving manner regardless of the salience of achievement cues. CEs, however, responded in a more striving fashion when such cues were present but less so when they were not.

Some preliminary evidence (Evans, 1976; Gilmore & Minton, 1974) also implies that the CE–DE breakdown may be usefully extended to include internals. It does not appear likely that the meaning will be exactly the same, however. Further, since the typical heterogeneity among internals is not as great as with externals (Hersch & Scheibe, 1967), it is also not as likely that the distinction will prove as useful predictively. At the same time, there is no reason to believe that all internals are free from anxiety. Consequently, some of them may be expected to behave defensively, much as a DE does. In addition, there is some evidence that an internal belief system is the more socially desirable one (Lefcourt, 1976). If so, it may turn out that not a few internals espouse their beliefs out of social desirability considerations. If so, then "false" internals might be identified using scores on a social desirability scale as a moderator variable.

Generalized Expectancies for Success and Anxiety

Implicit in all this discussion about defensiveness is the assumption that externals possess a lower generalized expectancy for success than do internals (thus fueling their defensive strategy). Considerable support for this exists (e.g., Nelson & Phares, 1971; Phares & Lamiell, 1974; Strassberg, 1973). Another way of stating this is that anxiety (low expectancy for success in an important need area) is more typical of externals than it is of internals. A wide array of data support this relationship (see Lefcourt [1976] and Phares [1976] for reviews of the relationship between I–E scores and anxiety).

A bit earlier, we discussed the defensive decisions of externals to perform on tasks that permit a rationalization of any subsequent failure (Phares & Lamiell, 1974). Unpublished data from another part of that project (Phares & Lamiell, 1973) revealed some additional things when internals, DEs (low-trust externals), and CEs (high-trust externals) were compared. First, DEs, CEs, and both high- and low-trust internals showed no differences as regards expectancies for success on the rationalizable tests. But DEs did state significantly lower expectancies for success on the nonrationalizable tests than did both groups of internals. There were no differences in expectancies on the nonrationalizable tests between CEs and either DEs or the internals. However, the location of the CE mean between the means of DEs and of the internals replicates work by Davis (1970) and provides an encouraging air of stability to these results. In terms of preferring to perform on one kind of test rather than another, high-trust internals showed significantly less preference for the rationalizable tests than the other three groups. External low-trusters (DEs) showed a significantly greater preference for the rationalizable tests than the other three groups.

In addition, a minimal-goal-level measure (the lowest score that a subject will consider reinforcing) was employed. On this measure, there were no differences among CEs, DEs, and internals for the rationalizable tests. On the nonrationalizable tests, however, both internals and DEs showed a tendency toward higher minimal-goal statements than CEs. There were no minimal-goal differences between DEs and internals.

What all this suggests is the possibility that DEs differ from CEs primarily with respect to the *value* attached to success in achievement situations, whereas DEs differ from internals primarily with respect to *expectancies* for success in achievement situations. Thus, the inconsistent behavioral patterns of DEs (as compared with internals and CEs) are not capricious but are mediated by two crucial variables: (1) the nature of the situation (i.e., whether or not the behavior in question is one on which a judgment of success or failure is likely to be made); and (2) the expectancy of success for that behavior. The foregoing data and analysis converge once again upon the defensive properties of external beliefs.

CONCLUSIONS

An individual's perceptions of control in a given situation are not completely a function of the objective characteristics of that situation. They are determined in part by generalizations from the past. What is more, the individual's stated perceptions of control (e.g., as based on an I-E scale) cannot always be relied upon in our predictions without the additional consideration of certain moderator variables. Such variables will enable us to capitalize on the defensive possibilities inherent in externality. Failure to consider such moderator variables will surely lead to errors in prediction. For example, relying solely upon I–E scores may be misleading when we observe that on certain occasions, an external individual makes external attributions but in other ways performs like an internal.

Based on the research and discussion in this chapter, it would appear, then, that we are justified in concluding that there are substantial defensive properties in the external belief systems of many individuals. In addition, there seems to be real utility in distinguishing between two classes of externals as an aid to prediction.

But research into defensiveness and perceived control is just beginning, and there is much still to be learned. For example, sex differences here are not well understood. Some studies (Davis, 1970; Hochreich, 1975) have used only males. Others (Hochreich, 1968, 1974) have used both males and females but could only produce the predicted defensive behaviors with males. Yet Lloyd and Chang's (1977) population was 60% female, and they still obtained the expected defensive data (using a criterion behavior involving social sensitivity rather than a more conventional achievement task).

Additional research is needed to determine the most useful way of identifying DEs and CEs (or at least to identify the specific correlates of each method). It would also be important to learn something about the developmental history of DEs and CEs.

Finally, to illustrate ways of more firmly establishing the credibility of the DE–CE distinction, the following kinds of research questions might be pursued:

1. How does the behavior of DEs, CEs, and internals compare in situations where the threat of failure is present as opposed to those where it is absent?
2. When the expectancies for success on the part of DEs are high (either through experience or experimental manipulation), will they not behave more like internals than like CEs?
3. If it is true that DEs possess a viable defense, will their anxiety levels *immediately* following failure be lower than in the case of internals? Similarly, if the presumed defenses of DEs are attacked, will they display a greater level of discomfort?
4. In attributing blame of one's own performance as compared to the failures of others, will DEs be consistently external, or will they blame others for the latter's shortcomings but not themselves for their own failures?

REFERENCES

Burnes, K., Brown, W. A., & Keating, G. W. Dimensions of control: Correlations between MMPI and I–E scores. *Journal of Consulting and Clinical Psychology*, 1971, *36*, 301.

Crandall, V. C., Katkovsky, W., & Crandall, V. J. Children's beliefs in their own control of reinforcemnts in intellectual-academic achievement situations. *Child Development*, 1965, *36*, 91–109.

Davis, D. E. *Internal-external control and defensiveness.* Unpublished doctoral dissertation, Kansas State University, 1970.

Davis, W. L., & Davis, D. E. Internal-external control and attribution of responsibility for success and failure. *Journal of Personality*, 1972, *40*, 123–136.

Efran, J. *Some personality determinants of memory for success and failure.* Unpublished doctoral dissertation, Ohio State University, 1963.

Evans, R. G. *Defensive externality as an extension of the I-E construct.* Unpublished master's thesis, Southern Illinois University, 1973.

Evans, R. G. *Situational generality of reaction to success and failure by defensive and nondefensive internals and externals: A test of three models of the relationship between locus of control and defensiveness.* Unpublished doctoral dissertation, Southern Illinois University, 1976.

Gilmore, T. M., & Minton, H. L. Internal versus external attribution of task performance as a function of locus of control, initial confidence, and success–failure outcome. *Journal of Personality*, 1974, *41*, 159–174.

Gore, P. M., & Rotter, J. B. A personality correlate of social action. *Journal of Personality*, 1963, *31*, 58–64.

Hamsher, J. H., Geller, J. D., & Rotter, J. B. Interpersonal trust, internal-external control, and the Warren Commission report. *Journal of Personality and Social Psychology*, 1968, *9*, 210–215.

Hersch, P. D., & Scheibe, K. E. Reliability and validity of internal-external control as a personality dimension. *Journal of Consulting Psychology*, 1967, *31*, 609–613.

Hochreich, D. J. *Refined analysis of internal-external control and behavior in a laboratory situation.* Unpublished doctoral dissertation, University of Connecticut, 1968.

Hochreich, D. J. Defensive externality and attribution of responsibility. *Journal of Personality*, 1974, *42*, 543–557.

Hochreich, D. J. Defensive externality and blame projection following failure. *Journal of Personality and Social Psychology*, 1975, *32*, 540–546.

Hochreich, D. J. Defensive externality and level of aspiration. *Journal of Consulting and Clinical Psychology*, 1978, *46*, 177–178.

Julian, J. W., & Katz, S. B. Internal versus external control and the value of reinforcement. *Journal of Personality and Social Psychology*, 1968, *8*, 89–94.

Lefcourt, H. M. *Locus of control: Current trends in theory and research.* Hillsdale, N.J.: Lawrence Erlbaum Associates, 1976.

Levenson, H. Perceived parental antecedents of internal, powerful others, and chance locus of control orientations. *Developmental Psychology*, 1973, *9*, 260–265. (a)

Levenson, H. *Reliability and validity of the I, P, and C scales—a multidimensional view of locus of control.* Paper presented at the meeting of the American Psychological Association, Montreal, August 1973. (b)

Lipp, L., Kolstoe, R., James, W., & Randall, H. Denial of disability and internal control of reinforcement: A study using a perceptual defense paradigm. *Journal of Consulting and Clinical Psychology*, 1968, *32*, 72–75.

Lloyd, C., & Chang, A. F. *The usefulness of distinguishing between a defensive and a nondefensive external locus of control.* Unpublished paper, University of Texas Health Science Center at Houston Medical School, 1977.

Nelson, P. C., & Phares, E. J. Anxiety, discrepancy between need value and expectancy, and internal-external control. *Psychological Reports*, 1971, *28*, 663–668.

Phares, E. J. Expectancy changes in skill and chance situations. *Journal of Abnormal and Social Psychology*, 1957, *54*, 339–342.

Phares, E. J. Internal-external control and the reduction of reinforcement value after failure. *Journal of Consulting and Clinical Psychology*, 1971, *37*, 386–390.

Phares, E. J. *Locus of control in personality.* Morristown, N.J.: General Learning Press, 1976.

Phares, E. J., & Lamiell, J. T. *Internal-external control, interpersonal trust, and defensive behavior.* Unpublished paper, Kansas State University, 1973.

Phares, E. J., & Lamiell, J. T. Relationship of internal-external control to defensive preferences. *Journal of Consulting and Clinical Psychology*, 1974, *42*, 872–878.

Phares, E. J., & Lamiell, J. T. *Locus of control, defensiveness, and activity preference: A test of alternative explanations.* Unpublished paper, Kansas State University, 1975.

Phares, E. J., & Lamiell, J. T. Personality. In M. R. Rosenzweig & L. W. Porter (Eds.), *Annual review of psychology*, (Vol. 28). Palo Alto, Calif.: Annual Reviews, 1977.

Phares, E. J., Ritchie, D. E., & Davis, W. L. Internal-external control and reaction to threat. *Journal of Personality and Social Psychology*, 1968, *10*, 402–405.

Phares, E. J., Wilson, K. G., & Klyver, N. W. Internal-external control and the attribution of blame under neutral and distractive conditions. *Journal of Personality and Social Psychology*, 1971, *18*, 285–288.

Prociuk, T. J., & Breen, L. J. Defensive externality and its relation to academic performance. *Journal of Personality and Social Psychology*, 1975, *31*, 549–556.

Prociuk, T. J., & Lussier, R. J. Internal-external locus of control: An analysis and bibliography of two years of research (1973–74). *Psychologocial Reports*, 1975, *37*, 1323–1337.

Rotter, J. B. *Social learning and clinical psychology.* Englewood Cliffs, N.J.: Prentice-Hall, 1954.

Rotter, J. B. Generalized expectancies for internal versus external control of reinforcement. *Psychological Monographs,* 1966, *80* (1, Whole No. 609).

Rotter, J. B. A new scale for the measurement of interpersonal trust. *Journal of Personality*, 1967, *35*, 651–665.

Rotter, J. B. Generalized expectancies for interpersonal trust. *American Psychologist*, 1971, *26*, 443–452.

Rotter, J. B. Some problems and misconceptions related to the construct of internal versus external control of reinforcement. *Journal of Consulting and Clinical Psychology*, 1975, *43*, 56–67.

Rotter, J. B., Chance, J., & Phares, E. J. (Eds.). *Applications of a social learning theory of personality.* New York: Holt, Rinehart & Winston, 1972.

Rotter, J. B., & Mulry, R. C. Internal versus external control of reinforcement and decision time. *Journal of Personality and Social Psychology*, 1965, *2*, 598–604.

Schneider, J. M. Skill versus chance activity preference and locus of control. *Journal of Consulting and Clinical Psychology*, 1968, *32*, 333–337.

Schneider, J. M. Relationship between locus of control and activity preferences: Effects of masculinity, activity, and skill. *Journal of Consulting and Clinical Psychology*, 1972, *38*, 225–230.

Seeman, M. Alienation and social learning in a reformatory. *American Journal of Sociology*, 1963, *69*, 270–284.

Seeman, M., & Evans, J. W. Alienation and learning in a hospital setting. *American Sociological Review*, 1962, *27*, 772–783.

Strassberg, D. S. Relationships among locus of control, anxiety, and valued-goal expectations. *Journal of Consulting and Clinical Psychology*, 1973, *41*, 319.

Thornhill, M. A., Thornhill, G. J., & Youngman, M. B. A computerized and categorized bibiliography on locus of control. *Psychological Reports*, 1975, *36*, 505–506.

15 Locus of Control for Specific Goals

Herbert M. Lefcourt
University of Waterloo

INTRODUCTION

In the research literature pertaining to the perception of control, there has been evidence presented attesting to the importance of perceived control for predicting both life satisfaction and depression. What is most compelling is that the methods used in the study of control have been diverse whereas the results and conclusions have been congruent.

Most recently, Langer and Rodin (1976) described a study conducted in a nursing home residence in which some of the elderly residents were induced to have a greater sense of control within their milieu. That is, certain residents were encouraged to believe that they could affect their surroundings so as to maximize their satisfactions. Others were offered the same satisfactions but without any sense of active decision making, participation, or control.

Subsequent assessments of residents' morale revealed that those who believed that available reinforcements were forthcoming in response to their own behaviors rated themselves and were judged by others to be more active and happier and (as indicated in a follow-up investigation, Rodin & Langer, 1977) lived longer than did those residents who were offered the equivalent amenities through the largess of the institution staff.

At about the same time that Langer and Rodin were reporting their results, Reid and Ziegler (1977) were analyzing data from a series of nine studies in which they sought correlations among a number of life satisfaction and activity measures with a scale entitled the "Locus of Desired Control." The results of these studies, also conducted among nursing home residents, bear similarity to those of Langer and Rodin.

Reid and Ziegler initiated their investigations with a survey in which elderly persons were questioned regarding the daily events that they believed were important for their feelings of happiness, contentment, and adjustment. From the interview data, a questionnaire was devised, half the items of which concerned the degree to which the individual desired or valued the particular satisfactions in question. The remainder of the questionnaire consisted of items pertaining to the degree to which the individual anticipated the possibility of attaining those satisfactions through his or her own abilities and initiatives. The product of these two scores—value and perceived control— was then correlated with a number of self-reports and observer ratings of the person's well-being. This measure, referred to as the locus of desired control, was found to be highly related to measures of life satisfaction, "subjective age," and to ratings made by nurses and interviewers of the residents' zest for life and assertiveness. Cross-lagged correlations indicated that locus of desired control correlated strongly with life-satisfaction scores collected a year later and, as in Rodin and Langer's (1977) follow-up study, was predictive of poor physical health—serious illness being predicted significantly in one sample and at a borderline significance level in another sample of elderly persons.

These findings also bear similarity to those reported by Naditch, Gargan, and Michael (1975) and by Naditch (1974). In these latter studies, locus-of-control-scale scores were found to be related to measures of depression and anxiety in interaction with an index of "relative discontent." That is, persons who expressed greater discrepancies between their aspirations and their achievements and who reported external control expectancies as well, were most apt to report depressive symptoms on the Cornell Medical Index. With another large sample, Naditch (1974) has found similar interactive effects between discontent and locus of control in the prediction of hypertension.

In each of these studies, then, the perception of control has been related to certain indices of well-being and has been used with reference to the actual concerns of the individual tested. Langer and Rodin emphasized the potential for controlling amenities within the nursing home, amenities that were the major satisfactions available in that nursing home. Likewise, Reid and Ziegler evaluated residents' concerns and assessed their beliefs regarding their ability to control the events pertaining to those concerns. Naditch and his colleagues, though not particularizing their subjects' concerns, assessed the degree to which they felt that their concerns or aspirations were not likely to be realized.

In each instance, the absence of a belief that the individual could be instrumental in determining the occurrence of desired ends resulted in what this writer has referred to as "devitalization" (Lefcourt, 1976)—the decline of life functions that are reflected in alertness, responsiveness, and the pursuit of satisfactions.

The importance of these studies, however, goes beyond the immediate stimulation value of the reported results. Although much of the information pertaining to locus of control has derived from research conducted within the confines of laboratories, these studies reveal the potency of the construct for illuminating very real phenomena such as illness and, perhaps, mortality. In so doing, these investigations have focused upon people's real concerns and have attempted to assess perceptions of control over reinforcements or satisfactions that matter to people in their daily lives.

DEVELOPMENT OF GOAL-SPECIFIC MEASURES OF LOCUS OF CONTROL

Rotter's original 23-item locus-of-control scale (I–E) (Rotter, 1966) was derived from a considerably larger scale that contained items that sampled different areas of concern. That is, there were items focusing upon achievement, affiliation, social recognition, etc. However, factor analyses of this early I–E scale failed to isolate clusters of items divisible by reinforcement concerns. Consequently, the now familiar, short, and relatively homogeneous 23-item scale came to be used in most of the early research pertaining to locus of control as an individual-difference variable.

The primary exception to this trend was evident in research conducted with children that made use of the Crandalls' Intellectual Achievement Responsibility questionnaire (IAR) (Crandall, Katkovsky, & Crandall, 1965). The Crandalls' scale focused entirely upon achievement and provided separate scores for attributions made in response to successes and failures. As such, it was both the first goal-specific device and the first measure to afford a more differentiated conceptualization of locus of control. That separate locus-of-control scores for successes and failures have utility has been demonstrated in several investigations. Ducette, Wolk, and Soucar (1972), for example, found that "inappropriate" imbalances between attributions for successes and failures were associated with maladaptive behavior in school; and Mischel, Zeiss, and Zeiss (1974) found that an internal locus of control for positive outcomes predicted persistence in the pursuit of rewards, whereas the internal locus of control for negative outcomes predicted effort expended to avoid punishments.

Evidence in support of a more differentiated conception of locus of control also is found in the research of attribution theorists. Weiner and his colleagues (Weiner, Frieze, Kukla, Reed, Rest, & Rosenbaum, 1971; Weiner, Russell, & Lerman, 1978) have examined the impact of specific causal perceptions upon both behavioral and affective responses to success and failure. These investigators have differentiated among various internal and external sources of outcomes with regard to achievement such as ability (a stable internal attribute) and effort (an unstable or alterable internal attribute). It is Weiner's contention that ability attributions result in feelings of confidence and competence given success experiences or feelings of incompetence and inadequacy following failure. In contrast, effort results in feelings characterized as "good" or "delighted" subsequent to success and "humble" or "guilty" following failure. Similar differentiations are made among external attributes such as task difficulty, other's influence, luck, etc., each with their assumed affective concomitants. In the studies by Dweck (1975) and Dweck and Reppucci (1973), these specific attributions were put to good test, revealing that ability attributions led to diminished efforts subsequent to failures, whereas effort attributions led to renewed output in the same circumstances. These investigations indicated that internality per se was less powerful as a predictor of goal-directed behavior than was the more specified causal attribution.

In recent years there have been some attempts to create assessment devices offering measurement of more specific aspects of locus of control. Among these are the scales constructed by Levenson (1973), which discriminates among sources of external control (powerful others vs. chance); by Reid and Ware (1974), which contains measures of self- or impulse control as well as fatalism and social system control; and by Kirscht (1972), which assesses beliefs about the control of health via disease-related practices.

More recently, Wallston, Maides, and Wallston (1976) and Wallston, Wallston, Kaplan, and Maides (1976) have published another health-related locus-of-control scale and have presented some evidence regarding discriminant validity for their measure in contrast to Rotter's I–E scale. In brief, persons who expressed the belief that health is at least partially determined by their actions were more apt to seek out health-related information than were those who perceived health more fatalistically. In addition, "health internals" were more satisfied with weight reduction programs that were self-directing than were "health externals," who preferred the more externally directed group program. In both instances, Rotter's I–E scale failed to predict the criteria.

The scales constructed by Kirscht, the Wallstons, and by Reid and Ziegler (discussed earlier) are distinctive in that they measure the locus of control with respect to particular areas of concern. Whereas the former assess beliefs regarding the control of health and illness, Reid and Ziegler focus upon satisfactions valued by elderly persons such as privacy, keeping personal possessions, socializing, and so forth.

In our laboratories, we have also been engaged in the construction of goal-specific locus-of-control measures. Our assessment devices are not to be regarded as "finished products." However, they are sufficiently developed and have produced enough interesting data to warrant their presentation.

THE UNIVERSITY OF WATERLOO PROJECT

As described in my book, *Locus of Control* (Lefcourt, 1976), one approach to the assessment of goal-specific expectancies is to conduct structured interviews in which subjects are queried about their major concerns and the means that are likely to contribute to particular outcomes relevant to those concerns. We did conduct a number of such interviews in accord with the schedule presented in the appendix of the book. From these interviews it was possible to discriminate among subjects with regard to locus of control to some degree. However, it was also obvious that our subjects' specific causal attributions varied substantially, with many of their responses classifiable via Weiner's fourfold classification scheme. We were offered stable internal attributes such as abilities, skills, talent, and intelligence as explanations for outcomes as well as unstable internal attributes such as effort, motivation, moods, affective states, etc. Likewise, external stable attributes such as "human nature," the kinds of settings in which one lived, and the difficulty in fulfilling particular ambitions were offered as explanations for possible outcomes as well as external unstable attributes such as other's moods and motivations, accidents, luck, etc.

To better assess these particular attributes offered by our subjects, we subsequently set out to design scales that would allow for measurement of specific causal agents and provide total locus-of-control scores as well. The result has thus far been two 24-item Likert scales, one assessing the locus of control for achievement, the other for affiliation. The scales, to which we hope to add others, are referred to as the Multidimensional-Multiattributional Causality Scales (MMCS) (Lefcourt, VonBaeyer, Ware, & Cox, 1978).

Each 24-item scale is composed of 12 items pertaining to successes and 12 to failures. The items are also divided into four groups of six items, each cluster representing one sort of causal attribution: stable internal causes, stable external causes, unstable internal causes, and unstable external causes. For each of the four sorts of attributions, half of the six items are possible reasons for successes, half for failures.

Examples of affiliative locus-of-control items are as follows:

There's not much use in my trying to please people. If people like me, they like me.

If I don't get along with others, it would probably be because I hadn't put much effort into it.

It seems to me that getting along with people is a skill.

In my experience, making friends is largely a matter of having the right breaks.

These items represent, respectively, a stable external attribution for success, an unstable internal attribution for failure, a stable internal cause for success, and an unstable external cause for success.[1]

Reliability estimates have been obtained from varied sources and with different samples. Norman (1977) administered the MMCS to 177 students at Centennial College near Toronto and found Cronbach's alpha of .67 for the achievement and .68 for the affiliation locus-of-control scales. Given the rather heterogeneous items included in the scales, these are reasonably high measures of internal consistency. With a sample of 232 university freshmen and sophomores, we have found alphas of .58 for each of the scales. Split-half Spearman–Brown correlations are .67 for achievement and .65 for affiliation locus of control. Although the scales are relatively consistent within themselves, the correlations between the two measures are low ($r = .21$, $p < .001$, $N = 282$), though significant. Test–retest reliability coefficients of .62 and .70 for achievement and affiliation, respectively, have been found with an earlier sample of 68 subjects. Further test–retest data will soon become available.

Beyond the intratest data, we have examined the MMCS opposite other scales with which relationships are anticipated. Opposite Rotter's I–E scale, both the affiliation and achievement locus-of-control scales produce rs of about .45, revealing both similarity to and difference from the former, as intended. Opposite the depression scale of Jackson's Differential Personality Inventory (Jackson & Messick, 1964), the affiliation locus-of-control scale produced correlations ranging between .37 among a sample of 134 females and .41 among a mixed-sex sample of 47 community college students. Within the same samples, the achievement scale produced rs of .27 and .03, respectively, whereas Rotter's I–E scale produced rs of .30 and .08. Paradoxically, in an entirely male sample, the relationship between affiliation locus of control and depression failed to materialize ($r = .13$), whereas achievement locus of control ($r = .28$) and Rotter's I–E scale ($r = .47$) were significantly associated with depression. Apparently, affective responses have differing correlates with locus of control for each sex and for differing areas of concern. Achievement seems to have greater affective consequences for males, affiliation for females.

Other data indicating utility in the separation of analyses for sex and areas of concern have been found with Jackson's Personality Research Form (PRF) (Jackson, 1967). Locus of control for achievement has been found to be negatively related to achievement propensities ($r = -.39$, $p < .05$) and to social recognition ($r = -.53$, $p < .01$) among males, as measured by the PRF. The more external with regard to achievement, the less achieving and social

---

[1]The full scale and description of same is available from the author.

recognition seeking were male subjects. Females, on the other hand, produced insignificant relationships among those scales ($r = -.16$ and $.29$, respectively).

Correlates of a more interesting sort have been obtained with recalled life events. Bryant and Trockel (1976) have reported that affectively significant life stresses recalled from the preschool years are related to statements of external control in adulthood on Rotter's I–E scale. With a sample of 44 subjects, we have also obtained correlations between the affiliation ($r = .34$, $p < .05$) and achievement ($r = .29$, $p < .06$) locus-of-control scales and the recall of negative life changes in the preschool years. Even more pronounced was the affiliation ability–preschool negative events correlation ($r = -.52$, $p < .001$). The more undesirable events recalled from the preschool years, the less likely were subjects to attribute affiliation outcomes to social ability. This finding was particularly marked among females for whom the $r = -.72$, $p < .001$ between affiliation ability and recalled preschool undesirable events.

Among another sample of 39 subjects, we have found the affiliation locus-of-control measure to be negatively related to the recall of positive preschool events ($r = -.26$, $p < .05$); the more subjects could recall positive early life events, the more internal with regard to affiliation were their scores. This was an interesting finding given the very low incidence of negative preschool events found in this sample, suggesting a complementarity between positive and negative events in predicting later locus-of-control scores.

These findings are of more than passing interest. Preschool time is a period of life during which affection and social intimacy play a prominent role. As such, one could hypothesize that the more memorable events occurring in the preschool years would be related to social attachments and that later social-affiliative behaviors may be mediated by expectancies derived from these early experiences. Research by Hetherington (1972) has indicated that certain social behaviors of adolescent girls were predictable from social traumas, death, or divorce during earlier years, as were personality measures such as Rotter's I–E scale. Our own data revealed that the relationship between early life events and expressions of externality are of a higher magnitude when the reinforcement area, in this case affiliation, is more relevant to the early life events in question. Although this point is obvious, the utility of more specific goal-related scales also becomes evident, and it is possible to envision that the locus-of-control-for-affiliation scale will be useful for investigating shyness, social withdrawal, and social competence.

In addition to these correlational explorations, we have experimented with the MMCS in a series of studies in which we have observed the role of specific area locus-of-control measures opposite achievement or affiliation criteria.

In one such study, subjects were engaged in an achievement-demanding task, one that required their solving a series of anagrams under time pressure similar to those described in a previous investigation (Lefcourt, Hogg, Struthers, & Holmes, 1975) with one important difference. In the earlier study, subjects worked alone with no distracting social cues present. Subjects paced themselves so that they could finish sets of anagrams in a certain limited time period. In another study that we conducted at about the same time as the anagram study (Lefcourt, Hogg, & Sordoni, 1975), we had found that internals became more distracted and uncomfortable while performing at a task when they were made aware of the presence of observers. Externals, in contrast, were at their worst when working in solitary, being isolated with their task.

The anagram study had been conducted with this isolation that internals appear to prefer, and it was noted in that study that externals were more distraught throughout the task and were even more so when failures were experienced.

In this first experimental investigation with the MMCS, subjects were presented with a facsimile of the anagram task described previously. However, the procedures for test administration varied considerably from the "ideal isolation" favored by internals. The experimenter sat next to the subject, stopwatch in hand. Whereas subjects in the earlier anagram study turned the anagram cards over themselves, finishing sets of 10 at their own pace, in this study the experimenter handed each card to the subject and removed it after a lapse of 30 seconds. The procedure was hurried, subjects were harried, and it was our expectation that persons who were internal for achievement would give evidence of greater discomfort (the reverse of the results from the previous study) than would those who were external for achievement.

The data offered some support for the hypotheses. The data consisted of body movements, particularly fidgetlike movements referred to as adaptors, and shifts in posture, the search for a more comfortable position as it were. Significant main effects were found for both adaptors and posture shifts, with internals for achievement producing more of each movement than their external counterparts. The adaptor movements increased as the difficulty of the items increased among internals but surprisingly declined in frequency among externals. Posture shifts, on the other hand, did not vary with difficulty level, internals shifting about more than externals throughout the test procedure.

In contrast to the results with the achievement measure, affiliation locus of control proved to be irrelevant to manifestation of adaptors. On the other hand, those who were more external for affiliation were found to shift their postures more than their internal peers in this socially embedded achievement task. Although more experimentation is required before definitive comments can be offered, let it suffice to suggest that the mixing of cues that stress social interaction and achievement within one experiment may offer some interesting and perhaps confusing criteria for combination measures deriving from the MMCS.

Another set of data in this study underlines the value of developing more goal-specific locus-of-control measures. Rotter's I–E scale was unrelated to the criteria, producing neither main effects nor interactions.

The availability of meaningful subtests in the MMCS also allows for a closer evaluation of significant results. In this investigation, the subscale for achievement effort proved to be the most robust predictor of discomfort-indicating body movements. Those who ascribed achievement outcomes to effort were the most likely to appear distraught as the task proceeded. Perhaps the guilt, embarrassment, or humility that Weiner and his colleagues associated with effort attributions for failure were the sources of discomfort that we witnessed in our study. However these initial findings are interpreted, the accessibility of subscales measuring specific attributes is appealing, especially as they may allow us to predict particular affective responses to given experiences.

In addition to the achievement-oriented study, the MMCS has been used in several investigations involving affiliative behaviors. In one study concerned with listening skills and self-presentation, we found that after subjects had spent a period of time interacting with each other, males' ratings of their partners' attentiveness were highly related to their locus-of-control-for-affiliation scores ($r = -.54$, $p < .01$, $N = 22$). That is, the more internal for affiliation was an individual, the more highly was he rated as a listener by the person with whom he had interacted. This relationship was not found with a female sample, however, nor with the achievement locus-of-control scale.

When particular nonverbal components of attentiveness were measured, the aforementioned ratings became comprehensible. Subjects who scored high on affiliation ability (the internal-stable factor) were more apt to nod affirmatively while listening ($r = .61$, $p < .01$), were more apt to provide visual acknowledgments in response to their partner's verbalizations ($r = .52$, $p < .02$), and were in turn more self-disclosing ($r = .46$, $p < .05$). Females exhibited a similar trend with regard to self-disclosure ($r = .41$, $p < .10$).

On the other hand, males who scored high in affiliation-situation attributions were rated as less accepting during the interaction ($r = -.43$, $p < .05$), less disclosing ($r = -.51$, $p < .02$), and less warm ($r = -.35$, $p < .10$).

In an earlier study in which we assessed the frequency of self-disclosures during a social interaction, ability and effort attributions for affiliation proved to have predictive utility for both sexes. When the conditions in the investigation called for more personal disclosures, those who were more internal for affiliation, scoring high on both ability and effort, were more likely to become self-disclosing ($r = .30$, $p < .05$).

Our research with the affiliation locus-of-control scale is still in progress, and we have been further encouraged by other data in which we have examined the role of affiliation attributions for predicting social behavior criteria. At this time, it would be premature, however, to describe our findings at length. Let it suffice to say that we have found both encouragement and uncertainty from our results. The manner in which the subscales operate opposite one another, for example, generates some confusion. For example, affiliation ability seems to have more value with regard to the prediction of social behaviors than the other three attributes. People apparently have ready generalizations about their stable social skills that seem reliable and important for predicting their social behavior. However, effort seems to be considerably more important than ability attributions when achievement behavior is being predicted. In fact, a perusal of the interrelationships between subscale scores and factor structure of the achievement locus-of-control scale suggests that ability attributions more often cohere with external attributes for achievement, a finding that bears similarity to the behavioral observations reported in Dweck's (1975) and Dweck and Reppucci's (1973) research that we noted previously.

Our data, thus far, are not conclusive, and we are not even committed to the exact forms of our scales at this time. However, between our initial findings with the MMCS, the Wallstons' health locus-of-control scale, and Reid's locus-of-desired-control measure, there seem to be ample support and encouragement for those interested in developing goal-specific locus-of-control measures.

FUTURE PROSPECTS

I would now like to take the opportunity to share a fantasy, one that has been in the back of my mind during the three years that I have been working on the development of the MMCS. Much has been reported in the literature about the relationship between locus of control, helplessness, depression, and devitalization. Enough substantial data has been amassed that recent descriptions of affective disorders such as those by Beck (1976), Becker (1977), and Klinger (1977) have emphasized helplessness and locus of control as central features in the development of depression. Nevertheless, it is my impression that formulations of depression emphasizing the perception of control have had more impact upon academicians and researchers than upon clinicians, who have to cope with problems such as depression in their daily practices.

If some assessment devices were to become available, however, that queried persons about their values or desired satisfactions and also probed for their control expectancies relevant to those ends, it is possible that the clinical utility of the research pertaining to control would be more quickly realized.

That Reid and Ziegler (1977) were able to conduct such assessments with elderly persons and could produce results congruent with experimental studies such as those of Langer and Rodin (1976) and Rodin and Langer (1977) attests to the potential value of such assessment procedures. I can imagine preventative programs built from findings that certain groups, or individuals occupying given positions or status, suffer an exacerbated sense of helplessness in some important realms of reinforcement. I can also imagine the use of individual assessments that would offer a clinician information about the precise concerns that people feel helpless to achieve. Such knowledge could suggest focal goals toward which therapeutic intrusions could be directed. In turn, the availability of focal goals could help to sharpen the testing and use of given therapeutic procedures much in the way that specification of the sources of anxiety has aided in the progress of behavior modification.

Our work thus far has merely scratched the surface with regard to the creation of goal-specific measures of locus of control. It is my hope, however, that the interest in helplessness and locus of control that exists today will be sustained and that research will proceed in some of the directions that I have described here. If such should become the case, the potential clinical utility that I have described now as a fantasy may in fact become operational tomorrow.

ACKNOWLEDGMENT

This paper was written while the author was receiving research support from the Canada Council Grant #410-77-0342.

REFERENCES

Beck, A. T. *Cognitive therapy and the emotional disorders.* N.Y.: International Universities Press, 1976.

Becker, J. *Affective disorders.* Morristown, N.J.: General Learning Press, 1977.

Bryant, B. K., & Trockel, J. F. Personal history of psychological stress related to locus of control orientation among college women. *Journal of Consulting and Clinical Psychology,* 1976, *44,* 266–271.

Crandall, V. C., Katkovsky, W., & Crandall, V. J. Children's beliefs in their control of reinforcements in intellectual-achievement behavior. *Child Development,* 1965, *36,* 91–109.

Ducette, J., Wolk, S., & Soucar, E. Atypical pattern in locus of control and nonadaptive behavior. *Journal of Personality,* 1972, *40,* 287–297.

Dweck, C. S. The role of expectations and attributions on the alleviation of learned helplessness. *Journal of Personality and Social Psychology,* 1975, *31,* 674–685.

Dweck, C. S., & Reppucci, N. D. Learned helplessness and reinforcement responsibility in children. *Journal of Personality and Social Psychology,* 1973, *25,* 109–116.

Hetherington, E. M. Effects of father absence on personality development in adolescent daughters. *Developmental Psychology,* 1972, *7,* 313–326.

Jackson, D. N. *Personality Research Form.* Goshen, N.Y.: Research Psychologists Press, 1967.

Jackson, D. N., & Messick, S. *The differential personality inventory.* London, Ontario: University of Western Ontario, 1964.

Kirscht, J. P. Perception of control and health beliefs. *Canadian Journal of Behavioral Science,* 1972, *4,* 225–237.

Klinger, E. *Meaning and void.* Minneapolis: University of Minnesota Press, 1977.

Langer, E. J., & Rodin, J. The effects of choice and enhanced personal responsibility for the aged: A field experiment in an institutional setting. *Journal of Personality and Social Psychology,* 1976, *34,* 191–198.

Lefcourt, H. M. *Locus of control: Current trends in theory and research.* Hillsdale, N.J.: Lawrence Erlbaum Associates, 1976.

Lefcourt, H. M., Hogg, E., & Sordoni, C. Locus of control, field dependence, and the conditions arousing objective versus subjective self-awareness. *Journal of Research in Personality,* 1975, *9,* 21–36.

Lefcourt, H. M., E., Hogg, E., Struthers, S., & Holmes, C. Causal attributions as a function of locus of control, initial confidence and performance outcomes. *Journal of Personality and Social Psychology,* 1975, *32,* 391–397.

Lefcourt, H. M., Von Baeyer, C., Ware, E., & Cox, D. *The multidimensional-multiattributional causality scale: The development of a goal-specific locus of control scale.* Paper presented at the meeting of the American Psychological Association, Toronto, 1978.

Levenson, H. Multidimensional locus of control in psychiatric patients. *Journal of Consulting and Clinical Psychology,* 1973, *41,* 397–404.

Mischel, W., Zeiss, R., & Zeiss, A. Internal–external control and persistence: Validation and implications of the Stanford preschool internal–external scale. *Journal of Personality and Social Psychology,* 1974, *29,* 265–278,

Naditch, M. P. Locus of control, relative discontent and hypertension. *Social Psychiatry,* 1974, *9,* 111–117.

Naditch, M. P., Gargan, M., & Michael, L. Denial, anxiety, locus of control, and the discrepancy between aspirations and achievements as components of depression. *Journal of Abnormal Psychology,* 1975, *84,* 1–9.

Norman, D. Unpublished data with the MMCS. Toronto: Centennial College, 1977.

Reid, D., & Ware, E. E. Multidimensionality of internal versus external control. Addition of a third dimension and non-distinction of self versus others. *Canadian Journal of Behavioral Sciences,* 1974, *6,* 131–142.

Reid, D., & Ziegler, M. *The contribution of personal control to psychological adjustment of the elderly.* Paper presented at the Canadian Psychological Association Convention, Vancouver, 1977.

Rodin, J., & Langer, E. J. Long-term effects of a control-relevant intervention with the institutionalized aged. *Journal of Personality and Social Psychology,* 1977, *35,* 897–902.

Rotter, J. B. Generalized expectancies for internal versus external control of reinforcement. *Psychological Monographs,* 1966, *80* (1, Whole No. 609).

Wallston, B. S., Wallston, K. A., Kaplan, G. D., & Maides, S. A. Development and validation of the health locus of control (HLC) scale. *Journal of Consulting and Clinical Psychology,* 1976, *44,* 580–585.

Wallston, K. A., Maides, S., & Wallston, B. S. Health-related information seeking as a function of health-related locus of control and health value. *Journal of Research in Personality,* 1976, *10,* 215–222.

Weiner, B., Frieze, I., Kukla, A., Reed, L., Rest, S., & Rosenbaum, R. M. *Perceiving the causes of success and failure.* Morristown, N.J.: General Learning Press, 1971.

Weiner, E., Russell, D., & Lerman, D. Affective consequences of causal ascriptions. In J. H. Harvey, W. J. Ickes, & R. F. Kidd (Eds.), *New directions in attribution research* (Vol. 2). Hillsdale, N.J.: Lawrence Erlbaum Associates, 1978.

16 Internal–External Expectancies and Cardiovascular Functioning

Bonnie R. Strickland
University of Massachusetts—Amherst

The internal–external control-of-reinforcement construct (I–E) has been one of the few individual-difference variables within personality theory that has proved to be of continued viability and validity (Lefcourt, 1966, 1976; Phares, 1976; Rotter, 1966, 1975; Strickland, 1977). No doubt, this occurs for a number of reasons. At a very general level, the development of the I–E construct paralleled shifting attitudes in the United States for large numbers of people. The faceless bureaucracies and "groupthink" of the fifties gave way to the individual and social unrest of the sixties. Although young people reported themselves as increasingly more external (Rotter, 1975), they began to act as if they could change society through their own efforts. Many of us now seem to be engaged in rethinking and consolidating individual goals in the seventies. Over the last quarter of a century, we have turned from a concern with conformity to an interest in individualism, from a reliance on authority to an examination of our own influence. Not only do we look at the stars and our astrological charts for clues to our future; we also receive messages from the satellites that we have thrown into space. Within this social and psychological milieu, numerous investigators turned their attention toward a consideration of internal–external beliefs about control of behavior. Although the I–E construct has often been poorly defined and even ill-used, many psychologists—working primarily within a theoretical framework of social learning theory (Rotter, 1954; Rotter, Chance, & Phares, 1972)—have through rigorous programs of research developed a clearer understanding of the parameters of I–E expectancies. The theoretical and practical importance of this variable has been furthered in such diverse areas as achievement behavior, social action, defensiveness and psychopathology, alertness and attention. In a less systematic way, the I–E dimension has been related to a number of health attitudes and behavior. This research has been reviewed in detail elsewhere (Strickland, 1978), and I do not try to cover all aspects of the relationship of I–E expectancies to health. For present purposes, I concentrate on one specific area within the general health arena, namely cardiovascular functioning. An examination of this important area covers those most salient and significant aspects of I–E-health relationships and gives us the advantage of pursuing one specific health concern in depth.

This year, in the United States, some 650,000 people will die of myocardial infarction (heart attack). Another 250,000 will die of stroke. Whereas most of us have an abiding fear of cancer, the fact is that cardiovascular disease accounts for 55% of all deaths in the United States—almost a million people a year (*Vital Statistics of the United States,* 1976). Within the age range of 35 to 54 years, heart disease is the leading cause of death among men and second to breast cancer among women. Strokes are the fifth leading cause of death among men and third among women. One man in three will have symptomatic arterial disease before age 60, and early death from heart attack will be the only symptom in 40% of these cases (Cooper, 1977). As we know, the rate of cardiovascular disorder appears to be growing among women, many of whom are entering the job market and facing the often considerable strain that has been a part of our contemporary male work world for many years. We do have some reason to believe, however, that the rate of death from cardiovascular disorders may be dropping after an all-time high a few years ago. This is probably occurring not only because of improved medical technology and care but also because many of us are changing our personal life-styles. Most of us now know fewer smokers and more joggers. This brings me to a second reason for choosing cardiovascular disorder as an area of focus. We have been accumulating evidence that certain personal characteristics contribute to heart and arterial disease. The impressively thoughtful and important work of David Glass and others (Glass, 1977a, b; Jenkins, 1976) has demonstrated a relationship between susceptibility to heart attack and what Glass labels Type A behavior—behavior characterized by such predispositions as competitive achievement striving, a sense of time urgency, and hostility. Glass further asserts that Type A individuals are engaged in a struggle for control over environmental demands. This control aspect of Type A behavior appears somewhat similar to the efforts engaged in by individuals who profess beliefs in internal control of reinforcement. Yet there are a number of unanswered questions here. The general I–E-health relationships suggest that internal individuals take precautions to guard against illness and disease and are less likely to have high blood pressure or to be victims of heart attack than are externals. It is difficult to align the possible adaptive strategies of internals with the tragic consequences of heart disease, which apparently affects overstriving, overcontrolling persons. I would like to consider these questions and offer some speculation as to the role of perceived control in cardiovascular disease. Much of what I propose may not be new (see Stokols, 1974, for a review of social learning perspectives in relation to the reduction of cardiovascular risk), but I do hope to add a consideration of I–E expectancies as one of the contributing components, although perhaps only to a minimal degree, of cardiovascular functioning. Moreover, the I–E literature has implications for treatment strategies once cardiovascular functioning is impaired.

Although the etiology of cardiovascular disease is not clearly understood, a number of antecedent conditions have been suggested as leading to increased susceptibility to heart attack (Brand, Rosenman, Sholtz, & Friedman, 1976). These include individual differences such as genetic predisposition, age, sex, and certain biochemical and physiological conditions (e.g., increased serum cholesterol, hypertension) as well as interactive aspects of individual characteristics and situational or environmental demands such as the reaction to work role, smoking and substance abuse, overeating, and physical inactivity. These latter precursors appear to be more actively under the control of the individual than do some of the more specific physiological characteristics, although even some of these, as I note later, may be modified by perceived control.

Within the theoretical network of the I–E construct, it is reasonable to assume that individuals who generally expect that reinforcements occur as a function of their own behavior will do what they can to maximize rewards and avoid punishment. These coping behaviors are also dependent on the degree to which persons recognize that their individual behaviors do make a difference. Internals note contingencies between their actions and subsequent events. (Actually these two factors, perception of contingencies and success striving, have both been included in the definition of internality, possibly leading to considerable confounding with I–E research.) Externals, on the other hand, are more likely to assume that the events that happen to them occur as a function of fate, luck, chance, or power beyond their personal control and understanding (Rotter, 1966). In regard to health behaviors, it does appear that individuals who hold internal expectancies, as opposed to externals, are more likely to seek out information about health maintenance when they value their health (Wallston, Maides, & Wallston, 1976; Wallston, Wallston, Kaplan, & Maides, 1976) and to engage in precautionary health practices (Williams, 1972a, b). Internal patients, in comparison to externals, learn more about their physical ailments when they are stricken with life-threatening disorders such as tuberculosis (Seeman & Evans, 1962) and pulmonary emphysema (Ireland, 1973). With regard to some of those activities that have direct relevance for heart disease, internals are more likely than externals to attempt to protect their health and guard against risk. For example, Sonstroem and Walker (1973) found that internal college males reported more positive attitudes about physical exercise and cardiovascular fitness than did external male students. The internal men were also more likely to participate in voluntary exercise. A number of studies have been conducted that demonstrate that persons who do not smoke and people who have stopped smoking are more internal than individuals who do smoke (Coan, 1973; Hjelle & Clouser, 1970; James, Woodruff, & Werner, 1965; Mlott & Mlott, 1975; Platt, 1969; Steffy, Meichenbaum, & Best, 1970; Straits & Sechrest, 1963; Williams, 1973). However, these results have not always been replicated (Bernstein, 1970; Best & Steffy, 1971; Danaher, 1977; Keutzer, 1968; Lichtenstein & Keutzer, 1967), and later evidence suggests that possibly the most appropriate manipulation for changing smoking behavior is to arrange smoking cessation treatment conditions that are congruent with I–E beliefs. Best and Steffy (1975) involved internals and externals in one of two smoking modification procedures. The most profound changes occurred when I–E beliefs and experimental conditions were congruent. That is, internals responded to an aversive satiation procedure and externals to an agent who decided the rate at which smoking would be reduced. These results were essentially replicated by Best (1975). I should note, however, that in general, the relapse rate following smoking cessation is quite high, close to 80% (Hunt, Barnett, & Branch, 1971).

The findings about I–E beliefs and weight control or weight loss are less clear. Some investigators report that internal in contrast to external subjects are more likely to successfully complete weight control programs (Balch & Ross, 1975) or to be more satisfied with treatment, again within congruent conditions (Wallston, Wallston, Kaplan, & Maides, 1976). However, other experimenters have not been able to relate I–E beliefs to attempts at weight loss (Bellack, Rozensky, & Schwartz, 1974; Manno & Marston, 1972; Tobias & MacDonald, 1977), although some report overweight individuals to be external—a finding also demonstrated by O'Bryan (1972).

Thus, when one considers precautionary health practices, it appears that persons who hold internal expectancies are more likely than externals to engage in behaviors that reduce the risk of heart attack. If this is the case, then one would naturally expect that internals would be less likely than externals actually to suffer from cardiovascular disease. Although the evidence is quite limited, in at least two research investigations, experimenters have suggested that this indeed may be the case. Naditch (1974) had access to the records of over 400 black adults who lived in six American cities. These persons were diagnosed as suffering from essential hypertension (high blood pressure), a disorder that is prevalent among a large number of black people in the United States and that is thought to lead to an increased susceptibility to heart attack and stroke. These individuals had been assessed as to I–E beliefs and had also rated their degree of life satisfaction on a scale ranging from highly content to highly discontent. That group of persons who reported that they were highly discontent with their lives and who also were external had a significantly higher percentage of hypertension (46%) than did any of the other groups (mean of 21%). Those persons who reported themselves as highly content and who were also internal had only a 7% hypertension rate. These results appeared to be primarily a function of the male respondents in the sample and not the females.

In a second extensive study of coronary disease, Cromwell and his colleagues (Cromwell, Butterfield, Brayfield, & Curry, 1977) studied 229 hospitalized patients who, by careful diagnosis, were judged to have suffered heart attacks. A group of 80 medical patients who were ill with disease of comparable seriousness but without cardiovascular involvement served as controls. Overall, coronary patients, as assessed by the Rotter scale, were significantly more external than the medical controls. Of particular interest in this research were the findings that I–E scores were differentially predictive of responses to hospital care. Cromwell et al. manipulated nursing care, patient participation in various activities, and information about heart attack and then considered a number of dependent variables, including stay in intensive care, stay in hospital, rate of alarms (heart rate changes while on the unit), a number of biochemical and physiological indices, rehospitalization, and that ultimate response, death. No patient who was involved in congruent conditions of I–E beliefs and participation in self-treatment either returned to the hospital following dismissal ($p < .06$) or died within 12 weeks following hospital stay ($p < .06$). The 12 who were rehospitalized and the five who died had all been involved in incongruent conditions. Since both these findings are only at the .06 level, one cannot accept these results with great confidence. However, the findings are in the predicted direction, and the very small number of cases may have contributed to the lack of statistical significance. In trying to explain the results, Cromwell et al. (1977) suggest that since these are long-term effects, they may be intimately tied to feelings the patient had about returning to the hospital. Patients whose treatment was incongruent with personal expectancies may have resisted a decision to return to the intensive treatment unit when symptoms of another heart attack occurred, if they did, thus denying themselves adequate care. It appears that incongruent conditions were particularly unpleasant for the participants in spite of the fact that the treatment approaches were relatively standard and apparently helpful when delivered in congruent conditions whether structured or individually controlled. Of other major import in this study are the findings that I–E beliefs were also related to many of the ongoing physiological and biochemical indices that were monitored during the patients' hospital stay. Except in two cases, where internality was linked with high anxiety, external beliefs were always associated with undesirable physical characteristics. These included high temperature, high sedimentation rates, high serum glutamic oxalacetic transaminase, high lactate dehydrogenase levels, and high cholesterol. Also, internal patients were more cooperative in response to treatment demands and left the coronary unit and the hospital earlier than external patients.

It should be noted, however, that in dissertation research completed by Marston (1969), no relationship was found between I–E scores and compliance behavior among a group of coronary patients. Further, in a sample of 58 males, Garrity (1973) found a relationship between a belief in external control (as assessed by responses to five items from the Rotter scale) and return to work after first heart attack.

So with some exceptions we have indications that individuals who report internal expectancies engage in preventive health practices, are less likely to have essential hypertension (depending on life contentment), are less likely to suffer heart attack, and may have a better overall prognosis once heart attack occurs with regard to specific physiological indices. Congruence of expectancies and remedial conditions appears to enhance response to treatment. Why should this be? Would these findings result only from the social and personal characteristics associated with internal expectancies, such as beliefs in control, attempts to master one's destiny, achievement striving, and so on? Or are these results also occurring as a function of more basic physiological responding that we do not yet understand very well? Do people stay healthy because they engage in appropriate health maintenance behaviors of which they are fully aware, or do individuals also reduce the risk of heart attack because at some level below awareness, they have developed appropriate and adaptive bodily responses to stress?

Again, we have several empirical studies, specific to blood flow, that give some indications that cognitive interpretations of threat and perceptions about one's ability to respond to stress modulate autonomic functioning. For example, Hokanson and his colleagues (Hokanson, DeGood, Forrest, & Brittain, 1971) were able to demonstrate that subjects who actually had control over rest periods in a shock-avoidance procedure reduced systolic blood pressure levels relative to yoked control subjects who had comparable rest periods imposed upon them. In biofeedback paradigms, internals appear to be more proficient at increasing heart rate and externals at decreasing heart rate than comparison subjects (Gatchel, 1975; Ray, 1974). Fotopoulos (1971) found that internal subjects could increase heart rate without either reinforcement or external feedback whereas external subjects could increase heart rate only under reinforcement conditions. Again, it appears that enhanced functioning occurs when subjects are in conditions congruent with their I–E expectancies. DeGood (1975) ran 24 internal and 24 external subjects under one of two aversive shock-avoidance procedures. Half the subjects could arrange for rest periods and half had rest periods imposed by the experimenter. Control over rest had an arousal-reducing effect on systolic blood pressure for all subjects. Diastolic blood pressure change appeared to be a function of congruency of conditions. Elevations were lowest for internals in conditions of self-initiated rest and for externals under imposed rest.

Thus, we do have evidence that I-E expectancies are related to basic physiological responding with specific focus on blood flow and/or heart rate. It is likely that the mechanisms through which this occurs are quite complex and probably tied to the perceptual and attentive vigilance of the subject (Berggren, Ohman, & Fredrikson, 1977). However, we still have the puzzle of relating I-E to Type A behavior, and we would be remiss, I think, if we were to assume that this heightened or enhanced autonomic functioning in relation to internality is always adaptive and positive. For instance, Carlson (in press) ran 24 male and 24 female college students who equally represented three distinct ethnic groups—Caucasians, Japanese, and Chinese—on a biofeedback task in which they were asked to lower muscle tension as indicated via frontal electromyographic (EMG) levels. Although no consistent differences in EMG levels were obtained in the control condition as a function of I-E [as assessed by the adult version of the Nowicki-Strickland Locus of Control Scale (Nowicki & Strickland, 1973)], internal subjects in the feedback condition did acquire significantly lower EMG levels than did externals. These results were consistent and stable across both sexes, all three ethnic groups, and two replications. However, internals in the feedback condition— the group that achieved the lowest frontal EMG levels—reported feeling less relaxed during training than their counterparts in the control condition and externals in the feedback condition. Carlson suggests that in their efforts to perform well, internals may have actually sacrificed their subjective state of general relaxation.

Houston (1972) ran college student subjects, assessed as to I-E beliefs, under one of two experimental conditions. One group of subjects was told that they could avoid electric shock by not making mistakes on a subtest of the WAIS, an intelligence measure. The other group was told that there was no way to avoid shock. Subjects who perceived that they had some control over shock reported less anxiety but actually evidenced greater physiological arousal than the no-control group. Although they did not report more distress, internal subjects increased heart rate significantly more than did externals across both conditions. Apparently, internals were more aroused in the control-of-shock condition but failed to admit anxiety about the situation. Externals may have found it easier to "accept" the threat of shock and "resign" themselves to having no control.

Evidently, we must be concerned with the degree to which the continued vigilance of the internal and his or her attempts to maintain control takes a toll in personal functioning, particularly when tasks are difficult or events are actually beyond one's control. As Wortman and Brehm (1975) note: "When an organism is confronted by outcomes that are truly uncontrollable, the most adaptive response may be to give up [p. 331]." Glass (1977b) makes a similar point about the detrimental consequences that may occur for the Type A individual who persists in "hyper-responsiveness" during prolonged exposure to uncontrollable stress. Those individuals who persist in attempts to control stressful life pressures apparently experience a concomitant increase in biochemical and pathologic phenomena that may lead to coronary disease. We might also expect that a failure in control would be more personally devastating for the internal, or Type A person, who has had a history of success and competence than for the external, or Type B person, who is more relaxed about personal abilities or who has attributed responsibility for life events to fate or to powerful others.

I would like to suggest, as do many others in this volume, that the relationship(s) between real control and perceived control is (are) complex and unlikely to be understood through any simple hypotheses linking control and adaptive functioning. I further believe that while we continue to investigate parameters of cognitive mediating variables, we must also consider what may be an even more fundamental phenomenon—namely, perceptions about contingencies of behavior and reinforcement that do actually reflect reality. Efforts at controlling or changing aversive life situations can only be successful if these attempts are functionally linked to the events that one is trying to manipulate. Continued attempts at influence that have no relation to the situation or event that one is trying to change obviously cannot be successful. Individuals may be best served by learning more about their own personal characteristics and values as well as coming to understand as clearly as they can the structural reality of the situations in which they find themselves. Adaptive processes most likely occur within a balance of beliefs and behaviors in which congruence of expectancies and situational demands coalesce for facilitation of desired results. The perception of control may prove to be of value in many general life situations where people take responsibility for their actions and engage in activities that lead them to desired goals. However, perceived control in situations where control is truly unavailable may lead to continued frustration, failure, disappointment, and despair. Moreover, the construct of control may also be only one of many cognitive factors operating as people engage in attempts to change life events. As Wortman and Dintzler (in press) suggest, individual attributions such as perceived control or learned helplessness may be embedded in a net of numerous other cognitions that would be expected to interact with behavior. These include phenomena such as the meaning that one attaches to life events, whether or not a life outcome was expected, the assessed cost of attempting to influence outcome, and the likelihood of further occurrence. Certainly, the perceived control literature and the I–E research have offered important and intriguing findings in relation to individual influence and health, including such life-threatening disorders as heart disease. These findings are important, but they may be only a small part of those complex interactive factors that are precursors of health functioning.

REFERENCES

Balch, P., & Ross, A. W. Predicting success in weight reduction as a function of locus of control: A unidimensional and multidimensional approach. *Journal of Consulting and Clinical Psychology*, 1975, *43*, 119.

Bellack, A. S., Rozensky, R., & Schwartz, J. A comparison of two forms of self-monitoring in a behavioral weight reduction program. *Behavior Therapy*, 1974, *5*, 523–530.

Berggren, T., Ohman, A., & Fredrikson, M. Locus of control and habituation of the electrodermal orienting response to nonsignal and signal stimuli. *Journal of Personality and Social Psychology*, 1977, *35*, 708–716.

Bernstein, D. A. The modification of smoking behavior: A search for effective variables. *Behaviour Research and Therapy*, 1970, *8*, 133–136.

Best, J. A. Tailoring smoking withdrawal procedures to personality and motivational differences. *Journal of Consulting and Clinical Psychology*,1975, *43*, 1–8.

Best, J. A., & Steffy, R. A. Smoking modification procedures tailored to subject characteristics. *Behavior Therapy*, 1971, *2*, 177–191.

Best, J. A., & Steffy, R. A. Smoking modification procedures for internal and external locus of control clients. *Canadian Journal of Behavioral Science*, 1975, *7*, 155–165.

Brand, R. J., Rosenman, R. H., Sholtz, R. I., & Friedman, M. Multivariate prediction of coronary heart disease in the Western Collaborative Group Study compared to the findings of the Framingham Study. *Circulation*, 1976, *53*, 348–355.

Carlson, J. G. Locus of control and frontal electromyographic response training. *Biofeedback and Self-Regulation*, in press.

Coan, R. W. Personality variables associated with cigarette smoking. *Journal of Personality and Social Psychology*, 1973, *26*, 86–104.

Cooper, K. H. *The aerobics way*. New York: Evans, 1977.

Cromwell, R. L., Butterfield, E. C., Brayfield, F. M., & Curry, J. L. *Acute myocardial infarction: Reaction and recovery*. St. Louis, Mo.: Mosby, 1977.

Danaher, B. G. Rapid smoking and self-control in the modification of smoking behavior. *Journal of Consulting and Clinical Psychology*, 1977, *45*, 1068–1075.

DeGood, D. E. Cognitive control factors in vascular stress responses. *Psychophysiology*, 1975, *12*, 399–401.

Fotopoulos, S. Internal vs. external control: Increase of heart rate by thinking under feedback and no-feedback conditions. *Dissertation Abstracts International*, 1971, *31A*, 3703–3704.

Garrity, T. F. Vocational adjustment after first myocardial infarction: Comparative assessment of several variables suggested in literature. *Social Science and Medicine*, 1973, *7*, 705–717.

Gatchel, R. J. Change over training sessions of relationship between locus of control and voluntary heart-rate control. *Perceptual and Motor Skills*, 1975, *40*, 424–426.

Glass, D. C. *Behavior patterns, stress, and coronary disease*. Hillsdale, N.J.: Lawrence Erlbaum Associates, 1977. (a)

Glass, D. C. Stress, behavior patterns, and coronary disease. *American Scientist*, 1977, *65*, 177–187. (b)

Hjelle, L. A., & Clouser, R. Internal–external control of reinforcement in smoking behavior. *Psychological Reports*, 1970, *26*, 562.

Hokanson, J. E., DeGood, D. E., Forrest, M. S., & Brittain, T. M. Availability of avoidance behaviors in modulating vascular-stress responses. *Journal of Personality and Social Psychology*, 1971, *19*, 60–68.

Houston, B. K. Control over stress, locus of control, and response to stress. *Journal of Personality and Social Psychology*, 1972, *21*, 249–255.

Hunt, W. A., Barnett, L. W., & Branch, L. G. Relapse rates in addiction programs. *Journal of Clinical Psychology*, 1971, *27*, 455–456.

Ireland, R. E. Locus of control among hospitalized pulmonary emphysema patients. *Dissertation Abstracts International*, 1973, *33a*, 6091.

James, W. H., Woodruff, A. B., & Werner, W. Effect of internal and external control upon changes in smoking behavior. *Journal of Consulting Psychology*, 1965, *29*, 184–186.

Jenkins, C. D. Recent evidence supporting psychologic and social risk factors for coronary disease. *New England Journal of Medicine*, 1976, *294*, 1033–1038.

Keutzer, C. S. Behavior modification of smoking: The experimental investigation of diverse techniques. *Behaviour Research and Therapy*, 1968, *6*, 137–157.

Lefcourt, H. M. Internal versus external control of reinforcement: A review. *Psychological Bulletin*, 1966, *65*, 206–220.

Lefcourt, H. M. *Locus of control: Current trends in theory and research*. Hillsdale, N.J.: Lawrence Erlbaum Associates, 1976.

Lichtenstein, E., & Keutzer, C. S. Further normative and correlational data on the internal–external (I–E) control of reinforcement scale. *Psychological Reports*, 1967, *21*, 1014–1016.

Manno, B., & Marston, A. R. Weight reduction as a function of negative covert reinforcement (sensitization) versus positive covert reinforcement. *Behaviour Research and Therapy*, 1972, *10*, 201–207.

Marston, M. Compliance with medical regimens as a form of risk taking in patients with myocardial infarctions. *Dissertation Abstracts International*, 1969, *30A*, 2151.

Mlott, S. R., & Mlott, Y. D. Dogmatism and locus of control in individuals who smoke, stopped smoking, and never smoked. *Journal of Community Psychology*, 1975, *3*, 53–57.

Naditch, M. P. Locus of control, relative discontent, and hypertension. *Social Psychiatry*, 1974, *9*, 111–117.

Nowicki, S., & Strickland, B. R. A locus of control scale for children. *Journal of Consulting and Clinical Psychology*, 1973, *40*, 148–154.

O'Bryan, G. G. The relationship between an individual's IE orientation and information seeking, learning, and use of weight control relevant information. *Dissertation Abstracts International*, 1972, *33B*, 447.

Phares, E. J. *Locus of control in personality*. Morristown, N.J.: General Learning Press, 1976.

Platt, E. S. *Internal–external control and changes in expected utility as predictions of the change in cigarette smoking following role playing*. Paper presented at the meeting of the Eastern Psychological Association, Philadelphia, Pa., April 1969.

Ray, W. J. The relationship of locus of control, self-report measures, and feedback to the voluntary control of heart rate. *Psychophysiology*, 1974, *11*, 527–534.

Rotter, J. B. *Social learning and clinical psychology*. Englewood Cliffs, N.J.: Prentice-Hall, 1954.

Rotter, J. B. Generalized expectancies for internal versus external control of reinforcement. *Psychological Monographs*, 1966, *80*(1, Whole No. 609).

Rotter, J. B. Some problems and misconceptions related to the construct of internal versus external control of reinforcement. *Journal of Consulting and Clinical Psychology*, 1975, *43*, 56–67.

Rotter, J. B., Chance, J. E., & Phares, E. J. *Applications of a social learning theory of personality*. New York: Holt, Rinehart & Winston, 1972.

Seeman, M., & Evans, J. Alienation and learning in a hospital setting. *American Sociological Review*, 1962, *27*, 772–783.

Sonstroem, R. J., & Walker, M. I. Relationship of attitudes and locus of control to exercise and physical fitness. *Perceptual and Motor Skills*, 1973, *36*, 1031–1034.

Steffy, R. A., Meichenbaum, D., & Best, J. A. Aversive and cognitive factors in the modification of smoking behavior. *Behaviour Research and Therapy*, 1970, *8*, 115–125.

Stokols, D. *The reduction of cardiovascular risk: An application of social learning perspectives.* Paper presented at the American Heart Association, Behavioral Science Conference on Cardiovascular Risk, Seattle, Washington, June 1974.

Straits, B. C., & Sechrest, L. Further support of some findings about the characteristics of smokers and non-smokers. *Journal of Consulting Psychology*, 1963, *27*, 282.

Strickland, B. R. Internal–external control of reinforcement. In T. Blass (Ed.), *Personality variables in social behavior*. Hillsdale, N.J.: Lawrence Erlbaum Associates, 1977.

Strickland, B. R. Internal–external expectancies and health-related behaviors. *Journal of Consulting and Clinical Psychology*, 1978, *46*, 1192–1211.

Tobias, L. L., & MacDonald, M. L. Internal locus of control and weight loss: An insufficient condition. *Journal of Consulting and Clinical Psychology*, 1977, *45*, 647–653.

Vital Statistics of the United States. Rockville, Md.: U.S. Department of Health, Education and Welfare, Public Health Service, National Resources Administration, National Center for Health Statistics, unpublished data, 1976.

Wallston, B. S., Wallston, K. A., Kaplan, G. D., & Maides, S. A. Development and validation of the health locus of control (HLC) scale. *Journal of Consulting and Clinical Psychology*, 1976, *44*, 580–585.

Wallston, K. A., Maides, S. A., & Wallston, B. S. Health-related information seeking as a function of health-related locus of control and health value. *Journal of Research in Personality*, 1976, *10*, 215–222.

Williams, A. F. Factors associated with seat belt use in families. *Journal of Safety Research*, 1972, *4*(3), 133–138. (a)

Williams, A. F. Personality characteristics associated with preventive dental health practices. *Journal of American Dentists*, 1972, *39*, 225–234. (b)

Williams, A. F. Personality and other characteristics associated with cigarette smoking among young teenagers. *Journal of Health and Social Behavior*, 1973, *14*, 374–380.

Wortman, C. B., & Brehm, J. W. Responses to uncontrollable outcomes: An integration of reactance theory and the learned helplessness model. In L. Berkowitz (Ed.), *Advances in experimental social psychology* (Vol. 8). New York: Academic Press, 1975.

Wortman, C. B., & Dintzler, L. Is an attributional analysis of the learned helplessness phenomenon viable?: A critique of the Abramson–Seligman reformulation. *Journal of Abnormal Psychology*, in press.

17

Perceived Locus of Control and Task Performance

Richard M. Ryckman
University of Maine at Orono

The focus on relationships between individual differences in locus of control and task performance by contemporary research investigators had its origins in Rotter's (1954) social learning theory. In this theory, individuals are assumed to acquire generalized expectancies to perceive reinforcing events as contingent or noncontingent upon their own behavior. Internals are people who believe that reinforcing outcomes are subject to their own control and occur as a result of displaying their skills or abilities. Externals, in contrast, typically perceive these reinforcing events as being determined by luck, fate, or powerful others. Differences in the control orientations of subjects have been assessed primarily through the use of skill versus chance instructional sets or through the use of a variety of paper-and-pencil personality measures. The most notable and popular personality scale currently in use is Rotter's (1966) I–E scale.

In his seminal monograph on the locus-of-control construct, Rotter (1966) pointed out that problems and issues associated with performance could be better understood by accounting for the role played by individual differences in control orientation. Specifically, he maintained that if individuals perceived reinforcers or punishers as contingent on their own behavior, then the occurrence of these events will strengthen or weaken the potential for that behavior to occur again in the same or similar situations. If, on the other hand, people perceive that reinforcers or punishers are not contingent upon their behavior, then the occurrence of these events will be less likely to strengthen or weaken the potential for that behavior to reoccur in the same or similar situations. Thus, people who perceive contingencies between behavior and outcomes would be likely to perform differently than individuals who perceive that outcomes are beyond their control.

The purpose of this chapter is to review and critically evaluate the many research studies that have been conducted to identify and explicate the nature of these differences between internally and externally oriented people. I focus on several research areas of relevance for understanding these differences, including: (1) activity preference and choice behavior; (2) risk-taking strategies; (3) expectancy shifting; (4) achievement motivation and behavior; and (5) schedules of reinforcement. Finally, I examine the many possible explanations of why internals outperform externals and also outline suggestions for possible new research directions aimed at overcoming deficiencies in the current literature.

ACTIVITY PREFERENCE
AND CHOICE BEHAVIOR

First, I would like to focus on research concerning the activity preferences and choice behavior of internals and externals and their implications for performance. In social learning theory, situations are assumed to serve as cues that arouse in individuals expectancies for reinforcers following displays of behaviors. Investigators have assumed that internals would tend to prefer situations that arouse expectancies of contingent relationships between behavior and reinforcers, whereas externals would perhaps prefer participating in situations where outcomes are chance determined. If this assumption could be shown to be valid, then it would suggest that learning and performance between internals and externals would differ in these two kinds of situations. For example, if internals did not value outcomes in chance situations, it is doubtful they would learn much or perform well. On the other hand, if they did value outcomes in skill-determined situations, they would probably show learning and performance that is superior to those shown by externals.

A number of studies have been conducted to test these propositions. Rotter and Mulry (1965), for example, hypothesized that internals and externals would differ in the value they placed on the same reward depending upon whether it was perceived by people as being contingent upon the exercise of their skills or upon the operation of chance. Specifically, they predicted that internals would value performing more in a skill situation than in a chance situation—as evidenced by their taking more time to make decisions on an angle-matching task under skill conditions—whereas externals would value performing more under chance conditions—as manifested by longer decision times under such conditions. The data clearly supported the first hypothesis but were only marginally supportive of the second hypothesis. A study by

Julian, Lichtman, and Ryckman (1968) did provide indirect support for Rotter and Mulry's hypotheses, however. We suggested that internals had a greater need to control outcomes than externals in a dart-throwing situation where their outcomes were clearly determined by the exercising of their skills. This greater "need for control" was assumed to occur because internals chose to throw darts (unblindfolded) from a lesser distance to the target than externals, even though this distance had been equated for the probability of success with farther distances. Externals, in contrast, showed that they valued performing more in a chance situation, since they expressed more concern than internals over criticism of their performances by experimenters in a chance-determined situation in which they threw darts blindfolded. Ryckman, Stone, and Elam (1971) replicated the study of Julian et al. and also explored possible sex differences in performance. We found that internal women were more irritated and embarrassed than external women by experimenter criticism of performance under skill conditions, whereas external women reacted more strongly to criticism under chance conditions. There was, however, no interaction between sex and task requirements for men. Men expressed less irritation and embarrassment than women when their performances were disrupted irrespective of whether or not outcomes on the task were skill or chance determined. The lack of an interaction between locus of control and task requirements for men was interpreted as resulting from their reluctance to display emotion, in accordance with cultural role expectations.

Ryckman, Rodda, and Stone (1971) extended this work, maintaining that a time latency measure might be a more sensitive indicator of the subject's concern with his or her performance than the verbal self-report measure used previously. Longer times were assumed to be positively correlated with concern. Using a dart-throwing task, we found that internal men had longer performance times than externals under skill conditions, whereas external men had longer time latencies under chance conditions. A similar interaction was not obtained for women. Instead, women had shorter performance times under skill than under chance conditions regardless of their locus-of-control orientations. Again, these findings were interpreted in terms of sex-role behaviors expected of men and women in our society. Women were hypothesized to be reluctant to engage in "masculine" behavior; hence they took less time to complete their performances in the skill situation than in the chance one. In brief, the studies using the dart-throwing task can be seen as providing general support for Rotter and Mulry's (1965) initial hypotheses, although they are moderated by the sex of the subject.

Julian and Katz (1968) tested the same hypotheses and found only partial support. In their study, subjects were required to compete against an opponent in a word game. They were asked to judge which of 42 pairs of words were synonyms or antonyms and were further informed that task outcomes were skill or chance determined. Specific hypotheses were that internals would avoid relying on their opponents for answers in the skill condition, even though such reliance might help them to win the competition, whereas externals would avoid relying on opponent help under chance conditions. Julian and Katz stated that confirmatory findings could be interpreted as supporting Rotter and Mulry's (1965) contention that self-determined rewards are of greater value to internals under skill conditions, whereas such rewards are of greater value to externals under chance conditions. The data, however, were not entirely supportive. Internals not only avoided relying on their opponent more than externals under skill conditions but under chance conditions as well. These investigators maintained that these latter results were not due to the possibility that internals perceived the chance task as involving skill-determined outcomes, since their postsession data analyses showed that subjects did perceive that the opponents in the chance situation were luckier than opponents in the skill situation and that the use of strategies to win the game was seen as more important under skill than under chance conditions. Although these data are suggestive, they do not provide direct evidence of a differential perceptual set by subjects under the two conditions. Subjects may have seen the opponent, but not themselves, as luckier under the chance condition. Subjects also may have perceived that strategies were less important under chance than skill conditions, because the task was perceived under chance conditions as so difficult that the use of strategies would have been meaningless. In fact, the instructions in this study do mention that the task under chance conditions is fairly difficult.

The difficulty in insuring that the proper perceptual sets have been established is one that recurs continually in the I-E literature. Typically, investigators intimate to subjects that the task is so difficult that the outcomes are essentially random. It may be, however, that internals interpret such instructions to mean that the task is a difficult one but one allowing of solution. It seems necessary, therefore, for investigators to separate the effects of the difficulty-chance dimensions in future research.

A more direct test of the hypothesis that internals prefer skill-determined activities and externals chance-determined ones was conducted by Schneider (1968). He simply asked internals and externals to state their liking for various sports and found that internal men picked more skill sports than chance sports for possible participation. Internal men chose to participate in skill activities such as football, soccer, and hockey; whereas external men picked chance activities such as dice throwing, dog-race betting, and horse-race betting. It does not seem surprising even today that the interaction between I-E and activity choice held only for men, since the tasks are ones that traditionally have appealed to men and not to women.

Gold (1966) gave internals and externals an opportunity to engage in skill and chance activities under conditions of high or moderate risk. She found that both internal and external men and women selected skill-determined rather than chance-determined tasks under high-risk conditions in which expectancies for success were only 10%, whereas internals and externals chose skill- and chance-determined tasks about evenly under moderate-risk conditions in which expectancies for success were 50%. These results suggest that choice selection may not only depend on the nature of the task but also on the probability of goal attainment.

In a follow-up study, Gold (1967) asked subjects to choose either skill or chance tasks without informational feedback about expectancies for success. She found that internal men picked skill tasks more often than chance tasks, whereas external men opted for chance over skill tasks. There were no differences in the choice behavior of internal and external women.

Finally, Ryckman and Sherman (1974) showed that internals not only value outcomes highly in skill situations but also that they will devise strategies to maximize control over them. In our study, internals were given an opportunity to exercise control by being allowed by an experimenter to select team partners of varying ability levels on an anagram task in advance of a competitive effort against other teams. We found that internals with good ability selected partners of equal ability, even though selection of superior-ability partners would have enhanced their teams' chances for success in the projected interteam competition. We believe that this result occurred because such choices would allow internals to maximize personal control of their outcomes and also their feelings of personal satisfaction if their teams had won in the interteam competition. In brief, they could take maximum personal credit if their team won. Selection of partners with superior ability was thought potentially to lessen satisfaction in the event that the team won, and the choice of inferior-ability partners was thought to jeopardize seriously chances for team success and, hence, personal success and satisfaction. Interestingly, we found some externals who selected inferior-ability partners under the same conditions, thus virtually ensuring defeat for their teams. Despite the fact that these externals had demonstrated objectively good ability on practice trials on the task earlier, they reported lacking confidence in themselves just before the start of the interteam competition. Thus, by choosing inferior-ability partners, they could absolve themselves of blame for the team defeat that they were certain would occur because of their own lack of confidence in their abilities.

In summary, the evidence in this area generally supports the idea that internals tend to prefer performing in skill-determined situations more than chance determined ones in comparison to externals, but these effects are moderated by sex differences and the probability of goal attainment.

RISK TAKING AND DECISION MAKING

The research picture concerning the risk-taking and decision-making behavior of internals and externals is less clear. The general hypothesis guiding research in this area seems to be that people who use more cautious and rational betting strategies will prove to be more successful performers than those who use impulsive and unrealistic tactics and decision making. In an early study, Liverant and Scodel (1960) examined the betting strategies of internals and externals in a dice-throwing situation. Before throwing the dice, subjects were asked to indicate the amount of money they wanted to wager and the kind of bet they wanted to make where the odds for winning were either high or low. They found that internals used a more conservative betting strategy than externals in that they selected more high-probability bets with smaller payoffs and did not vary their betting strategies over a series of trials as much as externals. A study by Strickland and Rodwan (1964) provided support for these initial findings. They examined the decision-making performances of internals and externals in a guessing experiment. Subjects were given 100 3 × 5 cards—75 of which contained circles and 25 of which were blanks. After a practice session, subjects were presented with the cards in randomized fashion and asked to guess before seeing each card whether it contained a circle or was blank. The results showed that internals had fewer false-positive errors than externals. That is, they made fewer wrong guesses about which alternative (a circle or a blank) was on the next card. A reasonable interpretation of these data might be that internals were more conservative in their betting, taking less risk than externals of being proved wrong. Indirect support for the hypothesis that internals may be conservative risk takers is also shown in a study by Wolk and DuCette (1973) where internals with high need for achievement tended to prefer taking intermediate risks on various motor performance tasks. Julian and Katz (1968) also found that internals preferred taking intermediate risks on a dart-throwing task. A study by DuCette and Wolk (1972) likewise indicated that internals preferred moderate risk taking, whereas externals were characterized by more extreme risk taking. Finally, El-Gazzar, Saleh, and Conrath (1976) showed that internals were more cautious than externals in their gambling behavior. They also found that I–E interacted with need for achievement in that high-achievement externals took great risks, whereas low-achievement internals tended to take little risk.

Despite this evidence, Rettig (1969) found no difference between internals and externals in risk-taking behavior where subjects were asked to predict the probability with which an unethical decision would be made under varied circumstances. Studies by Gold (1966), Butterfield (1964), and Minton and Miller (1970) were also characterized by a lack of differences between internals and externals in risk-taking behavior. Furthermore, an investigation by Strickland, Lewicki, and Katz (1966) even showed that internals were greater risk takers than externals in a dice-throwing study similar to the one conducted by Liverant and Scodel (1960). However, as the authors themselves noted, their results might be explained by reference to the age differences of subjects in the two studies. Specifically, Liverant and Scodel used college students as subjects; but Strickland, Lewicki, and Katz employed high school students, who may not have understood the betting odds very well. Finally, Baron (1968) administered a variety of Wallach and Kogan (1959) choice-dilemma problems to subjects and found that internals tended to be greater risk takers than externals. Perhaps internals were more willing to take risks because the choices they made were hypothetical and the payoffs fictional.

In summary, the research findings in this area are mixed, and no firm conclusions can be drawn at the present time. Clarification might be forthcoming if researchers decide to use a wider range of age groups, tasks, and payoffs. The maximum payoff in the Liverant and Scodel study, for example, was only 40¢. Perhaps internals would take more risks if the rewards were greater.

LOCUS OF CONTROL
AND EXPECTANCY SHIFTING

I would like to turn now to a presentation of the research on expectancy shifting. Expectancies, of course, are considered to be a primary determinant of performance in Rotter's social learning theory, so that it is not surprising that researchers have explored issues in this area more thoroughly than others. An early study by Phares (1957) was designed to examine the relationship between I–E and expectancy shifting. He used line matching and color matching as experimental tasks, instructing half his subjects that outcomes on both tasks were a matter of chance and the remaining half that these outcomes were skill determined. He theorized that subjects in the skill condition (those with an induced internal locus of control) would utilize their past performances as a basis for generalizing to future performances. As effective agents in the situation, that is, as people who perceived that they could determine their own outcomes, internals could generalize from past similar experiences. Since the subjects in the chance condition (those with an induced external locus of control) were not determining agents, Phares hypothesized that they would disregard their past performances and not use them as a basis for generalization to future performances. Using this reasoning, Phares predicted and found that subjects had greater increases and decreases in expectancies following success and failure, respectively, under skill than under chance conditions despite the fact that both groups had received the same number and sequence of reinforcers. He also found that subjects shifted or changed expectancies in the typical direction more often under skill conditions and that subjects in the chance condition showed more unusual expectancy shifts, that is, shifts upward after failure and downward after success.

Although the Phares (1957) study involved a situational manipulation of perceived control, it should be noted that he also developed a Likert-type I–E scale during this time period and showed that individuals who scored at the external end of the continuum behaved as all subjects did when placed in a chance versus a skill situation. That is, externals tended to show smaller magnitude increases and decreases following success and failure, a lower frequency of shifts, and more unusual shifts than did subjects who were classified as internals. James (1957) utilized a revised version of Phares' test and found similar results for internals and externals placed in skill and chance situations. He also found that externals generalized their past experiences to other tasks less than internals. Incidentally, James' scale was later revised by Liverant in association with Rotter and Seeman (Rotter, 1966) and eventually culminated in the creation by Rotter of the current version of the I–E scale.

In addition to the James study, which essentially replicated the initial effort by Phares, there have been a number of other studies that have also provided supportive evidence (Battle & Rotter, 1963; DuCette & Wolk, 1972; Lefcourt & Ladwig, 1966; Lefcourt, Lewis, & Silverman, 1968; Walls & Cox, 1971). Furthermore, a host of studies have provided partial support (Feather, 1968; Klein & Seligman, 1976; Masterson, 1973; Miller & Seligman, 1976; Petzel & Gynther, 1970; Rotter, Liverant, & Crowne, 1961; Ryckman, Gold, & Rodda, 1971; Ryckman & Rodda, 1971). A study by Lefcourt (1967), however, did not provide support. He used a level of aspiration board task (cf. Rotter, 1954) where outcomes were clearly skill determined and found no differences between internals and externals in the amount of shifting or in the number of unusual shifts. Rotter, Liverant, and Crowne (1961) also found no differences between skill and chance subjects in the number of unusual shifts, although they did find more typical changes (up after success, down after failure) in the skill, as compared to chance, condition. Ryckman, Gold, and Rodda (1971) examined relationships between I–E, expectancy shifts, and performance using an anagram task where outcomes were linked to subjects' abilities. We noted that although Feather (1968) had found that internals made more typical expectancy shifts than externals over 15 trials of anagram problem solving, he did not find that locus-of-control personality differences between high- and low-responsive subjects during the initial five trials of the task eventuated in a difference in subsequent performance effectiveness over the last 10 trials, as he had expected. That is, he expected that internals who were more responsive to their initial task experiences would subsequently perform more effectively than internals who were not as responsive to their experiences. Responsiveness was defined as the extent or degree of expectancy change in the typical direction made by the subjects. As a result, we argued that a consideration of both locus-of-control and self-esteem differences might be necessary to explain Feather's unexpected finding. Specifically, we predicted and found that responsiveness following success and failure on the first 5 trials of the anagram task was positively related to subsequent performance (over the last 10 trials) for high-self-esteem internals ($r = .50$, $p < .05$) but not for their low-self-esteem counterparts ($r = -.23$). It was assumed that internals with high self-esteem are characterized by greater acceptance of both their success and failure experiences. We also expected and found that responsiveness for high- ($r = .17$) and low-self-esteem ($r = -.13$) externals was unrelated to subsequent performance, because these subjects were presumably not very concerned with reinforcement outcomes on a task involving the use of individual skills. This study suggests the importance of considering interactions between various personality variables in order to increase one's accuracy of prediction about performance. It is a strategy that fortunately has been increasingly adopted by I–E researchers in recent years (e.g., DuCette & Wolk, 1973; El-Gazzar et al., 1976; Hochreich, 1974).

In another study (Ryckman & Rodda, 1971) we had subjects respond on a line-matching task where outcomes were primarily chance determined. We found that externals made more typical expectancy shifts following success but that contrary to our expectations, externals made fewer such shifts than internals after failure. We attempted to explain this latter finding by citing a study by Teevan and Hartsough (1964) that showed that externals have a high fear of failure. Relatedly, Rotter (1966) has maintained that subjects may acquire an external view as a defense against failure. Thus we maintained that if these contentions are valid, then one indication of the externals' defensiveness would be a reluctance on their part to shift downward after failure. A reanalysis of our data indicated that externals did indeed have more cases than internals of no expectancy shifts following failure. These cases of no expectancy shifts are similar to Rotter's (1945) description of a rigid pattern of responding by subjects who are failure avoidant. It seems that further exploration of these so-called neutral cases is warranted.

Finally, a study of expectancy shifting was conducted by Masterson (1973) in which subjects were asked to use their abilities to judge (skill condition) or to make guesses about (chance condition) which one of two pairs of women's stockings fashion designers thought was a better fashion accessory. Before making each judgment or guess on each of 30 trials, they were asked to state how confident they were of being correct. They were then given feedback from the experimenter concerning their correctness on each trial. There were eight acquisition trials under both the skill and chance manipulation conditions in which the experimenter provided subjects with either 25%, 50%,

75% or 87.5% reward schedules. Acquisition was followed by 22 extinction trials in which each of their judgments was deemed incorrect by the experimenter. In general support of Phares' (1957) findings, Masterson found that subjects in the chance condition made more atypical expectancy increases during both acquisition and extinction than subjects in the skill condition, whereas atypical decreases were more frequent in the chance condition during extinction only. In line with Phares' results, Masterson also found that typical expectancy decreases were more frequent in the skill than in the chance condition during both acquistion and extinction. Contrary to Phares' theorizing, however, there was no difference in the percentage of typical expectancy increases in the skill and chance conditions. In terms of the amount of expectancy change from initial levels (1st trial) to terminal acquisition levels (8th trial), Masterson found that subjects showed greater changes in the skill than in the chance condition even though initial expectancies between the two groups were highly similar. This result is consistent with Phares' original theorizing.

In summary, a large number of studies provide general support for the idea that the locus-of-control orientation of people influences expectancy changes. They indicate that internals are more likely to use their past experiences as the basis for generalizing to future performances than are externals or people who believe that outcomes are chance determined. One implication of these data is that internals may be more likely to use their cumulative experiences on tasks to develop better problem-solving strategies or more accurate and realistic assessments of their skills, so that the result could be more effective performances.

Alternative Explanation for Expectancy Shifts: Weiner's Attribution Approach

Recently, however, Weiner and his associates have questioned the adequacy of Rotter's locus-of-control interpretation of expectancy changes (Weiner, 1972; Weiner, Heckhausen, Meyer, & Cook, 1972). In their attributional model of achievement behavior, it is assumed that individuals allocate the causes of their successes and failures to four factors: ability, effort, luck, and task difficulty. These four factors are classified in terms of two dimensions: locus of control (internal versus external factors) and stability (fixed versus variable factors). Thus, an internal orientation involves the assessment of a performance in terms of ability and effort, whereas an external orientation involves attributions to luck and task difficulty. Assessments along the stability dimension would involve attributions of performances to ability and task difficulty (fixed) or to luck and effort (variable factors). In terms of this classification scheme, Weiner (1972) and Weiner et al. (1972) maintain that it is attributions to factors along the stability dimension rather than the locus-of-control dimension that primarily influence changes in expectancies following success or failure; whereas attributions to factors on the locus-of-control dimension primarily influence affective states, that is, feelings of pride or shame, following success or failure.

In regard to expectancy changes, Weiner and his colleagues (Weiner, 1972; Weiner et al., 1972) believe that if a current outcome is attributed to a stable cause, then the present outcome will be expected to reoccur in the future when the behavior is performed again. If a current event is attributed to an unstable cause, then the present outcome will not be expected to repeat itself in the future. Thus he maintains that attributions to stable factors produce greater increments and decrements and more typical expectancy shifts following success and failure than attributions to variable factors. Specifically, success ascribed to high ability or an easy task should produce greater increases and more typical expectancy shifts than attributions of success to high effort and good luck. Conversely, failure ascribed to low ability or a hard task should produce greater decreases and more typical shifts than attributions of failure to a lack of effort or bad luck.

Weiner and his colleagues report strong empirical support for their view that stability factors affect expectancy changes (Fontaine, 1974; McMahon, 1973; Meyer, 1973; Weiner, 1972; Weiner et al., 1972, Weiner, Nierenberg, & Goldstein, 1976). In the Weiner et al. (1976) study, for example, subjects were required to match a block design (taken from the WAIS) shown by the experimenter. Various groups of subjects were then led to believe that they were either successful or unsuccessful on a series of these problems and were asked to make attributions for their performances to factors along the stabiity and perceived control dimensions. They found that the stability of causal attributions, and not locus of control, affected expectancy changes.

Although the aforementioned studies provide support for the position of Weiner and his collaborators, a study by Riemer (1975) did not show that stability attributions influence expectancy changes. She found that men and women who believed that they were participating in a piano practicum and who attributed successful performances to good ability and/or an easy task did not become more confident that they would perform the same on the same task than subjects who attributed their performances to trying hard and/or to good luck. She did find support, however, for Weiner's (1972) and Weiner et al.'s (1972) contention that locus of control influences affective states. Subjects who attributed their successful performances to internal factors (ability and effort) reported more pride in their accomplishment than those who attributed their performances to external factors (chance and task).

Despite the fact that not all the evidence strongly supports the theorizing of Weiner and his collaborators, their position does provide a new and interesting theoretical scheme that may help to clarify the ways in which expectancies are formed and changed by individuals following performance outcomes. There are, however, a number of problems with the position that need attention. For example, its treatment of locus of control as synonymous with the skill–chance distinction is inadequate, as Phares (1976) has already noted. The locus-of-control construct has additional meanings and is used to account for a broader range of behaviors and situations than those encompassed by the skill–chance distinction. Also, research based on locus-of-control theory attempts to deal with generalized expectancies that individuals have acquired on the basis of a variety of past experiences, whereas the Weiner (1972) model focuses primarily on the role that specific expectancies play in influencing subject judgments. A generalized expectancy concept may have helpful theoretical and research implications for the Weiner model. For example, the model assumes that ability and task difficulty are stable factors but that effort and luck are unstable factors. Yet people may, on the basis of past experiences outside the current experimental situation, acquire generalized expectancies concerning their ability levels, luckiness, and motivation to persist when performing certain tasks. They may also have generalized expectancies about the difficulty of a task on the basis of extensive past experiences with similar tasks. In brief, people may come to believe that they are lazy or hard-working or that they are unlucky or lucky. Thus effort and chance can be conceptualized as stable factors if long-term experiences are assessed, as Weiner (1972) himself acknowledges.

Ability and task difficulty, on the other hand, can be conceptualized as unstable factors if individuals have had little or no experience with similar tasks or situations. Even with some experiences on such tasks, ability and task difficulty may still be seen as unstable factors if those experiences were variable. They may also be seen as unstable even if the individual has had extensive, consistent experiences on similar tasks, because he or she may not have had sufficient experience on the current task to integrate those experiences with the prior ones. See Table 17.1 for an illustration of an expanded classification scheme and some examples.

Of course, some of these examples are more likely to be subjectively real to the individual than others. For example, the statements "I am a persistent person" and "I am a lucky person"seem commonsensically to be more a part of one's naive perception of events than the statements "On this task, I sometimes have good ability" and "This task is sometimes easy for me." Nevertheless, within that constraint, I think that by taking generalized, as well as specific, expectancies into account, it should be possible to predict more accurately the attributions of people following performance outcomes and also their expectations and future behavior.

The Weiner (1972) model can be reformulated to achieve this goal in the following way. The generalized and specific expectancy concepts can be incorporated into the attribution model by the introduction of an uncertainty dimension. For example, there seem to be two primary sources of

TABLE 17.1
Classification Scheme for the Perceived Determinants
of Achievement-Related Behavior
Based on Generalized and Specific Expectancies

	Locus of Control			
	Internal		*External*	
	Generalized Expectancy	*Specific Expectancy*	*Generalized Expectancy*	*Specific Expectancy*
Stable	I have good (poor) ability.	I have good (poor) ability on this task.	Tasks are easy (hard) for me.	This task is easy (hard) for me.
	I am a persistent (lazy) person.	I will (will not) persist on this task.	I am a lucky (an unlucky) person.	I am lucky (unlucky) on this task.
Unstable	Across many similar tasks, I sometimes have good (poor) ability.	On this task, I sometimes have good (poor) ability.	Across many similar tasks, the task is sometimes easy (hard).	This task is sometimes easy (hard) for me.
	Across many similar tasks, I sometimes try (do not try) hard.	On this task, I sometimes try (do not try) hard.	Across many similar tasks, I am sometimes lucky (unlucky).	On this task, I am sometimes lucky (unlucky).

information uncertainty for a person faced with making ability attributions prior to performance on a particular task. One source involves the uncertainty generated by the degree of similarity between the current task and past experiences on other tasks. The more closely the previous tasks resemble the current one, the more certain an individual would be concerning personal ability judgments and hence in his or her expectancy for success. The more dissimilar the previous tasks to the current one, the more uncertain the individual would be. The second source of uncertainty is based upon the number, percentage, and pattern of success experiences on prior tasks, as Weiner and his colleagues note (Weiner, 1972; Weiner et al., 1972). Uncertainty is either increased or decreased also by the same experience factors as the person proceeds on the current task. Thus, if the person is in the initial stages of performing on a task in which prior experiences on tasks resemble the current one and on which he or she has a large number and consistent pattern of successes, then a failure on a given trial should be attributed to a lack of effort or bad luck. If, on the other hand, the person is in the initial stages of performing on a task that does not resemble prior ones very much and on which he or she has had a small number of experiences and ones involving inconsistent success patterns, then a failure on a given trial might still be attributed to the ability factor. That is, the person may believe that the specific experience provides information about his or her ability. Perhaps the individual did not have as much ability as he or she thought.

In terms of much of the research literature involving ability attributions, it seems that experimental tasks are often being used that are trivial and relatively foreign to the subject's experience since initial confidence estimates hover around 50%. If this is the case, then it would seem reasonable that the person would be very uncertain about his or her abilities on that task and that a series of successive, consistent, short-term experiences of success would elicit increasing expectations of success based upon perceptions of increasing ability. In these cases, we would expect to see many typical shifts and shifts of considerable magnitude, but we should not label these ability judgments a stable or fixed trait, as most theorists do. Such labeling is confusing, because it suggests that there would be little change in the magnitude of the shifts with successive experiences.

We would be unlikely to see as many typical shifts following success experiences or shifts of great magnitude where the individual has had a very long series of trials (a rare event in most research in this area) and was highly certain of personal ability. After all, if a person was thoroughly convinced that he or she had only mediocre ability on a task, additional success experiences would be unlikely to change those expectations much.

A similar analysis that utilizes the uncertainty concept can be applied to attributions involving luck, effort, and task difficulty. The incorporation of the concept into Weiner's model makes it more dynamic and capable of accounting for long-term changes in the person's attributions and expectations. A demonstration of the revised model's validity awaits further empirical work.

LOCUS OF CONTROL
AND ACHIEVEMENT MOTIVATION

I would like to turn now to a brief treatment of the literature on achievement motivation, since Phares (1976), Lefcourt (1976), and others have already written extensively and well on the topic. To begin, it is clear that the performances of people should be determined by the value they place upon achievement as well as by their beliefs that their actions will be effective in securing desired outcomes. Rotter (1966) has pointed out further that logically, internals should show more striving for achievement than externals, although he thinks that the relationship would be weakened in college populations (the most studied population) by the operation of two factors. The first limiting factor involves the presence of defensive externals in college populations (i.e., people who have arrived at an external view as a defense against failure but who were initially highly competitive; see Phares, Chapter 14, this volume). Such individuals would still maintain a high achievement orientation in competitive situations. The second limiting factor involves the fact that the college situation is highly structured in terms of achievement. This insures that people's responses will be more determined, irrespective of control orientation, than would be the case in less structured situations. Despite Rotter's conjecture, Phares (1976) reports that there are only a few studies that indicate the presence of a moderate relationship between I–E and striving for achievement, whereas more studies show no significant relationship. In fact, one study showed that internality in children is associated with a lower need for achievement (Chance, 1965). Thus the two variables seem unrelated, at least at this stage of empirical investigation. One of the major problems centers on the fact that investigators have used a bewildering variety of need-for-achievement and locus-of-control measures of varying reliability and validity to establish the relationship, not to mention different subject populations and tasks.

Despite these results, Wolk and DuCette (1973) maintain that there is considerable overlap between theories of control and achievement motivation. They report that Feather (1967) has pointed out that predictions concerning task performance would probably be more accurate if the locus-of-control orientation as well as achievement needs of subjects were taken into account. In fact, the study by Wolk and DuCette showed that locus of control does have a moderating effect on the relationship between achievement motivation and performance. Specifically, they found that internals with high need for achievement preferred intermediate-risk tasks more and performed better on a classroom examination than did externals with similar achievement needs. Thus their study showed that achievement-related behavior in achievement-motivated subjects is elicited only when subjects have an internal orientation. A recent quasi replication of the Wolk and DuCette study by Schultz and Pomerantz (1976), however, failed to provide supportive evidence. Instead, Schultz and Pomerantz found that achievement motivation was as strongly related to various achievement-related tasks—e.g., classroom grades, scores on verbal and quantitative tests—for the entire sample (both internals and externals) as it was for internals alone. Thus it was concluded that the locus-of-control orientation of subjects does not have a moderating influence on the relationship between achievement motivation and task performance. One of the problems with the Schultz and Pomerantz study, however, is that the investigators used a different measure of locus of control than did Wolk and DuCette, so the lack of confirmatory results could be attributed to differences in the reliability and validity of the measures used. Schultz and Pomerantz used Crandall's Intellectual Achievement Responsibility Questionaire,and Wolk and DuCette used Rotter's measure. More importantly, Wolk and DuCette used college students as subjects, whereas Schultz and Pomerantz used junior high school students. In contrast to junior high school students who live in a relatively directive environment, college men and women exist in an institutional environment where the burden for their performance outcomes is placed primarily on them. Success in such an environment may come to those who are not only highly motivated to achieve but who also believe in and accept personal responsibility for determining their actions.

Locus of Control and Academic Achievement Behavior

Where investigators have examined the relationship between I–E and achievement-related performance more directly, the results have been more encouraging. A recent review of the literature by Bar-Tal and Bar-Zohar (1977) shows generally that the more internal the individual's orientation, the higher the person's achievement-related performance. There are, however, troublesome sex differences that the authors generally ignore. In any event, among the 36 studies reviewed by Bar-Tal and Bar-Zohar, 31 showed a positive relationship between I–E and achievement behavior, at least for one of the sexes; four did not detect a significant relationship; and only one found a negative relationship. Most of the 31 studies that found the positive relationship simply correlated I–E with grade point average. The subjects were elementary, high school, and college students. A few of the investigations examined correlations between I–E and various achievement tests, including the Iowa Tests for Basic Skills, the California Achievement Test, and the Stanford Achievement Test.

Generally, then, performance seems to be jointly determined by both the person's locus of control and his or her need for achievement, at least for college students who operate in relatively nondirective academic environments.

IMPACT OF REINFORCEMENT SCHEDULES
ON THE PERFORMANCE OF INTERNALS
AND EXTERNALS

The final area of consideration concerns the impact of schedules of reinforcement on performance. Research has focused primarily on three problems here: the reverse partial reinforcement effect, intrinsic versus extrinsic reinforcement, and learned helplessness. We now turn to an examination of these areas.

Reverse Partial Reinforcement Effect

Early research by Rotter and his associates (Holden & Rotter, 1962; James & Rotter, 1958; Rotter, Liverant, & Crowne, 1961) examined the effects of different reinforcement schedules on the acquisition and subsequent extinction of verbal expectancies by people who were provided with an internal or external task orientation through the use of instructional sets. In general, this research showed that the usual superiority of partial over continuous reinforcement in trials to extinction was found only for people under chance conditions. Under skill conditions, resistance to extinction was superior following continuous rather than partial reinforcement. The explanation for these effects was that under chance conditions, subjects who received 100% reinforcement during the extinction phase noticed that the situation had changed and concluded that positive reinforcers would not be forthcoming. For the 50% reinforcement groups, it was assumed that the beginning of the extinction series did not produce a new cue to indicate that the situation had changed, and thus extinction was more gradual. Under skill conditions, the explanation was that with 100% reinforcement, subjects came to believe that outcomes were under their own control, and thus during the extinction trials, they were less likely to recategorize the situation as having changed. Thus extinction was gradual. With 50% reinforcement in the skill condition, in contrast, subjects attributed nonreinforcement to a lack of skill and extinguished more rapidly.

Weiner (1972) has recently provided an alternative interpretation for these data based upon his attribution model. He maintains that subjects in the skill condition who are continuously reinforced come to believe that they have high ability and thus are more resistant to extinction than subjects who are only intermittently reinforced and come to believe that they only have moderate ability. The change in self-perception from high to low ability requires more failure information than the shift from moderate to low ability. Under chance conditions, Weiner admits the data provided by Rotter and his associates are less amenable to an attributional explanation. He believes that subjects in the 50% reinforcement indeed see their outcomes as a matter of good or bad luck. In the 100% condition, however, he thinks the reward schedule is incompatible with the task instructions. As he puts it, "Just as a coin's repeatedly turning up heads is not compatible with the belief that the outcome is determined by luck, repeated success at the task indicates that something in addition to luck is causing the outcome [p. 398]." But this conjecture is valid only if we assume that attributions to luck are made only when there are variations in performance. If we conceptualize luck as relatively stable under certain conditions, on the other hand, subjects could be seen as assuming that they are lucky and/or have a lucky "hot streak" going under the continuous reinforcement schedule, a streak that may come to an end (first trial of the extinction series) at any time. Thus they would be likely to extinguish more rapidly than subjects who are under a 50% reinforcement condition and who do not know clearly (no unambiguous cues) that their luck has changed. The end of the person's lucky streak following continuous reinforcement may signal to him or her the beginning of an unlucky streak and thus lead to rapid extinction. This interpretation would require a revision in the Weiner model, as noted earlier.

Although early research by Rotter and his associates found support for the reverse reinforcement effect, current research findings have not been encouraging. For example, although Altshuler and Kassinove (1975) found the effect in fifth-grade pupils, it held only for boys. Shepel and James (1973) found that internals performing on a skill task with 100% reinforcement demonstrated significantly more temporal persistence than internals on the same task with 33.33% reinforcement. Under chance conditions, locus of control did not interact with reinforcement schedule, as expected. In addition, using trials to extinction as a criterion, Shepel and James found no significant interaction between I–E and reinforcement schedules under skill and chance conditions. Studies by DiCiaula, Martin, and Lotsof (1968), Keller (1971), Fazio and Hendricks (1970), James and Senn (1965), Nickels and Williams (1970), and Rest, Frieze, Nickel, Parsons, and Ruble (1972) have all failed to find a reversal of the partial reinforcement effect under skill conditions. Thus, there is a definite need for more research in this area with an explicit assessment of the subject's subjective interpretation of the meaning of the 100% chance situation as a high priority for experimenters.

Intrinsic Versus Extrinsic Reinforcement and I–E

A recent interest on the part of locus-of-control researchers concerns the impact of intrinsic versus extrinsic reinforcement (reinforcement provided by an experimenter) on the performance of internals and externals. The determination of which types of feedback are most effective in influencing the performance of different types of individuals would have far-reaching implications for the socialization process, ranging from childhood disciplinary practices to curriculum development and implementation in the schools. Is it better for internals, for example, to be involved in classroom situations where the teacher provides extrinsic feedback (social approval, letter grades, and so forth) or where they are allowed to discover the solutions to problems by themselves? Do externals perform better on tasks when reinforcers are mediated by others? Baron and his associates (Baron, Cowan, Ganz, & McDonald, 1974; Baron & Ganz, 1972) maintain that self-discovery procedures should enhance the performance of internals but not externals, whereas experimenter-mediated reinforcement should enhance the performance of externals but not internals. They reasoned that internals have a higher need for achievement than externals, whereas externals appear to be more responsive to the demands of others. Consequently, success based on self-discovery should trigger pride in accomplishment in internals more than externals and motivate them (internals) to excel. This view is also consistent with Weiner's (1972) position. Since externals are motivated primarily by social approval needs, they reasoned that externals would be more motivated to perform well following praise from the experimenter. Baron and Ganz (1972) found support for their theorizing in a study where fifth-grade students were required to learn a simple form discrimination in order to find a hidden object. They had to identify which one of three boxes contained an object where the boxes differed only in that each one had either a red square, a red triangle, or a red circle on its surface. Under the intrinsic reinforcement condition, the experimenter simply lifted the box indicated by the subject as correct. Under the extrinsic reinforcement condition, the boxes were hidden from the subjects' view after they made their choices, and the experimenter simply informed them whether they were correct or incorrect. In a follow-up study, Baron et al. (1974) showed the generalizability of these findings following a repetition of the original study, using a different population, locus-of-control measure, task, and new procedures for providing feedback.

A study by Taub and Dollinger (1975) also focused on the impact of intrinsic versus extrinsic reinforcement on the performances of internals and externals. Following a lead provided by Lefcourt's research (1967) that suggested that externals, but not internals, needed explicit cues regarding the purpose of and methods of succeeding at a task in order to perform effectively, they predicted and found improved performance by external children on a boring coding task (e.g., placing a subtraction sign symbol inside an appropriate geometric figure in a series of such figures) under conditions of heightened cue explication. Heightened cue explication was defined in terms of a purpose being given to the subjects by the experimenter for performing the task and a reward of candy being given to them for doing well. It was also predicted and found that internals would perform better under conditions where no instructional set outlining the meaning or purpose of the task and no rewards were promised.

Although the foregoing studies provide support for the position suggesting a positive relationship between internality and task performance under intrinsic reinforcement conditions, other research (Hall, 1973; Kumchy & Rankin, 1975; Unmacht & Obitz, 1974) fails to provide support. One possible explanation for this failure may be the fact that different authors define intrinsic and extrinsic motivation and reinforcers differently. Deci (1971), for example, defines intrinsic motivation as the satisfaction a person experiences as he or she performs a task when receiving no apparent reward. The emphasis in the Deci definition is on satisfactions provided by the activity itself. Baron and Ganz (1972), on the other hand, have a definition of intrinsic reinforcement that corresponds closely to self-reinforcement. In their study, subjects were assumed to be satisfied with the activity when they discovered that their choices were correct. Thus knowledge of results was assumed to be the source of reinforcement. This definition is clearly not isomorphic with the one provided by Deci. In Deci's definition, the emphasis is on the activity itself, not the outcome. In the Hall (1973) study, also, there is latitude for questioning whether the reinforcement used was equivalent to intrinsic reinforcement. He required subjects to write continuously the letters *ab* for 10 minutes. The index of productivity was the total number of responses produced during that period. Subjects were asked to reward themselves with a letter grade for their performance at different points during the 10 minute time period. Internals and externals did not differ in their performances. A possible explanation for this finding may be that the reinforcers were not a direct outgrowth of the internals' experience on the task but were provided to them by the experimenter ready-made. Since the reinforcers were only partially under their control, internals may not have been motivated to succeed. Internals may perform best under conditions where they are the originators as well as the appliers of reinforcers to their behavior. Alternatively, the task may have been so artificial and boring that it failed to engage the interest of the internal subjects.

In both the Baron and Ganz (1972) and Hall (1973) studies, it seems reasonable to conclude that the phenomenon under consideration was self-reinforcement, not intrinsic reinforcement. More research on the impact of both kinds of phenomena on the performances of internals and externals is sorely needed.

I-E, Learned Helplessness, and Task Performance

Finally, recent research based upon Seligman's (1975) theory of learned helplessness has shown that aversive stimuli have differential effects on learning and performance depending upon whether subjects perceive that they have or do not have control over their outcomes. In many of these studies, investigators report that people who believe that they have control over their outcomes (internals) show more effective learning and performance than people who believe that they have no control over their outcomes (externals) (Benson & Kennelly, 1976; Dweck & Bush, 1976; Dweck & Reppucci, 1973; Eisenberger, Park, & Frank, 1976; Fosco & Geer, 1971; Gatchel, Paulus, & Maples, 1975; Glass & Singer, 1972; Hiroto, 1974; Hiroto & Seligman, 1975; Klein, Fencil-Morse, & Seligman, 1976; Krantz, Glass, & Snyder, 1974; Roth & Kubal, 1975; Tennen & Eller, 1977; Thornton & Jacobs, 1971).

The paradigm used to study learned helplessness typically involves subjecting people to a training phase on a task in which they are given either contingent or noncontingent feedback following their performances. Control subjects receive no training. Afterwards, performances of the subjects in these groups are compared during a testing phase. Learned helplessness is assumed to occur when people receiving noncontingent feedback in the training phase show learning and performance deficits in the test phase in comparison to the contingent reinforcement and control groups.

In a study that is particularly relevant for personality research on individual differences in locus of control, Hiroto (1974) investigated the relationship between both perceived and instructed locus of control and learned helplessness. He subjected perceived and instructed internals and externals to one of three experimental training treatments. The first group was presented with unavoidable/inescapable aversive stimuli (loud tones). The second group received unavoidable/escapable stimulation, and the third group received no treatment. Following this preliminary training, the test performances of all subjects were assessed on a shuttle-box-type task in which subjects had to shift a knob on a "stick-shift"-type lever from one side of a center point on one trial to the other side on the next trial in order either to avoid or escape presentation of the loud tone. Hiroto found that perceived externals were more helpless than internals and that chance-set subjects were more helpless than skill-set subjects, as evidenced by the fact that both perceived and instructed externals were slower to escape or avoid the aversive tone, required more trials to reach avoidance criterion, and made fewer avoidance responses.

Despite all this evidence, other studies have actually shown improved performances following learned helplessness training, not deficits (Hanusa & Schulz, 1977; Roth & Bootzin, 1974; Roth & Kubal, 1975; Thornton & Jacobs, 1972; Wortman, Panciera, Shusterman, & Hibscher, 1976). In addition to the difficulties that these data present for Seligman's (1975) model, there are other serious methodological flaws in some of the studies in the literature and also plausible alternative explanations other than learned helplessness for why subjects in the testing phase in some of these studies show learning and performance deficits. See Wortman and Brehm (1975) for a detailed discussion of these problems and possible ways of eliminating them.

WHY DO INTERNALS OUTPERFORM EXTERNALS?

Most of the research that we have reviewed indicates that internals generally outperform externals. There are a number of possible reasons for this fact. As mentioned earlier, internals may use their cumulative experiences in skill situations to generate higher and more realistic expectations concerning the probability of success in like situations in the future, whereas externals do not. High expectations for success should be related to superior perform-ances, at least in certain situations. In addition, internals value skill-determined outcomes more than externals and thus are more motivated to succeed in such situations. The fact that internals generally persist longer than externals in trying to solve problems also implies that they are more likely to be successful eventually. They have also been found to show more pride in accomplishment than externals (Phares, 1976). Internals with high self-esteem who have experienced failure are also more likely to perform more effectively than externals with high self-esteem later on, presumably as a result of their willingness to learn from their failures (Ryckman, Gold, & Rodda, 1971).

Internals may also outperform externals because they are more task oriented (Pines & Julian, 1972). They are also more cognitively active (cf. Lefcourt, 1976). That is, they seek more information about their situations (Davis &Phares, 1967) and have more information about various issues critical to their welfare (Ryckman & Sherman, 1976; Seeman, 1963; Seeman & Evans, 1962). They also pay more attention to cues in skill situations that help them organize information that may help them solve problems (Lefcourt & Wine, 1969). In such situations, they also show both better intentional and incidental learning (Wolk & DuCette, 1974).

Finally, internals may outperform externals because they are better adjusted generally (cf. Phares, 1976). Studies have shown that internals have higher self-esteem than externals (Fish & Karabenik, 1971; Fitch, 1970; Ryckman & Cannon, 1975; Ryckman & Sherman, 1973), lower anxiety levels (e.g., Butterfield, 1964; Strassberg, 1973; Watson, 1967), and are less dogmatic (Clouser & Hjelle, 1970; Sherman, Pelletier, & Ryckman, 1973).

Most of these explanations unfortunately are post hoc in nature. For example, there is little evidence that links the cognitive activity of internals directly to task performance. Cognitive activity is viewed as a dependent measure in most of the studies just reviewed, and differences between internals and externals on this dependent measure are considered to be (and are) performance differences. Yet cognitive activity is generally conceded to be an intervening variable (loosely speaking) by researchers. This means that it might also be examined in terms of its effects on other behavioral, problem-solving performance criteria. Relatedly, we know that internals persist longer on skill-determined tasks, but we are not certain that such persistence results in more effective performances. Again, a motivational variable has been treated as a dependent measure of performance, not as an intervening variable. In the same vein, we do not know whether the fact that internals value skill-determined outcomes and have different expectancies for success produces superior performances. In terms of Rotter's social learning theory, for example, the concepts of reinforcement value and expectancy are treated as intervening variables that are assumed to influence performance outcomes.

In general, researchers have tended to examine relationships between locus of control and a variety of cognitive and motivational factors but not to link them to performance criteria. Where researchers have examined the relationships between I–E and performance directly, they have proceeded to ignore the contribution of cognitive and motivational mediators. This has certainly been the case in the area of achievement behavior, where the typical strategy has been to correlate I–E scores with grade point averages and other test scores. What seems to be needed are more studies that explicitly adopt a stimulus–organism–response (S–O–R) theoretical and research framework so that the linkages between control orientations, cognitive and motivational variables, and performances in given situations can become more clearly understood.

RECOMMENDATIONS FOR FUTURE RESEARCH

There are several other possible suggestions that might be considered by I–E researchers interested in this problem area. For example, there is a clear need for I–E researchers to tie their work more closely to social learning theory. This idea also suggests the assessment of the impact of the importance of the reinforcer upon the individual's willingness to perform well. Many of the tasks used by researchers to assess performance differences are trivial, boring, and tedious. Internals may be unwilling to exercise their skills and to expend much effort on such tasks. The result may be a lack of performance differences between internals and externals.

Many of the tasks currently being used are not only unarousing; they are ones that are traditionally associated with one sex or the other. It is not surprising, therefore, to find a lack of performance differences between internals and externals for a sample of women on a task considered by most people to be male associated in nature. In light of the fact that a number of studies have found interactions between I–E and the sex of the subject, it might be wise to control the problem in advance by establishing subjects' perceptions of the sex-role characteristics of the task in the population that is about to be sampled.

Since many of the tasks utilized in the experimental laboratory involve performance based upon the use of physical skills (e.g., pursuit rotor, reaction-time, visual discrimination tasks), there seems to be a need for the construction of a subscale to assess individual differences in that sphere. We are currently in the process of constructing such a scale (Ryckman, Robbins, Thornton, & Cantrell, 1978). Eventually, we hope to demonstrate that reliable and logical predictions can be made from it to behaviors involving the use of a variety of physical abilities and that the subscale can produce a higher relationship with these criteria than global I–E-test scores.

There is also a need to expand research efforts on the effects of reinforcement schedules on the performances of internals and externals. We know little about the effects of different patterns or arrangements of reinforcement on performance or about the impact of reinforcers that differ in magnitude. We know even less about the effects of punishment. Also, although there is considerable evidence that internals prefer to wait for reinforcers that are larger than to take smaller ones immediately available to them, few of these studies have examined the effects of such reinforcement delay upon subsequent performance.

A critical area that is only in an exploratory stage concerns the effects of self-reinforcement on performance. There are only a few studies extant and a lack of clear-cut results, so it is premature to draw any firm conclusions concerning whether self-reinforcement enhances or hinders the performances of internals. Also needed are studies that examine the impact of intrinsic reinforcement on the performance of internals and externals.

Finally, as Rotter (1975) has noted, it is clear that some psychologists have assumed that it is good to be internal and bad to be external. A questioning of this assumption may lead to a new series of researchable ideas. Although internals fit the positive American ideal of self-contained and achievement-oriented individualism, their strong concern for control over outcomes and for maximizing personal satisfactions may sometimes lead them to reject help from authority figures, a decision that may prove harmful to themselves and others (cf. Ryckman & Sherman, 1974). Would internals perform less well than externals under conditions where they need information dispensed by authority figures in order to solve problems? Their focus on the demands of the task may lead to successful problem solving in many situations, but is it always helpful and useful for them to focus on the task and not on the cues provided by the experimenter? How would internals perform in cooperative situations where unified action was necessary to move the group toward the attainment of its goals? Since they perceive themselves as ingenious, egotistical, and competent (Hersch & Scheibe, 1967), what would their reaction be in involuntary situations (e.g., the military and some classroom situations) where they were paired with partners who were less competent than they? How would they perform in situations where they were subordinate to others? Would they perform as well as externals in situations where rewards are expected to be shared with others? These are just a few of the questions that could be translated into researchable terms and that might serve to redress the imbalance in this interesting and important research area.

ACKNOWLEDGMENTS

My thanks to Gordon Kulberg and Colin Martindale for their constructive comments on an earlier draft of the article.

REFERENCES

Altshuler, R., & Kassinove, H. The effects of skill and chance instructional sets, schedule of reinforcement, and sex on children's temporal persistence. *Child Development*, 1975, *46*, 258–262.

Baron, R.A. Authoritarianism, locus of control and risk taking. *Journal of Psychology*, 1968, *68*, 141–143.

Baron, R. M., Cowan, G., Ganz, R. L., & Mc Donald, M. Interaction of locus of control and type of performance feedback: Considerations of external validity. *Journal of Personality and Social Psychology*, 1974, *30*, 285–292.

Baron, R. M., & Ganz, R. L. Effects of locus of control and type of feedback on the task performance of lower class black children. *Journal of Personality and Social Psychology*, 1972, *21*, 124–130.

Bar-Tal, D., & Bar-Zohar, Y. The relationship between perception of locus of control and academic achievement. *Contemporary Educational Psychology*, 1977, *2*, 181–199.

Battle, E.S., & Rotter, J. B. Children's feelings of personal control as related to social class and ethnic group. *Journal of Personality*, 1963, *31*, 482–490.

Benson, J. S., & Kennelly, K. J. Learned helplessness: The result of uncontrollable reinforcements or uncontrollable aversive stimuli? *Journal of Personality and Social Psychology*, 1976, *34*, 138–145.

Butterfield, E. C. Locus of control, test anxiety, reactions to frustration, and achievement attitudes. *Journal of Personality*, 1964, *32*, 355–370.

Chance, J. E. *Internal control of reinforcements and the school learning process.* Paper presented at the biennial meeting of the Society for Research in Child Development, Minneapolis, March 1965.

Clouser, R. A., & Hjelle, L. A. Relationship between locus of control and dogmatism. *Psychological Reports*, 1970, *26*, 1006.

Davis, W. L., & Phares, E.J. Internal-external control as a determinant of information-seeking in a social influence situation. *Journal of Personality*, 1967, *35*, 547–561.

Deci, E. L. Effects of externally mediated rewards on intrinsic motivation. *Journal of Personality and Social Psychology*, 1971, *18*, 105–115.

DiCiaula, P. J., Martin, R. B., & Lotsof, E. J. Persistence and intermittent reinforcement. *Psychological Reports*, 1968, *23*, 739–742.

DuCette, J., & Wolk, S. Locus of control and extreme behavior. *Journal of Consulting and Clinical Psychology*, 1972, *39*, 253–258.

DuCette, J., & Wolk, S. Cognitive and motivational correlates of generalized expectancies for control. *Journal of Personality and Social Psychology*, 1973, *26*, 420–426.

Dweck, C. S., & Bush, E. S. Sex differences in learned helplessness: I. Differential debilitation with peer and adult evaluators. *Developmental Psychology*, 1976, *12*, 147–156.

Dweck, C. S., & Reppucci, N. D. Learned helplessness and reinforcement responsibility in children. *Journal of Personality and Social Psychology*, 1973, *25*, 109–116.

Eisenberger, R., Park, D. C., & Frank, M. Learned industriousness and social reinforcement. *Journal of Personality and Social Psychology*, 1976, *33*, 227–232.

El-Gazzar, M. E., Saleh, S. D., & Conrath, D. W. Situational and individual difference variables in chance-determined activities. *Journal of Personality and Social Psychology*, 1976, *34*, 951–959.

Fazio, A. F., & Hendricks, D. E. Effects of chance versus skill instructional set and partial reinforcement on resistance to extinction. *Proceedings of the 78th Annual Convention of the American Psychological Association*, Washington, D.C., 1970.

Feather, N. T. Valence of outcome and expectation of success in relation to task difficulty and perceived locus of control. *Journal of Personality and Social Psychology*, 1967, *7*, 372–386.

Feather, N. T. Change in confidence following success or failure as a predictor of subsequent performance. *Journal of Personality and Social Psychology*, 1968, *9*, 38–46.

Fish, B., & Karabenik, S. A. Relationship between self-esteem and locus of control. *Psychological Reports*, 1971, *29*, 784.

Fitch, G. Effects of self-esteem, perceived performance, and choice on causal attributions. *Journal of Personality and Social Psychology*, 1970, *16*, 311–315.

Fontaine, G. Social comparison and some determinants of expected personal control and expected performance in a novel task situation. *Journal of Personality and Social Psychology*, 1974, *29*, 487–496.

Fosco, E., & Geer, J. H. Effects of gaining control over aversive stimuli after differing amounts of no control. *Psychological Reports*, 1971, *29*, 1153–1154.

Gatchel, R. J., Paulus, P. B., & Maples, C. W. Learned helplessness and self-reported affect. *Journal of Abnormal Psychology*, 1975, *84*, 732–734.

Glass, D. C., & Singer, J. E. *Urban stress experiments on noise and social stressors.* New York: Academic Press, 1972.

Gold, D. Preference for skill or chance tasks and I–E scores. *Psychological Reports*, 1966, *19*, 1279–1281.

Gold, D. Preference for skill or chance tasks in ambiguous situations. *Psychological Reports*, 1967, *20*, 877–878.

Hall, H. V. Effects of direct and self-reinforcement as a function of internal–external control. *Perceptual and Motor Skills*, 1973, *37*, 753–754.

Hanusa, B. H., & Schulz, R. Attributional mediators of learned helplessness. *Journal of Personality and Social Psychology*, 1977, *35*, 602–611.

Hersch, P. D., & Scheibe, K. E. Reliability and validity of internal-external control as a personality dimension. *Journal of Consulting Psychology*, 1967, *31*, 609–613.

Hiroto, D. S. Locus of control and learned helplessness. *Journal of Experimental Psychology*, 1974, *102*, 187–193.

Hiroto, D. S., & Seligman, M. E. P. Generality of learned helplessness in man. *Journal of Personality and Social Psychology*, 1975, *31*, 311–327.

Hochreich, D. J. Defensive externality and attribution of responsibility. *Journal of Personality*, 1974, *42*, 543–557.

Holden, K. B., & Rotter, J. B. A nonverbal measure of extinction in skill and chance situations. *Journal of Experimental Psychology*, 1962, *63*, 519–520.

James, W. H. *Internal versus external control of reinforcement as a basic variable in learning theory.* Unpublished doctoral dissertation, Ohio State University, 1957.

James, W. H., & Rotter, J. B. Partial and 100% reinforcement under chance and skill conditions. *Journal of Experimental Psychology*, 1958, *55*, 397–403.

James, W. H., & Senn, D. J. *Acquisition and extinction in skill and chance learning.* Paper presented at the annual meeting of the Midwestern Psychological Association, Chicago, 1965.

Julian, J. W., & Katz, S. B. Internal versus external control and the value of reinforcement. *Journal of Personality and Social Psychology*, 1968, *8*, 89–94.

Julian, J. W., Lichtman, C. M., & Ryckman, R. M. Internal-external control and need to control. *Journal of Social Psychology*, 1968, *76*, 43–48,

Keller, H. R. Children's acquisition and reversal behavior in a probability learning situation as a function of programmed instruction, internal–external control, and schedules of reinforcement. *Journal of Experimental Child Psychology*, 1971, *11*, 281–295.

Klein, D. C., Fencil-Morse, E., & Seligman, M. E. P. Learned helplessness, depression, and the attribution of failure. *Journal of Personality and Social Psychology*, 1976, *33*, 508–516.

Klein, D. C., & Seligman, M. E. P. Reversal of performance deficits and perceptual deficits in learned helplessness and depression. *Journal of Abnormal Psychology*, 1976, *85*, 11–26,

Krantz, D. S., Glass, D. C., & Snyder, M. L. Helplessness, stress level, and the coronary-prone behavior pattern. *Journal of Experimental Social Psychology,* 1974, *10,* 284–300.

Kumchy, C. G., & Rankin, R. E. Locus of control and mode of reinforcement. *Perceptual and Motor Skills,* 1975, *40,* 375–378.

Lefcourt, H. M. The effects of cue explication upon persons maintaining external control expectancies. *Journal of Personality and Social Psychology,* 1967, *5,* 372–378.

Lefcourt, H. M. *Locus of control: Current trends in theory and research.* Hillsdale, N. J.: Lawrence Erlbaum Associates, 1976.

Lefcourt, H. M., & Ladwig, G. W. Alienation in Negro and white reformatory inmates. *Journal of Social Psychology,* 1966, *68,* 153–157.

Lefcourt, H. M., Lewis, L., & Silverman, I. W. Internal versus external control of reinforcement and attention in a decision-making task. *Journal of Personality,* 1968, *36,* 663–682.

Lefcourt, H. M., & Wine, J. Internal versus external control of reinforcement and the deployment of attention in experimental situations. *Canadian Journal of Behavioral Science,* 1969, *1,* 167–181.

Liverant, S., & Scodel, A. Internal and external control as determinants of decision making under conditions of risk. *Psychological Reports,* 1960, *7,* 59–67.

Masterson, J. H. Expectancy changes with skill-determined and chance-determined outcomes. *Journal of Personality and Social Psychology,* 1973, *27,* 396–404.

McMahon, I. D. Relationships between causal attributions and expectancy of success. *Journal of Personality and Social Psychology,* 1973, *28,* 108–114.

Meyer, W. U. *Leistungsmotiv und Unsachenerklärung von Erfolg and Misserfolg.* Stuttgart: Ernst Klett, 1973.

Miller, W. R., & Seligman, M. E. P. Learned helplessness, depression, and the perception of reinforcement. *Behavior Research and Therapy,* 1976, *14,* 7–17.

Minton, H. L., & Miller, A. G. Group risk-taking and internal–external control of group members. *Psychological Reports,* 1970, *26,* 431–436.

Nickels, J. B., & Williams, C. B. Effects of locus of control and frequency of reinforcement on two measures of reinforcement expectancy. *Proceedings of the 78th Annual Convention of the American Psychological Association,* Washington, D. C., 1970.

Petzel, T. P., & Gynther, M. D. Effects of internal–external locus of control and skill or chance instructional sets on task performance. *Journal of General Psychology,* 1970, *82,* 87–93.

Phares, E. J. Expectancy changes in skill and chance situations. *Journal of Abnormal and Social Psychology,* 1957, *54,* 339–342.

Phares, E. J. *Locus of control in personality.* Morristown, N. J.: General Learning Press, 1976.

Pines, H. A., Julian, J. W. Effects of task and social demands on locus of control differences in information processing. *Journal of Personality,* 1972, *40,* 407–416.

Rest, S., Frieze, I., Nickel, T., Parsons, J., & Ruble, D. Effects of chance versus skill instructions, schedules of reinforcement, and locus of control on resistance to extinction. *Proceedings of the 80th Annual Convention of the American Psychological Association,* Honolulu, Hawaii, 1972.

Rettig, S. Locus of control in predictive judgments of unethical behavior. *Proceedings of the 77th Annual Convention of the American Psychological Association,* Washington, D.C., 1969.

Riemer, B. S. Influence of causal beliefs on affect and expectancy. *Journal of Personality and Social Psychology,* 1975, *31,* 1163–1167.

Roth, S., & Bootzin, R. R. Effects of experimentally induced expectancies of external control: An investigation of learned helplessness. *Journal of Personality and Social Psychology,* 1974, *29,* 253–264.

Roth, S., & Kubal, L. The effects of noncontingent reinforcement on tasks of differing importance: Facilitation and learned helplessness. *Journal of Personality and Social Psychology,* 1975, *32,* 680–691.

Rotter, J. B. Level of aspiration as a method of studying personality: IV. The analysis of patterns of responses. *Journal of Social Psychology*, 1945, *21*, 159–177.

Rotter, J. B. *Social learning and clinical psychology*. Englewood Cliffs, N. J.: Prentice-Hall, 1954.

Rotter, J. B. Generalized expectancies for internal versus external control of reinforcement. *Psychological Monographs*, 1966, *80*(1 Whole No. 609).

Rotter, J. B. Some problems and misconceptions related to the construct of internal versus external control of reinforcement. *Journal of Consulting and Clinical Psychology*, 1975, *43*, 56–67.

Rotter, J. B., Liverant, S., & Crowne, D. P. The growth and extinction of expectancies in chance controlled and skilled tasks. *Journal of Psychology*, 1961, *52*, 161–177.

Rotter, J. B., & Mulry, R. C. Internal versus external control of reinforcement and decision time. *Journal of Personality and Social Psychology*, 1965, *2*, 598–604.

Ryckman, R. M., & Cannon, D. W. Multidimensionality of locus of control and self-esteem. *Psychological Reports*, 1975, *37*, 786.

Ryckman, R. M., Gold, J. A., & Rodda, W. C. Confidence rating shifts and performance as a function of locus of control, self-esteem, and initial task experience. *Journal of Personality and Social Psychology*, 1971, *18*, 305–310.

Ryckman, R. M., Robbins, M., Thornton, B., & Cantrell, P. *Construction of a physical locus of control scale.* Unpublished manuscript, University of Maine at Orono, 1978.

Ryckman, R. M., & Rodda, W. C. Locus of control and initial task experience as determinants of confidence changes in a chance situation. *Journal of Personality and Social Psychology*, 1971, *18*, 116–119.

Ryckman, R. M., Rodda, W. C., & Stone, W. F. Performance time as a function of sex, locus of control, and task requirements. *Journal of Social Psychology*, 1971, *85*, 299–305.

Ryckman, R. M., & Sherman, M. F. Relationship between self-esteem and internal–external control for men and women. *Psychological Reports*, 1973, *32*, 1106.

Ryckman, R. M., & Sherman, M. F. Locus of control and perceived ability level as determinants of partner and opponent choice. *Journal of Social Psychology*, 1974, *94*, 103–110.

Ryckman, R. M., & Sherman, M. F. Locus of control and student reaction to the Watergate break-in. *Journal of Social Psychology*, 1976, *99*, 305–306.

Ryckman, R. M., Stone, W. F., & Elam, R. R. Emotional arousal as a function of perceived locus of control and task requirements. *Journal of Social Psychology*, 1971, *83*, 185–191.

Schneider, J. M. Skill versus chance activity preference and locus of control. *Journal of Consulting and Clinical Psychology*, 1968, *32*, 333–337.

Schultz, C. B., & Pomerantz, M. Achievement motivation, locus of control, and academic achievement behavior. *Journal of Personality*, 1976, *44*, 38–51.

Seeman, M. Alienation and social learning in a reformatory. *American Journal of Sociology*, 1963, *69*, 270–284.

Seeman, M., & Evans, J. W. Alienation and learning in a hospital setting. *American Sociological Review*, 1962, *27*, 772–783.

Seligman, M. E. P. *Helplessness: On depression, development, and death.* San Francisco: Freeman, 1975.

Shepel, L. F., & James, W. H. *Persistence as a function of a locus of control, task structure and reinforcement schedule.* Paper presented at the annual convention of the American Psychological Association, Montreal, 1973.

Sherman, M. F., Pelletier, R. J., & Ryckman, R. M. Replication of the relationship between dogmatism and locus of control. *Psychological Reports*, 1973, *33*, 749–750.

Strassberg, D. S. Relationships among locus of control, anxiety, and valued-goal expectations. *Journal of Consulting and Clinical Psychology*, 1973, *41*, 319.

Strickland, B. R., & Rodwan, A. S. Relation of certain personality variables to decision making in perception. *Perceptual and Motor Skills*, 1964, *18*, 353–359.

Strickland, L. H., Lewicki, R. J., & Katz, A. M. Temporal orientation and perceived control as determinants of risk-taking. *Journal of Experimental Social Psychology,* 1966, *2,* 143–151.

Taub, S. I., & Dollinger, S. J. Reward and purpose as incentives for children differing in locus of control expectancies. *Journal of Personality,* 1975, *43,* 179–195.

Teevan, R. C., & Hartsough, R. *Personality correlates of fear of failure vs. need achievement individuals—values scales* (Tech. Rep. No. 5). Lewisburg, Pa.: Bucknell University Press, 1964.

Tennen, H., & Eller, S. J. Attributional components of learned helplessness and facilitation. *Journal of Personality and Social Psychology,* 1977, *35,* 265–271.

Thornton, J. W., & Jacobs, P. D. Learned helplessness in human subjects. *Journal of Experimental Psychology,* 1971, *87,* 367–372.

Thornton, J. W., & Jacobs, P. D. The facilitating effects of prior inescapable/unavoidable stress on intellectual performance. *Psychonomic Science,* 1972, *26,* 185–187.

Unmacht, J. J., & Obitz, F. W. Verbal discrimination task performance as a function of self versus external reinforcement, I–E scale performance, and subject versus experimenter determination of response. *Journal of Psychology,* 1974, *86,* 139–148.

Wallach, M. A., & Kogan, M. Sex differences and judgment processes. *Journal of Personality,* 1959, *27,* 555–564.

Walls, R. T., & Cox, J. Expectancy of reinforcement in chance and skill tasks under motor handicap. *Journal of Clinical Psychology,* 1971, *27,* 436–438.

Watson, D. Relationship between locus of control and anxiety. *Journal of Personality and Social Psychology,* 1967, *6,* 91–92.

Weiner, B. *Theories of motivation.* Chicago: Markham, 1972.

Weiner, B., Heckhausen, H., Meyer, W. U., & Cook, R. E. Causal ascriptions and achievement motivation: A conceptual analysis of effort and reanalysis of locus of control. *Journal of Personality and Social Psychology,* 1972, *21,* 239–248.

Weiner, B., Nierenberg, R., & Goldstein, M. Social learning (locus of control) versus attributional (causal stability) interpretations of expectancy of success. *Journal of Personality,* 1976, *44,* 52–68.

Wolk, S., & DuCette, J. The moderating effect of locus of control in relation to achievement motivation variables. *Journal of Personality,* 1973, *41,* 59–70.

Wolk, S., & DuCette, J. Intentional performance and incidental learning as a function of personality and task dimensions. *Journal of Personality and Social Psychology,* 1974, *29,* 90–101.

Wortman, C. B., & Brehm, J. W. Responses to uncontrollable outcomes: An integration of reactance theory and the learned helplessness model. In L. Berkowitz (Ed.), *Advances in experimental social psychology* (Vol. 8). New York: Academic Press, 1975.

Wortman, C. B., Panciera, L., Shusterman, L., & Hibscher, J. Attributions of causality and reactions to uncontrollable outcomes. *Journal of Experimental Social Psychology,* 1976, *12,* 301–316.

18

Comments on Section IV: Individual Differences and Perceived Control

Julian B. Rotter
University of Connecticut

For the most part, the four preceding papers are reviews of research dealing with individual differences in beliefs in internal versus external control of reinforcement. Rather than review these reviews, I would like simply to react freely and comment on some selected aspects of these papers.

First, Phares (Chapter 14) raises the question of why I–E research has become so popular. At this time, there are well over 1000 published papers having to do with individual differences in internal vs. external control of reinforcement. And no one knows how many theses, dissertations, or unpublished studies have been done. This research began before the Vietnam War, the student revolution, the black riots, the political scandals of Watergate, and the assassinations. Although no one could have predicted in advance the popularity of the I–E concept, postdiction is something else.

These national disturbances have had far-reaching repercussions in our culture, social institutions, and in the everyday life of individuals. Certainly, these events have brought home to many both their inability to control events and the lack of predictability of events that are important in their lives. Perhaps less dramatic has been the ever-increasing complexity of life and the great increase in dependency on technical devices such as computers. Finally, the continuous increase in population and the constant increase in government control of individuals' lives in order to cope with the attendant problems has affected everyone's life. What all these forces add up to is that for many people, their lack of control over life events has been brought to conscious realization. Sociologists have dealt with the same concept for some time as alienation. In retrospect, it is not difficult to understand why psychologists have become so interested in problems of personal control. The interests and concerns of social scientists often reflect what is happening out there in the real world.

The second point in Phares' paper upon which I wish to comment has to do with the concept of defensive externality. Phares points out that support for the concept comes more strongly from male subjects that it does from female subjects. It is a persistent, if curious, finding. It seems to me that the question of why this is so relates to the question that Ryckman (Chapter 17) raises in his paper: When and under what circumstances do externals perform better than internals? Somewhat to our surprise in our early studies of internal–external control in college students, we did not find expected differences between the grades or the college entrance examination scores of internal and external subjects when we divided our distribution of I–E scores at the median. When we divided our samples by sex, there was no significant correlation for males of I–E scores with these standard indices of achievement. For females, however, there was a correlation of about -.22, indicating that female externals had lower college entrance scores than did internal females. This correlation is small statistically but significant, and it was consistent across samples. When we examined the distributions of scores, we found that there was a small sample of external males who outperformed most, if not all, of the internal males. In other words, we did not find a normal distribution of scores for external males on college entrance tests. There seems to be a subsample of male external subjects who state highly external beliefs on a questionnaire but nevertheless strive hard and perform very well. In trying to account for this group of subjects, I have assumed that they have experienced strong pressures for achievement and that they have internalized very high goals. They may have learned all the necessary skills in order to perform well in achievement situations, but having met with traumatic failures somewhere along the line, they learned to cope with these by projecting blame for their failures, particularly onto powerful others, bad luck, or unfairness. Once these defenses worked (i.e., once they were accepted by significant others), they began to generalize to other aspects of life in addition to academic achievement. Obviously, this is not a sequence that could happen only to males, but it is a sequence that might be more likely to happen to males in the area of achievement. It is also true that many of the studies involving externality have to do with achievement in a competitive academic skill situation. Perhaps we would find defensive externality more characteristic of women if we were to do studies involving potential failure in social or affectional satisfactions. I am not trying to stereotype sex differences but am merely pointing out differences that still exist in our culture, although overlap between the sexes tends to increase all the time. This sequence of internality, high goals, frustration, and defensive externality may have some significance for the study of depression and learned helplessness, which I comment on later.

I would like to go on now to some comments on Lefcourt's paper (Chapter 15). I have always spoken of belief in external or internal control as a generalized expectancy, which has led to some confusion for people who do not recognize that in social learning theory, an expectancy is determined both by a specific expectancy for a given situation and one or more generalized expectancies generalized from other related situations. It is never the case of either/or. It is doctrine in our brand of social learning theory that measurement in a specific area is enhanced by devising tests limited to that specific area, particularly if the specific area is one in which the individual has had a great deal of previous experience. It is only in a novel situation that a generalized expectancy may be expected to produce a higher degree of prediction. So the notion of specific scales to measure internal–external beliefs in specific areas is not only wise but is dictated by the theory. However, there are some limitations to devising specific scales, and these limitations are worth consideration.

The I–E scale that is now so widely used went through four different versions before it was finally published in 1966. We tried in at least two of these versions to devise specific subscales but found that the correlations between subscales were about as high as the internal reliability of the subscales. Although it is possible to devise separate scales, based on factor analyses of the old scale, they undoubtedly affect each other and reduce the specificity of responses to any single item. This was true in our early scale development and is evident in recent work by Levenson (1973), who has developed two subscales—one for chance and/or luck and the other for powerful others—as external scales. In a number of her studies, the two scales show fairly strong intercorrelations.

The other problem or limitation involves social desirability. In the development of the I–E scale, we correlated each item with the Marlowe–Crowne measure of the social desirability motive and eliminated those items that were heavily weighted with social desirability variance. We discovered that most of the items we had to eliminate had to do with academic achievement. It is socially desirable to say that hard work, effort, etc., will lead to personal accomplishment, and an adult scale of I–E and academic achievement that will show discriminant validity vis-à-vis social desirability may be hard to obtain.

Another type of specificity has to do with internal–external control beliefs for failure experiences versus success experiences. We also tried this in two earlier versions of our questionnaire and found, again, that scores for failure and scores for success correlated with each other almost as highly as the internal reliability of the subscales. However, our subjects were college students, and it is clear that college students feel some need for consistency in their responses. At the college level one cannot expect to get away with saying that good grades are a matter of hard work and ability but bad grades are a matter of luck. Not, at least, if one has to make both responses in a period of 15 minutes on the same test. For children, this need for consistency is apparently not so well developed, and both Crandall, Katkovsky, and Crandall (1965) and Mischel, Zeiss, and Zeiss (1974) have apparently successfully measured these two aspects of externality independently in young children.

The studies reported by Strickland (Chapter 16) were particularly gratifying to me—not only because it is reinforcing to find practical consequences of our theoretical ideas and laboratory studies, but also because differences obtained in some of these studies are of sufficient size to make me feel that the variable being measured is indeed internal versus external control rather than something having to do with test-taking attitudes. In addition to the study reported in detail by Strickland regarding hypertension in blacks and attitudes toward internal versus external control of reinforcement, there have been other studies dealing with patients with hypertension or cardiac problems that also show sizable differences between internal versus external control attitudes and attitudes toward treatment and treatment effectiveness.

A group of researchers at the Yale Medical School have been studying volunteering and pretreatment attrition in drug abuse treatment and the treatment of hypertension (Leigh, Ungerer, Ostfeld, Drake, & Reiser, in press; Ungerer, Harford, & Coloni, 1975). Their work shows some strong effects of locus of control in predicting both volunteering for treatment and remaining in treatment regimes. These studies raise a very practical question for the training of medical personnel. There is sufficient evidence now that internal versus external control beliefs will influence how actively patients will participate in treatment, follow treatment regimes, and devise their own ways of enhancing their suggested treatment regimes. It appears to be true for a variety of serious disorders; it may be true of minor disorders such as colds, sprains, etc., which, to my knowledge, have not yet been investigated. It seems to me that the medical profession needs to be alerted to the significance of this personality dimension in their plans for the treatment of patients. It might prove to be extremely useful in helping medical practitioners to differentiate which patients need something more than brief descriptions of treatment procedures and the benefits to be received from them if they are to follow the physician's prescriptions. Not covered in Strickland's paper, but perhaps related to this issue, is the whole question of increased motivation that follows from being given choice. The notoriously authoritarian methods of some physicians are certainly not well calculated to encourage the patient to follow the therapeutic regime that presumably will help cure him or her.

Ryckman (Chapter 17) raises the question of whether there are any instances in which externals outperform internals, noting that in most cases, it is the internals who outperform the externals. Of course, there are many studies where no differences between the two groups have been obtained, and there are several studies that show that internals are more resistant to verbal conditioning. It is a question of interpretation whether they are outperforming the externals in resistance to conditioning or whether the externals are outperforming them in speed of conditioning. Another area where externals may outperform internals is in the rote learning of ambiguous materials where it is not clear whether or not the learning can be enhanced by problem solving. Some of our early research suggested that internals given long, random sequences of lights to learn tend to seek logical solutions and are continuously trying out hypotheses. Although this may lead to quicker solutions of logical problems, it tends to interfere with the learning of random sequences, and perhaps this may be more generally true of rote learning.

Ryckman has reviewed some of the work on learned helplessness, depression, and locus of control that is currently attracting a great deal of interest. Presumably, depending on samples, depressive patients have been found to be more internal and more external in different studies, and the relationship between locus of control and susceptibility to learned helplessness has, similarly, not been consistent. However, the learned helplessness studies usually deal with a transitory state as a result of a relatively mild, continuous negative reinforcement, and the relationship of behavior in these investigations and long-standing personality characteristics may be far more complex than it appears.

The relationship of internal–external control to maladjustment may be relevant to interpreting the relationship of this variable specifically to depression or susceptibility to learned helplessness. Originally, on purely theoretical grounds, I hypothesized a curvilinear relationship between adjustment and internal–external control: namely, that both extreme internals and extreme externals would tend to be maladjusted. Extreme externals would be maladjusted, since they would not take the necessary steps to solve problems or to improve or cope satisfactorily with their environment. Extreme internals would be unhappy, because if they indeed believe that they can or should be able to control all their outcomes, then sooner or later they are going to meet with traumatic events, failures, accidents, or overpowering externally controlled events that will affect them negatively and leave them with the feeling that they have failed. Using a variety of tests of adjustment and anxiety, the findings, however, have always shown a moderate linear (positive) correlation between maladjustment and externality. This has always puzzled me. I wonder at this time if high internals faced with loss, failure, and inability to control important life events do not react in different ways—some perhaps feeling guilty and depressed, some projecting blame outward (i.e., acting like defensive externals), and some doing both. In other words, a low but consistent finding of a positive relationship between maladjustment and externality may in part be a function of the fact that many previous extreme internals have become defensive externals as a result of serious failure experiences or experiences of loss. It seems reasonable that it is the high internal who is most likely to be susceptible to serious disturbance following trauma. If one really believes in fate, one is much more likely to be able to cope with catastrophe, and it is not surprising that fatalistic religions flourish in parts of the world where deprivation, loss, and catastrophe are so common. So it may well be that the strong internal is the potential victim of depression, but if we see him after he is already depressed, he may turn out to be either a defensive external or an internal.

Since so many of the studies described in this section deal with the forced-choice I-E scale, I would like to make a general comment of caution about the use of this scale. There are 23 nonfiller items in the I-E scale, and current means for college students fall between 10 and 12. In 1966 the means typically fell between 8 and 9. For college student distributions, this is an extremely large difference. What is clear, and perhaps what leads to results that cannot be replicated, is that by using median splits and analysis of variance designs, we are now characterizing subjects as internal who were characterized as externals in earlier research. The problem is obviated at least in part by the use of correlational methods. If we are to continue to use analysis of variance and median splits, certainly awareness of this problem is important when comparing findings obtained over several years.

Finally, I would like to comment on the relationship of perceived choice to internal versus external control. It seems apparent that individuals cannot develop a feeling that they can control outcomes if they are not given choices. Only if we accept the notion that we have had real choices can we feel that an outcome is a result of our own decisions and efforts. How should this relate to individual differences in a belief in internal versus external control? It seems reasonable that a history of being given more choices would lead to a greater feeling of internality, and in fact, some of the work with the children's locus-of-control scale (Crandall, Katkovsky, & Crandall, 1965) supports this in relating Internal Achievement Responsibility scores to greater independence training and greater freedom for children.

Whether or not individual differences in internal versus external control relates to behavior in choice situations is a question of considerable interest. Much of the research reported in this volume suggests to me that the effects of giving choice on improved performance are essentially motivational. That is, subjects get more involved, work harder, and enjoy tasks more if given choice. Obviously, however, this is not true of all subjects to the same degree. It may well be that internals place a greater value on choice than do externals, although both may prefer choice situations. I would like to suggest some hypotheses that perhaps can be followed up regarding the relationship between internal versus external control and the benefits of perceived choice. One of these is that in situations where there is a high probability of success, there will be relatively little difference among groups of internals, defensive externals, and congruent externals. But in situations in which there is a high probability or expectancy of failure, defensive externals will either not prefer choice situations at all or prefer them less. If externality for some subjects is clearly defensive, then it loses its defensive value if there is perceived choice. Some responsibility for outcome must be taken by the subject who makes the choice. It is also possible that the general preference for choice may be a function of the number of choices presented, and this may also be differential for internals, defensive externals, and congruent externals. As the number of choices increases, the probability of making a wrong choice may subjectively also increase. There is anecdotal evidence to suggest that this may be the case. At any rate, it seems to me that more precise relationships between internal–external control as an individual-difference variable and perceived choice may be investigated profitably, using both expected failure versus success and number of choices available as experimental parameters.

REFERENCES

Crandall, V. C., Katkovsky, W., & Crandall, V. J. Children's beliefs in their own control of reinforcements in intellectual-academic achievement situations. *Child Development*, 1965, *36*, 91-109.

Leigh, H., Ungerer, J. C., Ostfeld, A., Drake, R. G., & Reiser, M. F. Borderline hypertensives volunteering for follow-up and biofeedback: Locus of control characteristics. *Journal of Psychotherapy and Psychomatics*, in press.

Levenson, H. Multidimensional locus of control in psychiatric patients. *Journal of Consulting and Clinical Psychology*, 1973, *41*, 397-404.

Mischel, W., Zeiss, R., & Zeiss, A. Internal–external control and persistence: Validation and implications of the Stanford Preschool Internal–External Scale. *Journal of Personality and Social Psychology*, 1974, *29*, 265-278.

Ungerer, J. C., Harford, R. J., & Coloni, R. S. Identification of dropouts at the initial stage of drug abuse treatment. *Psychological Reports*, 1975, *37*, 945-946.

V

DETERMINANTS AND CONSEQUENCES OF PERCEIVED FREEDOM AND PERCEIVED CONTROL

Greatness with private men esteem'd a blessing is to me a curse; and we, whom, for our high births they conclude the only freemen, are the only slaves.
Happy the golden mean.
—Philip Massinger

Without doubt, most would agree that freedom and choice have been most extensively investigated by social psychologists. In examining the chronology of the field, the early contributions of Lewin and Festinger cannot be ignored. However, the contemporary approach includes the armamentaria of an ever-expanding and interdisciplinary aggregate ranging from clinical psychologists through computer-based math modelers. In the first chapter in this section, Harvey, Lightner, and Harris examine a variety of paradigms used to study perceived freedom. Early in their chapter they sagely recommend sanitizing the language that is used to describe the phenomenon of freedom and choice. They then selectively review the effects of perceived freedom as they relate to reactance and attribution research and mention the commonly held assumption that subjects are motivated by the need for freedom. In support of this contention, they cite some of the reactance literature that shows that subjects will attempt to restore their freedom when it is threatened. Alternatively, we might suggest that this so-called attempt at the restoration of freedom might be understood as an example of countercontrol. This explanatory problem exemplifies one of the major difficulties encountered by those who study freedom and control. That is, to what degree can freedom be considered axiomatic, and to what degree is it merely a reflection of an alternate reactive process? Are people motivated to protect or exercise their freedom, or do people employ the illusion of freedom to counter the more pessimistic implications of its absence?

Continuing with their review, they bring together research concerned with freedom in the physical environment, including such contemporary topics as privacy and crowding. From there, they move to the effects of freedom and control on learning and performance and thence to decision theory and perceived freedom in mental institutions. They conclude the chapter with a discussion of some of their recent work on perceived freedom in an area they call close relations.

The second chapter in this section examines the consequences of attenuated control through a series of experiments conducted in both experimental and naturalistic settings. In this paper, Professor Langer looks at the relinquishment of control through the development of incompetence. She makes the novel distinction between incompetence based on situational inferences versus action-induced incompetence. An example of the former is the experience of helplessness whereas an example of the latter is incompetence that paradoxically may grow from the requirement that an individual pay attention to the various segments of a highly practiced or automatized action. Langer shows how certain experiences for the elderly can serve to establish and strengthen feelings of dependence as a result of allowing others to do things for them that they formerly had performed themselves. Conversely, she provides evidence that these detrimental processes can be retarded and even reversed.

Schulz and Hanusa continue with the theme of control and its absence in the elderly with respect to environmental influences that can importantly moderate perceived control. In a series of experiments in naturalistic settings, they demonstrate that the perception of control and the positive consequences attendant to it can be enhanced by environmental settings. However, environmental influences may also set a definite ceiling on the continued growth of the perception of control and may in fact conflict with the individual's self-concept and lead ultimately to an increased helplessness and general deterioration.

Finally, as a discussant and reviewer of the preceding three papers, Professor Singer takes a rather pessimistic view of our science in general and this field in particular. In recognizing that the scientist's personal ambition to become an adjective (e.g., the Schmartfarb effect; see Singer, Chapter 22) may retard progress as a result of the needless, redundant, and confusing generation of terms, Singer asks that we adopt certain procedural criteria as we move forward in our understanding of perceived control. Arguing that variables that provide more immediate and practical returns should be considered with greater esteem than isolated *de novo* findings, he asks that we order our research priorities in accord with these subjective criteria.

Further, he recommends that we focus on general issues relating to the variables affecting control as well as those that are affected by control. Suggesting that we may have to accept as axiomatic the fact that people do want control, he points out (subsequent to preparing his chapter; personal communication, 1978) that people nevertheless do not try to control everything. He went on to say that certain events are considered beyond our control either because of their simplicity or conversely because of their complexity. Within some midrange of events, we strive for control. Most likely, the range of events over which we believe we possess control depends on individual-difference factors (e.g., Rotter's internality, Arnkoff and Mahoney's neuroticism) as well as on the degree to which people permit their behavior to grow—in Langer's term—mindless.

19

Perceived Freedom as a Central Concept in Psychological Theory and Research

John H. Harvey
Vanderbilt University

Ben Harris
Vassar College

Jean M. Lightner
University of Virginia

INTRODUCTION

In this paper, we examine the concept of perceived freedom by reviewing some of its many roles within contemporary psychology. In this selective review, we focus on:

1. The relationship between perceived freedom and perceived control.
2. The centrality of perceived freedom in social psychology, illustrated by research in the areas of psychological reactance, social attribution, and the environment and behavior.
3. The varieties of perceived freedom hypothesized by Ivan Steiner (1977).
4. The role of perceived freedom in experimental research on human learning and in decision theory.
5. The possible role of perceived freedom in the attribution of mental health and illness.
6. Possible future directions for research on perceived freedom.

PERCEIVED FREEDOM AND CONTROL

For both researchers and theorists, there seems to be a tendency to use the terms *perceived freedom*, *choice*, and *control* interchangeably to refer to a single broad concept or experience. We have reservations about this tendency

275

and begin by proposing a distinction between the concepts of perceived freedom and control. Perceived freedom may be thought of as an experience associated with the *act* of deciding upon the alternatives that we will seek. It is a feeling or perception that accompanies a decision to engage in a certain action(s) as opposed to another or others. This assertion that the act of deciding is a core element of perceived freedom is in essential accord with Rollo May's focus on a *pause* in deliberation when options are considered. May (1977) offers this general definition of freedom: "the capacity to pause in the face of various stimuli, and then to throw one's weight toward this response rather than that one [p. 7]."

Compared to perceived freedom, perceived control does not seem to be so wedded to the act of deciding. Often, we may feel free to choose from a wide range of actions but feel little ability to gain control over the course that we have chosen. Following this reasoning, we characterize perceived control as more of a continuing experience than perceived freedom.[1]

This point may be illustrated by a popular song by Paul Simon, *Slip-Slidin' Away*. When this song asserts that "you know, the nearer your destination the more you're slip-sliding away . . . ," it seems to be referring to the problem of reaching the elusive goals that humans often seek. To us, this reference speaks to the point that initial freedom in selecting a course of action does not guarantee control over one's subsequent behavior and that the experience of control may be viewed as more continuous than that of freedom.

As an illustration of this continuing, regulating quality of perceived control, Henslin (1967) reports an interesting participant-observation study of crapshooting behavior. In this study, he found that feelings of control over the dice were maximized if the shooter displayed concentration and effort. In his initial efforts at crapshooting, Henslin was advised, "Take your time! Don't throw 'em out so fast! Take your time and work on it! [p. 319]." From our perspective, this advice was aimed at maximizing the shooter's sense of control by making his act of throwing a more continuous, long-duration behavioral sequence.

Although this distinction between perceived freedom and perceived control seems necessary to clarify their theoretical independence, research shows that these experiences often are positively related and occur in almost a simultaneous manner. For example, Harvey and Harris (1975) found a positive relationship ($r = .38$) between perceived choice in making a selection about which task to perform and expectancy about control over behavior on the subsequent task. Also, these investigators found evidence that in

---

[1]This definition of perceived control does not relate to the question of possible differential effects associated with perceived control versus predictability (see Reim, Glass, & Singer, 1971; Schulz, 1976). For our purposes, perceived control is conceived as an experience involving the continuing belief that one can predict events.

conditions producing high perceived choice (e.g., when decisions involved positive options), expectancy about feelings of internal control was higher than in conditions producing low perceived choice (e.g., when decisions involved negative options).

Our wish to distinguish theoretically the concepts of perceived freedom and perceived control may or may not have empirical implications. If an investigator asks subjects whether they sense control when they indicate they perceive high freedom at the time of decision, subjects also are apt to report a high feeling of control. But the control experience in this instance relates to the decision just as the freedom experience does. Unlike the type of perceived control measured by Harvey and Harris (1975), the feeling of control here does not relate to the events (outcome, behavior, or whatever) expected to occur subsequent to the decision. We agree with Edward Jones' (1978) recent comment that perceived freedom results depend to a considerable degree on how one asks the question about perceived freedom (cf. Gurwitz & Panciera's, 1975, conclusion based upon evidence from a study in which multiple measures of perceived freedom were taken). However, this subtlety of measurement issue is not particular to the area of perceived freedom research (any more than it is to attribution work in general or attitude or memory work, either, for that matter). And, most important, the methodological issue should not be used to cloud the seemingly reasonable argument that there are demonstrable conditions associated with fluctuations in individuals' perception of freedom and that these conditions may or may not correspond in a parallel way to these same individuals' perception of control.

PERCEIVED FREEDOM IN CONTEMPORARY SOCIAL PSYCHOLOGY

Would social psychological theory and research exist in their present forms if individuals did not perceive themselves to have a certain degree of freedom regarding the decisions they make? Possibly it would not. If we did not perceive ourselves as relatively free sometimes, and also did not perceive others to be relatively free on occasion, major areas of social psychological work would be so drastically altered as to be virtually unrecognizable. For instance, without the perception that we are free to perform certain behaviors or to hold various beliefs, we might not react against others' attempts to limit our range of behavior or belief. Also, we might be less likely to explain another individual's behavior by placing its origin within that individual. We would most often attribute it to that person's environment, that is, to forces not under his or her control. Finally, our relations with our own physical environment would probably be greatly altered if we did not perceive the possibility of achieving some freedom in our reactions to it and in our actions within it. It is difficult indeed to imagine what life in general, let alone the specific area of social psychology, would be like without the perception that we sometimes are free in our actions and beliefs.

To illustrate how much the concept of freedom permeates this field, we briefly review its role in relation to three areas of interest to social psychologists: psychological reactance, social attribution theory, and environmental social psychology. Of course, there are other theoretical and research areas in social psychology that are tied to the concept of freedom. For instance, it has been argued and data have been provided showing that perceived freedom is necessary for the arousal of cognitive dissonance in attitude change research (Brehm & Cohen, 1962; Wicklund & Brehm, 1976). In this chapter, however, we focus only on three contemporary topic areas as exemplifying the role of freedom in social psychologists' theorizing.

Perceived Freedom and Psychological Reactance

If we did not perceive ourselves to be free, we could not worry about the possibility of losing that freedom, and the theory of psychological reactance could not have been formulated. As stated by Brehm (1966), this theory asserts that the loss of or threat to an individual's freedom will cause the individual to experience psychological reactance, a motivational state directed toward the reestablishment of that freedom. The perception that one is free, therefore, is a basic element in the arousal of reactance; unless an individual believes that he or she can "significantly control personal destiny [p. 2]," he or she cannot feel threatened (Wicklund, 1974). Once the person feels a sense of freedom, however, even the slightest threat to that freedom may arouse reactance (Andreoli, Worchel, & Folger, 1974).

In reviewing the relationship between freedom and reactance, it is noteworthy that both quantitative and qualitative factors are involved. That is, the extent of one's ability to experience reactance depends on both the number of one's freedoms that are threatened and the felt importance of whatever freedom is seen to be in jeopardy. The former effect, relating the number of threatened freedoms to the amount of reactance aroused, was demonstrated by Sensenig and Brehm (1968) in a study of attitude change caused by attempted coercion. The latter effect, relating reactance to the importance of a threatened freedom, was shown by Worchel and Andreoli (1974) in a study of how reactance can be aroused by reciprocity-invoking behavior (e.g., personal favors).

Not only are there multiple ways in which changes in perceived freedom can arouse reactance, but there are also many ways in which freedom may be reasserted by those experiencing reactance. Two possibilities cited by Wicklund (1974) are the direct reassertion of freedom (i.e., by doing something that one is told not to do) and the more indirect route of performing a prohibited behavior after the prohibition has been lifted. An even more indirect restoration of freedom was described by Worchel and Brehm (1971), who showed how an individual could watch another person be assertive and thus perceive one's own freedom as being restored.

A final method for presumably reducing the amount of reactance evoked by a threatened freedom is worth mentioning because it involves a redirection of one's attributions rather than any behavioral change. This method was shown by Worchel and Andreoli (1974), who gave some subjects the opportunity to attribute a threat to their freedom to the environment rather than to a threatening person. For those who were offered this opportunity to attribute the threat to the environment, reactance-related behavior occurred to a significantly lesser degree than it did for those who were not given the opportunity.

A final comment about reactance research and perceived freedom is that although this perception presumably is integral to the operation of reactance, we know of no work in the area in which feelings of freedom have been probed as dependent variables or mediators between independent and dependent variables.

Perceived Freedom in Attribution Theory

In the general area of attribution theory, perceived freedom has been studied both as an independent and a dependent variable. As a dependent variable, freedom is often operationalized as perceived freedom of choice in selecting alternate behaviors, rewards, etc. This research fits well into the broad domain of attribution work, because it relates to people's daily attempts to determine the underlying causal structure of actions and events (Heider, 1958). In the attribution approach, perceptions of freedom are postulated to influence causal understanding; and in this approach, it has been predicted and found that various factors may influence an individual's understanding of the freedom possessed by self or others (Harvey, 1976).

Most research on what makes people feel that they have freedom and choice has been based on the two somewhat different theoretical conceptions of Steiner (1970) and Mills (1970). Since Steiner's work is discussed in Chapter 2, and is mentioned later as well, this review of freedom as a dependent variable sketches the major findings of another program of research by Harvey and his colleagues (see Harvey, 1976, for details). This work by Harvey et al. was given impetus by Mills' seminal (1970) analysis of perceived choice.

Briefly stated, perceived freedom can be affected by a number of factors related to the choices that one encounters in the decision making of everyday life. One of the most significant of these factors is the degree of similarity (in attractiveness) between choice options. As studied by Harvey and Johnston (1973) and Jellison and Harvey (1973), one perceives greater freedom when one is faced with small differences between options that are identical in kind. Also, greater freedom is perceived when options are close, *but not equal*, in attractiveness (Harvey, Barnes, Sperry, & Harris, 1974).

Another influence on one's perception of freedom is the valence of available options: Individuals have been found to perceive more freedom when choosing between positively valenced alternatives than when choosing between negatively valenced ones (Harvey & Harris, 1975). Further, it has been found that in making a decision, the number of options available interacts with perceived time taken to evaluate the options in influencing the amount of choice reported (Harvey & Jellison, 1974). Greater perceived choice was indicated, the greater the number of options when a person felt that he or she had expeditiously evaluated the options—perhaps indicating that the decision task was not burdensome. However, when the person felt that he or she had taken a relatively long time to evaluate the options, perceived choice was greater for a moderate as opposed to a large number of options.

Much of this evidence on determinants of perceived freedom has been interpreted in terms of Mills' (1970) assumptions that in order for choice to be perceived, people (1) have to be able to make distinctions among options, and (2) must feel some degree of uncertainty over which option is the best one to select. In this conception, perhaps the sense of uncertainty is the most basic dynamic underlying perceived freedom. Making distinctions is essential, but the distinctions cannot be too clear-cut lest a sense of choice be removed. And if they are not clear-cut, there is uncertainty about which alternative is best. Thus, we would refine Mills' analysis slightly to suggest that one's perception of freedom is perhaps most importantly based upon a feeling of uncertainty about the outcome of the decision. However, as pointed out by Kehoe and Newman in Chapters 5 and 9, respectively, there has been too little attention given to direct probing of uncertainty and other presumed mediators of perceived choice.

This description of work by Harvey and his associates on determinants of perceived freedom has not included mention of a class of variables whose effects may be mediated by processes other than the perceptual and elementary feeling processes already described. It seems clear that when decisions have negative societal or personal consequences, decision makers may be motivated to present themselves as having had little freedom, or indeed may sincerely feel that way, in making the decisions (Harris & Harvey, 1975; Harvey, Harris, & Barnes, 1975). We briefly mention this idea again later, but a central point is that we do not know very much at present about self-presentational strategies in either perceived freedom or perceived control phenomena.

Effects of Perceived Freedom on Social Attributions.   In almost every major theoretical statement of social attribution theory (e.g., Heider, 1958; Jones & Davis, 1965; Kelley, 1967), perceived freedom has played an important, if not crucial, role. Much of the emphasis on freedom has been in relation to the question of how we attribute dispositional qualities (such as attitudes to other people). Jones (1978) suggests that the theory of correspondent inference was based in large part on the idea that you can tell what a person is like if the person has choice in taking an action. In general, studies of the question of how dispositions are inferred have found that our perception of another's freedom is a key determinant of our perception of that person's attitudes (Jones, Davis, & Gergen, 1961; Jones & Harris, 1967; Jones, Worchel, Goethals, & Grumet, 1971; Steiner & Field, 1960). More specifically, when an individual expresses a certain opinion with apparent freedom to do so or not to do so, others seem to be more confident in their attribution of a corresponding attitude to the individual. When an individual is seen to have no freedom in choosing which position to support, others have been found to ignore the behavior and base their attributions on other factors such as the individual's past behavior and attitudes (Jones et al., 1971).

Freedom not only affects our attribution of attitudes and dispositions but also affects our perception of the basic qualities of personal responsibility and causality for interpersonal events. As described by Heider (1958), the central factor in our attributing causality (and hence, responsibility) for an event to another person is our perception of the *intentional nature* of that person's behavior. Intentionality, in turn, depends on freedom from outside coercion; thus our causal attributions to others depend on our perception of their freedom. This point has been demonstrated recently by Harris (1977), who found that adults faced with a minor misfortune (the breakage of a chair) only attributed significant responsibility to the person involved in that misfortune when that person was perceived to act in a *free, intentional manner*. (In addition to this effect of perceived freedom on subjects' attribution of responsibility, even their attributions of simple causality for the observed event were significantly affected by this variable.)

To summarize, it seems as if contemporary attribution theory would be radically changed by elimination of the concept of freedom. As noted in the introduction to this section, attributions made to individuals hinge on the perception that they are free to choose their behaviors and beliefs. Without this perception, personal attributions would be worth little in allowing us to understand and predict others' social behavior.

Perceived Freedom in the Physical Environment

All behavior takes place in some physical setting; all choices are felt and all decisions made in the context of some physical surroundings. The field of environmental psychology has sprung from the need to understand more fully this interplay between behavior and environment. In this section, we consider the importance of perceived freedom in relation to the physical environment by describing work emerging from the literature of environmental social psychology. Specifically, we are interested in how one may use or rely on the environment to increase one's freedom and, finally, in what happens in settings in which freedom is curtailed or limited for whatever reason.

Proshansky, Ittelson, and Rivlin (1970) view perceived freedom as an integral component in the relationship of the individual to the physical surroundings. According to Proshansky and colleagues, any individual in any setting has certain purposes he or she wishes to accomplish in that setting. Satisfying these purposes is facilitated if there is a wide range of possible options available. Proshansky et al. (1970) therefore conceive of freedom as depending on the *number* of options available and note that the individual reacts to the environment so as to maximize these options and, concurrently, his or her perceived freedom.

According to this conception, the individual works actively to maximize his or her freedom in the physical setting. These efforts are often overt, noticeable ones, as in the case of changing from a smoking to a nonsmoking section on a bus or plane. But some theorists also note the existence of more subtle, less noticeable ways of using the environment to enhance one's freedom, with one of the more widely discussed ways being the individual's protection of personal privacy (Altman, 1975; Proshansky et al., 1970; Westin, 1967).

Privacy, according to Westin (1967), is "the claim of individuals, groups or institutions to determine when, how, and to what extent information about them is communicated to others [p. 71]." Westin also notes that privacy is not merely a matter of physical separation from others; the individual who is "alone in a crowd" experiences a state of privacy in anonymity. Privacy may also be experienced as "intimacy" by members of a dyad or small group. Finally, although in the presence of familiar others, an individual may feel private by controlling the sensory input he or she receives from the others present.

Kelvin (1973) postulates that privacy, of whatever type, increases an individual's freedom because it decreases the influence of others over that individual. Both Kelvin and Altman view privacy as a positive state: By giving others less power over the individual, it makes that individual less vulnerable as well as freer in regard to his or her own actions. Social isolation, on the other hand, is viewed as a negative state because it *blocks* freedom—that is, the freedom *to have contact* with other people.

Proshansky et al. (1970) take a somewhat similar stand, noting that though the specific conditions under which a sense of privacy is experienced may vary, it does in all cases help to maximize perceived freedom. They propose that the removal of social constraints that privacy affords aids the individual in increasing the range of available options, thereby increasing the freedom that he or she feels. They summarize the relationship of privacy to perceived freedom as follows: "Other things being equal, privacy affords the individual the opportunity, in both thought and action, to attempt any and all alternatives and to make his choice accordingly [p. 182]."

Indirect support for these assumptions may be found in the previously discussed social psychological work on reactance. As mentioned, the private individual is, through whatever means, removed from the influence attempts of others, attempts shown in reactance research to reduce perceived freedom. As a specific example, he or she is removed from behaviors that evoke a norm of reciprocity (e.g., a favor that dictates a similar action in return), behaviors that have been shown to arouse reactance and prompt the reassertion of freedom through various means (Worchel & Andreoli, 1976).

We can think, however, of certain cases in which an individual may seek publicity rather than privacy to maximize personal freedom. For example, although an actor rehearsing a role in private may feel a great deal of freedom, it is also possible that he or she may perceive a high degree of freedom when doing so in front of an audience; the actor may feel that the audience enhances the possibilities for variations in performance, and thus a sense of freedom may be high. It might be fruitful for theorists and investigators examining Proshansky et al.'s thesis on the relationship between privacy and perceived freedom to entertain this alternative perspective.

Proshansky et al. (1970) also suggest that a desire for privacy is really at the heart of another environmental means of enhancing perceived freedom—that means being territoriality. They note that humans need not only a minimum space in which to satisfy their physical or biological needs but also a minimum space in which to satisfy their psychological needs, including that for privacy. By controlling a particular area and the activities occurring there, one can again maximize his or her options and thus increase perceived freedom.

Though postulating privacy and territoriality as environmental factors increasing perceived freedom, Proshansky et al. (1970) also discuss crowding, a third one that *decreases* perceived freedom. Crowding decreases one's control over territory and limits the type and amount of privacy that can be achieved. Crowding is seen as a relative rather than an absolute phenomenon: One may feel crowded in the presence of two other people or not feel crowded in the presence of a hundred. As a criterion for crowding, Proshansky et al. (1970) note: "Crowding occurs when the number of people an individual is in contact with is sufficient to prevent him from carrying out some specific behavior and therefore restricts his freedom of choice [p. 182]."

Proshansky and his colleagues (1970) conclude their provocative discussion of perceived freedom as it relates to privacy, territoriality, and crowding by stressing the importance of being able to maximize that freedom:

Whether the individual's freedom of choice represents a decision to use the least crowded of a variety of routes, to read in his bedroom rather than in the living room, or to formulate any of many other decisions that he faces each day, broadening the available possibilities open to him can only enhance his dignity and human qualities, making him less an automaton and more a fulfilled individual [p. 183].

VARIETIES OF PERCEIVED FREEDOM

In the following discussion, we comment on Steiner's latest and enriching theoretical contribution to perceived freedom research in social psychology. We assume some knowledge of Steiner's discussion in this volume (Chapter 2) of "Three kinds of reported choice" and his recent (1977) theoretical statement entitled "Attribution of choice." These works provide the most comprehensive examination currently available of the various types of perceived freedom. We briefly review what Steiner refers to as evaluative, discriminative, and autonomous choice and present our general comments on this conception.

Steiner notes that his three types of choice emanate from comparison processes related to the options available to be acted upon. These available options may be compared as a set with some other set of appropriate or perhaps ideal options not immediately available. Or available options may be compared with one another within the set.

Steiner says that evaluative perceived choice, or "good choice," pertains to the experience in which a person feels that the utility of his or her options is at least as high as that of the appropriate alternatives that serve as a personal comparison set for the decision in question. This type of perceived choice is postulated to be a function of the disparity between available options and comparison options. Presumably, this feeling will be directly related to the goodness of one's set of available options as compared to an ideal set for the decision.

Whereas in the evaluative choice process, comparisons between available options are actually minimized, in the discriminative choice process, such comparisons are emphasized. Discriminative perceived choice, or "clear choice," relates to a comparison between or among options. It is predicted to be greater to the degree that the best of the alternatives exceeds the second best. Thus, a big difference in attractiveness between or among options would enhance this type of perceived choice.

Lastly, Steiner defines autonomous perceived choice as involving a decisional situation with options having approximately equal utilities. In contrast to discriminative perceived choice, autonomous perceived choice is reduced by large discrepancies between or among options. Why the term *autonomous*? Steiner does not say explicitly, but he makes it clear that in this type of perceived choice, the person feels that he or she, rather than something in the environment, is the principal causal agent—that is, feels a high degree of control over personal actions.

As Steiner (1970) did in his pacesetting paper, he again has produced an important theoretical analysis that should serve as a stimulus for much research on variables influencing these varieties of perceived choice. Indeed, if one tries to think of all possible types of meanings of perceived choice that may be viable in people's decision making, it is apparent that Steiner's analysis is quite comprehensive and perceptive. Also, in his paper in this volume (Chapter 2), Steiner reviews emerging evidence pertaining to the distinctive phenomenological validities of these types of reported choice. We do, however, wish to pose a few questions about which this analysis seems somewhat silent and to suggest some dynamics of perceived freedom that are not implied by Steiner's statement.

An area of some contention with Steiner's analysis is his apparent characterization of the decision maker as a relatively rational, clear-thinking processor of a more than modest amount of information. His analysis is qualified at points in terms of the frailties of information processing (cf. Kahneman & Tversky's, 1973, thesis) and in terms of the role of commitment in affecting retrospective inferences of choice. We do not believe that Steiner—or any of the writers in this area, including ourselves—has given enough attention to how judgments of choice or freedom that are publicly communicated in some form (possibly via only the response to a questionnaire item that presumably will be seen only by the experimenter) sometimes evolve from a desire to present oneself in a desirable way to others and/or to relieve oneself of cognitive discomfort. We believe that our work in the studies by Harris and Harvey (1975) and Harvey, Harris, and Barnes (1975) alludes to this important facet of perceived freedom but clearly in no definitive way. We would like to suggest the need for research on relatively public versus relatively private judgments of perceived freedom. It could well be true that similar to attributions of causality (Wells, Petty, Harkins, Kagehiro, & Harvey, 1977), public and private judgments of freedom represent different phenomena that are governed by different psychological processes.

Further, we have reservation with an implication of Steiner's analysis that actors and observers exhibit similar tendencies in their perceptions of an actor's freedom in making a decision or taking an action. The work by Gurwitz and Panciera (1975) and by Harvey, Harris, and Barnes (1975) shows some notable occasions when divergence occurs.

PERCEIVED FREEDOM
AND LEARNING PHENOMENA

As a result of the novel work of Monty and Perlmuter and their colleagues (see Perlmuter & Monty, 1977), perceived choice has become an important variable in contemporary learning research. Essentially, these investigators have shown that learning may be enhanced if individuals are allowed to exercise choice over a portion of the materials to be learned. In this discussion, we highlight briefly some findings emerging from this program of work on choice and learning and offer some comments on how the general interpretation of the findings relates to ideas drawn from social psychological work on perceived freedom.

Using a paired-associate learning task, the standard research paradigm in this work, Monty and Perlmuter (1975) gave subjects in a choice condition an opportunity to select response words with which they wished to associate stimulus words. In contrast, they assigned each subject in a force condition the responses chosen by the previous subject in the choice condition. Thus, yoked pairs of subjects learning identical materials were exposed to the paired-associate learning task. Monty and Perlmuter found that choice condition subjects learned more rapidly and to a higher level than did force condition subjects. Subsequent research by these investigators reduced the possibility that the beneficial effect associated with the choice was due to certain mnemonic cues that aided in the formation or retrieval of the learned associations. A principal explanation for this effect presented by Monty and Perlmuter focused on a presumed increase in general level of motivation when choice was available.

Further work by Perlmuter, Monty, and their associates has revealed that individuals who are given the opportunity to choose on a paired-associate task but who subsequently are denied the opportunity to learn the chosen materials do not learn as well as individuals not given the opportunity to choose (Perlmuter, Monty, & Cross, 1974). This effect was explained as due to a reactance-like frustration, with negative implications for performance, induced by denial of an opportunity to learn chosen materials. Also, Monty, Rosenberger, and Perlmuter (1973) reported that individuals given a choice on a few *initial* response items perform as well as individuals given a choice on all response items—but the items had to come at the outset of the choice procedure. Perhaps there may be a critical early period on a problem-solving/learning task when one either does or does not attain a feeling of control conveyed by choice.

Recent studies by Savage and Perlmuter (1976) and by Monty, Geller, Savage, and Perlmuter (1979) are most relevant to the previously described literature on social psychological work on perceived freedom. In this research, some subjects were given a choice from pairs of alternatives, each of which was high in meaningfulness as defined by Taylor and Kimble (1967). For other subjects, each pair of responses was comprised of one high- and one low-meaningful word. Savage and Perlmuter found that performance was significantly better when choice was made from similarly meaningful alternatives than when it was made from disparate alternatives. In their interpretation, the investigators emphasized the likelihood that it is the "perceived" nature of the choice rather than the actual fact of choice that facilitates learning. The high–low meaningfulness condition, though literally involving the choice act, apparently did not convey a high sense of choice, and therefore it did not have a positive impact on performance. As Monty, Perlmuter, Savage, and associates suggest, these data resonate well with the data deriving from the social psychology literature showing perceived choice to be greater when options are similar than dissimilar in attractiveness (Harvey & Johnston, 1973). They argue that it is the character of the nonchosen element that determines the consequences of choice; although some subjects chose one or more of the low-meaningful words, they suggest that such options (similar to unattractive alternatives in the perceived choice work in social psychology) may be readily eliminated from consideration by the subject. Hence, more unfamiliar words presumably do not constitute viable choice options.

This work on choice and learning shows the importance of perceived choice in basic learning situations. Our analysis of relevant data in the social psychological area is consistent with these investigators' focus on the motivating quality of perceived choice. Why does perceived choice have this motivating impact on learning? Some possible answers, which also involve a motivational theme, may be presented by examination of White's (1959) statement on competence motivation and of Mills' (1970) theoretical analysis of perceived choice.

According to White's notion of competence motivation, people are most fulfilled in situations in which they can engage in cognitive analysis and manipulation of the environment. Jellison and Harvey (1973) showed that conditions in which perceived choice is high, as opposed to those in which it is low, are conducive to people's feelings that they have gained information about their ability to analyze and manipulate the environment. In situations where perceived choice in making a decision is low, little thinking is required, and competence motivation should be low. Thus, Monty, Perlmuter, and associates appear to be enhancing competence motivation when they present subjects with choice in forming stimulus–response links on the paired-associate task. Subjects may feel that they can better test their learning ability under conditions of high perceived choice. In future work, it might be interesting to find out if indeed subjects do verbalize such objectives on learning tasks.

Part of Mills' analysis relates in an indirect manner to motivation. As we already have described, he suggests that on a decision task, a feeling of uncertainty about which option is best underlies a high perception of choice. Uncertainty may have a motivating impact on learning; it is somewhat unsettling cognitively and influences the individual to deliberate over and analyze the information to a greater degree (see also Mills' 1968 statement of a theory of choice certainty in decision making). We are not necessarily suggesting that differential deliberation induced by choice—with resulting uncertainty—explains the learning data that have just been reviewed. However, it seems likely that the element of uncertainty should have been present in the choice conditions, and this likelihood seems especially great for the work involving variations in the meaningfulness of the words in the response sets. The high–high-meaningfulness words should lead to the greatest amount of uncertainty and consequent perceived choice.

PERCEIVED FREEDOM AND DECISION THEORY

The area of decision theory, broadly defined, seems relevant to work on perceived freedom only in an indirect fashion at present. Unlike the work of Monty, Perlmuter, and associates in suggesting links between perceived freedom and learning, there has been no integrative work in this area that would link the study of decision making and choice behavior with the previously described social psychological literature on perceived freedom. However, the potential for such an integration would seem to be fairly substantial; it is intuitively appealing to think that people's feelings of choice in making decisions somehow relate to their decisional strategies and the decisions they actually make. In this discussion, we mention some possible areas for theoretical integration and fruitful research.

Choice behavior represents an extensive area of cognitive psychology and involves a vast number of important theoretical and empirical contributions. For example, Luce (1959), Berlyne (1960), Garner (1962), Tversky (1972), and Tversky and Kahneman (1973) have produced important and perhaps, in some cases, classic statements. An excellent review of recent work on behavioral decision theory and the more specific area of choice behavior is provided by Slovic, Fischhoff, and Lichtenstein (1977). In no way can we provide a sophisticated survey of this area of work. We will try only to alert interested researchers in cognitive psychology to what we see as possible convergences in the two domains. As a general orienting definition of the role of choice behavior in decision theory, Walker's (1964) definition may be helpful: "'Decision theory' amounts to an effort to predict choice of one event rather than another on the basis of objective probability and value or subjective probability and utility [p. 75]."

Based upon general reading in the literature on decision theory, what do we learn that may relate to social psychological work on perceived freedom? If we begin on a methodological level, we first notice that the work in social psychology on actor–observer differences (Harvey, Harris, & Barnes, 1975; Jones & Nisbett, 1971) does not seem to have a parallel in decision theory; decision theorists usually look only at the behavior and perceptions of those facing decisions (actors) rather than their audience (observers). However, it does appear that similar independent variables often are studied both by social psychologists concerned with perceived freedom and by decision theorists. For example, both sets of theorists are interested in the number of options confronting the decision maker and in various aspects of the options such as their complexity or similarity in attractiveness. On the other hand, a basic methodological difference is that social psychologists working in this area do not seem interested in predicting subjects' actual choice—they are more interested in the perceptions accompanying that choice. Prediction of choice and concomitant behavior is of central importance to decision theorists in their prolific work on model building. However, decision theorists appear to give little attention to perceptions accompanying decision and behavior such as perceptions of freedom, control, satisfaction, and competence.

Turning from the methodological to the theoretical domain, we find that there is an interesting amount of overlap between social psychological and decision theories, although the ideas are much richer and more elaborated in the decision-making area. Steiner (1977) seems to see some areas of potential convergence. For example, he inquires about the relationship between perceived choice and the strategies of "satisficing" and "maximizing" (March & Simon, 1958) in decision making. We may ask whether one or the other strategy produces a greater amount of perceived choice. Though Steiner does not answer these questions, his ideas might be used as a foundation for empirical inquiry.

The following quotes from writings in the literature of decision theory illustrate further the possibility for theoretical integration of these two areas:

1. "Uncertainty is a prerequisite to [psychological] structure" (Garner, 1962, p. 339).
2. "Features of the task that complicate the decision, such as incomplete data, incommensurable data dimensions, information overload, time pressures, and many alternatives seem to encourage strain-reducing noncompensatory strategies . . . " (Slovic et al., 1977, p. 8).

With respect to Garner's concept of uncertainty, we have described how Mills' analysis of perceived choice emphasizes uncertainty as a central underlying dynamic of perceived choice. In both these analyses, uncertainty is seen as related to amount of information—in an inverse fashion. If one has total information about choice options and if they are not identical in kind and valence, Mills proposes a rather diminished feeling of choice on the part of the decision maker. Garner's argument is more complex and stresses the close interconnection between information, uncertainty, and psychological structure. He posits that uncertainty always exists but that structure emerges as "related uncertainty." It does not seem too farfetched to assume that feelings of choice for important decisional situations are correlates of the psychological structure discussed by Garner. Given the tenability of this line of reasoning, integrative research is needed to examine concurrently how people make decisions, the nature of their decisions, cognitive structural properties, and, perhaps just as importantly, their perceptions of choice and control.

In considering the statement by Slovic et al. (1977), we think it is noteworthy that variables such as availability of information, perceived deliberation time in making a decision, and amount of information (number of options) all have been investigated either directly or indirectly in perceived choice research (see Harvey & Jellison, 1974; Harvey & Johnston, 1973; and for a more general statement encompassing a number of social psychological phenomena, see Taylor & Fiske, 1978). Also, the concern with stress in decision making mentioned by Slovic et al. has been studied in a general way in social psychology by Janis and Mann (1977) in their work on the effects of stress on decision making in various field settings. However, Janis and Mann were not explicitly concerned with the perception of freedom, and this relationship between stress and perceived freedom awaits empirical test. In general, the promise for an integrated view of decisional strategies, choice behavior, and the likely concomitants of perceived freedom and control seems great. But we know of no research programs now under way that are concerned with directly probing these interconnections.

PERCEIVED FREEDOM AND THE ATTRIBUTION OF MENTAL ILLNESS

Increasingly, social attribution theory has been used in the field of clinical psychology to explain the etiology of pathological behavior (e.g., Pennebaker, Burman, Shaeffer, & Harper, 1977; Storms & McCaul, 1976) and to develop possible new clinical treatments (Davison & Valins, 1969; Keltner & Marshall, 1976). In many cases, clinical uses of attribution theory have focused on the key role of perceived freedom and control in analyzing behavior disorders (e.g., Brehm, 1976; Wortman, Panciera, Shusterman, & Hibscher, 1976) and promoting positive behavior change (e.g., in the elderly, see Langer & Rodin, 1976; Schulz, 1976). One aspect of clinical psychology that has been relatively neglected by attribution theorists, however, is the attribution of mental illness and health. For psychologists and sociologists attempting to understand phenomena such as the effects of psychiatric labeling, an analysis of clinical attributions (e.g., informal diagnostic impressions) may be a worthwhile exercise. In this section, we present such an analysis, focusing on the possible effects of perceived freedom in clinicians' perceptions of psychiatric patients. In doing so, we agree with Bernard

Weiner's (1975) statement that "the inferential processes used by psychiatric diagnosticians are identical to those processes used in any attributional endeavor [p. 434]."

In most clinical settings, the process of finding (or "attributing") causes for a client's behavior is a crucial determinant of the institution's response to that client. In many cases, whether one attributes much of the client's behavior as due to psychopathology (an internal dispositional attribution) or due to environmental events (an external attribution) may be highly related to the client's institutional fate (see Batson, 1975).

According to some critics of psychiatric diagnosis and practice, attributions of mental health and illness are largely invalid in institutional settings (Rosenhan, 1973). Although most clinicians (e.g., Spitzer, 1975) would not agree with the view that "we cannot distinguish the sane from the insane" (Rosenhan, 1973, p. 257), many would agree that processes such as impression management by patients can significantly affect the reliability and validity of clinical attributions (Braginsky, Braginsky, & Ring, 1969). Moreover, enough patients believe in their ability to voluntarily affect the validity of psychiatric diagnoses that many hours of patient discussion are devoted to theorizing about the determinants of clinical attribution (see, for example, Bukovsky & Gluzman, 1975).

Observers of clinical diagnosis have often commented on the difficulty of "un-becoming" a mental patient (Scheff, 1966). One aspect of this problem is what Rosenhan (1973) calls "the stickiness of psychodiagnostic labels [p. 252]." Take, for example, the case of a male psychiatric inpatient who is admitted suffering from what is termed manic-depressive psychosis, depressed type, and whose subjective experience improves enough that he no longer feels the need of hospitalization and begins seeking discharge. From the viewpoint of attribution theory, the task of such a patient might be seen as the changing of others' perceptions of the causes of his behavior. More specifically, the perception in need of change would be that the patient's behavior is caused by a disorder of his personality (a negative, internal attribution). As an alternative to this perception, the patient might want his behavior attributed to internal, positive factors such as adequate coping mechanisms, ego strength, etc. Despite the existence of this potential alternative attribution (i.e., the attribution of health), we argue that it is extremely difficult for observers to adopt such new attributions for many patients. In fact, it is our position that changing the attributions of others is a herculean task for anyone who has been in the role of a psychiatric patient.

For an understanding of how clinicians perceive illness and health in patients, an important variable would seem to be the amount of freedom that is attributed to the patients in question. In the example of our patient trying to unstick the label of manic-depressive psychosis, Jones and Davis' (1965) theory of correspondent inferences would stress that new, healthier behavior will result in new, healthier attributions to the patient only if he is seen as free. More specifically, correspondent inferences theory would suggest that if the patient were seen as free to choose from a number of alternate behaviors (e.g., to seek employment, to socialize, to enroll in school, etc.), then whatever choice was actually made could be attributed to the patient's personality or personal dispositions (e.g., a healthy ego).

Based on research on this topic (e.g., Jones et al., 1961), we could further predict that observers might see our hypothetical patient as internally motivated to the extent that he acts in a manner inconsistent with environmental constraints. In other words, only when a patient's behaviors are deviant with the established environmental reward structure (e.g., of an institution) could that patient be seen as a relatively free agent. Thus, for a recently improved patient's behavior to be attributed to that patient, he would have to be seen as breaking out of the normative constraints of his environment; he would have to be seen as a "threateningly free spirit," to embellish somewhat Steiner's (1972) use of this term.

Unfortunately, in most institutional environments, patients are rewarded for being emotionally calm and behaviorably manageable rather than for being either overly demanding or passive. Thus for a patient to be seen as engaging in free behavior, he or she would probably have to be somewhat demanding and obstreperous. Such behavior, of course, is probably similar to that which caused the patient's original diagnosis as being disturbed.[2] If, on the other hand, the patient is consistently calm and well behaved, this behavior may either go unnoticed or be attributed to institutional constraints.[3] Such institutionalized behavior, Jones and Davis (1965) might predict, may eventually result in the awarding of discharge as its reward but has little hope of resulting in the attribution of "normality" to the patient.

---

[2]This attributional no-win rule for a patient is clearly seen if we apply to such a patient the results of Kruglanski and Cohen's (1973) study of the relationship between deviance, personality (or "character"), and attributed freedom. As shown by these authors' data, "only when an act is inconsistent with the actor's character... is greater freedom attributed upon its duration" (Kruglanski & Cohen, 1973, p. 249). Of course, for a mental patient, any deviancy can be seen as in-role behavior, even by relatively sophisticated professionals. This point is recognized not only by Kruglanski and Cohen (1973) but also by Ivan Steiner (1972) in a theoretical discussion of Don Quixote's behavior. Steiner makes the point that even deviant behavior is not seen as free if it becomes predictable. In the case of Don Quixote, for example, one can see how initially deviant behavior becomes predictable when it is seen as consistent with his elaborate delusional system.

[3]One cause of this attribution is the limited freedom in most institutional environments. As noted by Osmond (1970): "Ironically, the organizational and architectural structure of mental hospitals has managed, in the matter of exercising choice, to meet the patient's needs almost exactly in reverse....People incarcerated in these places have their everyday choices—food, clothing, recreation—limited, whereas they have to choose intimate companions from a mob of equally sick strangers—a choice we are seldom faced with in normal living [p. 286]."

Evidence of how difficult it is to reliably control clinical attributions comes from a recent study by Weary and Harvey (1977). In this experiment, Weary and Harvey manipulated clinicians' perceptions of simulated patients' freedom of choice and tested the effects of this manipulation on attributions of patients' psychological difficulties. The clinicians for this study were 20 male and female PhD candidates in clinical psychology who were being trained in psychotherapy and most of whom identified their theoretical orientation as psychodynamic. All subjects saw a videotape of and read case notes concerning a moderately depressed or a severely depressed female patient who was interviewed for pretherapy evaluation. Half the clinician-observers were told that the patient referred herself for evaluation, and half were told that a physician referred the patient without her consent. All clinicians were asked to rate how much they saw the patient's problem as located within herself (internal attribution) and how much they saw the problem as located within her environment (external attribution).

From Jones and Davis' (1965) theory, one might predict the following for this study: In the free-choice (uncoerced) condition, the patient's free discussion of personal problems should induce the attribution that she possesses clinical insight and motivation to change (internal qualities). Based on these attributes, this uncoerced patient would then be seen as having less pathology than the nonfree (coerced) patient. Although Weary and Harvey (1977) apparently were successful in manipulating the freedom attributed to their patients in seeking therapy, their experimental results were not as has been predicted. Instead of perceived freedom of patient affecting clinicians' dispositional (internal) attributions, it affected only their attributions to the patient's environment. Specifically, patients in the high-choice (noncoerced) condition were seen as having more of an *environmentally* located problem than were patients in the low-choice (coerced) condition. At the same time, however, all patients were seen as having a high degree of internally caused difficulty.

In explaining these results, we first look at what was found (the difference in external attribution) and then at what was not found (any difference in internal attribution) as an effect of manipulating the perception of a patient's choice. Increased environmental attribution of problems for self-referred patients is a phenomenon that may be familiar to clinicians. It is based on the observation that a person's environment often must drastically deteriorate (e.g., the breakup of a close relationship, a death in the family, prolonged unemployment) for the person to seek counseling or psychotherapy. Thus, the environment of concerned voluntary patients is perceived to contain more problem-related cues (and more of the problem) than the environment of involuntary patients. Although this pattern of attributions may reflect some projection by the clinician, it seems like a logical perception to make.

A more theoretically significant result of Weary and Harvey's study was that the factor of high- versus low-perceived choice in seeking help had no effect on clinicians' internal attributions of patient problems. A logical but speculative interpretation of this finding is that it is part of the same no-win attributional rule that was presented to explain the durability of negative clinical attributions. That is, if a patient freely discusses his or her problem, then one may attribute some motivation and insight to that patient; but one may also attribute enough of an internally located problem to help produce that insight. "After all," a dynamically oriented clinician might say, "one is not motivated toward therapy over a problem that exists entirely in one's environment."

Although there needs to be more research and careful theorizing done on how perceived freedom affects client and therapist attributions (see Harris & Harvey, 1978), we have presented some evidence that psychiatric patients are caught in a difficult situation. Often, almost any unusual behavior that they might exhibit could be seen as part of their illness (see, for example, the contrasting defense mechanisms of acting out and reaction formation); no matter how free and uncoerced a client's or patient's behavior may seem, therapists eventually may see it as determined and repetitive. As such, the behavior cannot be the basis of much new attribution about their improvement by observers, and therefore any previously labeled patient's characteristics would seem unusually fixed and unchanging. Thus, in the context of the concept of perceived freedom, we see an attributional reason for "the stickiness" of both psychodiagnostic labels and psychodynamic clinical attributions.[4]

POSSIBLE FUTURE DIRECTIONS
IN RESEARCH

We already have alluded to several areas for possible future work on perceived freedom. In our discussion of social psychological work and of varieties of perceived freedom, we suggested that the unexplored issue of public versus private judgments of freedom might be fruitful for examination. Further, we have noted in the context of our discussion of clinical processes the need for more work on how perceived freedom affects client and therapist

---

[4]In her book, *The Application of Social Psychology to Clinical Practice* (1976), Sharon Brehm suggests, "For most clinical efforts, it is probably helpful for the client to perceive his own freedom and to take the responsibility for his own actions [p. 196]." This position seems quite persuasive and concurrent with the general humanistic picture of a free, responsible agent of action and change. According to our analysis, however, Brehm's suggestion seems insensitive to some facets of the processes of labeling and the institutionalization of behavior.

attributions. Finally, in light of the theoretical links that now exist, some explicit work on the interconnections between perceived freedom and the environment and variables in the areas of learning and decision and choice behavior seems warranted.

One area of social psychology in which the concepts of perceived freedom and control deserve investigation and that we would like to discuss briefly is that of close relations. This area is relatively new in social psychology. It relates to much more substantial and intensely affective relationships than have been studied over the last two decades in interpersonal attraction research. The recent edited collection by Levinger and Raush (1977) provides some perspective on the scope of a social psychological undertaking in the area of close relations. Although the concept of perceived freedom has received a paucity of attention in the vast clinical and sociological literatures on marriage, Haley (1963) gives an illustration of the possible import of perceived freedom in marriage. He suggests that in a relationship that is strongly bounded by external norms (e.g., where divorce is not morally possible), participants may continually question whether their commitment is voluntary or involuntary. However, in a marriage that lacks external constraints, even the most minor conflict is apt to be seen as threatening to personal freedom and as a cause for disengagement.

The present authors along with other colleagues have begun some exploratory work on the import of perceived freedom and control in close relations. Some of the questions we have investigated include: Would people express more satisfaction with relationships, the more freedom they perceived in the relationships to pursue their own personal interests and career? Would they indicate less conflict in their relationship, the more free they felt to pursue personal interests and career? Would number of significant emotionally and physically supportive others in one's life be positively related to satisfaction with relationships? (In asking the foregoing question, we have assumed that number of significant others indirectly relates to whether or not people feel free in their close relations.) Would perceived control in interpersonal relations be related to number of significant others? Would there be differences for these feelings of satisfaction and control as a function of sex of subject and/or sex of other?

In one study, reported as part of a work on attribution in conflicted close relations (Harvey, Wells, & Alvarez, 1978), senior undergraduates and graduate students who had been engaged in relatively exclusive close relationships for between 6 months and 2 years were given a detailed questionnaire probing various facets of their relationships. The data revealed a very strong positive correlation ($r = .63$) between perceived freedom to pursue personal interests and career and satisfaction with the relationship. Also, the perceived freedom measure was significantly negatively correlated with a measure of conflict in the relationship ($r = -.37$). These correlations did not differ significantly as a function of sex of subject. Although of course no cause–effect relationship is indicated by these data, they do suggest that the feeling of being relatively unconstrained by a relationship in pursuit of one's interests and profession is conducive to satisfaction and inhibitive of conflict.

Finally, in a more recent study conducted by the present authors, junior and senior college students were asked about the number of significant (i.e., emotionally supportive) others of both sexes whom they had relied upon in recent months. Each sex indicated more significant others of the same sex than they did of the opposite sex: The 31 males in the study averaged 5.5 male significant others and 3.4 female significant others; the 83 females averaged 5.3 female significant others and 2.8 male significant others. Other data more relevant to this manuscript showed that for males, there was a strong positive relationship ($r = .52$) for number of female significant others and satisfaction with the relationship. Also, males' satisfaction with relationships was not correlated with their number of significant male associates. In terms of perceived control, males indicated more control in interpersonal areas of their lives, the greater the number of significant female relationships ($r = .30$) and the greater the number of significant male associates ($r = .49$). Again, for females the results showed no significant correlations.

Overall, these data suggest that number of significant others in one's life (presumably related to perceived freedom, though not directly documented in this work) makes more difference in contributing to males' sense of satisfaction with and control in relationships than it does in contributing to these feelings for females. Why might these sex differences exist? Is it possible that quality of interaction is of much importance to females in close relations relative to number of people with whom such interactions can be transacted and that, on the other hand, number is of much importance to males (not to say that quality is not important to males too)? Of course, this is a speculative possiblity. We simply do not know the answers—though we are intrigued by the potential for discovery in this area. These sex differences indicate a need for much more theoretical work in connecting perceived freedom and control and central feelings in intimate relations. As in other parts of the domain of phenomena associated with close relations, these perceptions may be experienced in quite different ways by females and males (see, for example, Bernard's conception of his and her marriage in *The Future of Marriage,* 1973).

CONCLUDING COMMENT

In this paper, we have attempted to describe a part of the breadth and importance of perceived freedom in the expanses of psychological inquiry and in human life in general. As scientists we may agree with the implication of Skinner's (1971) thesis that people in point of fact do not possess freedom of choice. We contend, however, that whether or not people actually do have freedom, ample evidence is now available showing that people's perceptions of freedom influence a variety of thoughts and actions and that these perceptions have discernible, empirically verifiable determinants. Further, the potential for future work on this concept is great, and is little restricted by boundaries of specialization in psychological research.

ACKNOWLEDGMENTS

The work reported in this paper was supported in part by a grant from the Vanderbilt Research Council and the Spencer Foundation to the first author. The authors wish to thank Gifford Weary, Jon Lightner, and Ivan Steiner for valuable comments on an earlier version of this manuscript.

REFERENCES

Altman, I. *The environment and social behavior.* Monterey, Calif.: Brooks/Cole, 1975.

Andreoli, V. A., Worchel, S., & Folger, R. Implied threat to behavioral freedom. *Journal of Personality and Social Psychology,* 1974, *30,* 765–771.

Batson, C. D. Attribution as a mediator of bias in helping. *Journal of Personality and Social Psychology,* 1975, *32,* 455–466.

Berlyne, D. E. *Conflict, arousal and curiosity.* New York: McGraw-Hill, 1960.

Bernard, J. *The future of marriage.* New York: Bantam Books, 1973.

Braginsky, B. M., Braginsky, D. D., & Ring, K. *Methods of madness: The mental hospital as a last resort.* New York: Holt, Rinehart & Winston, 1969.

Brehm, J. W. *A theory of psychological reactance.* New York: Academic Press, 1966.

Brehm, J. W., & Cohen, A. *Explorations in cognitive dissonance.* New York: Wiley, 1962.

Brehm, S. S. *The application of social psychology to clinical practice.* Washington, D.C.: Hemisphere Publishing, 1976.

Bukovsky, V., & Gluzman, S. A manual on psychiatry for dissidents. *Survey,* 1975, *21*(1/2), 180–199.

Davison, G., & Valins, S. Maintenance of self-attributed and drug-attributed behavior change. *Journal of Personality and Social Psychology,* 1969, *11,* 25–33.

Garner, W. B. *Uncertainty and structure as psychological concepts.* New York: Wiley, 1962.

Gurwitz, S. B., & Panciera, L. Attributions of freedom by actors and observers. *Journal of Personality and Social Psychology,* 1975, *32,* 531–539.

Haley, J. *Strategy of psychotherapy.* New York: Grune & Stratton, 1963.

Harris, B. Developmental differences in the attribution of responsibility. *Developmental Psychology,* 1977, *13,* 257–265.

Harris, B., & Harvey, J. H. Self-attributed choice as a function of the consequence of a decision. *Journal of Personality and Social Psychology,* 1975, *31,* 1013–1019.

Harris, B., & Harvey, J. H. Social psychological concepts applied to clinical processes: On the need for precision. *Journal of Consulting and Clinical Psychology,* 1978, *46,* 326–328.

Harvey, J. H. Attribution of freedom. In J. H. Harvey, W. J. Ickes, & R. F. Kidd (Eds.), *New directions in attribution research* (Vol. 1). Hillsdale, N.J.: Lawrence Erlbaum Associates, 1976.

Harvey, J. H., Barnes, R. D., Sperry, D. L., & Harris, B. Perceived choice as a function of internal–external locus of control. *Journal of Personality*, 1974, *42*, 437–452.

Harvey, J. H., & Harris, B. Determinants of perceived choice and the relationship between perceived choice and expectancy about feelings of internal control. *Journal of Personality and Social Psychology*, 1975, *31*, 101–106.

Harvey, J. H., Harris, B., & Barnes, R. D. Actor–observer differences in the perceptions of responsibility and freedom. *Journal of Personality and Social Psychology*, 1975, *32*, 22–28.

Harvey, J. H., & Jellison, J. M. Determinants of perceived choice, number of options, and perceived time in making a selection. *Memory & Cognition*, 1974, *2*, 539–544.

Harvey, J. H., & Johnston, S. Determinants of the perception of choice. *Journal of Experimental Social Psychology*, 1973, *9*, 164–179.

Harvey, J. H., Wells, G. L., & Alvarez, M. D. Attribution in the context of conflict and separation in close relationships. In J. H. Harvey, W. J. Ickes, & R. F. Kidd (Eds.), *New directions in attribution research* (Vol. 2). Hillsdale, N.J.: Lawrence Erlbaum Associates, 1978.

Heider, F. *The psychology of interpersonal relations*. New York: Wiley, 1958.

Henslin, J. M. Craps and magic. *American Journal of Sociology*, 1967, *73*, 316–330.

Janis, I. L., & Mann, L. Decision making: A psychological analysis of conflict, choice, and commitment. San Francisco: Free Press, 1977.

Jellison, J. M., & Harvey, J. H. Determinants of perceived choice and the relationship between perceived choice and perceived competence. *Journal of Personality and Social Psychology*, 1973, *28*, 376–382.

Jones, E. A conversation with Edward E. Jones and Harold H. Kelley. In J. H. Harvey, W. J. Ickes, & R. F. Kidd (Eds.), *New directions in attribution research* (Vol. 2). Hillsdale, N.J.: Lawrence Erlbaum Associates, 1978.

Jones, E. E., & Davis, K. E. From acts to dispositions. In L. Berkowitz (Ed.), *Advances in experimental social psychology* (Vol. 2). New York: Academic Press, 1965.

Jones, E. E., Davis, K. E., & Gergen, K. J. Role playing variations and their informational value for person perception. *Journal of Abnormal and Social Psychology*, 1961, *63*, 302–310.

Jones, E. E., & Harris, V. A. The attribution of attitudes. *Journal of Experimental Social Psychology*, 1967, *3*, 1–24.

Jones, E. E., & Nisbett, R. E. *The actor and the observer: Divergent perceptions of the causes of behavior*. Morristown, N.J.: General Learning Press, 1971.

Jones, E. E., Worchel, S., Goethals, G. R., & Grumet, J. Prior expectancy and behavioral extremity as determinants of attitude attribution. *Journal of Experimental Social Psychology*, 1971, *7*, 59–80.

Kahneman, D., & Tversky, A. On the psychology of prediction. *Psychological Review*, 1973, *80*, 237–251.

Kelley, H. H. Attribution theory in social psychology. In D. Levine (Ed.), *Nebraska Symposium on Motivation* (Vol. 15). Lincoln: University of Nebraska Press, 1967.

Keltner, A., & Marshall, W. A. Attribution and subject control factors in experimental densensitization. *Behavior Therapy*, 1976, *7*, 626–633.

Kelvin, P. A social psychological examination of privacy. *British Journal of Social and Clinical Psychology*, 1973, *12*, 248–261.

Kruglanski, A. W., & Cohen, M. Attributed freedom and personal causation. *Journal of Personality and Social Psychology*, 1973, *26*, 245–250.

Langer, E. J., & Rodin, J. The effects of choice and enhanced personal responsibility for the aged: A field experiment in an institutional setting. *Journal of Personality and Social Psychology*, 1976, *34*, 191–198.

Levinger, G., & Raush, H. L. *Close relationships: Perspectives on the meaning of intimacy*. Amherst: University of Massachusetts Press, 1977.

Luce, B. D. *Individual choice behavior: A theoretical analysis*. New York: Wiley, 1959.

March, J. G., & Simon, H. A. *Organizations*. New York: Wiley, 1958.

May, R. Freedom, determinism and the future. *Psychology Today,* April 1977, pp. 6–9.

Mills, J. Interest in supporting and discrepant information. In R. P. Abelson, E. Aronson, W. J. McGuire, T. M. Newcomb, M. J. Rosenberg, & P. H. Tannenbaum (Eds.), *Theories of cognitive consistency: A sourcebook.* Chicago: Rand McNally, 1968.

Mills, J. *Unpublished analysis of perceived choice.* University of Missouri—Columbia, 1970.

Monty, R. A., Geller, E. S., Savage, R., & Perlmuter, L. C. The freedom to choose is not always so choice. *Journal of Experimental Psychology: Human Learning and Memory,* 1979, *5,* 170–178.

Monty, R. A., & Perlmuter, L. C. Persistence of the effects of choice on paired-associate learning. *Memory & Cognition,* 1975, *3,* 183–187.

Monty, R. A., Rosenberger, M. A., & Perlmuter, L. C. Amount and locus of choice as sources of motivation in paired-associate learning. *Journal of Experimental Psychology,* 1973, *97,* 16–21.

Osmond, H. Function as the basis of psychiatric ward design. In H. M. Proshansky, W. H. Ittelson, & L. G. Rivlin (Eds.), *Environmental psychology: Man and his physical setting.* New York: Holt, Rinehart & Winston, 1970.

Pennebaker, J. W., Burman, M. A., Shaeffer, M. A., & Harper, D. C. Lack of control as a determinant of perceived physical symptoms. *Journal of Personality and Social Psychology,* 1977, *35,* 167–174.

Perlmuter, L. C., & Monty, R. A. The importance of perceived control: Fact or fantasy? *American Scientist,* 1977, *65,* 759–765.

Perlmuter, L. C., Monty, R. A., & Cross, P. M. Choice as a disrupter of performance in paired-associate learning. *Journal of Experimental Psychology,* 1974, *102,* 170–172.

Proshansky, H. M., Ittelson, W. H., & Rivlin, L. G. Freedom of choice and behavior in a physical setting. In H. M. Proshansky, W. H. Ittelson, & L. G. Rivlin (Eds.), *Environmental psychology: Man and his physical setting.* New York: Holt, Rinehart & Winston, 1970.

Reim, B., Glass, D. C., & Singer, J. E. Behavioral consequences of exposure to uncontrollable and unpredictable noise. *Journal of Applied Social Psychology,* 1971, *1,* 44–56.

Rosenhan, D. L. On being sane in insane places. *Science,* 1973, *179,* 250–258.

Savage, R. E., & Perlmuter, L. C. *Choice and control: Perceptual and contextual determiners.* Undergraduate honors thesis, Virginia Polytechnic Institute and State University, 1976.

Scheff, T. J. *Being mentally ill: A sociological theory.* Chicago: Aldine, 1966.

Schulz, R. Effects of control and predictability on the physical and psychological well-being of the institutionalized aged. *Journal of Personality and Social Psychology,* 1976, *33,* 563–573.

Sensenig, J., & Brehm, J. W. Attitude change from an implied threat to attitudinal freedom. *Journal of Personality and Social Psychology,* 1968, *8,* 324–330.

Skinner, B. F. *Beyond freedom and dignity.* New York: Knopf, 1971.

Slovic, P., Fischhoff, B., & Lichtenstein, S. Behavioral decision theory. *Annual Review of Psychology,* 1977, *28,* 1–39.

Spitzer, R. L. On pseudoscience in science, logic in remission, and psychiatric diagnosis: A critique of Rosenhan's "On being sane in insane places." *Journal of Abnormal Psychology,* 1975, *84,* 442–452.

Steiner, I. D. Perceived freedom. In L. Berkowitz (Ed.), *Advances in experimental social psychology* (Vol. 5). New York: Academic Press, 1970.

Steiner, I. D. *Some antecedents and consequences of attributed freedom.* Paper presented at the American Psychological Association meeting, Honolulu, Hawaii, September 1972.

Steiner, I. D. *Attribution of choice.* Unpublished manuscript, University of Massachusetts—Amherst, 1977.

Steiner, I. D., & Field, W. L. Role assignment and interpersonal influence. *Journal of Abnormal and Social Psychology,* 1960, *61,* 239–246.

Storms, M. D., & McCaul, K. D. Attribution processes and emotional exacerbation of dysfunctional behavior. In J. H. Harvey, W. J. Ickes, & R. F. Kidd (Eds.), *New directions in attribution research* (Vol. 1). Hillsdale, N.J.: Lawrence Erlbaum Associates, 1976.

Taylor, J. D., & Kimble, G. A. The association value of 320 selected words and paralogs. *Journal of Verbal Learning and Verbal Behavior,* 1967, *6,* 744–752.

Taylor, S. E., & Fiske, S. T. Salience, attention, and attribution: Top of the head phenomena. In L. Berkowitz (Ed.), *Advances in experimental social psychology* (Vol. 11). New York: Academic Press, 1978.

Tversky, A. Elimination by aspects: A theory of choice. *Psychological Review,* 1972, *79,* 281–299.

Tversky, A., & Kahneman, D. Availability: A heuristic for judging frequency and probability. *Cognitive Psychology,* 1973, *4,* 207–232.

Walker, E. L. Psychological complexity as a basis for a theory of motivation and choice. In D. Levine (Ed.), *Nebraska Symposium on Motivation.* Lincoln: University of Nebraska Press, 1964.

Weary, G., & Harvey, J. H. *Effects of attributed freedom to seek therapy and severity of disturbance on perceived locus of control problem.* Paper presented at Southeastern Psychological Association meeting, Hollywood, Florida, May 1977.

Weiner, B. "On being sane in insane places": A process (attributional) analysis and critique. *Journal of Abnormal Psychology,* 1975, *84,* 433–441.

Wells, G. L., Petty, R. E., Harkins, S. G., Kagehiro, P., & Harvey, J. H. Anticipated discussion of interpretation eliminates actor–observer differences in attribution of causality. *Sociometry,* 1977, *40,* 247–253.

Westin, A. F. *Privacy and freedom.* New York: Atheneum, 1967.

White, R. W. Motivation reconsidered: The concept of competence. *Psychological Review,* 1959, *66,* 297–333.

Wicklund, R. A. *Freedom and reactance.* Hillsdale, N.J.: Lawrence Erlbaum Associates, 1974.

Wicklund, R. A., & Brehm, J. W. *Perspectives on cognitive dissonance.* Hillsdale, N.J.: Lawrence Erlbaum Associates, 1976.

Worchel, S., & Andreoli, V. A. Attribution of causality as a means of restoring behavioral freedom. *Journal of Personality and Social Psychology,* 1974, *29,* 237–245.

Worchel, S., & Andreoli, V. Escape to freedom: The relationship between attribution of causality and psychological reactance. In J. H. Harvey, W. J. Ickes, & R. F. Kidd (Eds.), *New directions in attribution research* (Vol. 1). Hillsdale, N.J.: Lawrence Erlbaum Associates, 1976.

Worchel, S., & Brehm, J. W. Direct and implied social restoration of freedom. *Journal of Personality and Social Psychology,* 1971, *18,* 294–304.

Wortman, C. B., Panciera, L., Shusterman, L., & Hibscher, J. Attributions of causality and reactions to uncontrollable outcomes. *Journal of Experimental Social Psychology,* 1976, *12,* 301–306.

20 The Illusion of Incompetence

Ellen J. Langer
Harvard University

Research in the area of control has been concerned primarily with the negative consequences that arise from the perceived loss of control. The most typical finding is that a perceived loss of control results in stress and psychological reactance when it is acute and learned helplessness when the loss is chronic (e.g., Glass & Singer, 1972; Seligman, 1975; Wortman & Brehm, 1975). In contrast to this approach, research conducted by myself and my colleagues has focused instead on the positive psychological consequences that accrue when people are provided with an enhanced sense of control. In studies dealing with chance situations (Langer, 1975, 1977; Langer & Roth, 1975), the preoperative hospital experience (Langer, Janis, & Wolfer, 1975), divorce (Langer & Newman, in press–a; Newman & Langer, 1978), crowding (Langer & Saegart, 1977), and old age (Langer & Rodin, 1976; Rodin & Langer, 1977), we assessed the facilitating effects of providing control. Although both the negative and positive approaches appear to have yielded interesting and useful findings, more recent research suggests that neither gives a complete version of the perception of control phenomenon. It is the intent of the present paper to review some of this recent work.

One of the most basic issues, which has not been adequately addressed, is how and why people give up control. In the most frequently studied instances (e.g., learned helplessness), control is given up as a function of an inference drawn from the present situation. Here, present events lead one to infer incompetence. There are many instances, however, where individuals are not incapacitated in the present situation but where their very actions in that situation induce a subsequent illusion of incompetence. Here, present actions are undertaken without knowledge of the potential implications of those actions. Although psychological research has been concerned almost exclusively with the situation-inferred case, it may be the action-induced one that is both more pervasive and more debilitating to the individuals involved due to its insidious nature. For people who infer a loss or lack of control from their present situation, it is unnecessary to look beyond the perceived loss to understand the motivation for their subsequent behavior. The reasons for people taking actions that may lead to a *subsequent* perception of less control, however, are multiple and varied. To mention a few: The effort involved in trying to control an outcome may outweigh the potential benefit of obtaining it (e.g., "I would like to be a doctor, but it's not worth four years of graduate school"); the outcome may be obtained more readily by letting another obtain it for you (e.g., "My physician knows more about illness than I do, so I'll do what she says"); engaging in the behavior required to bring about the outcome may be demeaning (e.g., "I want my data analyzed, but now that I have my degree, I should let a graduate student research assistant do it for me"); roles may demand giving up control (e.g., "I'm only an employee, I have to do what I am told...."); and so on.

Researchers may have ignored these instances where actions may induce relinquishing control because on the face of it, the consequences for the people in these circumstances do not appear to be psychologically costly. In most of these and similar instances, the individuals involved typically do not perceive themselves as relinquishing control, and concomitantly, they do not assume that such active passivity was paid for at a high price. The purpose of this chapter is to demonstrate how all instances of relinquishing control (both situation-inferred and action-induced) may lead to an illusion of incompetence and therefore may, indeed, be costly. There are, of course, ways in which the two cases differ. For example, the effects of situation-inferred lack of control may be felt immediately, whereas the effects of action-induced relinquishing control are more often delayed. Nevertheless, the major point to be made is that whether the loss of control is situation-inferred or action-induced, whether the effects are immediate or delayed, the consequences may be negative and the debilitation severe.

SITUATION-INFERRED LACK OF CONTROL

Before expounding on instances in which action-induced lack of control may have negative consequences, attention is given to a broader examination of those instances whereby inferences drawn from present events may lead one to an illusion of incompetence, the situation-inferred case.

Learned Helplessness

I only discuss the work on learned helplessness briefly, since detailed analyses can be found elsewhere (e.g., Seligman, 1975). The major purpose in discussing it now is so that it may be seen as part of a larger picture. In the learned helplessness paradigm, an individual comes to perceive response/outcome independence in situations where the outcome is in fact response contingent. This perception occurs as a result of generalization from prior experiences with uncontrollable aversive outcomes. What is crucial to this paradigm is repeated experience with failure. Such experience leads the individual in that situation to the inaccurate belief that he or she is incompetent, hence the individual gives up and becomes passive. The result, then, of this form of relinquishing control is clearly negative. Learned helpless individuals are not receiving the positive outcomes they could be receiving, they are not learning what could be learned from the situations they are in, and reflections on these consequences will result in lowering of their self-esteem. Seligman and his colleagues have suggested that the effects of such experience with uncontrollable aversive outcomes may be so debilitating as to eventuate in reactive depression (cf. Seligman, 1975).

Outcome-Independent Situational Factors

Another determinant of relinquishing control as a function of an inference drawn from present circumstances derives from situational factors that may be independent of repeated experience with failure. In a series of studies testing the illusion of control (Langer, 1975, 1977; Langer & Roth, 1975), it was found that the more similar a chance situation was to a skill situation, the more likely the illusion of control would occur. What was interesting about these skill-relevant factors was that they were objectively orthogonal to success on the task in question. Nevertheless, their presence resulted in an increase in confidence of success for the individuals involved. In contrast to the work on perceived control, the illusion of control dealt with situations that were completely chance determined—like lotteries, drawing for high card, or coin flipping—where it was clear that the illusion would dissipate if the chance nature of the situation was made salient to the participant.

The factors responsible for inducing an illusion of control that were tested in those earlier studies included competition, active and passive involvement, stimulus and response familiarity, choice, and the particular sequence of outcome. Competing with someone who looks incompetent in a chance game, flipping a coin oneself as opposed to watching someone else do it, thinking about the chance outcome and strategies to obtain it, possessing a lottery ticket with a familiar rather than an unfamiliar symbol on it, practicing the chance activity, choosing your own lottery ticket, or receiving several chance-determined hits in a row all seem to result in further behavior that implies an expectation for success that is inappropriately higher than the objective probability would warrant.

Just as the presence of skill-relevant factors may lead to an illusion of control in chance situations, the absence of these factors in skill situations may lead to an illusion of incompetence. For example, many people may deduce that they are incompetent at tasks that they in fact can perform quite effectively when put in a situation with an overtly confident individual. This would be an illusion of incompetence, since the potential success of the confident individual would not actually diminish the success of the former individual if he or she engaged in the behavior rather than gave up unless they were engaging in a zero-sum task, which is not characteristic of most of the circumstances in which we find ourselves. Giving up may be unwise for a number of reasons, including the possibility that the confident exterior of the assumed competitor may be a misleading indicator of that person's skill.

Similarly, when placed in an uninvolving position, as when waiting in a physician's office during a physical examination or awaiting surgery, one often relinquishes more control to the physician than may be wise. The whole medical situation is set up such that the patient is the passive recipient of services; yet research (e.g., Langer, Janis, & Wolfer, 1975; Langer & Rodin, 1976; Rodin & Langer, 1977) has already provided evidence of increased benefits to one's health that follow a cognitively more active participation in medical environments.

The potential debilitating effects associated with the presence of an apparently competent competitor, and with the absence of active involvement, are probably also involved with the other skill-relevant factors tested in the illusion-of-control studies. Let us consider familiarity with the task, or more precisely, the lack thereof. A person faced with a novel task may conclude incompetence erroneously after a superficial analysis of what the task entails. If people do not question how this "new" object or "new" response is similar to something familiar that is within their range of competence, they may give up rather than attempt the task, or they may attempt the task with more stress than is necessary or productive. So, for example, if a student of an elementary chemistry class who is about to conduct an experiment from a workbook attends to the novelty of the beakers, test tubes, and chemicals instead of likening the experience to following a cookbook (assuming that is familiar to him or her), the experiment may never be conducted; or if it is, the illusion of incompetence may hinder its successful completion. Without looking for something familiar in that which is new, feelings of incompetence are almost inevitable. Ironically, although the skills involved are often precisely those at which the person may be most competent, attention to the novel packaging may rob the individual of the confidence that is in fact warranted. These are just a few of the many examples in which the absence of factors closely related to controllable situations (but that are not necessarily outcome relevant) may lead an individual to unquestioningly perceive incompetence, just as their presence may lead to an illusion of control.

ACTION-INDUCED LACK OF CONTROL

Earlier it was stated that action-induced relinquishing control also may result in the illusion of incompetence. Again, whereas the debilitating effects of the situation-inferred case are largely immediate (i.e., occurring within the training session itself), here the consequences are more often delayed than not. In these cases, the individual is unaware that the present circumstances may lead to a decrement in a sense of competence at a later point in time. Therefore the person doesn't do anything to oppose it, with the effect that on that later occasion, he or she may experience the debilitation.

Mindlessness

One action-induced way people relinquish control is through repeated experience with an activity as they achieve a state of mindlessness. In contrast to the situations already described, in this instance, the consequences are not necessarily negative; nor is the person's response likely to be passive. When an individual first approaches a task, he or she is necessarily attentive to the particulars of the task at hand. With repeated experience with that task, less and less attention to those particulars is required for successful completion of the task. If the behavior is engaged in often enough, the original stimulus for the behavior may now cue in an entire sequence of behaviors, allowing rather complex action to unfold automatically, without conscious attention. In recent papers (Langer, 1978; Langer, Blank, & Chanowitz, 1978; Langer & Newman, in press-b), we have argued that mindlessness may be the preferred mode of interacting with one's environment and that mindlessness with respect to ostensibly thoughtful action may be rather pervasive. The studies conducted to demonstrate mindlessness were all very simple in design. Basically, subjects in compliance paradigms were given information that was either semantically sound or senseless and that was either structurally congruent or incongruent with their past experience. Equivalent responding to semantically sound and senseless information suggests that subjects are not thinking about what is being communicated to them. One of the hypotheses was that unless the structure of the communication is novel—i.e, incongruent with past experience—such mindlessness would occur, regardless of novel semantics.

Briefly, for example, in one of these studies, subjects were approached while using a copying machine and were asked to let a confederate use it instead. One of three requests was made: "Excuse me, may I use the Xerox machine"; "Excuse me, may I use the Xerox machine because I want to make copies"; "Excuse me, may I use the Xerox machine because I'm in a rush." From an information-processing perspective, the first and second requests are the same—what else would one do with a copying machine except make copies? Therefore if subjects were attending to what was being said, the first two requests should have resulted in the same rate of compliance. However, structurally they are different. In this regard, the redundant or placebic information ("Excuse me, may I use the Xerox machine because I want to make copies") is more similar to the last request, "Excuse me, may I use the Xerox machine because I'm in a rush." Similarity in compliance to the last two requests would imply attention to structure rather than conscious attention to content. That, in fact, was what was found. In the previously cited studies, whether the interactions were face to face or through written communications, whether they were semantically sound or senseless, they occasioned behavior that appeared mindless as long as the structure of the interaction triggered some overlearned sequence of behavior.

Virtually all researchers studying the importance of control will agree that the effects of objectively losing or gaining control will only have psychological significance if the person recognizes (accurately or inaccurately) the gain or loss. When behaviors are first engaged in, such recognition or awareness is present; hence, successful performance may have positive consequences for the individual. However, once the behavior or thoughts about the behavior become automatic, obviously such awareness is precluded by definition. Thus, at these times, the perception of control has been relinquished. The effect of relinquishing control in this way is neither positive nor negative. It is in fact not experienced. The consequences, however, may become either positive or negative, depending on other external circumstances. For example, if external circumstances lead to an evaluation of speed of responding or the ease with which the outcome now can be obtained, the effects of overpractice will be positive.

The potential negative effects of relinquishing control through mindlessness may be characterized as instances where practice makes imperfect. Some current research my students and I conducted suggests that once a cognition accompanying a behavior becomes automatic, it is no longer available for conscious processing in the same way nonoverlearned behaviors or cognitions are and that renewed attention to that which is overlearned tends to be disruptive. This would not necessarily be a problem if people were aware of this and just allowed themselves to go on automatic. However, there are many activities where people believe that they should be thinking about what they are doing while they are doing it. For example, putting in writing what you have said informally a hundred times before and giving a formal talk that you have practiced repeatedly and given repeatedly are just two of the countless instances where people think they should think before or while they act. Our data suggest that such attention to responses that were previously overlearned and unattended to will result in poorer performance. The unexpected experience of this poorer performance may have severe consequences for individuals and may lead them inappropriately to infer incompetence. That is, by not letting ourselves respond automatically in regard to something overlearned that we thought we could do well, we may stumble over our feet and then inaccurately conclude that we didn't know "it" as well as we thought we did.

All will acknowledge that there are few positive consequences of perceiving oneself successfully controlling a very easy task. Oddly enough, however, when one becomes expert at a task over which they *can* feel a sense of pride at being able to control the outcome completely, the very process of attaining such expertise—practice—often renders the person more vulnerable to situational factors that may lead to an illusion of incompetence with regard to that very task. (These factors are spelled out later in the discussion of self-induced dependence.) Expertise is attained by successively ignoring more and more of the particulars of the task in question. With repeated experience, the components of the task drop out (or to put it another way, the components of the task coalesce further and further to form a whole). The result of complete mastery, then, is that individuals are often in the position of knowing that they can perform the task without knowing the steps required to accomplish its performance. When circumstances lead these people to question their ability to perform that task successfully (e.g., perhaps even a single question from someone, "Are you *sure* you can do it?"), they may be unsure that they can, because they cannot supply as evidence the steps involved that are necessary to do it. (This effect, of course, will not occur when people can generate steps involved in doing the task, even if the self-generated parts objectively had virtually nothing to do with the whole.) Thus for tasks over which people should feel most confident, they may be most unconfident. Tasks that are very complicated—with so many component parts as to preclude complete mastery—would not of course, by this process, render the individual vulnerable.

Self-Induced Dependence

In work Judith Rodin and I conducted (Langer & Rodin, 1976; Rodin & Langer, 1977) with institutionalized elderly adults, we found that encouraging decision making, providing opportunities to make decisions, and giving these people something outside of themselves for which to be responsible (a plant) had the effect of rendering them more competent. They became more alert, more active, happier, and healthier relative to comparison groups. In fact, in a follow-up to that study, we found that half as many people died in the experimental group as in the comparison group. Originally we had conceived of the institutionalized elderly as "learned helpless" and then tried to provide control to see if the debilitation could be reversed. However, upon later reflection, it seemed unlikely to me that so many people had undergone exposure to the repeated uncontrollable aversive outcomes that is characteristic of the learned helplessness paradigm. Instead it seemed that contextual factors, which may be psychologically more important or as important as outcome valence, may have been responsible for the relative giving up of many of these people. Being assigned an explicit label that connotes inferiority relative to another person; engaging in a consensually defined demeaning task; no longer engaging in a previously performed task that is now engaged in by another; or allowing someone else to do something for you—all may lead an individual to an illusion of incompetence if these aspects of the situation are salient to that person. In contrast to the learned helplessness paradigm, these circumstances may lead an individual to infer incompetence even when prior experience resulted in success. This phenomenon whereby an individual erroneously infers incompetence from interpersonal situational factors was termed self-induced dependence (Langer & Benevento, 1978). In experiments testing these ideas (Langer & Benevento, 1978; Langer & Imber, 1978), we were studying the development of this debilitating process. Therefore we did not use the elderly as subjects. However, the elderly as a group would seem particularly vulnerable to self-induced dependence, because they bear negative labels; they do not engage in previously engaged-in activities; and people typically do things for them. The studies conducted thus far speak most directly to the first of these circumstances, wearing inferior labels. It was hypothesized that wearing a label that connotes inferiority relative to another person may render an individual less capable of performing tasks that are psychologically inconsistent with that role and that this may happen regardless of prior success experience with the task in question.

The subjects, tasks, and treatments changed from study to study, but the skeleton design remained the same. The experiments basically consisted of three phases. In the first phase, pairs of subjects *successfully* performed some task individually (e.g., solving arithmetic problems). In phase II they performed a different task together (e.g., solving anagrams), where one of the pair was the "boss" and the other was the "assistant" (or "worker," depending on the study) or where neither subject was labeled. In phase III subjects individually performed the original task again. Simply experiencing oneself in a subservient position had the effect of rendering the individual less able to perform the original task—a task on which the most recent experience had only been success. While these subjects showed a decrement in performance in phase III of the experiment, there was no difference among the groups in phase II. That is, they were able to perform well as "workers" or "assistants" but were rendered incompetent when faced with tasks that were now psychologically inconsistent with that role. Thus the debilitating effect was delayed rather than immediate. Performing a task while wearing the inferior label appears to have eventuated in these individuals inferring incompetence. They performed only about half as well as they did originally. Similarly, the superior label had a significantly facilitating effect. The tasks used in the original studies were all familiar tasks to subjects—that is, ones that may be performed somewhat mindlessly. In more recent studies (Langer & Imber, 1978), task familiarity or practice was varied in an attempt to understand better the process mediating the performance decrement. As stated earlier, repeated practice with a task may result in obfuscation of the steps involved in successful performance of that task. This was hypothesized to make an individual vulnerable to circumstances that would make one question one's competence. Among the several possible circumstances that could bring such questioning about, the one that again was subjected to experimental investigation was being assigned a label that connotes inferior status relative to another person. In this study it was expected that being assigned the inferior label would result in self-induced dependence with respect to an overlearned task, just as it would for a task at which subjects have no experience. However, the label was expected not to have influence in regard to a *nonoverlearned* task with which subjects have *some* experience, since subjects here were expected to be able to recall the steps necessary to complete the task successfully when their competence is brought into question by the label. Thus, a curvilinear relationship between task experience and label influence was predicted. In phase I of this study, one group of subjects performed a novel "do-able" task to a set criterion, whereas a second group performed the same task beyond mastery. In phase II, with the inclusion of a no-prior-experience group, all three groups performed a different task after being assigned a label. In phase III they were tested on the task used originally in phase I. Results reveal that subjects who either had been overpracticed at the task or who had no practice showed the self-induced dependence effect, whereas moderate-task-experience groups did not show a decrement in performance following the assignment of the inferior label.

In another study, we were interested in seeing if the effect could be reversed now that the vulnerability seemed to be a function of people losing sight of the components involved in the task at hand. To do this, we simply had subjects attend to the steps involved in the task to be performed when giving them their instructions. In phase I, one group of subjects performed the task in this way while the comparison group performed the same task without this salience manipulation. The next two phases were the same as those already described. The results of these studies suggested again that self-induced dependence can result from the imposition of an inferior label and that the debilitation can be reversed by leading subjects to attend to the smaller skills that are involved in successfully completing the task, skills that are progressively overlooked with practice. All the completed research has dealt with the effects of being explicitly assigned a label that connotes inferiority. Research in progress is aimed at testing some of the other determinants of self-induced dependence. For example, in one study, subjects are encouraged to let someone complete a task for them. It is expected that simply letting someone else do the task for them will render them less capable of subsequently performing the task themselves. Again, this should be particularly true for either a relatively unfamiliar or an overlearned task. Parenthetically, if this turns out to be true, it may be interesting to question our experiments on perceived control in which the experimenter typically gives the subject control. Does having someone give you control have as much impact as taking it on your own? Does being given control legitimize its exercise, or would self-initiated control attempts be more meaningful to the individual involved?

Self-induced dependence, thus, is an instance whereby people are engaging in actions—allowing themselves to wear labels or perhaps allowing other people to do things for them—without knowledge of the implications of those actions. This results in delayed rather than immediate effects.

Premature Cognitive Commitment

The final category of relinquishing control that may lead to an illusion of incompetence to be discussed is that of making premature cognitive commitments. When a person is exposed to information, there are two aspects of the information that the individual can choose to evaluate—its internal logic or its relevance for him or her. A recognition that this information is irrelevant and therfore does not apply personally relieves the individual of the necessity for closely examining the substantive assertions of that information. If at some later point in time, the individual is exposed to evidence that the information may in fact apply to him or her, that individual becomes vulnerable to the substantive implications of that previously accepted information. The earlier judgment of irrelevance has unwittingly prematurely committed the person to its validity and its consequences. By originally assuming its irrelevance to oneself, there is an implicit assumption of relevance, validity, and consequence of this information for others, thus making the person vulnerable. In contrast, a person who believes that the issue is relevant to him or her will examine the information or at least will not accept the conclusions and when later faced with the issue, can defend against it. This may occur for social, psychological, or physical symptoms. For example, assume that a person who is financially solvent and who expects to remain that way is led to believe that once a person is poor, there is nothing he or she can do to remedy the situation, or that people who are poor are worthless. Compare this person with another who is also financially solvent but who believes that his or her financial status may not remain that way. Assume that this latter person is also told that being poor is hopeless or that poverty makes one completely worthless. According to this formulation, it would be expected that this latter person who believes that it could happen to him or her will defend against the consequences at the time the information is first given, whereas the former person will accept the consequences, since at that time there is no personal danger. If at a later time both people lose all their money, the person who prematurely made a cognitive commitment to accepting the conditions of poverty—that is, its hopelessness—will continue to accept the inevitability of this situation, since it would not occur to him or her to do otherwise, whereas the other individual—faced with the same circumstances—will not.

Another example, and one more germane to my other interests, has to do with the elderly. On some level we all know that if we live long enough, at some point we will become old. Nevertheless, for the large majority of people, their own late adulthood has no psychological reality for them. Thus for all intents and purposes, some people act as if they believe that although others may get old, they themselves never will. Therefore, if these people are led to believe, for example, that senility, which is characterized by forgetfulness, accompanies old age, there is little reason for them to defend against this conclusion. That is, since it doesn't have any psychological reality for them, there is little justification to spend time thinking about external circumstances that may result in what looks like senility. For example, since the elderly are often ignored for many reasons, they may not be given as many reminders as their younger counterparts; or they overlook the fact that young, nonsenile people also are not infrequently forgetful. When this younger person then becomes old and either sees him- or herself forget things or is called forgetful by someone else, the person may very well erroneously assume that he or she is becoming or is senile. The potential negative consequences of the rest of this self-fulfilling prophecy should be obvious.

We conducted a study to determine the validity of these ideas (Chanowitz & Langer, 1978). Specifically, the experiment was designed to assess whether or not a premature cognitive commitment resulted in an illusion of incompetence. This was accomplished in the following way. Subjects were led to believe that the incidence in the general population of a certain disorder ("field dependence") was either 10% or 80%, the implication being that they were either unlikely or likely to have the disability. In the 80% condition, then, the information about the disability was relevant to the person. Though it wasn't made explicit, the symptoms were ones that would interfere with some of the very tasks they would be called upon to perform. Half of each group were asked to think about the consequences of having the disability and how they would cope with it if they had it, so that we could put their suggestions to use for other people. The other half were not given these instructions. All subjects then performed these tasks and "discovered," on the basis of performance standards posted on the data sheets they used to record their responses, that they had the disability. Subsequent task performance was the primary dependent measure. As predicted, regardless of how likely it originally seemed that they would have the disorder, subjects who were given instructions to think about the consequences of having the disability performed as well after hearing that they did have the disorder as before. Similarly, subjects who were not given these instructions, but who were originally led to believe that the information regarding the disability was relevant for them, also performed as well after learning that they had the disorder as before. This suggests that this group dealt with the information in a similar way. In contrast to these groups, however, the subjects who were originally led to believe that it was unlikely that they would have the disorder, and therefore presumably wouldn't have to defend against it, showed a severe decrement in performance after learning that they were so afflicted. They performed considerably more poorly than the other three groups did. Again, as with self-induced dependence, this decrement in performance occurred in spite of previous success at the task. This study suggests that accepting information uncritically, because it has no immediate consequences for the individuals involved, may indeed render people incompetent at a later point in time, a time when such incompetence may be illusory.

SUMMARY

In the foregoing analysis, I have tried to show how there are several different ways in which one may relinquish control—both from situational inferences and inadvertent actions—and how both cases may result in an illusion of incompetence. In the situation-inferred case, one may relinquish control, for example, as a result of learned helplessness training, or perhaps as a result of outcome-independent situational factors that may be characterized as the converse of those elements that foster the illusion of control. The processes suggested by which action may induce people to relinquish control leading to an erroneous belief in incompetence were through mindlessness, where practice may lead to imperfect, self-induced dependence and premature cognitive commitment. These initial experiments should be viewed as tests of capacity. Clearly, further investigation is required to determine the boundary conditions for each of the debilitations. Nevertheless, the results of these recent investigations suggest that although the consequences in each case may be severe, they also may be prevented or reversed.

ACKNOWLEDGMENTS

Preparation of this paper was facilitated by a grant from N.S.F. (BNS 76-10939) to the author. I am grateful to the following people for their comments on an earlier version of this paper: Benzion Chanowitz, Carol Dweck, Phyllis Katz, and Jeremy Miransky.

REFERENCES

Chanowitz, B., & Langer, E. J. *Premature cognitive commitment.* Mimeograph. Harvard University, 1978.

Glass, D., & Singer, J. *Urban stress: Experiments on noise and social stressors.* New York: Academic Press, 1972.

Langer, E. J. The illusion of control. *Journal of Personality and Social Psychology,* 1975, *32,* 311–328.

Langer, E. J. The psychology of chance. *Journal for the Theory of Social Behavior,* 1977, *7,* 185–208.

Langer, E. J. Rethinking the role of thought in social interaction. In J. H. Harvey, W. J. Ickes, & R. F. Kidd (Eds.), *New directions in attribution research* (Vol. 2). Hillsdale, N.J.: Lawrence Erlbaum Associates, 1978.

Langer, E. J., & Benevento, A. Self-induced dependence. *Journal of Personality and Social Psychology,* 1978, *36,* 886–893.

Langer, E. J., Blank, A., & Chanowitz, B. The mindlessness of ostensibly thoughtful action. *Journal of Personality and Social Psychology,* 1978, *36,* 635–642.

Langer, E. J., & Imber, L. *Mindlessness and susceptibility to the illusion of incompetence.* Mimeograph. Harvard University, 1978.

Langer, E. J., Janis, I., & Wolfer, J. Reduction of psychological stress in surgical patients. *Journal of Experimental Social Psychology,* 1975, *11,* 155–165.

Langer, E. J., & Newman, H. Post-divorce adjustment and the attribution of responsiblity. *Sex Roles,* in press. (a)

Langer, E. J., & Newman, H. The role of mindlessness in a typical social psychological experiment. *Personality and Social Psychology Bulletin,* in press. (b)

Langer, E. J., & Rodin, J. The effects of choice and enhanced personal responsibility for the aged: A field experiment in an institutional setting. *Journal of Personality and Social Psychology,* 1976, *34,* 191–198.

Langer, E. J., & Roth, J. Heads I win, tails it's chance: The illusion of control as a function of the sequence of outcomes in a purely chance task. *Journal of Personality and Social Psychology,* 1975, *32,* 951–955.

Langer, E. J., & Saegart, S. Crowding and cognitive control. *Journal of Personality and Social Psychology,* 1977, *35,* 175–182.

Newman, H., & Langer, E. J. *A cognitive arousal model of relationship formation, stabilization, and disintegration.* Mimeograph. Harvard University, 1978.

Rodin, J., & Langer, E. J. Long-term effects of a control-relevant intervention with the institutionalized aged. *Journal of Personality and Social Psychology,* 1977, *35,* 897–902.

Seligman, M. *Helplessness: On depression, development, and death.* San Francisco: Freeman, 1975.

Wortman, C., & Brehm, J. Responses to uncontrollable outcomes: An integration of reactance theory and the learned helplessness model. In L. Berkowitz (Ed.), *Advances in experimental social psychology* (Vol. 8). New York: Academic Press, 1975.

21

Environmental Influences on the Effectiveness of Control- and Competence-Enhancing Interventions

Richard Schulz
Barbara Hartman Hanusa
Carnegie-Mellon University

INTRODUCTION

Social psychologists and gerontologists are becoming increasingly aware that perceived choice and a sense of personal control are important determinants of the aged individual's physical and psychological well-being. Large quantities of observational and correlational research are now available documenting the fact that lack of personal autonomy may account for some of the negative effects observed among the aged in general and the institutionalized aged in particular (Schulz, 1978; Schulz & Brenner, 1977).

For example, in a recent review and analysis of the literature on relocation of the aged, Schulz and Brenner (1977) present a theoretical model that stresses the importance of control and predictability as mediators of relocation outcomes. Briefly, they argue that the response to the stress of relocation is largely determined by: (1) the perceived controllability and predictability of the events surrounding a move; and (2) differences in environmental controllability between pre- and postrelocation environments. Support for this model is found in numerous relocation studies where mortality rates are typically used as dependent measures. Available findings indicate that: (1) the greater the perceived choice the individual has in being relocated, the less negative the effects; (2) the more predictable the new environment is, the less negative the effects of relocation; and finally (3) decreases in environmental controllability are associated with negative outcomes, and increases in controllability are associated with positive outcomes. One could extend the perceived choice and control analysis to other health-related areas such as recovering from coronary disease (Krantz

& Schulz, in press), response to a kidney transplant (Schulz, in press), and the longevity (Schulz & Aderman, 1973) and physical well-being (Schulz, 1978) of terminal cancer patients.

Although the sheer quantity of data implicating the importance of control and predictability as determinants of health-related outcomes is compelling, these data are almost exclusively based on correlational research. It is not clear whether a sense of control is an antecedent or a consequence of the individual's physical well-being. Furthermore, since none of the research was specifically designed to test a control model, it is often necessary to make assumptions about the details of studies in order to invoke an interpretation based on such a model.

Fortunately, several recently completed studies have been carried out testing the impact of perceived choice and control on subjects' health status using experimental methodology. The first experiment on this topic was carried out by Schulz (1976), who hypothesized that some of the characteristics frequently observed among the institutionalized aged, such as feelings of depression and helplessness as well as accelerated physical decline, are at least in part attributable to loss of control and decreased environmental predictability. This hypothesis was supported by data obtained from a field experiment carried out in a retirement home. It was found that making a significant positive event either predictable or controllable had a powerful positive impact on health status and morale.

A conceptually similar experiment was carried out by Langer and Rodin (1976). In their study, aged residents of a nursing home who were induced to feel responsible for their outcomes exhibited greater activity, happiness, and increased alertness when compared to a similar group of patients who were told that the staff would take care of them and make them happy.

Rodin and Langer (1977) also collected health and psychological status data 18 months after their study was completed and found that subjects in the responsibility-induced condition evidenced better health and higher activity patterns. Furthermore, their mood and sociability did not decline as greatly, and mortality rates were lower when compared to the staff-support comparison group. In contrast to these positive long-term effects, Schulz and Hanusa (1978) found that the groups exposed to the predictability- or control-enhancing intervention exhibited only temporary positive effects. Once the study was terminated, the improved groups declined back to baseline levels.

A third experiment examining the effects of a predictability-enhancing intervention was recently completed by Schulz and Hanusa (1977). This experiment tested the hypothesis that an intervention designed to enhance the predictability of an institutional environment should facilitate adaptation and decrease some of the physical and psychological deficits typically associated with relocation. Newly admitted persons who were provided with predictability-enhancing information were judged to be physically and psychologically healthier than persons given either no information or irrelevant information. Furthermore, the positive effects achieved persisted over time. Eight weeks after the study was completed, the groups provided with the predictability-enhancing information had shown no decline in health or psychological status.

In summary, the completed experimental research in this area has provided information regarding the impact of control and predictability-enhancing interventions on the institutionalized aged, the long-term effects of these interventions, the generality of the effect across widely divergent populations, and the relationship between these interventions and individual differences (see Schulz, in press). Although these findings provide some important answers to questions regarding social–psychological aspects of aging, they raise several new questions as well. One persistent theme in much of the completed research is that the intervention used may not only affect perception of environmental control but may also enhance feelings of competence. Thus, both Schulz (1976) and Langer and Rodin (1976) suggested that their control manipulation may have made subjects feel generally more competent. The control-enhancing message used by Langer and Rodin (1976), for example, explicitly stated that subjects were responsible for making some important decisions regarding their lives, implying that they were competent enough to make these decisions. We might ask, therefore, what is the relationship between competence and control? The remaining portion of this chapter is devoted to the discussion of two experiments addressing this issue.

Competence and Control

Existing laboratory research (Dweck & Reppucci, 1973; Hanusa & Schulz, 1977; Hiroto, 1974) suggests that lack of control is most devastating when it carries with it broad implications against the individual's self-worth. Conversely, manipulations that increase control and at the same time elevate feelings of competence should have a greater and longer-lasting positive impact than control-enhancing interventions that do not affect competence attributions. This may account for the differences in long-term effects found by Rodin and Langer (1977) and by Schulz and Hanusa (1978). It is likely that the responsibility intervention used by Langer and Rodin (1976) encouraged subjects to make positive self-attributions, whereas Schulz's (1976) intervention did little to cause subjects to change their overall self-concept. Given this analysis, one would expect the impact of the responsibility-enhancing intervention to persist over time.

Aged individuals may be especially susceptible to competence-enhancing interventions because of the decline in physical and psychological functioning typically associated with aging. Schaie and Schaie (1977), for example, have suggested that an aged person's functioning "could be enhanced if negative feelings about adequacy and perceived value were modified [p. 715]." Similarly, Kuypers and Bengtson (1973) suggest that the social breakdown of the elderly, a process whereby the elderly person is defined as and eventually views him- or herself as incompetent, can be counteracted by interventions that enhance feelings of competence in three areas: social-role performance, adaptive capacity, and personal feelings of mastery and inner control. Kuypers and Bengtson make specific suggestions for accomplishing these goals, but to date there are no experimental demonstrations documenting the effects of competence-enhancing interventions.

EXPERIMENT 1

Experiment 1 was designed to test the combined effects of control- and competence-enhancing interventions on the institutionalized aged. Two levels of competence and two levels of control were manipulated in a 2 × 2 design. In addition, two control groups were run to collect baseline data (no-treatment group) and to assess the effects of the increased attention (attention group) subjects received in the experimental treatment conditions. It was expected that the impact of the control- and competence-enhancing interventions would be additive. Thus subjects who were made to feel highly competent and who were given control over an important outcome should exhibit better health and psychological status than subjects exposed to just the competence- or just the control-enhancing intervention. It was further expected that being exposed to either the competence- or the control-enhancing intervention should improve outcomes relative to groups who received neither.

Method

Subjects and Setting

Experiment 1 was conducted at a large (1600 bed), county-run, long-term-care facility for the aged. The hospital residents are typically white, single, and of low socioeconomic status. They are assigned to an area of the hospital based on their physical condition and the degree of nursing attention needed. Physical problems vary from cardiovascular diseases to central nervous system disorders (e.g., multiple sclerosis) to general deterioration of physical and mental capacities due to advancing age. The severity of the physical problems ranges from minimal to totally involving.

Subjects for this study resided either in the moderate care area (known as the Pavilion) or the minimal care area (the Infirmary). They ranged in age from 52 to 91 years (mean age was 74 years) and had been in the hospital anywhere from 1½ to 20 years, with a mean stay of 5 years. One hundred and ten potential subjects were identified by the social workers. After the initial interviews, 65 residents were selected for the study. These residents were over 50 years of age, oriented, capable of answering questions posed by the interviewers, and ambulatory. Subjects were randomly assigned to one of six treatment groups that were matched for sex, age, and length of stay. The experimental design consisted of a 2 × 2 factorial (two levels of control and two levels of competence) and two baseline control groups. The number of subjects in each experimental condition ranged from 9 to 11.

Procedure

Once eligible subjects were identified and preliminary data (activity level, orientation level, and attitudes toward the hospital) had been collected, subjects were approached by one of three female experimenters. Permission was obtained from each subject to include them in a study being conducted by psychologists at Carnegie-Mellon University. All subjects agreed to participate, and the procedure for each condition was initiated.

Subjects assigned to one of the four experimental treatment conditions were told that they would be working on a series of cognitive and social skills tasks involving several sessions distributed over a 5-week period. The cognitive tasks used included mazes, simple problems from Raven's Progressive Matrices, semantic ability questions, and simple reaction time. To test their social skills, subjects were asked to generate questions useful in getting to know someone. Although all subjects in the four treatment groups worked on these tasks, the payoff contingencies and feedback they received varied according to the specific treatment condition.

Competence Manipulation. Subjects assigned to the *high-competence* condition were told that these tasks had been tested on many other people their age and that they would be given feedback about their performance. The feedback they received was always positive, and subjects were repeatedly told that they were "better than others their age," "better than others within the institution," "really good," "very impressive," and so on.

Subjects assigned to the *low-competence* condition were also given high rates of feedback indicating that they had solved the problems. However, the meaning of this feedback was left ambiguous. Subjects were told that these tasks had never been tested on aged persons before, "so we really don't know how difficult or easy they are. They may all be very easy or they may be hard."

Control Manipulation.   Control was manipulated by varying the contingency of reinforcement. For *high-control* subjects, payment was made to appear contingent upon task performance by giving subjects a store coupon after completing one or several trials on a task. Subjects assigned to the *low-control* condition were given store coupons before performing a task for "helping us with the study." All subjects received equal amounts of money.

No-Treatment Condition.   Subjects assigned to this condition received the same quantity of coupons given subjects in other conditions but were not exposed to any treatments. Subjects were informed that the coupons were payment for participating in our study and providing us with information.

Attention Condition.   To control for the increased attention paid to members of the treatment groups, subjects in this condition were visited by an experimenter as often as subjects in the treatment groups. Subjects typically chatted with the experimenter and were given the same quantity of store coupons received by other participants. The coupons were given them in payment for participating in the study and providing us with information.

A sample protocol illustrating the application of the high-competence, high-control manipulation to the maze task is now presented:

After explaining to subjects how the mazes are solved, each subject was told: "I'd like you to do as well as you can. For each one you do correctly, I'll give you 20¢ in store coupons. These mazes have been tested on a lot of people your age, so I'll be able to tell you how good you are compared to them. And remember, you can control how much money you make by doing well. The better you do, the more store coupons you'll get."

After completing maze one, the subject was told, "That's right. You've got 20¢ now. You did pretty good on that one. Are you ready for a little harder one?"

After maze two: "You're really good. Most of the others your age have had a harder time doing these, and you're breezing right through. You're up to 40¢ now."

After maze three: "I'm really impressed, you're doing very well. You know, most people have a lot of trouble with this maze—not just people at Kane, but other places also. You're up to 60¢ now."

After maze four: "You're really good at these mazes. You're up to 80¢ now. Let's do one more and we'll quit."

After maze five: "You're better than other people here, and you're better than most people your age. Let me give you your store coupons now."

Dependent Measures

Three types of data assessing the impact of the intervention were collected. Subjects' perception of contingency and performance expectations served as manipulation checks for the control and competence manipulations, respectively. Health and psychological status as well as activity level served as the major dependent variables in the study. Subjects provided self-assessments on these measures and were in addition rated by the caretaker staff. Finally, subjects were assessed on a variety of cognitive functioning measures to determine to what extent experience with such tasks generalized to new, similar tasks. The data were collected by four interviewers blind to experimental condition.

Results

The data were analyzed using an analysis of variance procedure suggested by Winer (1962, pp. 263–267) for a design involving a complete factorial with additional control groups. Thus, a 2 × 2 analysis of variance procedure was used to test for the main effects and interaction of control and competence, and the t statistic was used to assess differences between the treatment and control groups.

Manipulation Checks

Subjects in the treatment conditions were asked why they received the store coupons. Eleven of 20 persons in the high-control condition reported that they received them for performing well on the experimental tasks, whereas only four of 20 subjects in the low-control condition felt this, $X^2(1) = 5.24$, $p < .05$.

Manipulation checks for the competence intervention were more difficult to obtain. Subjects were asked if they perceived themselves to be better than others their age, but few were willing to admit this, probably because there were often other persons in the room when these questions were asked. A more indirect check on the competence intervention was obtained by asking subjects to evaluate their task performance. As expected, subjects exposed to the high-competence intervention evaluated their performance to be significantly higher than those in the low-competence condition, $F(1,27) = 14.87$, $p < .001$.

Self-Ratings[1]

Health Status. At the completion of the study, all subjects were asked (1) to rate their own health now, and (2) whether or not they perceived their health to have changed in the last month. A 2 × 2 analysis of variance carried

---

[1]Collecting useful data from this population proved to be a difficult task. All scales used were either dichotomous or trichotomous, and subjects were not always willing to answer all questions. This differential response rate is reflected in the degrees of freedom for each question.

TABLE 21.1
Mean Self-Ratings by Condition

			Condition			
	No Treatment	*Attention*	*Low Competence, Low Control*	*Low Competence, High Control*	*High Competence, Low Control*	*High Competence, High Control*
Health status	2.09	1.70	2.44	2.40	2.33	2.80
Change in health status	2.00	1.90	2.00	2.50	2.56	2.00
Satisfaction with life	2.36	2.20	2.50	2.60	1.78	2.30
Number of things done to keep busy	1.63	2.00	3.44	3.30	3.44	2.45
Have say in what you do all day	1.4	1.6	1.78	1.70	1.78	1.36

out on subjects' health ratings at the end of the study yielded no significant effects. As the means in Table 21.1 indicate, the differences between the four treatment groups were negligible. The means for the two control groups were also not reliably different. However, when the four treatment groups were combined and contrasted to the two comparison groups, a reliable difference was found. Persons in the four treatment groups perceived themselves to be significantly healthier than persons in the control groups, $t(53) = 2.63$, $p < .05$. A 2×2 analysis of variance carried out on subjects' perception of *change* in health status yielded no significant main effects but did yield a significant Control × Competence interaction, $F(1,33) = 5.73$, $p < .02$. Inspection of the means displayed in Table 21.1 shows that subjects who were exposed to either the high-competence or high-control manipulation perceived more positive change in health status than persons who were exposed to neither or both.

Activity and Life Satisfaction. Activity levels were in part assessed by having subjects list the number of things they do to keep busy. A 2×2 analysis of variance yielded no significant main effects or interactions. Nor were the two control groups different from each other. However, when the four treatment groups were combined and contrasted to the two control groups, it was found that subjects in the treatment groups listed significantly more items than subjects in the two comparison groups, $t(54) = 2.52, p < .05$. It should be noted, though, that one of the treatment groups (high competence plus high control) did not differ from the two comparison groups.

A similar pattern of results was obtained in answer to the question, "Do you have a say in what you do all day?" The treatment groups were more likely to answer yes to this question than the two control groups. Of the control subjects, 50% answered yes to this question, whereas 64% of the treatment subjects responded affirmatively. However, only 30% of the subjects exposed to both the high-competence and high-control manipulation responded positively to this question.

Finally, all subjects were asked how satisfied they were with their lives at present. A 2×2 analysis of variance yielded a significant effect for competence, $F(1,33) = 6.16$, $p < .02$. The means in Table 21.1 show the low-competence groups to be more satisfied than the high-competence groups. The main effect for Control and the Control × Competence interaction failed to reach significance at the .05 level of confidence.

In sum, the self-report data do not support the conclusion that the effects of control and competence interventions are additive. In fact, these data suggest the reverse. Having both appears to have no beneficial effects relative to the control groups, but having either control or competence appears to be of some benefit.

Nurse's Ratings

Since no one social worker was familiar with all the subjects, three different persons were used to rate different subsets of the study population. Each nurse rated several subjects in each condition, and deviation scores were computed in order to combine the ratings made by different nurses. Deviation scores were computed by averaging the assessments made by each nurse and calculating each subject's deviation from the mean of each nurse's group. It was necessary to use deviation scores instead of absolute ratings because the scales were used differently by different nurses. All nurses used 9-point Likert scales to rate subjects on health status, zest for life, and activity. Mean deviation scores are presented in Table 21.2.

Analysis of the health status data yielded no significant differences. However, a 2 × 2 analysis of variance yielded a significant Competence × Control interaction for zest, $F(1,35) = 8.46$, $p < .01$, and a marginal interaction for activity, $F(1,35) = 3.31, p < .078$. As the means in Table 21.2 show, subjects exposed to either the high-competence or high-control intervention exhibited positive effects, whereas subjects exposed to both or neither evidenced no positive effects and were no different from the two control groups.

Cognitive-Motor Ability

Several cognitive performance tasks were included as dependent measures to determine whether the experience gained during treatment would generalize to new tasks and improve performance on old tasks. A variety of tasks were used. The results for the four tasks listed in Table 21.3 are representative. Of the four, subjects had previous experience only with the reaction-time task.

There were no differences among treatment groups on any of the four tasks, nor were there differences between the two comparison groups. Contrasts between the four treatment groups combined and the two comparison groups combined yielded significant effects for three of the four tasks. Subjects who had participated in the teatment procedure were better on the forward digit span, $t(53) = 2.98$, $p < .01$; could generate more rhyme words, $t(52) = 1.89$, $p = .05$; and had faster reaction times, $t(28) = 3.22, p < .01$. Although the differences among the four treatment groups were not significant, these data do hint of the possibility of additive effects attributable to the combined effects of the control- and competence-enhancing interventions. The means in Table 21.3 show that the group exposed to the high-competence and high-control intervention evidenced the best performance on all measures.

TABLE 21.2

Mean Deviation Scores for Nurses' Ratings of Subjects by Condition

			Condition			
	No Treatment	*Attention*	*Low Competence, Low Control*	*Low Competence, High Control*	*High Competence, Low Control*	*High Competence, High Control*
Health status	.05	–.83	–.12	+.42	–.01	.02
Zest	–.57	–.85	–.37	+.38	+.74	–.70
Activity	–.57	–1.80	–.61	+.75	+.62	–.39

TABLE 21.3
Mean Scores on Cognitive-Motor Tasks by Condition

		Condition				
	No Treatment	Attention	Low Competence, Low Control	Low Competence, High Control	High Competence, Low Control	High Competence, High Control
Forward digit span	5.3	5.8	6.4	6.6	6.3	6.8
Backward digit span	2.7	2.8	3.2	3.3	3.2	4.0
Number of correct rhyme words generated in response to specific stimulus word	.73	1.10	1.22	2.60	2.11	3.36
Simple reaction time in milliseconds	1445	10005	764	704	746	610

Discussion

The most compelling feature of these data is that the group exposed to both competence- and control-enhancing interventions was relatively worse off on indicators of health, psychological status, and activity when compared to groups exposed to only one of these enhancing interventions. The control- and the competence-enhancing interventions appear to have equivalent impact when presented alone. The reason for this latter effect probably resides in the nature of the manipulations used in this study. Although an attempt was made to manipulate control and competence orthogonally, it is likely that each caused subjects to infer the presence of the other. Thus, the competence manipulation undoubtedly contributed to feelings of perceived control, and the control manipulation enhanced feelings of competence.

Viewed from this perspective, the combined effects of the competence and control manipulations very likely resulted in feelings of heightened self-esteem and great potency among subjects exposed to both. Why should these same subjects exhibit the paradoxical effect of decreased health and psychological status? An answer to this question may be found by examining more closely the theoretical perspectives that guided this study.

The design of this field experiment was in part based on the theoretically derived assumption that increasing an individual's level of perceived competence and control should facilitate functioning. This assumption is critical to the reactance-control model proposed by Wortman and Brehm (1975) and to the learned helplessness model described by Seligman (1975) and by Abramson, Seligman, and Teasdale (in press). Both theories propose that maladaptive behaviors result when the individual lacks control or perceives the self as incompetent, and both suggest interventions designed to enhance feelings of control and competence. In brief, these theories focus on what happens to the organism when control is lost and suggest interventions aimed at returning the individual to normal functioning. However, neither theory explicitly asks what the impact of a control- or competence-enhancing intervention is upon someone who is already functioning adaptively within a given environment. Most of us have assumed that even for populations functioning adaptively within a particular setting, increasing perceived control and competence will still improve level of functioning. Several gerontologists have suggested that this may not always be true.

The possibility that increased competence may have negative effects within some contexts has been suggested by Lawton (1975). The adaptation level theory proposed by Lawton focuses on individual competence and environmental press. Press is defined as the demand quality of an environment and can be either positive or negative and can vary in strength. Whether press is negative or positive depends on its ability to elicit adaptive or nonadaptive behaviors. With a given level of press, the occurrence of adaptive or nonadaptive behaviors will depend on the individual's level of competence.

Positive behavior or affect occurs when the individual's level of competence is adequate to deal with the press level of a given environment. Negative behaviors or affect occur (1) when press level is excessively high, making it impossible for an individual of a given level of competence to deal with the environment; or (2) when press level is excessively low—that is, the environment is not challenging enough for the individual to exercise his or her perceived level of competence. This latter hypothesis may explain the unexpected results obtained for the group exposed to both the competence- and control-enhancing interventions. Their competence may have been raised to a level where the environment was unable to provide them with the necessary opportunities to exercise their competence.

One important implication of this interpretation of the data is that environmental context may be a limiting factor on the effectiveness of interventions aimed at the individual. In a very constrained environment such as an institution, person-oriented interventions may have to be supplemented with changes in the environment for maximal benefits to the individual. On the other hand, this is unlikely to be a problem in environments that offer a large latitude in their ability to accommodate different levels of competence. It should therefore be possible to demonstrate additive effects for control- and competence-enhancing intervention in unconstrained environments. To test this notion, a conceptual replication of Experiment 2 was carried out in a college environment.

EXPERIMENT 2

Experiment 2 was designed to replicate conceptually the intervention used in Experiment 1 but with a college population in a college environment. It was hypothesized that the opportunities to exercise one's competencies in a college environment are almost infinite, and it should therefore be possible to obtain additive effects for the combined impact of control- and competence-enhancing interventions.

Experiment 2 was aimed at investigating the importance of perceived control and competence in adapting to the first year of college life. The design of the experiment was identical to the one used with the institutionalized aged. Freshman volunteers were assigned to one of six groups: four treatment groups in which two levels of competence were crossed with two levels of control and two baseline comparison groups.

Method

Subjects and Setting

First-year college students at a moderate-sized, private, urban university were asked on the first day of orientation to volunteer for a program designed to improve their communication skills. Seventy-one students agreed to participate and were randomly assigned to one of six conditions. The design consisted of a 2 × 2 factorial (two levels of competence crossed by two levels of control) plus two baseline comparison groups comprised of a no-treatment group and an attention group. The number of subjects in each condition were as follows: no treatment (n = 11), attention (n = 9), high competence plus high control (n = 8), high competence plus low control (n = 8), low competence plus high control (n = 10), low competence plus low control (n = 8). In order to create a no-treatment group, all subjects were initially informed that there might not be enough room to accommodate everyone. Subjects randomly assigned to the no-treatment group were later called and informed that we could not fit them into the schedule. Subjects assigned to the remaining condition were also called and asked to report for a 4-hour evening session.

Procedure

Subjects assigned to the four treatment groups and the attention control group were asked to spend an evening working on communication and problem-solving skills. Each group was scheduled for a different evening of the week. When all participants arrived, the experimenter, a trained counseling psychologist, introduced herself and briefly explained the purpose of the new orientation programs. With this completed, the manipulations were begun.

Competence Manipulation

Perceived competence was manipulated by teaching subjects that they were personally capable of dealing with important interpersonal problems. In the *high-competence* condition, subjects were given a set of problems they were likely to encounter and were asked to generate solutions to them and act them out. The set of problems included:

1. asking a professor for more credit on tests
2. asking a roommate to stop borrowing things
3. dealing with being pressured for sex
4. informing parents of low grades
5. discussing what bothers them when criticized
6. being generally more assertive

After acting out these problem situations, all subjects received positive feedback about their ability to generate and act out good solutions to these problems.

Subjects assigned to the *low-competence* condition were given the same problem but were not allowed to generate their own solutions. Instead, they were given prepared scripts and asked to perform them. (The scripts were in fact identical to the solutions generated by the high-competence group). After role playing the scripts, these subjects also received positive feedback about their performance.

Control Manipulation. Control was manipulated by varying the perceived responsibility for outcomes subjects were likely to experience. Persons in the *high-control* condition were informed that the "university provided many opportunities but it was their job to take advantage of them." They were further told that they "would likely encounter a variety of new problems and that there were people on campus who could help, but it was their job to seek help."

Persons in the *low-control* condition were simply told that "college life was interesting and exciting, but they would also encounter a variety of problems."

Attention Condition. Persons in this condition were given relaxation training, were taught verbal and nonverbal communication skills, and performed several exercises designed to familiarize them with other members in the group.

No-Treatment Condition. Persons in this group did not participate in an evening session but were asked to provide data at midterm and at the end of the semester.

Dependent Measures

Four types of dependent measures were collected. One, manipulation checks consisted of questions asked shortly after the group session and at midterm concerning whether or not they would use the skills they learned and how confident they felt about using the skills. Two, subjects were asked about their participation in a variety of activities other than going to class and studying. Three, grade point averages were obtained for each subject both at midterm and at finals. Finally, approximately half the subjects in each condition were interviewed at the end of the semester by a clinical psychologist blind to subject's condition. Each person was interviewed for 30 minutes and rated on adjustment, social competence, and assertiveness.

Results

Manipulation Checks

After completing the 4-hour treatment session, subjects were given questionnaires asking them to indicate on 4-point scales how useful they thought the skills were, whether they would personally use the skills, and how confident they felt about using the skills taught them. Data for the four treatment groups were analyzed using a 2 × 2 analysis of variance procedure. For the question assessing the usefulness of the skills, a marginal main effect for the competence manipulation was obtained, $F(1,29) = 3.57, p < .07$. As indicated by the means in Table 21.4, the high-competence group tended to find the skills more useful. When asked whether they would personally use the skills, significant main effects were obtained for both competence, $F(1,29) = 5.03, p < .05$, and control, $F(1,29) = 6.04, p < .05$. Both the high-competence and high-control groups thought that they would be more likely to use the skills. Similar effects were obtained for the question assessing subjects' confidence in their ability to use the skills, $F(1,29) = 4.04, p < .05$. The effect for the competence manipulation was in the same direction, but it was not significant, $F(1,29) = 3.11, p < .12$.

Similar questions asked at midterm yielded comparable results. For the question assessing the usefulness of the skills, a main effect for the competence manipulation was obtained, $F(1,33) = 9.63, p < .01$. High-competence subjects perceived them to be more useful. On this same variable, there was also a significant interaction between competence and control, $F(1,33) = 4.96, p < .05$, which was primarily attributable to the group exposed to both the high-competence and high-control manipulation. Persons in this condition were significantly higher on this variable than the other groups, $F(1,33) = 10.04, p < .001$, for the comparison between high competence and high control and the three other groups combined.

Finally, when subjects were asked how much they had used the skills, a significant main effect for the control manipulation was obtained, $F(1,32) = 9.26, p < .01$. High-control subjects used them more.

In sum, these data show that the control and competence manipulations had significant impact on both judged usefulness of the tasks and their likelihood of being used.

Grade Point Averages

Grade point averages for all participants were obtained from university records at midterm and at the end of the semester. A 2 (competence) × 2 (control) × 2 (time) repeated measures analysis of variance of these data yielded a significant main effect for time, $F(1,29) = 5.23, p < .03$, and a nearly significant interaction between competence, control, and time, $F(1,29) = 3.84, p < .06$. Although all groups experienced increases in grade point average, only the high-competence-plus-high-control group evidenced a significant increase in grade point average, $F(1,29) = 7.38, p < .05$.

Activity

At the end of the semester, subjects were asked to list all the activities they had participated in excluding studying and going to classes. A 2 × 2 analysis

TABLE 21.4
Mean Skill-Ratings by Condition (Data Collected Immediately After Treatment Session)

	Attention	Low Competence, Low Control	Low Competence, High Control	High Competence, Low Control	High Competence, High Control
			Condition		
How useful are the skills?	3.67[a]	3.38	3.3	3.0	2.25
Would you personally use skills?	3.33	4.88	3.6	3.71	2.38
How confident are you about being able to use skills?	3.89	4.75	3.40	3.57	2.75

[a]The lower the number, the higher the rating.

of variance of the four treatment groups yielded a significant interaction, $F(1,29) = 5.29$, $p < .05$. This interaction is due to the fact that the high-competence-plus-high-control group engaged in significantly more activities than the other treatment groups did, $F(1,29) = 5.36$, $p < .05$, for comparison between high control plus high competence against all other treatment groups combined.

Clinical Assessment

Four subjects were randomly selected from each condition, interviewed by a trained clinician, and rated on a 10-point scale assessing adjustment, social competence, academic competence, and assertiveness toward peers. Subjects within each condition were divided into two groups using a median split procedure. The number of subjects below and above the median for each condition and for each of the three assessment scales is reported in Table 21.5. The Fisher exact probability test was used to analyze these data.

Analysis of these data showed that subjects in the high-competence groups were judged to be significantly more socially adjusted than persons in the low-competence (Fisher's exact probability = .011) or comparison groups (Fisher's exact probability = .055). Neither the main effect for control nor the interaction between control and competence was significant. Analysis of the social competence data yielded identical results. Subjects in the high-competence conditions were judged to be more socially competent than those in the low-competence (Fisher's exact probability = .013) or the two comparison groups (Fisher's exact probability = .010). Analysis of assertiveness toward peer ratings yielded similar although slightly weaker effects. As before, the high-competence groups were judged more assertive than the low-competence (Fisher's exact probability = .055) or comparison groups (Fisher's exact probability = .020). Finally, analysis of the ratings of academic competence and adjustment yielded no significant effects.

GENERAL DISCUSSION

The results of Experiment 2 supported the hypothesis that within a college environment, the combined effects of control- and competence-enhancing interventions are greater than the impact of either intervention alone. Across several dependent measures, persons exposed to both the high-competence and high-control interventions exhibited greater positive gains than other treatment groups or the baseline comparison groups. These findings stand in sharp contrast to the results obtained in Experiment 1, where aged subjects exposed to similar interventions exhibited declines relative to other treatment groups.

TABLE 21.5
Ratings of Adjustment, Social Competence, and Assertiveness by Condition

	No Treatment		Attention		Condition — Low Competence, Low Control		Low Competence, High Control		High Competence, Low Control		High Competence, High Control	
	Number Above Median	Number Below Median	Number Above Median	Number Below Median	Number Above Median	Number Below Median	Number Above Median	Number Below Median	Number Above Median	Number Below Median	Number Above Median	Number Below Median
Adjustment	0	4	1	3	0	4	0	4	1	3	4	0
Social competence	0	4	0	4	0	4	0	4	1	3	4	0
Assertiveness toward peers	0	4	2	2	1	3	2	2	3	1	4	0

What might account for these different outcomes? Although there are many important differences between the two experiments, perhaps the most notable is the environmental context in which these interventions were carried out. It was suggested earlier that a college environment provides infinite opportunities for exercising individual competencies, and there may therefore be no upper limit to the impact of competence- and control-enhancing interventions. The opportunities to exercise individual competencies in a long-term-care facility for the aged are undoubtedly more limited. With the exception of participating in some recreational activities and interacting with other patients, there are few opportunities that would challenge persons of moderate or high levels of perceived competence.

Persons in a college environment have the additional option of moving from one environment to another. An individual whose level of competence is enhanced can choose to participate in more complex and challenging environments or, if a particular environment is too challenging, can choose to retreat to one that is more commensurate with his or her abilities. Aged persons residing in public long-term-care facilities are essentially captives in their environment. They have no choice other than to make do with whatever opportunities their environment offers. As a result, it is not uncommon to find that some of the most capable persons in such institutions are also some of the most dissatisfied and unhappy.

What can we say about the applied implications of these data? More specifically, do these findings challenge the desirability of using competence-enhancing interventions with the institutionalized aged? At the least, the data suggest that close attention be paid to contextual factors, so that competency levels are appropriately matched with environmental opportunities. Ideally, interventions aimed at improving self-concept should, if necessary, be accompanied by appropriate environmental alterations. Unfortunately, specifying the type of environmental opportunities sufficient for a given level of competence will undoubtedly prove to be a difficult task, although some headway is being made on this front by researchers such as Lawton (1975), Kahana (1975), and Moos, Gauvain, Lemke, and Mehren (1977).

Finally, there exists the theoretical possibility that competence-enhancing interventions will raise an individual's self-concept to unrealistically high levels. Attempts to exercise these competencies may result in failure experiences whose net impact is likely to be damaging to the individual.

Much of the theory and research in the past decade has emphasized the negative effects of loss of perceived control and competence on individual functioning and, by implication, has emphasized the benefits to be derived from increased control and enhanced competence. The research reported here suggests that we take a closer look at the potential impact of increasing perceived control and competence, paying special attention to the context in which this is done. There may be a real danger in making people too competent or in giving them freedoms that constrain rather than liberate.

ACKNOWLEDGMENTS

This research was in part supported by National Institute on Aging Grant AG00525. We are grateful to Irvin Foutz, M.S.W., Stephen W. Lenhardt, M.S.W., and the staff of John Kane Hospital for their support and cooperation in carrying out this research.

REFERENCES

Abramson, L. Y., Seligman, M. E. P., & Teasdale, J. Learned helplessness in humans: Critique and reformulation. *Journal of Abnormal Psychology,* in press.

Dweck, C. S., & Reppucci, N. D. Learned helplessness and reinforcement responsibility in children. *Journal of Personality and Social Psychology,* 1973, *25,* 109–116.

Hanusa, B. H., & Schulz, R. Attributional mediators of learned helplessness. *Journal of Personality and Social Psychology,* 1977, *35,* 602–611.

Hiroto, D. S. Locus of control and learned helplessness. *Journal of Experimental Psychology,* 1974, *102,* 187–193.

Kahana, E. A congruence model of person–environment interaction. In P. G. Windley, T. O. Byerts, & F. G. Ernst (Eds.), *Theory of development in environment and aging.* Manhattan, Kansas: Gerontological Society, 1975.

Krantz, D., & Schulz, R. Personal control and health: Some applications to crisis of middle and old age. In A. Baum & J. Singer (Eds.), *Advances in environmental psychology* (Vol. 2). New York: Academic Press, in press.

Kuypers, J. A., & Bengtson, V. L. Social breakdown and competence. *Human Development,* 1973, *16,* 181–201.

Langer, E. J., & Rodin, J. The effects of choice and enhanced personal responsibility for the aged: A field experiment in an institutional setting. *Journal of Personality and Social Psychology,* 1976, *34,* 191–198.

Lawton, M. P. Competence, environmental press and the adaptation of older people. In P. G. Windley, T. O. Byerts, & F. G. Ernst (Eds.), *Theory development in environment and aging.* Manhattan, Kansas: Gerontological Society, 1975.

Moos, R., Gauvain, M., Lemke, S., & Mehren, B. *The development of a sheltered care environment scale.* Paper presented at the annual meeting of the American Gerontological Society, San Francisco, November 21, 1977.

Rodin, J., & Langer, E. J. Long-term effects of a control-relevant intervention with the institutionalized aged. *Journal of Personality and Social Psychology,* 1977, *35,* 897–902.

Schaie, K. W., & Schaie, J. P. Clinical assessment and aging. In J. E. Birren and K. W. Schaie (Eds.), *Handbook of the psychology of aging.* New York: Van Nostrand Reinhold, 1977.

Schulz, R. The effects of control predictability on the physical and psychological well-being of the institutionalized aged. *Journal of Personality and Social Psychology,* 1976, *33,* 563–573.

Schulz, R. *The psychology of death, dying and bereavement.* Reading, Mass. Addison-Wesley, 1978.

Schulz, R. Aging and control. In M. E. P. Seligman & J. Garber (Eds.), *Human helplessness: Theory and applications.* New York: Academic Press, in press.

Schulz, R., & Aderman, D. Effect of residential change on the temporal distance to death of terminal cancer patients. *Journal of Death and Dying: Omega,* 1973, *4,* 157–162.

Schulz, R., & Brenner, G. Relocation of the aged: A review and theoretical analysis. *Journal of Gerontology,* 1977, *32,* 323–333.

Schulz, R., & Hanusa, B. H. *Facilitating institutional adaptation of the aged: Effects of predictability enhancing intervention.* Paper presented at a meeting of the American Gerontological Society, San Francisco, November 21, 1977.

Schulz, R., & Hanusa, B. H. *Long-term effects of control and predictability enhancing interventions: Findings and ethical issues.* Unpublished manuscript, 1978.

Seligman, M. E. P. *Helplessness: On depression, development, and death.* San Francisco: Freeman, 1975.

Winer, B. J. *Statistical principles in experimental design.* New York: McGraw-Hill, 1962.

Wortman, C. B., & Brehm, J. W. Responses to uncontrollable outcomes: An integration of reactance theory and the learned helplessness model. In L. Berkowitz (Ed.), *Advances in experimental social psychology (Vol. 8).* New York: Academic Press, 1975.

22

Diverse Comments on Diverse Papers About Choice and Perceived Control

Jerome E. Singer
Uniformed Services University of the Health Sciences

A reader of this volume cannot help but be impressed by the enormous number of distinctions, differences, variables, and concepts that have been discussed: control, competence, expectation, beliefs, stability, instability, and even more. Not only have such distinctions proliferated, but each one came complete with two or three data points, usually from a single study, and all the definitions were just different enough to be not mutually substitutable. In the 1960s there was a letter in the *American Scientist* in which the author extrapolated both the rate at which elementary particles were being discovered and the rate at which PhDs in physics were being produced and predicted that the two curves were going to cross in about 2025. I think that psychologists who are interested in control and perceived choice are a little ahead of that game. We're going to have a variable for every investigator in the field in about three years. Why are there so many conflicting variables? They serve two functions, one of which understandably, but uncharitably, is territoriality. Each of us doing research in the field wants to be original and creative. An easy way to do that is to notice a loose end, then resolve the issue by drawing a difference or a distinction that nobody else has made. Then that's yours, you're responsible for the Schmartfarb effect, or whatever. In addition there seems to have been a widespread naive belief, which I think this volume can go a long way to dispel, that somehow we are going to discover a magic bullet—that we are going to hit upon the particular variable or concept that in one or two experiments will clean up the whole field and tie everything together. Anybody who reads this volume should be disabused of that notion.

On the other hand, there is no reason to be too negative. It is true that we have seen so many differences, so many distinctions, and so many theories that are about 30° out of phase with each other that it's impossible to make a translation from one to the other. When one person talks about control, it's another person's expectancy and a third person's environmental attribution. Although it's not clear how to fit these all together, it is possible that despite the lack of a complete fit, there may be some common core that is worth investigating. This is illustrated by the well-known anecdote of the parents whose son was overly optimistic. They were concerned that he was destined for a life of disillusionment because he was always such a Pollyanna. So in order to disillusion him gently at an early age, when his birthday came, they took a fancy gift box, filled it with horse manure, and gave it to him. They watched him as he opened the box, saw him discover the contents and react with great joy; he began flinging it around and playing with it. Since their strategy hadn't worked, the parents asked him, "Why are you so happy?" Still laughing, the boy said, "Well, with all this horse shit, there's got to be a pony around somewhere."

Our task is to find the pony of choice and perceived control. We cannot do this by assembling a huge model attempting to incorporate all the variables that have been proposed. Some of the papers that have been presented are multivariate, assembling models using five, ten, fifteen different factors. It's clear that a paper of that sort cannot be easily digested even in written form, given the quality and amount of data we have. It is even more depressing to realize that for perceived control and choice, no matter how complex your model is, somebody else is going to crosscut it with yet an equally complex model.

What then should we do? My suggestion is that we should begin to make judgments between what are the powerful variables and what aren't. We seem to be in general agreement that people who exercise choice over events in their environment get some beneficial effects from this, that somehow this choice is mediated by a feeling of control. If the control works, good things happen; if the control is taken away or if they are unable to exercise it, bad things happen. What affects control? What does control affect? That's the heart of the problem.

To illustrate the nature and difficulty of solving the problem, let us consider Chapter 19 by Harvey, Harris, and Lightner. This is a masterful attempt to integrate much of the material on control and choice into one coherent model. The paper is complex because the model is complex, and the model is complex because there are so many variables to be considered and tied together. This chapter is probably as coherent an attempt as is possible to integrate the findings that were of concern to the authors at the time they did the paper. Yet if we must consider the issues that have been raised in this volume, at least a dozen other variables, distinctions, qualifications, or new areas of research must be incorporated into an already complicated model. The task is not to add just 12 more sections. We must add their multiple higher-order interactions. It is not likely that even Harvey et al. could successfully combine all the material we have in this volume together with all the material that went before and still come up with a coherent model embracing this diversity of findings on choice and control. If, then, there is too much material for a single model, how are we to proceed? Logically, there are several alternatives. We could separate the field into its components. The group of us who work on locus of control and the I–E scale would work at refining our particular model and set of findings; those of us who work on choice would proceed with our area and so on in a similar fashion for attribution, perceived control, and all the other subfields. This would postpone a reconciliation for an assemblage of the micro-theories for a number of years until each of the subareas was complete.

Aside from the fact that such a strategy would undercut the rationale for the entire volume, there is another reason why this might not be the best way to work. There are definitions and postulates made by the subtheories on an arbitrary basis that differ from each other in significant ways. By attempting an early amalgamation, some of the reconciliation of divergent types of research would ultimately be made easier. By keeping our ways separate from the beginning, the ultimate reconciliation would become harder and harder as each subarea became more specialized. But to attempt to integrate the subfields now requires that the complexity of the total field somehow be reduced. Although I have no specific variables that are candidates for elimination from further consideration, there are several strategies and general principles of variable reduction that seem to me sensible to follow:

1. *Foreground Variables.* In any field there are a number of relatively atheoretical factors that are known to influence results; these are attended to by everyone doing experimentation in the field without necessarily becoming part of the theoretical structure. Every area of psychology has its folklore (i.e., those things that must be done in the laboratory if the work is to come out correctly but that do not appear in the theories). The care, feeding, and housing of laboratory rats, for instance, must be done in certain special ways or the animals will be unfit for experiments on learning, motivation, or whatever. Yet very few theories of learning or motivation have explicit rules on how the animals are to be housed and maintained. In many studies of operant behavior, for example, little mention is made that the birds used as subjects are at 80% of their normal body weight. That reduction is not a part of the theory or relationship of reward contingencies to the shaping of behavior, yet it is very much a necessary component of the research. In similar fashion, many of the variables we are talking about have little theoretical import. They are the sort of background variables that are necessary to ensure that the study is done right. These variables are intended to ensure proper experimental conditions and to keep unwanted alternatives from creeping

into the studies. For instance, the use of randomization to assign subjects to experimental conditions is an integral part of our craft; these procedures serve to eliminate the effects of unmanipulated variables. A discussion of the unmanipulated variables, so controlled, is usually not germane to the experiment. These factors can be regarded as background variables. Unlike the theoretically important foreground variables—those variables that figure in the underlying theory's development—they need not be incorporated into the theory. The background variables can be mentioned merely as a way to conduct better research, but they hardly need to be a part of the structure or fabric of the larger concept of choice and perceived control. It is foreground variables that deserve our attention.

2. *Outcome Measures.* The studies reported in this volume embrace a wide variety of outcomes in which different independent variables are related to different outcomes. Some of the outcomes are paper-and-pencil tests, others are behavioral, still others are somewhere in between. Those outcomes that deal with prima facie important and relevant events in people's lives seem to me much more compelling than those that deal with situation-bound behaviors or self-reports. Consider, for example, the outcomes in Schulz and Hanusa's paper (Chapter 21)—the morbidity and mortality of residents in old-age homes. What could be a more important outcome than the life or the death of their subjects? Clearly, variables that have a bearing or an influence on life or death are ones that must be included first in any sensible and comprehensive theory of choice and perceived control. Such independent variables have a much stronger claim on our attention than do ones that, although perhaps equally potent in terms of the amount of variance accounted for in an experiment, affect not life and death outcomes but self-reports, modified attitudes, or changed attributions. All these latter events may be important in themselves and may have significance for the establishment of a theory, but surely they have to take a back seat to outcomes of great personal significance and attachment. Given a choice between simplifying a model by dropping a variable that affects attitude change or dropping one that affects the life expectancy of the subjects, the choice appears to be clear: Drop the attitude change variable. The focus on important outcomes is not, of course, a hard and fast rule but a useful guide toward needed simplification.

3. *Experimental Availability.* Many of the variables proposed in this volume as modifications or additions to theories of choice or perceived control were actually used in an after-the-fact manner to explain complicated results or to clear up a puzzling inconsistency between experiments. In such capacities they serve a utilitarian purpose. Their status for theoretical inclusion in our comprehensive model will depend either on their direct availability, through experimental manipulation of one form or another, or

on their indirect availability as hypothetical constructs. Since as a general rule it is always easier to illustrate something simple than something complicated, those variables that are themselves experimentally manipulable (or have readily measurable indicants) and that when so manipulated show important effects have a compelling claim for being included in the model. This point is illustrated by some of the distinctions proposed by Langer in Chapter 20. Her distinction, for example, between situation-incurred and action-induced loss of control is rooted in a number of experimental operations, and the results of making this distinction can be shown to have effects through the application of these manipulations. As such, these variables have a greater claim to being included in the comprehensive model than similar distinctions utilized only after the fact in a reconciling explanation or used in some mediating status not directly tied to operations.

4. *Previous Work.* Several of the variables discussed in this volume relate to phenomena that have been studied in other theories at other times in other fields of psychology. Variables such as these, which have a history and a pedigree, would seem to be more relevant for inclusion in a comprehensive theory of choice and control than variables arrived at *de novo*. Throughout this volume, we see discussions of choice, the effects of choosing between alternatives in various situations, and the enhancement of certain kinds of performance as a result of the choice. Unmentioned was the series of studies that started with Brehm (1956), in the dissonance literature, and a later reinterpretation by Bem (1967), which focused exactly on the effects of perceived choice. In these studies, subjects rate a number of objects, then select one. Lo and behold, after the choice, subjects will increase their perceived value of the object they have chosen and denigrate the alternative they haven't selected—presumably as a function of the dissonance aroused by the choice. Bem's alternative interpretation is one of operant self-observation, but for the purposes of illustration it doesn't matter. The same reevaluations occur. Whether you believe these explanations or not, they produced a number of relevant studies (e.g., Festinger, 1964).

This body of literature is instructive in several ways. It suggests that the act of choosing is separate from consequences of choosing. They are two related questions: (a) why do people want a choice; and (b) what are the consequences of exercising choice? The consequences are the better explored question—changes in the value of the selected and rejected alternatives. For both the dissonance and the Bem explanations, subjects are not aware of what the consequences of their choice will be at the time they exercise the choice. At the time they select, say, a toaster instead of a waffle iron, they are not aware that they are going to increase the value of the toaster for themselves just as a function of having selected it. I think this helps us understand some of the perceived choice literature, for it suggests that choice may be reinforcing for reasons other than those that make the perception of choice desirable.

This still leaves the basic question: Why do people desire choice? I've concluded that we don't have a good answer to that question. Perhaps there isn't one. Any theory or any set of constructs we use to explain this desire for choice has to have some primitive terms. It may be more fruitful at this time to avoid rumination about the fine-grained analysis of why people want choice and simply postulate a need to have some control over the environment—some choice in outcomes. Once a need like that is started in motion, it can be maintained by any number of mechanisms. For example, people in search of control exercise choice and are reinforced by a set of positive consequences to want more of it, thus strengthening a need to achieve control and the use of choice to obtain it. If, in fact, most of our interests lie in the effects and consequences of choice and control, it may be advantageous to defer the more basic motivational questions and build on our past and present knowledge of these outcomes. It may well be that paradoxically, although we can construct complicated schematas, we have insufficient data on which to build a simple model of why people want control and choice.

There is one other caveat that I would add, because I think the field is important enough to be done right. We run the danger of a belief in metaphor and word magic. It is very easy to use the same words for different meanings and assume that we are talking about the same things even when we are not. We have a tendency to employ buzzwords instead of precise language. For example, information processing is a current buzzword. When one writes about information processing, referring either to some precisely coded amount of material that a subject has to analyze or referring to the observation that people must cognize a stimulus-rich environment, the assumption that these diverse uses are manifestations of the same phenomenon is, at best, a metaphor. All of us have the task of being precise in designating where we have commonalities with others and where our interests are. The issues are important enough and the outcomes are worthwhile enough to make all this a reasonable effort.

REFERENCES

Bem, D. J. Self-perception: An alternative interpretation of cognitive dissonance phenomena. *Psychological Review*, 1967, *74*, 183–200.

Brehm, J. W. Post-decision changes in the desirability of alternatives. *Journal of Abnormal and Social Psychology*, 1956, *52*, 384–389.

Festinger, L. *Conflict, decision, and dissonance*. Stanford, Calif.: Stanford University Press, 1964.

VI

OVERVIEW AND APPRAISAL

> *Necessity is the plea for every infringement of human*
> *freedom. It is the argument of tyrants; it is the creed*
> *of slaves.*
> —William Tipp

Difficult as it is to summarize and critically review the research on perceived control within one area of psychology, it is perhaps almost futile to attempt a review of the entire area within a single chapter. Nevertheless, the final chapter is dedicated to this mission.

In conforming with the pleas of Singer and others for conceptual simplicity and parsimony, Seligman and Miller suggest that perceived control and freedom be incorporated under the conceptually unifying rubric of power. Following Lacey's dichotomization of control into agenda control and outcome control, Seligman and Miller suggest that the concept of power be reserved only for agenda control. Although this matter requires empirical resolution, they argue by metaphor that the true perception of control (power) resides only with the master and not with the slave, despite the multitude of decisions (outcome control) permitted the slave. In the interest of conceptual unification, they also propose the adoption of expectancy as a core hypothetical construct. At one level of analysis, and in a variety of situations, it would be difficult to deny the expectancy construct a vital role. On the other hand, it is a somewhat slippery construct that is often not easily subject to empirical disproof.

In addressing what may be one of the major unresolved themes in the area of perceived control, Seligman and Miller wrestle with the question of why people value or desire control. Can it be considered a basic need or an acquired one, and if the latter, what role do cultural factors have in its development and expression? The culture-free results of relevant animal experiments strongly support the idea that the need for control be considered axiomatic. Further, Seligman and Miller support the view that the need for control is neither interchangeable with nor satisfied by predictability. That is, if the subject knows in advance when an event will occur, this knowledge does not contribute to the subject's perception or belief that it is in fact controllable. On the other hand, the need to control may be satisfied vicariously or through certain others.

In contradistinction to the idea that the need to control is axiomatic, we would like to suggest that the conscious desire for control may only be the penultimate expression of this need, whereas its terminal statement may be in consigning or ceding control to an automatized (Kimble & Perlmuter, 1970) or mindless (Langer, Chapter 20) state. That is, in seeking control, individuals may be testing their competence and their ability to deal effectively with the environment. Upon attaining a certain level of mastery, further testing and evaluation are discontinued, and this in turn is followed by more routinized activity. Being subject to novel or noxious stimulation disallows both the immediate possibilities of control as well as mindlessness and thus serves as a source of disturbance until either the organism is separated from the stimulation or mastery and automatized control once again eventuates.

And finally, we would like to make one observation not tied exclusively to perceived control that relates to Seligman and Miller's discussion of some recent work dealing with depressed and nondepressed subjects. That is, they point out that Alloy and Abramson reported that depressed college students more veridically report the degree to which their behavior influences the outcome of environmental events than do nondepressed students, who report being in control when this is not the case. Similarly, in Chapter 12, Arnkoff and Mahoney discuss the idea that neurotics, stripped of their defenses and deprived of comforting illusions, likewise reflect the environment more accurately. Perhaps it is the depressed and the neurotic who understand most clearly what the poet Shelley meant when he defined freedom as "that sweet bondage."

REFERENCE

Kimble, G. A., & Perlmuter, L. C. The problem of volition. *Psychological Review,* 1970, *77,* 361–384.

23

The Psychology of Power: Concluding Comments

Martin E. P. Seligman
Suzanne M. Miller
University of Pennsylvania

This volume illustrates the steady growth and emergence of a new field: the psychology of power. The field cuts across many of the traditional areas of psychology and has particular relevance to learning, personality, emotion, and psychopathology. Although the contributors to this volume represent many differing vantage points, a few critical issues and concerns have surfaced again and again. This paper represents an attempt to highlight the issues that we believe to be both substantive and pervasive in the field as it stands today. Toward this end, we are going to focus on three major types of issues. The first is philosophical issues, the second is theoretical issues, and the third is applications. We conclude by summarizing what is known in the field and what is, as yet, unknown or uninvestigated but should be. In this way, we hope to thread the various areas together and provide an integrative framework from which to proceed. One rider should be noted, however. Our remarks with regard to each issue are highly selective and even idiosyncratic and are concentrated on the ways in which they articulate with our own thinking and the thinking of our collaborators.

CONCEPTUAL ISSUES

The first set of remarks are concerned with philosophical and conceptual issues. We discuss three such issues that emerged and that we take to be of considerable importance.

Agenda Control Versus Outcome Control.   Perhaps the most significant new idea in this volume stems from Lacey's notion of "agenda setting"

(Chapter 1). Lacey tries to distinguish between having control over an outcome—for example, the slave putting a brick on the left or on the right—and having control over the agenda—for example, making pyramids versus making sphinxes.

When the senior author taught at Cornell about 10 years ago and the place exploded with revolution, everyone ran around forming committees. The board of trustees even asked the students and faculty to write a new constitution. But it began to seem as if the conjugation of the verb *restructure* went as follows: "I restructure, you restructure, he/she/it restructures, we restructure, you restructure, they control." This, we believe, is the essence of the distinction between outcome control and agenda setting.

Most of the experiments in the field to date have been concerned with manipulating control over outcomes, not over agendas. And yet the notion of *power*, which may be the central notion throughout this volume, deals largely with setting agendas. Lacey pointed out the need to distinguish between these two instances of control but did not provide us with necessary and sufficient conditions for making this difficult distinction. It seems important to us to attempt to define these notions and to examine them experimentally in the future if that is possible.

As a starting point, let us enumerate several possible distinctions: Perhaps agenda control versus outcome control simply breaks down into goals versus subgoals, that is, choice over the goals themselves versus choice over the ways one achieves those goals (subgoals). A second way of trying to make the distinction is to consider what happens when one party exercises control. In the case of outcome control, there is generally a reciprocal relationship between the parties involved. That is, if one party exercises control, the other party usually makes some response in return. This is not necessarily so in the case of agenda control. Take as an example a pigeon pecking for grain on a given schedule. When the pigeon pecks (outcome control), the experimenter (who has agenda control) does something back: He delivers grain. Yet when the experimenter sets the agenda—thou shalt peck on a FI 60, or when the slave driver sets the building agenda—there is no reciprocity. A third possible way of getting at the distinction has to do with an issue that arose peripherally several times and that we feel should have been accorded more attention. When you exercise outcome control, it is sometimes a zero-sum game; that is, when you have control, someone else loses it. Other times, it is not a zero-sum game. With agenda control, however, it almost always seems to be a zero-sum game. To illustrate the point, if you are a slave and you unionize (agenda control), you take power away from the slave driver. In other words, unionization of slaves is a zero-sum game. Conversely, when the slave decides to build the pyramid from left to right rather than from right to left (outcome control), he is not taking anything away from anyone else; rather something is merely added to the situation. Similarly, when the pigeon chooses the left key or the right key (outcome control), it is not taking anything away from the experimenter; but when it escapes from the Skinner box (agenda control), the experimenter loses something—a pigeon. So a third possible way of distinguishing agenda control from outcome control is that the former is usually a zero-sum game: When one person gets control, someone else loses it. Outcome control, on the other hand, can either be a zero-sum game or it can be a non-zero-sum game. Each of the above possibilities for defining agenda control seems incomplete or inadequate. Therefore, we do not endorse any of them here. However, we heartily endorse all future efforts to delineate this distinction.

We are dwelling on this philosophical issue for an important reason. Much of the research reported in this volume seems to be more relevant to the notion of agenda control than to the notion of outcome control. By way of illustration, let us just list about 10 such instances: Houts, Quann, and Scott (Chapter 11) discussed the conditions that lead employees in institutions to like or dislike their clients. Perhaps this is related to whether the client or patient is perceived to be exercising outcome control versus agenda control. The former type of control would not be construed as very threatening by staff members (and so they would like their clients). In contrast, the latter type of control would be construed as threatening (and so they would dislike their clients). Moyer (Chapter 6) talked about countercontrol, where the subject does something that he knows the experimenter does not want done. It seems to us that when subjects assert countercontrol, they are engaged, not in outcome control, but in agenda control; that is , they are setting the agenda for the experiment in a different way than the experimenter wants.

Kanfer (personal communication) has mentioned resistance in therapy. Again, it seems that when a patient resists an interpretation offered by the therapist, it is an example of agenda control rather than outcome control. Death and resignation were also discussed. Once a dying individual realizes that death comes to everyone and that he or she has no control over it , the person becomes resigned by saying, "That's the way of nature. I'm part of the Darwinian flow. New living creatures grow out of dying ones." Here, too, the action being taken consists not of controlling the outcome but rather of redefining the agenda. Newman (Chapter 9) mentioned the experiment in which subjects engaged in a learning task and either were told to employ a strategy recommended by experts or were encouraged to invent their own personal strategy. The results showed superior learning when subjects invented their own strategies, and this also seems to be an instance of agenda control.

In his discussion, Rotter (Chapter 18) commented that subjects in many experiments are not "given a choice" but rather are "forced to make a choice." This may be another way of distinguishing between the two classes of control, where outcome control is exemplified by being forced to make a choice and agenda control is exemplified by having choices available. So, for example, when the thief "offers" you a choice between your money or your life or when the Godfather makes you "an offer you can't refuse," these are forced choices and do not represent agenda control. The notion of "autonomous" choice emerged in Steiner's discussion (Chapter 2): Although he was not writing in this context, it is likely that feelings of autonomy are more related to agenda control than to outcome control. In other words, decisions about whether to build the pyramid from left to right or from right to left do not lead to feelings of autonomy; whereas decisions about whether to build pyramids or sphinxes, or to forego building altogether, do lead to feelings of autonomy. Similarly, a profound notion of being an origin in deCharms' sense (Chapter 3) is not just derived from the sense of touching something and seeing it move. The notion of personal causation seems to have more to do with deciding what gets moved, that is, with setting agendas. Finally, Langer (Chapter 20) presented data about the differential effects of being labeled a worker or a boss on subsequent "inferred" helplessness. Here the label sets the agenda, and one important question that Langer's work raises is how the lack of agenda control influences the action one takes with respect to outcome control. Taken together, the aforementioned examples highlight the importance of agenda control and point up the need to operationalize the distinction between this type of control and the more commonly investigated outcome control.

The well-known Milgram (1965) experiments are relevant here. The majority of his subjects engaged only in outcome control. That is, they made decisions about how high the subsequent shock level would be. The precious few of his subjects who said in the words of Olaf, glad and big, "There is some shit I will not eat," engaged in agenda control. But consider how far Milgram had to push his subjects to get that effect. This illustrates just how difficult it may be to operationalize any form of agenda control in the laboratory. Nonetheless, although the prospect of defining and operationalizing agenda control seems daunting, we cannot underscore enough the importance of undertaking such research. Until this is done, the field cannot claim to be studying the psychology of power.

Hypothetical Constructs.   The second conceptual issue arose out of some remarks of Steiner (Chapter 2) and it has to do with the status of our explanatory mechanisms. We are particularly concerned with the status of such crucial notions as "expectancy" and "perception" of control. We would take Steiner's contented cows analogy even further and unabashedly recognize that an expectancy is a hypothetical construct, not an intervening variable (MacCorquodale & Meehl, 1948). On the one hand, it is not a tautology, it does not have a single definition, and it is not exhausted by any one operation. On the other hand, it is not a real thing, like a microphone.

Rather it is a hypothetical construct, like the notions of "natural selection," "life," "reward," or perhaps "atom": There are a number of different converging operations for getting at it, but it is not a "real" thing. To illustrate, one can compare the notion of "expectancy" to the notion of "icon" or afterimage in visual memory. It is possible to measure the time course of an icon: how many bits of information are contained in it, how bright it is, as well as more subjective properties like what color it is. Nonetheless, it is not a "real" thing, nor is it defined by any single property. So we are in the difficult, but wholly scientifically respectable endeavor of dealing with basic explanatory mechanisms that have the status of hypothetical constructs.

Let us illustrate how this seems to proceed using the logic of expectancy of not having control—that is, the expectancy of helplessness. As an example, we have some confidence that what underlies helplessness effects is the expectancy of noncontingency between responses and outcomes. This is because when we go through the operation of producing objective noncontingency, we observe consistent effects in a set of converging dependent variables: (1) people and animals who have been exposed to objective noncontingency subsequently become passive; (2) they subsequently have trouble learning contingent relationships; (3) they do not change their expectancies for future success in skill situations when they succeed and fail; and (4) human beings who have been exposed to noncontingency often also report that they have no control, that their responding does not matter. This further encourages us in our belief in an underlying state of an expectancy of helplessness. However, here is where we depart from Steiner's stance. In our view, the notion of expectancy is not rooted in phenomenology or in self-report. Individuals do not have to be able to report that they have no control in order for the expectancy of helplessness to exist. Nor do we believe that individuals necessarily find expectancies waiting to be plucked like tulips when they introspect (see also Nisbett & Wilson, 1977). Rather, subjective reports of noncontingency are just one— nonprivileged—instance of a number of converging operations that follow from assuming the hypothetical construct of expectancy of noncontingency.

In this regard, we would like to mention a recent finding, using a new technique for measuring perception of control. Alloy and Abramson (in press) first teach people to make quantitative estimates of how much control they have. In the experimental situation, there is a green light that occasionally goes on and off. The subject also has a button that he presses. After hearing a lecture on how to quantify control, the subject is exposed to different relationships between button pressing and the green light going on. Then subjects are asked to quantify how much control they had over the green light going on. A very surprising result emerges. Figure 23.1 shows the various experimental conditions. The black solid line reflects the quantitative estimate you would make if you were a perfect transducer of contingencies. In

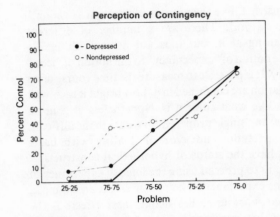

FIG. 23.1. Perception of contingency in depressed and nondepressed subjects. (From Alloy & Abramson, in press.)

the condition on the extreme right (75–0), the green light goes on 75% of the time if you press the button, and it never goes on if you do not press the button. In the 75–25 condition, the light goes on 75% of the time if you press the button, but it also goes on 25% of the time if you do not press the button. Similarly, in the 75–50 condition, the light goes on 75% of the time when you button press, but it goes on 50% of the time even when you do not button press. Then there are two noncontingent conditions, in which the light goes on 75% of the time (75–75) or 25% of the time (25–25) regardless of what you do. Alloy and Abramson were interested in differentiating subjective estimates of perceived control between nondepressed and depressed college students. The helplessness model predicts that the latter group should have strong expectancies of no control. As Fig. 23.1 shows, however, depressed individuals are extremely accurate in assessing how much control they have according to the measure of judged control. When they have control, they accurately report that they have control. When they do not have control, they also see the noncontingency. There is a clear distortion from reality, but surprisingly it emerges in the nondepressed group. Nondepressed subjects who are exposed to noncontingent outcomes believe they have control even when they do not. This is particularly the case when the noncontingent event occurs frequently. The theme of these results is that depressed people are "sadder but wiser."

To summarize, both the individual-difference literature and the general process learning literature on control make use of a similar explanatory notion—expectancy of control. This notion is a hypothetical construct that is accessed by a converging set of operations.

Terminological Confusion.   The third conceptual issue that we want to discuss has to do with the dismaying array of terms bandied about. There is a crying need for a more acute analysis of the interrelations between these terms, because they are by no means synonymous with one another. Thus far, however, this has not been clearly recognized. The result is that various terms that are not synonymous have been used interchangeably. We can briefly illustrate the point with respect to four sets of such terms: internal/external, having control/not having control, origin/pawn, and being free/not being free. Let us begin with the relationship between internal/external causal attributions and having control versus not having control. Although these two sets of terms appear to have considerable overlap, closer inspection shows them to be wholly orthogonal. Consider the following 2 × 2 table (Table 23.1) in which beliefs about oneself are plotted against beliefs about others. Here internal and external attribution for cause are defined independently of control and helplessness. Quadrants 3 and 4 both represent the situations in which helplessness occurs, and yet an internal attribution is made in one case, and an external attribution is made in the other. In cell 3, you believe that all responses in your own repertoire are independent of the outcome in question, but *other* people can make responses that produce the outcome. This leads you to make an internal attribution for your helplessness. That is, if other people can learn calculus and you cannot, then there is something wrong with you, and your helplessness is due to your own inability or lack of effort or some other similar personal problem. When you have no responses in your repertoire for producing the outcome and neither does anyone else (cell 4), then you have a situation of universal helplessness. Your child contracts leukemia, and there is nothing either you or medical science can do to save him. You make an external attribution for your helplessness— there is nothing wrong with you, it must be the situation—yet you are no less helpless. The same analysis applies to quadrants 1 and 2, where you have

TABLE 23.1
Personal Helplessness and Universal Helplessness

Other	Self	
	The person expects the outcome is contingent on a response in his repertoire.	*The person expects the outcome is not contingent on any response in his repertoire.*
The person expects the outcome is contingent on a response in the repertoire of a relevant other	1	personal helplessness 3 (internal attribution)
The person expects the outcome is not contingent on a response in the repertoire of any relevant other.	2	universal helplessness 4 (external attribution)

control. In cell 2, you have a response in your repertoire that works to produce the outcome—you can learn multiplication tables. But so can everyone else, and therefore you make an external attribution for having control—it is an easy task, any fool can do it. Conversely, if the response that produces the outcome is in your repertoire alone (climbing Mt. Everest) and other people do not have it, then you make an internal attribution for having control. In sum, although we have not attempted an exhaustive analysis of the relationship between internality/externality and controllable/uncontrollable, the two notions appear to be orthogonal.

The notion of internal/external also seems to be independent of the notion of origin/pawn by a very similar kind of logic. If you were to lift up your index finger right now, you would get that sense of personal causation that has to do with being an origin. As Professor deCharms (Chapter 3) argued, this is a primitive and very basic sense of causation from which we may derive some of our other senses of causation. However, lifting one's finger is an easy task, and so you would make an external attribution for your success. Thus, origin is not equivalent to internal.

Finally, let us consider the relationship between the notions of control, internality, and freedom. Perhaps the worst confusion of all exists with respect to these three sets of terms. By freedom here, we do not mean "perceived freedom" as discussed by Harvey, Harris, and Lightner (Chapter 19). Rather we are referring to the traditional, philosophical notion of freedom and its sometimes opposite, determinism. This issue is totally beyond the range of any of the current empirical work on control or causal attributions. Freedom is not equivalent to having control over outcomes, whether the outcomes are easy (an external attribution for success) or difficult (an internal attribution for success) to achieve. You can have control over an outcome, but your exercise of that control can be totally determined by your past experience or some other factor. Freedom is not even reducible to having control of agenda setting. How you set the agenda may be determined. The freedom/determinism issue hinges instead on questions like: Are choices that an individual makes about agenda setting influenced in a predictable manner by past experience? Is that individual responsible for personal choices?

This concludes the conceptual issues that we wanted to review. These issues figure prominently throughout this volume, and future work should help to refine and untangle the existing confusions.

THEORETICAL ISSUES

Now we would like to tackle two theoretical issues that we take to be of prime importance.

Stress. The first issue has to do with why people want to choose and control and why they are stressed when they do not have choice and control. Amazingly little was said in this volume about this important issue. It is also relevant to another theme mentioned, by Brown (Chapter 8) and others, having to do with the cultural bias that may exist in this type of research. It has been alleged that certain cultures do not value control. This seems to be the case for certain segments of Indian society and for Zen Buddhists. Moreover, there are clearly individuals in our own culture who do not want control and who are not stressed by the lack of control. Taken to its logical conclusion, this view argues that control is not a basic need but has been artificially inculcated into us by the capitalist ethic, Protestantism, and Madison Avenue. Hence the experimental results that emerge showing desire for control are correspondingly artificial and are only applicable to our own society.

The crux of this argument seems to be the belief that *predictability* is a more basic human need than controllability. That is, life essentially involves a struggle against randomness and unpredictability, and one way of promoting order and predictability is by having your own responses control outcomes. Another, perhaps more effective, way of finding order is by yielding up control to a higher authority such as a powerful individual or a political or religious system. So proponents of this view say that Westerners have been conned into a need for control. What is even worse, this need has been degraded to control over completely trivial outcomes, such as whether to eat at McDonald's or Gino's, or Roy Roger's. This is an interesting argument and one that should not be taken lightly. One could, of course, put forth the opposite contention. That is, the basic need is for control, but individuals will settle for mere predictability if control is out of the question.

One source of evidence that can be brought to bear on this dialogue—and is not corruptible by cultural values—is the animal literature. Inspection of these data shows that the same manipulations that produce ill effects in humans produce parallel ill effects in animals. Generally speaking, animals are stressed by the lack of choice and control and probably choose to have choice. These results speak against the view that we have been seduced into wanting control by the capitalistic ethic.[1] Indeed, the animal foundations suggest that it is in societies where famine and overcrowding are endemic that a distortion of basic needs exists. Somehow the need for control may get beaten out of people under such conditions and be replaced by a second best—the struggle against randomness and toward predictability, without individual control.

---

[1]See A. Antonovsky's letter to the editor and reply by L. C. Perlmuter and R. A. Monty (1978) in *American Scientist.*

Isaiah Berlin's paraphrase of De Maistre's criticism of Rousseau seems very appropriate here: 'To say that man is born free but everywhere he is in chains is like saying "The sheep is born carnivorous but everywhere he is nibbling grass."' In other words, the fact that the struggle for control is such a commonplace phenomenon in the real world, coupled with the fact that we generally find choice of control in the laboratory, should lead us to believe that it is a basic want.

About ten theories address the issue of why control is preferred and less stressful. These theories have recently been reviewed elsewhere by Miller (in press-a). The majority of these theories are inadequate, and we just briefly mention here what is wrong with some of the major ones: The operant view that choice of control is reinforcing is a tautology with no explanatory power whatsoever. Rather it simply redescribes the fact that individuals choose control. It has also been proposed (Glass & Singer, 1972) that individuals choose control in order to avoid feelings of helplessness. So "feelings of helplessness" are invoked to explain why individuals are stressed when they do not have control. This seems tautological because it is not evident how such feelings can be assessed independently of the fact of stress per se. Similarly, the Mandler and Watson (1966) claim—that uncontrollability is stress inducing—suffers from circularity. When boiled down to its essentials, the theory asserts that uncontrollability increases stress, because breaking up an accustomed or ongoing controlling sequence increases stress. Learned helplessness (Seligman, 1975) may be useful in accounting for why exposure to uncontrollability produces motivational and cognitive deficits. However, it fails to provide a mechanism for why lack of control may be stressful and dispreferred.

Finally, there is White's (1959) notion of the drive for "competence." Although this view should be applauded for its historical role in helping to create the field we work in, it is not particularly helpful in the present context. White takes the position that we are born with a need to achieve competence. But the existence of such a drive does not appear to be independently verifiable of the fact that control is preferred and less stressful. Closely allied to White's view are the functional explanations, which Renshon touched on in his paper (Chapter 4). Such views emphasize the evolutionary adaptiveness of having control, claiming that it was those organisms who wanted control and who felt stressed by the lack of control who survived and reproduced (e.g., Averill, 1973). Although this argument is not tautological, it is extremely difficult to assess. Moreover, it would be impractical to test, particularly because NIMH does not give grants that last for millennia.

There are three noncircular theories of control, which have in common the proposition that the desire for control is reducible to the desire for predictability. Included here are Seligman's (1968) safety signal theory, Weiss' (1971) relevant feedback theory, and the information-seeking theory associated with Berlyne (1960) and Sokolov (1963), as applied to control. Each provide a mechanism for why predictability is more preferred and less stressful than unpredictability. So predictability either increases safety (Seligman, 1968; Weiss, 1971) or reduces surprise and uncertainty (Berlyne, 1960; Sokolov, 1963). Where these theories fall down is in asserting that controllability adds nothing over and above predictability and that it is merely the provision of extra predictability that accounts for the stress-reducing effects of control. The problem with these accounts is that they are inconsistent with two sets of human experiments that have not been discussed at this conference (see Miller, in press–a and b, for a thorough review of this literature). The first set of experiments shows that individuals still prefer control and are less stressed by control even when they are given *equal predictability* in the no-control condition. By equal predictability, we mean that both controllable and uncontrollable conditions provide identical information about the onset, offset, and/or duration of the event in question. The second set of experiments shows that individuals still prefer control and are less stressed by control even when they never exercise the controlling response. This is the *potential control* paradigm of Glass and Singer (1972), in which subjects get a "panic button" that they can press to terminate the event, but they are asked not to use it. In fact, subjects never actually press the button. So here the group with control has neither more predictability nor more actual control than the group without control. Therefore, the theories that equate control with predictability do not provide an adequate explanation for the equal predictability data or for the potential control data.

There are two viable theoretical alternatives to account for these data, and we detail them now. The first is an extension of Church's (1964) yoked control artifact argument, the internality hypothesis; and the second is Miller's minimax hypothesis (Miller, in press–a and b). Let us begin with the internality view.

The yoked control argument may have seemed relatively trivial when it first appeared 15 years ago, but it seems much more important now. It is also a frightening argument, because it says that the majority of the results on control and choice may be an artifact of a given set of experimental circumstances. The yoked control paradigm was originally conceived as a way of unconfounding the effects of control or choice from the nature and extent of the physical stimulation received. In order to accomplish this, the organism without choice or control is presented with exactly the same physical stimuli as the organism with choice or control. Thus, the two organisms only differ in that one individual actually goes through the act of choosing or controlling.

Church (1964) challenges the premise that the two organisms are really receiving identical stimulation. That is, although the stimuli may be physically identical as administered by the experimenter, they are not necessarily experienced as identical by the two organisms. This view rests on the assumption that individuals typically undergo moment-to-moment fluctuations in their moods and internal physiological states. So in the aversive case, for example, shock is going to feel intolerable during those moments when the individual is in a highly vulnerable internal state. There are other moments, however, when exactly the same shock is going to feel less painful, because the individual is in a less vulnerable internal state.

Now consider a subject who has learned that he has control over shock termination. Anytime that shock is turned on at a moment when the subject is in a vulnerable internal state, it will have the net result of making the shock feel particularly painful. Hence the subject will be motivated to turn the shock off as quickly as possible. This means that the subject with control *never receives an intolerable shock of long duration.* This cannot be the case for the yoked subject, however. Shock is being turned on and off without regard to fluctuations in his internal state, and therefore he is bound to receive, *at some point,* an intolerable shock that is of long duration. Church argues that this artifact pervades the entire animal literature, and we now translate it into an explanation of why people want choice and control. The internality argument can be distilled as follows: It proposes that the only reason for opting for choice and control is in order to receive a better outcome. This is because choice and control enable an individual to match his internal state with external events, thereby making the overall outcome better.

The argument is equally applicable to the appetitive, as well as to the aversive, case. For example, it can handle some of the early experiments of Perlmuter and Monty (e.g., Perlmuter, Monty, & Kimble, 1971) by saying that in exercising choice over word association lists, the individual is able to choose those associations for which he already has a good cognitive schema.[2] In other words, "gog" and "fud" together remind him of his cousins, George and Fred. Therefore, he has a more usable outcome than the yoked subject, who does not have access to this idiosyncratic schema. Similarly, an individual will prefer to choose between getting a doll or getting candy, because she can then match her own momentary internal state with the approximate physical event—she likes candy better. So again, the overall outcome is better.

Now let us turn to Miller's hypothesis. It proposes that the reason why individuals want control over aversive events is that having control provides a guaranteed upper limit on how bad the situation can become (see also Bandura, 1977). The hypothesis is explicitly stated as follows (Miller, in press–a):

---

[2]This model is, however, unable to account for the beneficial results seen in list learning and reading comprehension tasks where choice subjects select only a very small portion of the materials to be learned but do better on the nonchosen items (Perlmuter & Monty, 1977).

An individual who has control over an aversive event insures having a lower maximum danger than an individual without control. This is because an individual with control attributes the cause of relief to an internal, stable source—his own response—whereas an individual without control attributes relief to a less stable source....

Consider two subjects, one of whom has instrumental control and one of whom does not. The one with instrumental control knows that all he has to do is execute the controlling response and shock will go off. That is, he knows that the maximum upper limit of duration of an intolerable shock will not be greater than his reaction time. He is also assured that any future shock will only occur up to some relatively low, maximum level. In contrast, the subject who does not have instrumental control has no guarantee that shock will go off quickly if it becomes intolerable. In the typical experiment, for example, subjects with control are told to turn off shock *as soon as* they feel intolerably stressed or tired. In contrast, uncontrollability subjects are simply told that shock will eventually be turned off. This means that whenever shock becomes intolerable for the controllability subject, he can obtain immediate relief. Whenever shock becomes intolerable for the uncontrollability subject he has no guarantee that the situation will not persist or even get worse....

[H]uman beings not only learn that they have control but, in Weiner et al.'s terms (1971), they go on to construe control as being caused by an internal, stable factor: their own responding. When trauma is controllable, the attribution of its effects are to oneself. When trauma is uncontrollable, the individual must make alternate, external attributions (e.g., the experimenter is controlling the shock; laws of nature; God; luck; bureaucracy). If a subject has control now, all he has to do is exercise that same response in the future and he can minimize the maximum danger. If a subject attributes the cause of relief to a stable, internal factor—such as his own response—he has a reliable predictor that in the future will occur only up to some relatively low, maximum amount. In contrast, if the attribution is to some unstable, external factor—such as the experimenter's whims—future danger is not guaranteed to be restricted to any relatively low maximum. Although the experimenter's actions have been reliable and predictable in the past, the subject cannot count on them for the future as reliably as he can count on his own response.

The main advantage of this hypothesis is that it makes systematic predictions about when subjects will relinquish control. Specifically, the hypothesis says that individuals will relinquish control for situations in which they believe that some factor other than their own responding provides a more stable guarantee of a maximum upper limit of danger. This is important because of cultural and individual-difference data showing that control is not always preferred. The hypothesis can also be extended to account for choice of control over positive outcomes—for example, choosing between dolls versus candies. This is because control provides a guaranteed lower limit on the goodness of the outcome to be received. That is, it enables an individual to maximize the outcome's minimum reward value.

The crucial difference between the two hypotheses is that the internality view depends on the *internality* (and not the stability) of the controlling response, whereas minimax depends on the *stability* (and not the internality) of the controlling response. According to the internality view, the mechanism by which an individual expects to improve an aversive outcome is by matching his internal state with external events; and having an internal controlling response enables him to accomplish this. In contrast, when the outcome is uncontrollable, the individual cannot accomplish this match and so he expects a worse outcome. Thus there is an inherent value to control per se (i.e., the individual must have the response to make the outcome better). The fact that an internal controlling response also tends to be more stable than most external factors is unimportant.

According to minimax, on the other hand, individuals expect to improve an aversive outcome by being provided with a guaranteed upper limit on how bad the situation can become. Having an internal controlling response is only important to the extent that it provides the most stable guarantee of minimized danger. Thus there is *no* inherent value to control per se (i.e., the individual does *not* have to have the response to make the outcome better). Rather, it is simply that internal factors (such as one's own response) are generally more stable than external factors.

Each of these hypotheses is able to explain a substantial portion of the control and stress phenomena, including the equated predictability and potential control data (see Miller, in press–a and b). However, there is a piece of evidence that discriminates between the two views. Bowers (1968) has shown that the level of shock that individuals choose for themselves is *twice* the intensity under conditions where they expect to control shock than under conditions where they do not expect to control shock. The internality view cannot explain these results, because an individual who is concerned with matching his internal state with external events should never consent to a level of shock that may, at a subjectively vulnerable moment, feel intolerable. In contrast, minimax can easily account for these data, on the basis that control provides a more reliable upper limit of maximum aversiveness. Therefore, controlling individuals are less concerned with leaving themselves a large safety margin.

There is yet another set of findings that is compatible with minimax but not with internality. As noted above, minimax specifies that individuals should yield up control when they believe that some external factor is a more stable guarantee of minimized aversiveness than their own response. Recent evidence supports this (see Miller, in press–b). In contrast to minimax, the internality hypothesis does not predict conditions under which individuals will choose to relinquish control. An aversive outcome is improved by taking account of one's internal state, and a given individual is obviously a better judge of his own moment-to-moment fluctuations than is any external factor.

In summary, there are presently only two viable hypotheses for explaining the choice and control data. Both views have no difficulty in explaining the appetitive as well as the aversive case. However, minimax is unique in that it also spells out the conditions under which individuals will relinquish control.

It is important to emphasize that the two views share one important feature in common: They are both outcome oriented. In other words, control and choice change the expected outcome—either by matching internal and external events (internality) or by providing a guaranteed upper limit of a bad outcome (minimax). Therefore *both hypotheses deny that choice and control have any value above and beyond improving the expected outcome.* Brigham's "blind choice" results (Chapter 10) are relevant here. He presented youngsters with two tin cans and told them that they could have the contents from one of the cans. The children were then asked whether they wanted to make the choice between the cans for themselves or whether they wanted the experimenter to make the choice for them. In neither case were they informed of the contents of the two cans. Most of the children preferred to choose for themselves even though the choice was blind. These results seem to suggest that individuals do value control and choice per se. That is to say, choice and control may not only be a means to an end—whether the end is upper limit or matching internal states with external events—but may be an end in itself. It would seem, then, that the mechanism underlying all of the choice and control data is still undetermined, and we believe that future experiments will illuminate this crucial issue.

Attributions. The last theoretical issue that we would like to address concerns the relationship between attributions and expectancies. Phares (Chapter 14) mentioned that there is not necessarily a tight relationship between one's perception of control or helplessness in the present and one's expectations of control or helplessness for the future. We believe that a systematic relationship does exist between the perception of control or no control and the expectancy of control or no control, and that the linkage lies in attributions. Figure 23.2 presents the flow diagram of interest here. We spell out the logic for the helplessness case, although the identical logic holds for control. When an individual is faced with an objective noncontingency (although this is neither necessary nor sufficient), it generally produces in that

FIG. 23.2.   Flow of events leading to symptoms of helplessness.

> Objective noncontingency → *Perception* of present and past noncontingency → *Attribution* for present or past noncontingency → *Expectation* of future noncontingency → *Symptoms* of helplessness.

TABLE 23.2

Formal Characteristics of Attribution and Some Examples

Dimension	Internal		External	
	Stable	Unstable	Stable	Unstable
Global				
Failing student	Lack of intelligence (Laziness)	Exhaustion (Having a cold, which makes me stupid)	ETS gives unfair tests. (People are usually unlucky on the GRE.)	Today is Friday the 13th. (ETS gave experimental tests this time which were too hard for everyone.)
Rejected woman	I'm unattractive to men	My conversation sometimes bores men.	Men are overly competitive with intelligent women.	Men get into rejecting moods.
Specific				
Failing student	Lack of mathematical ability (Math always bores me.)	Fed up with math problems (Having a cold, which ruins my arithmetic)	ETS gives unfair math tests. (People are usually unlucky on math tests.)	The math test was form No. 13. (Everyone's copy of the math test was blurred.)
Rejected woman	I'm unattractive to him.	My conversation bores him.	He's overly competitive with women.	He was in a rejecting mood.

Note. ETS = Educational Testing Service, the maker of graduate record examinations (GRE).

person the perception of present or past noncontingency. At this point, a human being—and probably an animal as well—attempts to make sense of, or explain, the situation. That is, the individual questions what the cause of his being in a noncontingent situation is. This is a crucial question because the nature of the cause to be chosen (i.e., the nature of the attribution the individual makes) determines precisely when and where future expectations for noncontingency are going to occur. These expectancies, in turn, determine the symptoms of helplessness: lack of response initiation, inability to solve problems, emotional changes, and so forth.

As Ryckman (Chapter 17) mentioned, there are eight relevant attributions that an individual can make for personal helplessness. Table 23.2 shows that an individual can make either an internal or external attribution for the cause (see above), a stable or unstable attribution, and a global or specific attribution. Let us just illustrate the point with two examples. If you fail on the math part of the GRE, you can make an internal, stable, global attribution for your failure (e.g., "I'm unintelligent"); or you might make an external, unstable, specific attribution for your failure (e.g., "The math test form was number 13, which is an unlucky number"). It is a knowledge of the individual's attribution that allows us to predict when the expectancy for helplessness will be generalized over a wide range of situations (i.e., following a global attribution for the cause) and when the expectancy will persist in time (i.e., following a stable attribution for the cause). What the internal/external dimension adds is that it allows us to predict when the expectancy for helplessness will be accompanied by lowered self-regard. The data show that self-esteem sometimes decreases following the expectation of helplessness but at other times remains unchanged. We propose that lowered self-esteem is dependent on making an internal attribution for helplessness.

This proposal was recently tested in Abramson's (1978) doctoral dissertation. She exposed college students to inescapable noise and manipulated whether they made an internal or external attribution for their helplessness. One group was made personally helpless (i.e., they were shown norms that indicated that other people usually learned to escape the noise); and a second group was made universally helpless (i.e., they were shown norms that indicated that almost no one could learn to escape). A third group was given typical helplessness (i.e., they were exposed to inescapable noise and shown no comparative norms). There were subsequent performance deficits in all three helplessness groups. This tells us that the helplessness effects follow directly from the expectancy of noncontingency. In contrast, self-esteem loss only occurred in two groups: in the personally helpless group and in the group not shown any norms. The group that made an external attribution for its helplessness (universal helplessness) did not show self-esteem loss.

There is one final aspect of attributional theorizing that bears some comment, and it has to do with Lefcourt's (Chapter 15) new questionnaire for measuring attributions. By coincidence, we have been involved in a similar endeavor. We are particularly interested in testing the hypothesis that depressed individuals may have an insidious attributional style. More specifically, we are hypothesizing that depressed individuals tend to make internal, global, and stable attributions for their failures; whereas nondepressed individuals tend to make the opposite attributions for their failures. The reformulated helplessness model of depression (Abramson, Seligman, & Teasdale, 1978) predicts this result. Accordingly, we have devised a questionnaire that is similar in logic to the one Lefcourt has devised. Briefly, there are 12 questions, 6 of which are achievement oriented and 6 of which are affiliation oriented. People are asked to imagine vividly a situation in which someone compliments them on their appearance, for example, and to name the most likely cause for receiving such a compliment. They are then asked to rate the cause according to: (1) the internal/external dimension (Is it due to you or due to other people or circumstances?); (2) the stable/unstable dimension (Will the cause persist in time?); and (3) the global/specific dimension (Is it going to affect many areas of your life?).

We recently administered the questionnaire to a sample of depressed and nondepressed college students, and the prediction was basically confirmed. The results showed that depressed individuals tend to make more internal attributions for their failures, and these attributions tend to be more stable and global. This effect only holds for those failure items that depressed people rate as being important to them. We are continuing to accumulate such data, with a view toward refining the predictive power of our model. The first step is to determine whether it is the attributional style that produces the depression or, instead, whether it is the depression that produces the insidious attributional style.

APPLICATIONS

Throughout this volume, we have been impressed by the range of real-life phenomena to which theorizing about choice, internality, helplessness, control, etc., has been applied. It is clear that research in this area has already proved useful in determining various strategies for helping people and has also been of aid in illuminating fresh, new possibilities for the future. We believe that such practical benefits justify our existence. There is at least one important area of application, however, that still remains a mystery and that we feel should be highlighted. This has to do with the developmental course of attributional styles. It seems likely that individuals do develop consistent attributional styles, which entail abiding belief structures about having control or being helpless. Once learned, these attributional styles appear to be relatively implastic. Yet we know almost nothing about the foundational learning involved in the development of such styles. When exposed to noncontingency, how is it that some children learn to make the attribution that their helplessness is global, stable, and due to something about them? When is such crucial learning laid down? Up until what point is it still reversible? There are already some potential avenues of inquiry that may be fruitful to pursue. It is possible that deCharms' (Chapter 3) origin training program, applied not to teachers but to youngsters, will illuminate the source of such attributional training and show how to reverse helplessness-type attributional styles. The reattribution training pioneered by Dweck (1975) also becomes very important in this regard.

We view this as a very acute problem area, particularly because of some new data that have been collected by Smith (1979) in her doctoral dissertation at the University of Pennsylvania. These data have to do with the black/white IQ controversy. At this point, the IQ data unequivocally show that American Blacks have lower IQ scores than do American Whites. The important issue really revolves around the meaning and interpretation of these data. The standard interpretation is that IQ is a measure of ability and that IQ differences accordingly reflect differences in ability, which are genetically determined. Based on Smith's data, however, we are going to suggest an interpretation that is contrary to the standard view. That is to say, we do not believe that the IQ difference reflects an inherited ability difference. Rather, we believe that the observed differences in IQ test scores reflect a learned difference in susceptibility to helplessness. Let us illustrate with an example. Assume that an individual has the ability of a Mozart but believes he is helpless at composing symphonies. If his symphony-composing performance is then tested, he will score zero. This score is not a reflection of lack of ability or skill, however. Instead, his low composition score reflects low motivation, which in turn is due to his belief in his own helplessness. Applied to the IQ issue, the question of interest is whether Blacks score lower in IQ tests than Whites because of an increased susceptibility to helplessness-inducing experiences.

In her dissertation, Smith asked if there is differential susceptibility to helplessness in black versus white individuals and in middle- versus lower-class individuals. She specifically hypothesized that black and lower-class individuals would be more prone to exhibit helplessness deficits after exposure to noncontingency. She used second and tenth graders, half of whom were black and half white and half of whom were middle class and half lower class. Within these groups, subjects were then exposed to one of three conditions: solvable cognitive problems, unsolvable cognitive problems, or no pretreatment. All subjects were then tested on a cognitive subscale of the WAIS, the block-design test. Several interesting results emerged. First of all, the usual helplessness effect was obtained, with prior exposure to unsolvable cognitive problems (noncontingency) producing impaired posttest performance. In addition, there was both a race effect and a class effect, with Blacks showing overall poorer performance than Whites and lower-class children showing overall poorer performance than middle-class children. Contrary to expectation, there was no grade effect.

The important results revolve around two crucial interactions. First, there was a Race × Group interaction, which shows that a black youngster who is exposed to helplessness (unsolvable cognitive problems) subsequently performs more poorly than a White who is exposed to helplessness. There was a similar Class × Group interaction, which shows that a lower-class youngster who is exposed to helplessness subsequently performs more poorly than a middle-class youngster. It is worth noting that these results still held, even when IQ was covaried out. There was one final finding of interest. A youngster who is black and lower class performs adequately if he is *not* exposed to helplessness. In contrast, once exposed to helplessness, this youngster subsequently shows very deteriorated performance. The child gives up.

Consider now how these results bear on the black/white IQ dispute. A youngster taking the IQ test does all right on problem one and goes to problem two. The child solves this and goes on to problem three. On problem three, however, he does badly. Smith's data suggest that a white, middle-class youngster will bounce back and simply continue with problems four, five, six, and so on. However, a black, lower-class youngster who fails on problem three will then do poorly. This suggests that the racial difference is not genetic but learned, and that it is not intellectual but motivational. However, it is probably learned very early on, perhaps well before the second grade. These results may be cause for optimism, since learned, motivational differences are probably more remediable than genetic, intellectual ones.

These results substantiate our belief that the psychology of power as a field is justified not only by its theoretical and conceptual endeavors but ultimately by its applications to human welfare.

SUMMARY AND CONCLUSIONS

Let us now summarize our comments by providing a brief overview of the state of our field as it presently exists. First and foremost, let us acknowledge and applaud the fact that we now have a field of the psychology of power. This volume has both served to confirm the existence of the field and to extend its boundaries. The inception of control and power as a field can be likened to the inception of psycholinguistics as a field. Chomsky (1957) showed people with a variety of interests in linguistics, mathematics, and developmental and cognitive psychology that they were addressing a common set of questions and that these questions comprised a discipline. Similarly, there are a common set of questions that unite those of us working in the discipline of control and power. Indeed, we suspect that there are about 500 psychologists presently doing research within the boundaries of this field.

Before we become too self-congratulatory, we would like to review briefly some of the deficits of our field. One glaring deficit is the lack of conceptual clarity. We are faced with a terminological mare's nest. In this nest are such terms as: *choice, control, perceived choice and control, freedom, perceived freedom, coercion, origin/pawn, internal/external, controllable/uncontrollable, incompetence/competence/helplessness, self-administration, autonomy,* and many others. We agree with Singer (Chapter 22) that the multiplication of terms has become counterproductive and that simplicity must be found. In the interests of such conceptual clarity, moreover, it must be emphasized that these terms are by no means synonymous. Nonetheless, they are not randomly related to each other, and we must parse out the various interrelationships.

A second problem with the field is the lack of a taxonomy of operations. The operations themselves are multifold, and included among them are actual control, choice, self-administration, inferred helplessness, potential choice, potential control, illusory control, etc. What we are missing is a rational taxonomy for classifying them.

The third deficit is the absence of a coherent theory of stress and choice in contrast to the presence of well-articulated theories of how choice and control may affect performance (e.g., Seligman, 1975). There is still no coherent and confirmed view of why choice and control are preferred and why they decrease stress.

A fourth problem revolves around the lack of cross-cultural data. The field abounds in cross-cultural speculations, but the decisive data for verifying these important speculations are missing. A wealth of animal data has accumulated, and this has been helpful. However, we need to supplement our knowledge with data from cultures other than our own.

A final deficit is related to our ignorance about the permanence of the effects of control and choice. We still do not know what is needed to render these effects permanent, as opposed to transient, foundational as opposed to superficial. In our view, the five issues mentioned represent the most salient deficits in the area.

On the other hand, the field has already achieved a great deal and deserves to be proud of its accomplishments. Let us touch on a few of the advances that have occurred: It is now known that control and choice, however they are operationalized, almost invariably have good effects. Moreover, this has been shown to be the case for a wide variety of situations and manipulations. For example, both people and animals are happier, healthier, more active, solve

368 SELIGMAN AND MILLER

problems better, and feel less stress when they are given choice and control. This field has uncovered these benefits, and this is a substantial contribution. The converse findings have also emerged. That is, the lack of choice and control are detrimental and are generally bad. Depression, dysphoria, stress, passivity, illness, retardation of performance, and even death are among the deficits produced.

Secondly, a great deal is now known about the role of individual differences in choice and control. Several scales measure these individual differences, mainly by asking people to make attributions about the causes of choice and control. Such individual differences have been found to be systematically related to behavior, to health, etc., and these findings are of practical and theoretical significance.

Third, there presently exist three or four conceptual frameworks within which to view the effects of choice and control. Each of these frameworks deals with some subset of the issues at hand, most successfully with the effects of choice and control on performance. At this point, it is important to attempt to unify these various approaches, thereby refining the predictive and explanatory power of all the models.

Finally, there are clearly the beginnings of several very successful applications. In fact, we are hard pressed to think of another area of psychology that has provided so many potential benefits for mankind in so short a time. The psychology of control and power has implications for cardiovascular functioning, retardation, IQ performance, job satisfaction, learning ability, child-rearing practices, therapy, psychopathology, poverty, and the lives of the elderly as well as the lives of college students.

As a closing comment, we believe that this volume contains within it the seeds of a unique collaboration. We are immensely grateful to our editors, Drs. Monty and Perlmuter, for bringing together two normally distinct traditions. One is the general process learning tradition, and the other is the individual-difference tradition. Obviously, there are a lot of different strands represented in this volume, but these represent the two major traditions. Although the two traditions are clearly complementary, they have rarely acted in concert in the past. We are hopeful that this volume signifies the unification of these two traditions in an effort to understand the effects of control and choice on the lives of our fellow men and women.

ACKNOWLEDGMENTS

This paper was supported by Grant MH-19604-07 from the National Institute of Mental Health and by Grant RR-09069 from the National Institute of Health. These remarks were delivered extemporaneously in reaction to the oral presentation of the papers that make up this book. We have attempted to preserve the spontaneity of these remarks by only lightly editing the written version.

REFERENCES

Abramson, L. *Universal versus personal helplessness: An experimental test of the reformulated theory of learned helplessness and depression.* Unpublished doctoral dissertation, University of Pennsylvania, 1978.

Abramson, L. Y., Seligman, E. P., & Teasdale, J. D. Learned helplessness in humans: Critique and reformulation. *Journal of Abnormal Psychology,* 1978, *87,* 49–74.

Alloy, L. B., & Abramson, L. Y. Judgment of contingency in depressed and nondepressed college students: A nondepressive distortion. *Journal of Experimental Psychology: General,* in press.

Averill, J. R. Personal control over aversive stimuli and its relationship to stress. *Psychological Bulletin,* 1973, *80,* 286–303.

Bandura, A. Self-efficacy: Toward a unifying theory of behavioral change. *Psychological Review,* 1977, *84,* 191–215.

Berlyne, D. E. *Conflict, arousal, and curiosity.* New York: McGraw-Hill, 1960.

Bowers, K. S. Pain, anxiety, and perceived control. *Journal of Consulting and Clinical Psychology,* 1968, *32,* 596–602.

Chomsky, N. *Syntactic structures.* The Hague: Mouton, 1957.

Church, R. M. Systematic effect of random error in the yoked control design. *Psychological Bulletin,* 1964, *62,* 122–131.

Dweck, C. S. The role of expectations and attributions in the alleviation of learned helplessness. *Journal of Personality and Social Psychology,* 1975, *31,* 674–685.

Geer, J. H., Davison, G. C., & Gatchel, R. J. Reduction of stress in humans through nonveridical perceived control of aversive stimulation. *Journal of Personality and Social Psychology,* 1970, *16,* 731–738.

Glass, D. C., & Singer, J. E. *Urban stress: Experiments on noise and social stressors.* New York: Academic Press, 1972.

MacCorquodale, K., & Meehl, P. E. On a distinction between hypothetical constructs and intervening variables. *Psychological Review,* 1948, *55,* 95–107.

Mandler, G., & Watson, D. L. Anxiety and the interruption of behavior. In C. D. Spielberger (Ed.), *Anxiety and behavior.* New York: Academic Press, 1966.

Milgram, S. Some conditions of obedience and disobedience to authority. *Human Relations,* 1965, *18,* 57–76.

Miller, S. M. Controllability and human stress: Method, evidence, and theory. *Behavior Research and Therapy,* in press. (a)

Miller, S. M. A minimax theory of controllability and human stress: If I can stop the roller coaster I don't want to get off. In M. E. P. Seligman & J. Garber (Eds.), *Human helplessness: Theory and application.* New York: Academic Press, in press. (b)

Nisbett, R. E., & Wilson, T. D. Telling more than we can know: Verbal reports on mental processes. *Psychological Review,* 1977, *84,* 231–259.

Perlmuter, L. C., & Monty, R. A. The importance of perceived control: Fact or fantasy? *American Scientist,* 1977, *65,* 759–765.

Perlmuter, L. C., & Monty, R. A. The authors reply. *American Scientist,* 1978, *66,* 274.

Perlmuter, L. C., Monty, R. A., & Kimble, G. A. Effect of choice on paired-associate learning. *Journal of Experimental Psychology,* 1971, *91,* 47–53.

Seligman, M. E. P. Chronic fear produced by unpredictable electric shock. *Journal of Comparative and Physiological Psychology,* 1968, *66,* 401–411.

Seligman, M. E. P. *Helplessness: On depression, development, and death.* San Francisco: Freeman, 1975.

Smith, R. *The black/white IQ discrepancy: Differential susceptibility to helplessness.* Unpublished doctoral dissertation, University of Pennsylvania, 1979.

Sokolov, E. N. *Perception and the conditioned reflex.* New York: Macmillan, 1963.

Weiner, B., Frieze, I., Kukla, A., Reed, L., Rest, S., & Rosenbaum, R. M. *Perceiving the causes of success and failure.* Morristown, N.J.: General Learning Press, 1971.

Weiss, J. Effects of coping behavior in different warning signal conditions on stress pathology in rats. *Journal of Comparative and Physiological Psychology,* 1971, *77,* 1-13.

White, R. W. Motivation reconsidered: The concept of competence. *Psychological Review,* 1959, *66,* 297-333.

Author Index

Italics denote pages with bibliographic information.

E

Easton, D., 51, *62*
Edelman, M., 53, *62*
Edwards, G., 184, *188*
Efran, J., 197, 198, *207*
Eisenberger, R., 252, *257*
Ekstrand, B. R., 125, *126*
Elam, R. R., 235, *260*
El-Gazzar, M. E., 238, 241, *257*
Eller, S. J., 252, *261*
Ellis, A., 176, *187*
Erickson, M. H., 84, *89*
Erikson, E., 46, *62*
Evans, I. M., 177, 180, *189*
Evans, J. W., 198, *208, 223, 230,* 254, *260*
Evans, R. G., 204, *207*

F

Farnum, M., 135, *141*
Fasnacht, G., 139, *141*
Faught, W. S., 155, 164, *172*
Fazio, A. F., 250, *257*
Feather, N. T., 108, *120,* 240, 247, *257, 258*
Felixbrod, J. J., 135, *141*
Fencil-Morse, E., 252, *258*
Festinger, L., 18, *27,* 119, *120,* 343, *344*
Fiedler, M. L., 37, *40*
Field, W. L., 281, *299*
Fine, M., 135, *141*
Fisch, R., 170, *174*
Fischhoff, B., 288, 289, 290, *299*
Fish, B., 254, *258*
Fiske, S. T., 290, *300*
Fitch, G., 254, *258*
Fitzgerald, R., 59, 60, *62*
Folger, R., 278, *297*
Fontaine, G., 243, *258*
Forrest, M. S., 169, *172,* 226, *229*
Fosco, E., 252, *258*
Fotopoulos, S., 226, *229*
Frank, J. D., 155, *172*
Frank, M., 252, *257*
Fredrikson, M., 227, *229*
Freud, S., 45, *62,* 166, *172*
Friedman, M., 223, *229*
Friedman, S., 167, *172*
Frieze, I., 26, *27,* 211, *220,* 250, *259,* 359, *370*
Fromm, E., 44, *62,* 160, *172*

G

Gajdos, E., 182, *187*
Ganz, R. L., 250, 251, 252, *257*
Gargan, M., 210, *220*
Garner, W. B., 288, 289, *297*
Garrity, T. F., 226, *229*
Gatchel, R. J., 119, *120,* 226, *229,* 252, *258,* 359, 360, *369*
Gauvain, M., 335, *336*
Geer, J. H., 252, *258,* 359, 360, *369*
Geller, E. S., 94, 95, 105, *106,* 286, *299*
Geller, J. D., 202, *207*
Gergen, K. J., 281, 292, *298*
Gibb, E., 136, *140*
Gilmore, T. M., 204, *207*
Glass, D. C., 26, *27,* 102, *105,* 160, *172,* 179, *188,* 222, 228, *229,* 252, *258, 259,* 276, *299,* 301, *313,* 356, 357, *369*
Gluzman, S., 291, *297*
Glynn, E. L., 135, *141*
Goethals, G. R., 281, *298*
Goffman, E., 144, *153*
Gold, D., 237, 238, *258*
Gold, J. A., 240, 254, *260*
Goldfried, M. R., 176, *188*
Goldstein, M., 192, *193,* 243, *261*
Golin, S., 166, 167, *172*
Goot, M., 57, *62*
Gore, P. M., 202, *207*
Greeno, J. G., 124, *126*
Greenwald, A. G., 19, *27*
Grumet, J., 281, *298*
Gurwitz, S. B., 277, 285, *297*
Gynther, M. D., 240, *259*

H

Haley, J., 56, *62,* 170, *172,* 295, *297*
Hall, H. V., 251, 252, *258*
Hamburg, D., 167, *172*
Hamsher, J. H., 202, *207*
Hansen, V., 136, *140*
Hanusa, B. H., 253, *258,* 316, 317, *336, 337*
Harford, R. J., 266, *269*
Harkins, S. G., 285, *300*
Harper, D. C., 290, *299*
Harris, B., 24, *27,* 67, 68, 69, 81, *81,* 276, 277, 280, 281, 285, 288, 294, *297, 298*
Harris, V. A., 281, *298*
Hartsough, R., 241, *261*

Subject Index